Teresa Ann Ellis
Gender in the Book of Ben Sira

Beihefte zur Zeitschrift für die alttestamentliche Wissenschaft

Herausgegeben von
John Barton · Reinhard G. Kratz
Markus Witte

Band 453

De Gruyter

Teresa Ann Ellis

Gender in the Book of Ben Sira

Divine Wisdom, Erotic Poetry, and the Garden of Eden

De Gruyter

ISBN 978-3-11-033079-3
e-ISBN 978-3-11-033089-2
ISSN 0934-2575

Library of Congress Cataloging-in-Publication Data

A CIP catalog record for this book has been applied for at the Library of Congress.

Bibliografische Information der Deutschen Nationalbibliothek

Die Deutsche Nationalbibliothek verzeichnet diese Publikation in der Deutschen
Nationalbibliografie; detaillierte bibliografische Daten sind im Internet
über http://dnb.dnb.de abrufbar.

© 2013 Walter de Gruyter GmbH, Berlin/Boston

Druck: Hubert & Co. GmbH & Co. KG, Göttingen
♾ Gedruckt auf säurefreiem Papier

Printed in Germany

www.degruyter.com

For Michael

Acknowledgements

A large project such as this book carries the influences of many people, and I appreciate this opportunity to thank those who have taught me and have encouraged the project. In the interval between the rather hurried completion of the dissertation that forms the basis for the book, and the book's current form, my sense of the project's scope has shifted. There have been many changes in organization and in content, some of which are both substantial and unexpected—such as the expanded sections of material from classical Greece.

The puzzle-solving aspect of the study refused to be hurried, and thus some essential pieces of the puzzles were missing until the most recent revisions. This was not an orderly progression. My incremental understanding of the important verse BBS 42:14 is an example of the leap-frogging process. The first half of the verse, "Better the evil of a man than the goodness of a woman," appears on the first page of the book with a comment on "the gendered nature of the taunt" and the declaration that such a statement "must either yield a kernel of wit as compensation, in the manner of a riddle, or else be dismissed as an empty hyperbole." Months after writing this, and after more work with the Greek texts, I suddenly realized the Hebrew word "taunt" in the second half of 42:14 is, literally, the "kernel of wit" that is my solution to the puzzle.

The study is now ready to go out into the world, and I thank Walter de Gruyter GmbH for including it as part of the BZAW series; also, I thank Sabina Dabrowski for her skills as Production Editor. I hope that the book's contents will suggest to readers a variety of directions for further investigations of topics related to the Book of Ben Sira and to Sirach.

The now-completed project began when I first read the Book of Ben Sira—the text captivated me, and many people have been instrumental in the project's development. First thanks go to the scholars with whom I began the study of Ben Sira: Drs. John Endres, S. J., Dina Stein, and Patricia Bulman. Special thanks go to Dr. Leo G. Perdue, my dissertation director, and to Drs. Carolyn Osiek, R. S. C. J., and Yvonne Sherwood, readers for the dissertation. I thank Drs. Claudia V. Camp and Benjamin G. Wright, III, for conversations about Ben Sira. Many thanks go to dear friends whom I met at Brite Divinity School/TCU, for continued conversations, laughter, and encouragement. And, to my husband, Michael H. Nadler, thanks for his computer-wisdom (such as writing scripts to sort index entries) and boundless thanks for everything else—he is present in the whole book.

Table of Contents

List of Contents

List of Charts

Chapter 1
Gender and Taxonomies

The ancient Hebrew text known as "the Book of Ben Sira" and its Greek translation, Sirach, include many harsh comments about women. Statements such as "Better the evil of a man than the goodness of a woman" (BBS 42:14a) are extreme enough to explain the label *misogynist* that is applied to the author.[1] However, the statement is an outrageous anomaly in the context of the author's stated views of bad, and good, behaviors. For Ben Sira's audience—living in a Hellenistic milieu in which gendered invective was an art form—the evaluation of "evil" as better than "goodness" might be more jarring than the gendered nature of the taunt. Still, a statement that is so discordant demands clarification and must either yield a kernel of wit as compensation, in the manner of a riddle, or else be dismissed as an empty hyperbole.[2] The current study considers this statement by Ben Sira, and others like it, in the context of relations in the Book of Ben Sira that are portrayed in terms of *gender*, examining textual devices that contribute to the construction of these gendered portrayals. I investigate *gender* as a discursive category, focusing on the effects of Ben Sira's choice of particular sets of human and non-human figures as the subjects of his sayings and on his use of biblical figures to extend, implicitly, the semantic range of the gender-commentary.

The end result of this project is a semantic analysis of the discourse of *gender* in the Book of Ben Sira. Elements of the title unfold in an orderly sequence—"divine Wisdom," "erotic poetry," and "the Garden of Eden" are

---

1   "Ben Sira est misogyne, répète-t-on," as Gilbert ("Ben Sira et la femme," 426) summarizes the situation, citing McKeating's comments as especially harsh ("Jesus ben Sira's Attitude," 85). The word recurs reflexively, appearing even in titles (e. g. Ilan's article, "'Wickedness Comes from Women' (*Ben Sira* 42:13): Ben Sira's Misogyny and Its Reception by the Babylonian Talmud," and Schroer's chapter title, "The One Lord and Male Dominance in the Book of Jesus Sirach: The Image of Woman and the Image of Wisdom in a Misogynist Document"). Some scholars reject the use of "misogynist" (Trenchard, *Ben Sira's View*, 185 n. 12) or qualify its scope (Camp, "Understanding," 37).

2   See Kohlenberger (*Parallel Apocrypha*, 572); according to footnote *a* in the Knox Translation, it is "a sentiment which could have little meaning, even in the mouth of the most determined cynic." Skehan and Di Lella (*Wisdom*, 90) call 42:14a "downright gross."

major topics for analysis, but, before they appear, it is necessary to delimit "the Book of Ben Sira" and "gender."

1.1 Texts

In the Talmuds, the term "the Book of Ben Sira" designates a Hebrew text or texts written by Ben Sira, "the son of Sira."[3] The Book of Ben Sira is remarkable among ancient Hebrew texts for being considered—in its origin— the work of one person. Thus I speak of the author by name as "Ben Sira," though without implying that every word of the extant Hebrew texts originated with that individual.[4] Ben Sira's work is an enormous semantic jumble: a haphazard mixture of genres that now exist in irreconcilable and/or incomplete versions in several languages.[5] The work was very popular, both in its original Hebrew and in the Greek translation.[6] The Hebrew version is cited in rabbinic literature twenty-two times with formulas reserved for biblical texts or for the sayings of the Rabbis,[7] while Sirach, the LXX Greek translation that

---

3   The work is cited in the Jerusalem Talmud (*y. Sanhedrin* 27b) as ספרי בן סירא "the Books of Ben Sira," and in the Babylonian Talmud (*b. Sanhedrin* 90a) as ספר בן סירא "the Book of Ben Sira." The relevant mishnah is *m. Sanhedrin* 10:1.

    The label is applied similarly in current scholarship. For examples, see titles by (alphabetic order) Balla, Beentjes, Ben-Hayyim, Calduch-Benages, Dihi, Egger-Wenzel, Gilbert, Labendz, Liesen, Marböck, Perdue, Reiterer, Stokes, Voitila, and Wright. Some scholars may include non-Hebrew texts as referents.

4   His personal name is a matter of contention, but the Hebrew of BBS 51:30, "one who is called 'son of Sira'" (שנקרא בן סירא) provides a neutral choice. The date of origin for the Book of Ben Sira is ca. 185 BCE. Beentjes (*Book of Ben Sira in Hebrew*, 6) gives a range from 190 to 180 BCE; Muraoka ("Sir 51, 13–30," 167) prefers 190 BCE; and Di Lella (Skehan and Di Lella, *Wisdom*, 7) chooses 180 BCE.

5   Latin and Syriac versions are not part of this project. The Latin versions ("Ecclesiasticus") are translations from the Greek, and the Syriac—though derived from Hebrew texts—is acknowledged to be greatly influenced by Christian ideologies (Wright, *No Small Difference*, 6; Skehan and Di Lella, *Wisdom*, 57; and Winter, Parts 1 and 2 of "Origins of Ben Sira in Syriac," esp. Part 2, p. 498, referring to changes that are "the systematic work of a translator or reviser who had a prejudice against the Law").

6   The date for the earliest Greek translation would be c. 120 BCE, based on remarks by the translator, who claims to be Ben Sira's grandson. The earliest extant text of Sirach is the "Codex Vaticanus," from the first half of the fourth century CE.

7   The Book of Ben Sira is cited thirteen times by the standard rabbinic introduction for a biblical quotation (ונאמר "and it is said," without naming the text) or by named citations (with variations of the verb root כתב). Quotations from a rabbinic figure are introduced by אמר or אומר, "says/said," or sometimes by the formula "Rabbi X said in the name of Rabbi Y." There are nine instances in which these forms introduce Ben Sira "as if Ben Sira were

was used by Jews and then by Christians, eventually became part of deuterocanonical scripture. The book's non-scriptural status for Jews contributed to the gradual disappearance of Hebrew versions of the book.[8] For over a thousand years, discussions of Ben Sira's work were conducted in terms of the Greek version, Sirach, which became, by default, the standard text. When fragments of Hebrew versions from the Middle Ages were found in the Cairo Genizah at the end of the nineteenth century, many scholars considered them retroversions; it was only when indisputably ancient fragments were found at Qumran and Masada that the Hebrew texts as a group were accepted as independent of the Greek.[9] We now have about two-thirds of the Greek text extant in at least one Hebrew manuscript.[10] Over time, "there has grown an opinio communis as to the reliability of the Hebrew text of the Book of Ben Sira. That is true both of the Masada Scroll and the Genizah manuscripts."[11]

---

himself a rabbinic sage" (Wright, "*B. Sanhedrin* 100b," 46). The twenty-two instances do not include the major discussion of Ben Sira in *b. Sanhedrin* 100b.

8   The scatological nature of *The Alphabet of Ben Sira* probably hastened the process. It is an anonymous and unrelated medieval (700–1000 CE) work in Aramaic and Hebrew that features Ben Sira as a character.

9   The medieval MSS closely match MS M, found at Masada. MS M dates from the "first half of the first century BCE" (Beentjes, *Book of Ben Sira in Hebrew*, 6). Among those who date MS M within that range are Muraoka ("Sir 51, 13–30," 169) and Gilbert ("Implications," 83). If MS M is dated 100–50 BCE, then the work, in at least one form, was in circulation within about a hundred years of its origin, c. 185. However, Martone dates MS M to "between 40 b.c.e. and 20 c.e." ("Ben Sira Manuscripts," 88). Dates for the Qumran fragments are the second half of the first century BCE for 2Q18 and the first half of the first century CE for 11QPs^a (Beentjes, *Book of Ben Sira in Hebrew*, 6).

10   For overviews and comparisons of the characteristics and provenance of the nine extant manuscripts, see Beentjes, *Book of Ben Sira in Hebrew*, 5–19 (information on present location of MSS leaves, pp. 13–19); Martone, "Ben Sira Manuscripts"; Skehan and Di Lella, *Wisdom*, 51–54 (list of the verses for each set of MS fragments on pages 52 and 53). For more detailed discussions see Adler ("Some Missing Chapters"); Baillet, et al. (*'Petites Grottes' de Qumran*); Cowley and Neubauer, *Original Hebrew*); Di Lella ("Newly Discovered Sixth Manuscript"); Egger-Wenzel ("Ein neues Sira-Fragment des MS C"); Elizur ("Two New Leaves"); Gaster ("New Fragment"); Gilbert ("Implications"); Lévi ("Fragments"); Marcus ("Fifth MS of Ben Sira)"; Margoliouth ("Original Hebrew"); Muraoka ("Sir 51, 13-30"); J. A. Sanders (*Psalms Scroll*); Schechter ("Fragment of the Original Text" and "Further Fragment"); Schechter and Taylor (*Wisdom of Ben Sira*); Scheiber ("Leaf of the Fourth Manuscript)"; Schirmann ("Dap hadas" and "Dappim nospim"); Yadin (*Ben Sira Scroll from Masada* [originally *Megillat ben-Sira mimmasada*]).

11   Beentjes, "Hermeneutics," 45. Though the Book of Ben Sira did not have the status of inspired literature (scripture) to protect it from random scribal tinkering, the high degree of uniformity between the early MS M from Masada and MS B from the Cairo Genizah attests to scribal concern to transmit the texts accurately. Leiman (*Canonization*, 100) defines the

Nevertheless, Sirach's uninterrupted history of liturgical use and scholarly commentary still constitutes it as a 'natural' standard, and gaps in the Hebrew MSS reinforce the effect of the Greek text's implicit status as the default. The lack of a Hebrew version for passages important to some major topics does entail reliance on the Greek text for those topics. For example, a study of *wisdom* in the Book of Ben Sira would be hampered by the absence of a Hebrew text for chapter 24, the fullest description of the figure of Wisdom. And, for almost any topic, there will be certain passages, verses, or words unavailable in Hebrew. Given this combination of habitual usage that favors the Greek version and textual limitations that disadvantage the Hebrew, it is unusual to find commentaries that are based primarily on the Hebrew texts or that distinguish explicitly between Greek and Hebrew sources for translations. Because the Greek translation of the Book of Ben Sira diverges significantly from extant versions of its source—and, for motifs related to *gender*, there can be divergence to the point of contradiction—translations that conflate the text traditions are not appropriate for semantic studies.[12] I emphasize separate identities for the two text-groups by using the name "Book of Ben Sira" (BBS) for the Hebrew MSS as a whole and "Sirach" (Sir) for the Greek texts.[13]

Separating the Hebrew and Greek lineages of Ben Sira's texts is analogous to the treatment of the Hebrew Bible and the Septuagint. The Septuagint is not equivalent to the Hebrew Bible—neither is the Septuagint's book Sirach the same as the Book of Ben Sira. Indeed, the translator of Sirach applies the LXX/Hebrew Bible analogy to his work. In the Prologue to Sirach, he asks the reader to

> exercise forbearance in cases where we may be thought to be insipid with regard to some expressions that have been the object of great care in rendering; for what was originally expressed in Hebrew does not have the same force when it is in fact rendered in another language. And not only in this case, but also in the case of the

---

rabbinic classification of BBS as "the category of uninspired canonical literature" and states that BBS "was accorded semi-biblical status in the tannaitic period" and later.

12 Semantic influence is presumed to be unidirectional (unless proven otherwise for specific cases), meaning that the Greek texts can comment on the Hebrew texts, but not vice versa. In this sense, the Hebrew texts are "original" with regard to semantic content.

13 For the contents of the Hebrew MSS, I rely on Beentjes (*Book of Ben Sira in Hebrew* and "Errata") and note the Ben-Hayyim text (Academy of the Hebrew Language, *Book of Ben Sira*; foreword by Zeev Ben-Hayyim) when it differs. The source for citations from the Hebrew Bible is the Hebrew text edited by Dotan (*Biblia Hebraica Leningradensia*, and from Sirach it is the Greek text edited by Ziegler (*Sapientia Iesu Filii Sirach*).

Law itself and the Prophets and the rest of the books the difference is not small when these are expressed in their own language.[14]

For some topics, the lack of essential passages in Hebrew forces reliance on the Greek texts, but a Hebrew text-base is practicable, now, for topics whose major pericopes are extant in Hebrew. The latter case applies to the topic of *gender*, for which enough important passages are extant in at least one MS.

The foundational premise for the current project is that semantic analyses of discursive topics are useful contributions to the field of Ben Sira studies. A corollary to that premise is that a single-language text-base is an appropriate choice for the project, since each linguistic strand will have a different semantic profile. Separate translations for the Hebrew and Greek texts are proposed by Egger-Wenzel, with separate commentaries, because "[a]ll standard translations offer mixed texts, which do not distinguish between the intentions of grandfather and grandson" and by Beentjes, who declares that the Hebrew and Greek texts "must be considered as *literary entities of their own*, which cannot be exchanged at pleasure."[15] In keeping with these opinions, I have chosen the Hebrew MSS of Ben Sira as the single text-base for this project because they are part of a Hebrew-language continuum that is the center of my academic work, but also because they are underrepresented in most commentaries.

In the translations that follow, the Greek text is given with the Hebrew in some cases where the Greek diverges significantly from the Hebrew. However, for two important verses related to *gender*—Sir 23:18 and 26:12—Sirach will be the source because there is no extant Hebrew.[16] The first of these, Sir 23:18, occurs in a poetic unit about *adultery* (Sir 23:16–27). The Greek text may imply that a married man's adulterous behavior is an offence against his own wife, which would be a major departure from the standard biblical definition of adultery as a man's relation with a married woman, without reference to the adulterer's own wife if he is married. The whole passage is a significant part of the gendered discourse, therefore I analyze the Greek text.[17] The second missing verse is 26:12, the notorious comment that a

---

14   Translation by Wright ("Sirach," 719) from the *New English Translation of the Septuagint*. In this study, translations of the Greek are from NETS or are by the author in cases where translating the Greek emphasizes a point with regard to the Hebrew version.

15   Egger-Wenzel, "Change of the Sacrifice Terminology," 90; Beentjes, "Reconstructions," 26 (emphasis original); although Beentjes says that the only "legitimate way [is] to investigate ... each text, each version, even each manuscript, on its own"(ibid. 27), I consider that the Hebrew MSS have sufficient semantic congruence on the topic of *gender* to justify a unified semantic analysis.

16   Sir 3:1–6a and 17:1–8 are given, also.

17   See chart 4-13, in chapter 4.

daughter will "sit opposite every stake and she will open quiver to arrow" (NETS). The comment is part of a continuation of BBS 25:13–26:3, a passage to be analyzed in detail from the Hebrew, and I expect that the Hebrew of BBS 26:12 would continue the pattern I describe for the earlier verses.[18] For the purpose of a comprehensive evaluation of *gender* in the Hebrew text-group, the two Greek texts—the passage I analyze (Sir 23:16–27) and that which I ignore (Sir 26:5–12)—must both carry the same judgment of "indeterminable" and remain as open questions, for without a Hebrew version any conclusion is tentative.

Unless otherwise indicated, all translations of Hebrew in this study are my own and are working-translations that incorporate a one-to-one rendering of the vocabulary. The choice to translate without variance reflects my convictions about how meaning is made in the Hebrew Bible, where the choice of words and their positioning often have semantic significance—for example, the substitution of a new word for a word that has been repeated throughout a passage can indicate a shift of meaning. The chart below gives some recurrent words (with vowels added for nouns) and the translations.

Vocabulary key for the Book of Ben Sira

אִישׁ	man-husband; man	גַּאֲוָה	pride	גּוע	to expire
בַּעַל	lord-husband; lord	עֲנָוָה	humility	מות	to die
אוֹהֵב	friend (male)	זָדוֹן	insolence	כבד	to honor
חָבֵר	an associate	חֶמְדָּה	desire	כָּבוֹד	honor; glory (God)
גֶּבֶר	a fellow	חֵפֶץ	delight	קלה	be dishonored
פתה	to be simple	פשע	to transgress	קָלוֹן	dishonor
שׂכל	to be intelligent	חטא	to sin	כלם	to humiliate
חכם	to be wise	עול	to do wrong	כְּלִמָּה	insult
בין	to understand	עָוֶל	wrongdoing	קלל	to declare cursed
צַדִּיק	righteous-man	עָוֹן	iniquity, guilt	חרף	to taunt, reproach
רֶשַׁע	wicked-man	בוש	to feel ashamed	חֶרְפָּה	a taunt, reproach
כְּסִיל	fool	בֹּשֶׁת	shame		
אֱוִיל	foolish	בייש\ת	modest, m./f.		

Formatting translations from the Hebrew texts requires care. It is important to distinguish between the MSS to "show respect for the work of the individual scribes"[19] and to accommodate the interests of Hebrew scholars, but it is

---

18   See chart 2-11, in chapter 2.
19   Perdue, in conversation 18 August 2010.

necessary, also, to provide an uncluttered text for all readers. For most passages that are extant in multiple MSS, there is a clear default and the other MSS supply only a few phrases. Each major passage is formatted so that the MS source for every word in Hebrew (and English) should be identifiable and any semantically-divergent versions are included.[20] NOTE: These are working-translations and are, therefore, rather lumpy, repetitious, and rough because they are entirely specific to the semantic goals of the project. In other words, these are *not* smooth translations that reproduce the beauty of the Hebrew originals and could appear in a literary translation of the Book of Ben Sira.

The MSS of the Book of Ben Sira have no consistent lexical or typographic demarcations for the beginning and end of textual units that are larger than a bicola. Therefore, because standardized units facilitate comparison of their contents, I posit the *poetic unit*. Rather than matching passages of the Book of Ben Sira with external definitions of the *poem*, I identify what constitutes a poetic unit in the Book of Ben Sira by describing a shared set of patterned arrangements in a core group of passages. Poetic units, which can include embedded proverbs, are my literary templates for analyzing passages from the Book of Ben Sira.

A typical poetic unit has a brief thematic introduction, two middle sections with variations on the theme, and a brief closing section that may refer back to the introductory verse(s);[21] in the chart where a poetic unit is analyzed, these sections are separated by solid horizontal lines. Chart 1-1, below, shows the bicola sequences for each passage analyzed as a poetic unit.[22]

---

20 The only unit for which no single source can serve as a default is BBS 42:9–14. Translations in the text appear with simplified formatting, for optimal legibility. Passages that are textually or hermeneutically complex appear again in section A.2 of the Appendix, with full notation of MSS in Hebrew and in English. There, the Hebrew has keyed inserts of letters that Ben-Hayyim (*Book of Ben Sira*) and Beentjes (*Book of Ben Sira in Hebrew*) read differently.

21 The passage BBS 51:13–30 does not fit the typical four-part pattern, though it has opening and closing segments. Several passages in chart 1-1 have variations on the pattern: BBS/Sir 3:1–16 has three middle segments, and BBS 9:1–9 and BBS 9:10–16 each have one middle segment but combine to make a 2/6/6/2 pattern. See the chart at the beginning of the Source Index for chart numbers for these fragments from larger units, which are not given in chart 1-1: BBS 33:14–15; 42:24–25 (chapter 1) BBS 11:29–31; 16:1–4; 30:11–13 (chapter 4); and BBS 13:14–20; 17:1–8 (Gr.); 26:1–3; 26:13–17 (chapter 5).

22 An important set of gender-focal verses that is not listed as a poetic unit is BBS 26:13–17, in chart 5-11.

Chart 1-1: Bicola sequences in poetic units of BBS/Sirach

Sequence (Poetic Unit)	3:1-16	4:11-19	4:20-28	6:18-31	7:18-26	9:1-9 ||	9:10-16	14:20-15:8	15:11-20	23:16-27	25:13-24/26:1-3	33:20-30	36:18-26 ||	37:16-26	40:18-27	41:15c-42:1d	42:1e-8	42:9-14	51:13-30
INTRODUCT'N	1	1	1	1	2	2	2	2	2	3	1	2	1	1	2	2	1	1	4,4
TOPIC 1	4	3	4	5	3	6	6	6	4	7	3	4	4	4	4	4	4	4	3,3,3,3,4,4
TOPIC 2	4	3	4	5	3	6	6	6	5	6	4	4	4	4	4	4	4	4	3,3,3,3,3
CLOSING	1	2	1	1	1	4	2	2	2	2	1/3	1/2	1	1	2	3	1	1	3,3
TOTAL BICOLA	14	9	10	12	9	12	10	16	13	18	12	11	10	10	12	13	10	10	26
FIG.#	4-1	3-1	2-7	3-2	4-8	4-9	4-10	3-4	5-1	4-13	2-11	4-5	5-6	5-7	5-9	2-8	2-9	4-16	3-5

Each column of the chart displays the bicola sequence for a single poetic unit. Columns with a grey background are double units in which a poem about a female figure is preceded or followed by a semantically-parallel unit about a male. The bottom row of chart 1-1 lists the chart number for the full analysis of each poetic unit.

  The demonstration of so many structurally-similar and structurally-coherent units, in chart 1-1, is evidence in favor of their being significant bearers of coherent discourse. The point is that I have not chosen a random collection of passages for analysis, taken without regard for context; the structural patterns, together with the genres and forms, are themselves important contributors of contexts by which to evaluate the passages' contents.

1.2 Methodologies

The current study operates through specific preconceptions about *gender*, and about the relation of the written text to its producers and their social environments, that are compatible with a methodological foundation of discourse theory. My understanding of the model is informed by Lincoln's synthesis of "theory" with "the detailed analysis of specific materials."[23]

---

23 Lincoln, *Discourse*, 172. Lincoln's theoretic model inherits from Foucault, among others (Foucault, *Archaeology of Knowledge*).

Discourse is understood to operate at both an individual and a societal level.[24] It is intrinsic to all human productions: "[m]anners, dress, food, orientation to time, divisions of labor, and so forth, are all elements of a social group's discourse, alongside its explicit words."[25] The inclusion of material objects as discursive effects means that archeological evidence of material culture becomes part of the 'text' under investigation, as well as being part of the context. Gender theory covers a similar range of data because *gender* is a cumulative product of the repetition of codified sets that include particular gestures, costumes, and vocal patterns.

Discourse constructs, or *constitutes*, its topics—bringing them into being, rather than describing a pre-existing set of conditions. People are produced by discourse as well as being producers of discourse, as the human process of organizing and classifying "the diverse data of the phenomenal world" also "comes to organize the organizers."[26] Through the process of the formation of the subject, an individual becomes 'a subject' in two ways, concurrently—by becoming 'subject' to the set of discourses in which she or he develops, the person grows into selfhood as an agent, 'a subject.' The Book of Ben Sira has as its ideological goal the formation of such subjects among the male Jewish population. These texts could, therefore, be regarded as a set of rather overt formulations of the discursive topics important to the author and his peers, but the mixture of genres and the cryptic quality of the Hebrew should discourage assessments based on single verses, or even a single passage, taken out of context. For a discursive trope such as *gender* that can function as a vehicle for other topics, the caution against simple conclusions is especially pertinent.

Discourse theory provides a framework that is shared by theories of gender and classification, especially a shared emphasis on the link between knowledge and power. Postcolonial theory is another model that relates to discourse through the topic of *power*. Ben Sira lived within an empire as an educated member of a deliberately-distinct colonized group, and the influence of that status on his writing is an important consideration in analyzing the texts—for instance, his use of Hellenistic modes cannot transparently identify the strategies they serve, since he may have used classical genres in the production of a literature of resistance.[27] In the current study, the upcoming

---

24   The unmodified word "discourse" (singular, without an article) denotes an abstract comment about the general topic, thus distinguishing the topic from specific instances of it, e.g., "several discourses in the Book of Ben Sira are the discourse of *gender* and the discourse of *speech*" (each with an article and a reference to a particular location/source).

25   Newsom, "Wisdom and the Discourse of Patriarchal Wisdom," 147–48.

26   Lincoln, *Discourse*, 137, n. 10.

27   See chapter 2, "*Gender* and Impersonal Speech."

section on classification is theory-laden, while the ongoing discussion of *gender* is more concerned with pragmatic identifications of semantic patterns than with abstract levels of theory, and the material on Ben Sira's colonial situation, also, is handled with a minimum of theoretical discussion.

The current study considers statements in the Book of Ben Sira in the context of relations that are portrayed in terms of *gender*. Explicitly, this is not a comparative analysis of *gender* in the texts that bear Ben Sira's name, but an analysis of *gender* in one specific linguistic strand. I presume there is sufficient semantic coherence among the extant Hebrew MSS that they can be *interpreted* together as a coherent discourse despite a span of more than a thousand years for their dates of production. The detailed analyses in later chapters demonstrate a high level of semantic equivalence between relevant gender-focal verses that are extant in multiple MSS. With this consideration in mind, the choice of discourse theory as the basic hermeneutical strategy permits a rigorous analysis of the production of meaning within a group of manuscripts that share ideological elements.[28]

The thirty passages I have chosen to translate from the Book of Ben Sira are, uniformly, members of the earlier stage in the development of the Hebrew texts of Ben Sira.[29] Together, the thirty passages have two hundred and sixty-eight Hebrew bicola, of which two hundred and sixty-five are part of the early textual-stratum of the Book of Ben Sira, called HTI.[30] The three bicola from the later addition, HTII, occur in a single pericope (BBS 30:11–13).[31] Thus, the provenance of my text-base exhibits a significant measure of uniformity.

Though the methodological range for this project is narrow, I want my work to be 'in conversation with' that of scholars using a broad range of analytical strategies. It is important, therefore, to situate this work in the chain

---

28 I do not presume that a particular unit would have the same discursive purposes in all the Hebrew manuscripts where it is present, but I expect that there is less difference among these units than between them and other textual witnesses.

29 For a chart of all the passages, see the table on page vi. Of the thirty translated units of BBS, four units in Sirach have a GII addition that is not part of the extant Hebrew (BBS 3:1–16 [fig. 4-1] has an addition at Sir 3:7; BBS 13:14–20 [fig. 5-3] at Sir 13:14; BBS 16:1–4 [fig. 4-4] at Sir 16:3; BBS 17:1–8 [fig. 5-2] has additions at Sir 17:5,8). The Greek text is from Ziegler, *Septuaginta XII/2: Sapientia Iesu Filii Sirach*.

30 For the terminology, see Skehan and Di Lella (*Wisdom*, 55–59, here 55; following Kearns, "Ecclesiasticus," 547–50), who mentions "HTI, the Hebrew original of Ben Sira; HTII, the expanded Hebrew text of one or more recensions; G1, the grandson's Greek translation of HTI; GII, the expanded Greek translation based on HTII."

31 In the unit BBS 30:11–13, one colon from verse 11 and two from verse 12 are part of the GII additions to Sirach. See chart A4-3, in the Appendix, for the cola in BBS 30:11–13 that match the GII additions according to Ziegler.

of tradition so that it is accessible to readers with varied perspectives. For those who wish to enlarge the range of hermeneutical perspectives, I suggest reading the current study in conjunction with Skehan and Di Lella's *Wisdom of Ben Sira*, which provides an excellent commentary on a variety of issues.[32]

In the analyses that follow, I evaluate the results on a scale from *probable* (very likely) through *possible* (less likely) to *conjectural* (suspended judgment, could be either likely or unlikely). Why do I include *conjectural* translations and interpretations? A phrase or sentence may ultimately be judged *impossible*, but that phrase might elicit a response from a reader, in the form of a new direction of investigation that could yield positive results. Thus, I give a full set of not-*impossible* data so as not to circumscribe the play of imagination, as a way of participating in the chain of tradition.

The difficult nature of the language of the Book of Ben Sira is another factor in the decision to include *conjectural* conclusions. The Hebrew is notoriously convoluted and rife with wordplay. My guide in this textual maze is Kister's comment that Ben Sira's book "is full of rare words and *hapax legomena*, and his love of puns leads to their extensive use. Some of these were already incomprehensible to readers two or three generations after his time."[33] His statement—which confirms my assessment of the Book of Ben Sira—encourages me to push the possibilities of wordplay to their limits, and perhaps beyond. One of the delights offered by the Hebrew language is its elasticity, its capacity to enfold multiple meanings. Though I do not expect to 'recover' Ben Sira's puns, I identify certain passages as likely sites for wordplay and suggest possible puns, and also offer conjectures for alternative readings based on perceptions of sustained wordplay.

---

32 For overviews of Ben Sira studies since that of Skehan and Di Lella, see Di Lella ("Wisdom of Ben Sira" [1996]); Reiterer ("Review of Recent Research on the Book of Ben Sira (1980–1996)") and Beentjes ("Some Major Topics in Ben Sira Research" [2005/6]), among others. Balla (*Ben Sira on Family*) gives both Greek and Hebrew for many of the passages I analyze, and she compares the two text traditions. For an alternative view of *gender* in the Ben Sira texts, see Camp (*Gender and the Rise of Canon Consciousness*). For a separate translation of the Greek, see Wright ("Wisdom of Iesous Son of Sirach," in NETS).

33 Kister, "Genizah Manuscripts," 39. Note that one of the "readers two or three generations after" Ben Sira could be the grandson who translated the work into Greek.

1.3 Classification

The process of theorizing about women and men as related categories has a lengthy history, which in the West made its formal debut with the ancient Greeks. Etiological stories—such as the poems of Hesiod and the early chapters of Genesis—construct implicit taxonomies that include *gender*, but the earliest formal, explicit taxonomies of gender are those by Athenian philosophers of the fourth century BCE. The Greek gender-taxonomy that emerged from this place and time became hegemonic with the expanded influence of Greek language and culture that characterized the Hellenistic empires that succeeded Alexander. Since Ben Sira wrote in the presence of this imperial Hellenistic cultural hegemony, any gender-related taxonomy in the Book of Ben Sira must be examined in relation to the pervasive Greek model that ordered the world around him. The Greek model was, and is, a successfully-naturalized taxonomy, meaning that it is largely invisible—thus, its workings require thorough exposition, a measure that is justified because classification has a weighty role in the production of gendered discourse.

There are essential differences between the model of *gender* that I perceive in the Book of Ben Sira and the corresponding model prevalent in the Hellenistic world within which Ben Sira produced his text. The two models use the same set of elements, but connections between the elements are organized differently, producing taxonomic systems that do not function in the same way. The fundamental difference I describe is the existence of an active *logos* component (Greek model), or a dormant one (BBS model), in the gender taxonomies. I compile an image of the Greek taxonomy by reference to a series of theorists whose work, taken together, delineates both the point at which the discourse of *gender* in the Book of Ben Sira diverges from the Hellenistic model and the implications of this divergence for gender studies. The goal is to produce "distinct articulations of gender asymmetry" for the two cultural systems.[34]

1.3.1 Binary Oppositions and Deconstruction

A *binary opposition* is a pair of categories that are considered to be, in essence, immiscible opposites. The hierarchical nature of binary thinking is manifest in this smallest, most basic unit of taxonomic logic—a binary opposition itself encodes hierarchy through the different valuation of its two components. Some standard binaries in Western systems are presence/absence,

---

34   Butler, *Gender Trouble*, 45-46.

male/female, life/death, light/darkness, right/left, culture/nature and good/evil. Binary oppositions are a feature of many models used for semantic analysis, although structuralists, poststructuralists, discourse theorists, and others do not presume the same sorts of epistemological baggage for binaries.

For structuralists such as the anthropologist Lévi-Strauss, binaries are the basic cognitive unit that organizes the timeless and universal structure of language. The structuralist model is the basis for the work of other theoreticians including poststructuralists and deconstructive analysts, who reinterpret the role of binaries. In a deconstructive system, binary oppositions retain their importance although the view of structures as unchanging is rejected. Instead, deconstructive systems emphasize the hierarchical aspect of binary-based systems by foregrounding the consistent and unequal valuation of the two terms within Western cultural traditions—the dominant term in each pairing, the *unmarked* taxon, is considered more desirable and assumes normative status.[35] The unmarked taxon functions as the unspoken default, so that the *marked* taxon's label must be stated for its presence to be recognized. Customarily, the unmarked taxon is listed first, as in "good/evil." Unlike the structuralist model's claim to universality and timelessness, the deconstructive approach posits an unstable situation in which the binaries operate locally.

A deconstructive system does not operate by reversing the values of the unmarked and marked taxa. Merely reversing the hierarchies is futile, because although "it is a powerful act to turn the world upside down, ... a simple 180-degree rotation is not difficult to undo. An order twice inverted is an order restored, perhaps even strengthened as a result of the exercise."[36] This rebound effect was the case with the ultimately-illusory destabilizations of binary order in Greek drama—Zeitlin describes a "mobility of temporary reversals and dialectical play with opposites" that pushed the interplay of taxa to a condition of "dangerous indeterminacy" that might perturb the elite male spectators, yet the disruption was temporary because the resolution of a play reinstated the dominant taxa.[37]

A fundamental relationship among binary oppositions in Western systems of classification is exposed by Derrida. His insight on phallogocentrism is the basis for my distinction between the Book of Ben Sira's discourse of *gender* and that of the Greek system, and I quote at length from his expositions. In

---

35 These definitions for *marked* and *unmarked* derive from Cultural Studies, and are unlike Lincoln's definition from Linguistics: "Those possessed of the property under discussion constitute the marked class; those who do not, fall into the unmarked class" ("Tyranny," 5).

36 Lincoln, *Discourse*, 159.

37 Zeitlin, "Playing," 86.

response to an interviewer's comment that "sexual difference is present in many of your texts," Derrida states:

> I speak especially ... about sexual **differences** rather than a single difference—dual and oppositional—that is indeed, with phallocentrism, with that which I also nickname "**phallogocentrism**," a structural feature of philosophic discourse that has prevailed in the tradition. Deconstruction passes through it, from any starting place. Everything comes back there. ... this powerful phallogocentric foundation that conditions almost all of our cultural heritage. ... it is represented, certainly in different but equal ways, in Plato, as well as in Freud or Lacan, in Kant as well as in Hegel, Heidegger or Lévinas. In any case, I've set myself to show it.[38]

The passage refers to the binary male/female as the "sexual difference" that is "dual and oppositional." It is an essential part of the phallogocentric structural system, in which it functions as a *center* of "philosophic discourse"—an irreplaceable element through which all others in the system have meaning. Presence/absence is the other central binary, and it gives its name "presence" (*logos*) to the title for such a system, "logocentric." Within a logocentric system, the unmarked term *male* instantiates *presence* by the presence of the phallus[39]—thus the term "phallogocentrism" names the two binaries as a linked center. By cross-referencing *male* (the phallus) with *presence* (*logos*), Derrida removes the option of deniability from both taxa. Discursive sleight of hand cannot naturalize either module when this powerful linkage explicitly implicates them, together. The enunciatory act breaks the apparent inevitability of the binary pattern so that the dominant taxa of the binaries can no longer evoke each other at the level of 'nature.'

Derrida elaborates on the ramifications of phallogocentrism in his response to comments by McDonald. The immediate context is her remarks on the biblical story of Adam and Eve, to which Derrida offers the following commentary on Lévinas' analyses of those figures.[40] Lévinas moves the origin of sexually-differentiated humanity to the building of Eve from Adam's side/rib in Gen 2:21, in order to preserve "the universality of moral laws" by deriving them from Gen 1, the sexually-undifferentiated Human.

> Once again, the classical interpretation marks as masculine sexuality that which it presents as a neutral originality or, at least, as prior and superior to any sexual

---

38 Derrida, "Autrui est secret," emphasis original; my translation (based on Baldridge's in Dely's article, "Jacques Derrida," 5).

39 Some theoretic models distinguish the physical object, "the penis," from the abstract concept, "the phallus," but the terms are interchangeable at the present taxonomic level of discussion—the physical presence of the penis signifies the symbolic potency of the phallus.

40 Lévinas, "Le judaïsme et le féminin"; "Et Dieu créa la femme."

marking. Lévinas indeed senses the risk there would be in erasing sexual difference. He maintains it thus: the human in general remains a sexed being. But he cannot do it, so it seems, without placing (differentiated) sexuality beneath humanity (that which holds at the level of the mind/spirit) and especially without simultaneously putting the masculine at the beginning and in command, at the *arkhè*, at the level of Spirit. Carrying the most self-interested contradiction, this gesture repeats itself since, let us say, "Adam and Eve"—and the analogy persists in "modernity" despite all the differences of style and of treatment. ... Whatever the complexity of the pathways and the knots of the rhetoric, don't you believe that the Freudian movement repeats this "logic"? Is it not also the risk run by Heidegger? One should perhaps say, rather, the risk **avoided** because phallogo-centrism is insurance against the return of that which is, without doubt, dreaded as the most distressing risk.[41]

The passage above demonstrates, through comments on the interpretation of a biblical text, Derrida's view of the instantiation and naturalization of phallogo-centric marking. The "most distressing risk" is that sexual differentiation is not binary—i.e., that the penis-or-phallus ceases to signify *presence* in its function as a taxonomizer, whereupon the system of mutually-reinforcing binaries breaks down, producing the possibility that, as stated in "Autrui est secret," there are "sexual differences rather than one sole difference [that is] dual and oppositional." In the analysis of Lévinas' formulation, Derrida describes how two binaries, first/second and spirit/body, are mapped with a third, male/female. Again, as in his comments on the *phallus*-and-*logos* combination he names "phallogocentrism," Derrida foregrounds the clustering aspect of the deployment of binary oppositions—they hunt in packs, so to speak, meaning that the clustered binaries reinforce each other. Attacking a single binary in this system is futile.

The list of binary oppositions, below, represents many of those cited as fundamental units of discourse.

(life/death)
male/female ——————— presence/absence
first/second ——————— primacy/subordinacy (original/derivative)
mind/body ——————— reason/emotion (or speech/writing)
light/dark; white/black —— good/evil
right/left ——————— forthright/devious
culture/nature ————— civilization/savagery
nature/culture ————— 'natural'/artificial

---

41   Derrida, "Chorégraphies," 109, emphasis original; my translation (based on McDonald's, "Interview," 73).

I sequence the elements in the two columns of the chart so that binaries in the left column are physically perceptible and those in the right-hand column are comparatively abstract. Binaries in the same row have some degree of relation in Western thought-systems, such as the link between presence/absence and male/female—likewise reason/emotion with mind/body, and good/evil with light/darkness. The two bottom rows show different orderings of the terms "culture" and "nature." The culture/nature binary links *culture* with *civilization* as unmarked terms, but the reverse case is also possible, with *culture* as the marked term matching *artificial*. Often, the observable binaries of these conglomerations naturalize those that are conceptual—the relation between physical and abstract is similar to that of metaphors, in which a physical category such as "vision" will lend its vocabulary to the elements of an abstract category such as "understanding," producing, in this case, the metaphoric statement "I see what you mean."

1.3.2 Binary Oppositions and Taxonomic Logic

Theories of classification provide a vocabulary to enunciate a distrust of naturalized discourse and to analyze the semantic maneuvers involved in the discursive construction and maintenance of power differentials. Practical application of these theories not only demonstrates the constructedness of hegemonic taxonomies that use the presumption of universality to naturalize social inequities, but also can describe the use of features such as anomalies to destabilize these taxonomic systems. The primary tool for these activities— the binary opposition, which is "the basic morpheme of taxonomic logic"—is itself an empty set of placeholders. "What is fundamental to classificatory logic is thus … the mere fact of polarity."[42]

Diagrams represent classificatory logic as a cascading series of binary oppositions, which together produce a hierarchical system. The binaries act as taxonomizers, each of which divides the group into a subset of those that match salient elements of one taxon and a subset of those that do not. The categories chosen as taxonomizers, and their sequence, determine the results of a taxonomy, producing a particular serial ranking for the subclasses of the diagram's taxonomic tree. Social hierarchies can thus be encoded in the form of taxonomies and, when more than one set of rankings is produced by a taxonomy, the implications of the social parameters expand dramatically. For example, Lincoln analyzes a hierarchical model of the soul, from Plato's works (*Timaios* and *Republic*), as a multimodular taxonomy achieved by the

---

42   Lincoln, "Tyranny," 3.

simultaneous "categorizing three different entities that are brought into correlation with one another: varieties of the soul, parts of the body, and social classes."[43] This hierarchical and artificial system comes to seem natural, pre-existing, and inevitable through conflation with the human form. The connection is established by combining the binaries mind/body and up/down (or, superior/inferior) in a metaphorical construct that maps the human form onto a scale of value—highest is most valuable, lowest is least, and *mind* is valued over *body*. Thus, whatever abstract category receives the "head/mind" role is naturalized as preeminent by its relation to the incontrovertible 'natural' fact that human heads are at the top of the organism. Naturalized systems blur their relationship with discourse's partner *force*,[44] and a successfully-naturalized discourse evades challenge because it remains implicit—its indistinct outlines provide camouflage. In this way, "that which is unsaid can be far more powerful than that which is openly asserted," because it forestalls criticism.[45]

1.4 Taxonomies of *Gender*

Significantly, the naturalizing "head" metaphor present in Plato's thought-system is not part of the taxonomies of the Book of Ben Sira. There is no instance of a head/body binary and, thus, no naturalizing discourse as a trope.[46] However, one external source of authority in the Book of Ben Sira is

---

43 Lincoln, *Discourse*, 135.

44 Lincoln, *Discourse*, 4–5. As an act of resistance to the "social hierarchy" constructed by the binary theory/practice, a corollary of the head/body binary, Lincoln (*Discourse*, 171–72) uses his own formulations to discuss themes such as the interrelation of "power" and "discourse" rather than perpetuating specific sets of vocabulary from Foucault, Bourdieu, Scott, or other theoreticians whose works he lists in the bibliography of *Discourse*. For example, when Lincoln notes that any given taxonomical system allows only a limited range of thought and precludes all other possibilities (ibid., 137 n. 10 [p. 197]), I hear echoes of Foucault's *episteme* and am reminded of Foucault's generous statement that he writes "for users, not readers," and thus would like his books to be "a kind of tool-box which others can rummage through to find a tool" and use it "however they wish in their own area" ("Prisons et asiles," 523–524).

45 Lincoln, "Tyranny," 17.

46 The semantic range for ראש, "head," includes "beginning" (nine instances, all seven that occur in Greek translated by ἀρχή) and "lift/lower a head" for an increase or a lessening of dignity (six times, all Greek translations as κεφαλή). For the lexical list for ראש in BBS, see chart AppLex-5 in the Appendix.

The linkage "superior = mind = head" does not develop in the Hebrew Bible or the Book of Ben Sira because the body part that is held responsible for volition and thought is more likely to be the heart than the head or brain. The *heart* cannot function as the "superior" portion of

the early chapters of Genesis, sometimes cited through allusions that include ראש as "beginning." Though the etiological appeal to Genesis parallels the Greek use of Hesiod, in the Book of Ben Sira the directions of inquiry, and the results, do not parallel the phallogocentric Greek model.

1.4.1 Ben Sira's *Taxonomy of Pairs* and *Affinity-Schema*

The Book of Ben Sira presents its readers with a simple taxonomic principle that is enunciated, distinctly, in the descriptions of God's "works" of creating the universe. Examples of Ben Sira's *taxonomy of pairs* are shown in chart 1-2, below.

Chart 1-2: BBS 33:14–15 (MS E, composite) and 42:24–25 (MSS B, M)

33:14	[Opposite bad-things] are good
	—and opposite life is death.
	Opposite a good man is a wicked one
	—and opposite light, darkness.
33:15	Regard all the works of God
	—all of them in pairs, this-one close by that-one.
42:24	All of them in pairs, this-one by that-one
	—and He has not made any of them deceptive.
42:25	This-one according to that-one renews their goodness
	—and who can have enough of beholding their splendor?

The pairs of opposites Ben Sira describes are, in current terminology, binary oppositions. [47] The semantic range for the preposition לעומת (לְעֻמַּת) in 33:15b, translated as "close by," includes "beside," "parallel to," or "corresponding to." Some pairs of opposites are mentioned, such as those given in 33:14 ("bad-things and good," "life and death," "light and darkness"), but there are no explicit examples related to sex or gender, such as "male and female" or "masculine and feminine." The absence of the male/female binary in the Book of Ben Sira—given the explicit fact that the opposites are presented as part of a universal divine pattern and not as random items—could be due to the invisibility of a foundational assumption, but it could also indicate that Ben Sira did not consider the two categories opposed. A non-oppositional connection

---

this naturalizing equation because the heart is located at the center of the body, and thus would signify in a hierarchy based on the binary center/periphery.

47 See *DCH* 4:555b–554a.; see chart 5:3, in chapter 5, for the Hebrew and a fuller discussion.

between the categories can be present in the Book of Ben Sira as an allusion to God's speech in Gen 2:18 that describes the plan for making a human female to match the male: she is to function as עֵזֶר כְּנֶגְדּוֹ "a helper/rescuer corresponding to him."[48] The allusion in the Book of Ben Sira would be made through עֵזֶר in BBS 36:24: קנה אשה ראשית קנין עזר ומבצר ועמוד משען, "Gaining a wife is primary-gain—helper/rescuer and fortress and pillar of support".[49]

Whether or not the male/female binary is part of Ben Sira's taxonomy of creation, in the Book of Ben Sira it functions in a set of four characters (Sage, Right Wife, Fool, and Wrong Wife) whose interrelations I describe as a *schema of affinities and antipathies*. The affinity-schema defines appropriate relationships for the central figure, the Sage, with regard to his choice of a spouse and his choice of male friends.[50] These schematic figures appear in a virulently anti-female passage, and I introduce them at the beginning of the discussions of gender taxonomies because they are a useful test-case.

A taxonomy can be derived from the schema, as shown below in charts 1-3a and 1-3b. Different rankings are produced for Ben Sira's figures by a reversal in the order of the taxonomizers. The selection and sequencing of taxonomizers is "something that must be done by induction because the text is mute on this point."[51] For the group in the Book of Ben Sira, the choice of taxonomizers is clear because the four figures of the taxonomy are composites of two binary oppositions, wise/foolish and male/female. The two taxonomizers are Piety ("Do they fear God?") and Sex ("Are they male?"). Because the Book of Ben Sira equates "fearing God" with Wisdom (BBS 15:1), the subgroup that fears God is labeled "wise." When the total set is separated first according to Piety and then those subgroups are separated according to Sex, the following ranked values result for the four figures:

---

48 See *DCH* 5:604b כְּנֶגֶד "corresponding to, fit for, ... Gen 2:18, 20." The preposition in BBS 33:14 that indicates a relation of opposition is נוכח.

49 See chapter 5, chart 5-6, for a detailed analysis of the passage, BBS 36:18–26.

50 Schematic aspects of the affinity-schema are presented in chapter 2, "*Gender and Impersonal Speech*," but are not relevant to the current discussion.

51 Lincoln, *Discourse*, 138. Given categorization's potential to determine the outcome of an analysis, it is important to test a range of taxonomizers in different sequences, and to cross-check the resulting rankings with data from the text—inevitably, a subjective process.

Chart 1-3a: Ranking of figures from BBS, in a religion-primary taxonomy

	ALL JUDEANS/JEWS			
Taxonomizers				
1. PIETY	+		-	
(God-fearing)	WISE		FOOLISH	
2. SEX	+	-	+	-
(male)	WISE MAN	WISE WOMAN	FOOLISH MAN	FOOLISH WOMAN
RANK	1	2	3	4
CODING	+ / +	+ / -	- / +	- / -
BBS FIGURES:	SAGE	RIGHT WIFE	FOOL	WRONG WIFE

"Fear of God" (יראת אלהים) is chosen as a taxonomizing attribute because it is the primary standard by which Ben Sira evaluates a Jewish male. Ben Sira's texts link phrases related to "fearing God" with Wisdom eight times (three of these include Torah) and declare five times that fearing God is the "greatest" value, including the statement that a ruler and a judge will be honored, but "there is none greater than one who fears God" (BBS 10:24).[52] Though Ben Sira does not link "fearing God" directly with any female figure, his allusion to the Valorous Wife (Prov 31:10–31) as the prototype for the Right Wife would encompass the statement that "a woman who fears YHWH, she is to be praised" (Prov 31:30), thus including women within the category of highest value.[53] However, when Sex is the first-order taxonomizer, the rankings change:

---

52   Seven of the eight associations of fear-of-God with Wisdom occur in Sirach, but are not extant in Hebrew. The eighth instance is BBS 15:1 (MSS A and B), linking one-who-fears-YYY ("YYY" stands for YHWH) with both Wisdom and Torah. Of the five links with "greatest," two are in BBS (BBS 10:24, MS A, and BBS 40:26, MS B).

53   The verse BBS 26:2 states that: "A 'valorous wife' fattens her husband—and [his years] … [rejoice]." See chapter 5, "Human Female, Biblical Females," for a discussion of possible prototypes for the Wrong Wife and Right Wife.

Chart 1-3b: Ranking of figures from BBS, in a gender-primary taxonomy

	ALL JUDEANS/JEWS			
Taxonomizers				
1. SEX (male)	+ MEN		− WOMEN	
2. PIETY (God-fearing)	+ WISE MAN	− FOOLISH MAN	+ WISE WOMAN	− FOOLISH WOMAN
RANK	1	2	3	4
CODING	+ / +	+ / −	− / +	− / −
BBS FIGURES:	SAGE	FOOL	RIGHT WIFE	WRONG WIFE

Reversing the sequence of the taxonomizers has major consequences for the hierarchy of the four figures: both male figures now rank above the females. However, an assertion that the taxonomy values the Fool above the Right Wife is precluded by verses such as BBS 40:23: "Friend and companion will give timely guidance—better than both, an intelligent wife (אשה משכלת)." Values attuned to the Sex-first hierarchy are not present in any extant Hebrew passage,[54] in contrast to the numerous verses in the Book of Ben Sira that stress values like fearing-God.[55] Therefore, the Piety-first model in chart 1-3a is more accurate for the derivation of the four figures in Ben Sira's affinity-schema. As shown in charts 1-3a and 1-3b, the first-order taxonomizer has priority in delineating which of the potential paths of discourse are available and which disappear—an illustration of the fact that any given taxonomical system "renders only *certain kinds* of thought and action possible, simultaneously precluding infinite others."[56] And, as a point of comparison with Greek taxonomic maneuvers, the Book of Ben Sira shows no examples of reversals in its first-order taxonomized categories, unlike Greek drama, which deploys the previously-mentioned device of a temporary, blatant reversal

---

54 The only exception is BBS 42:14, "Better the evil of a man than goodness of a woman," discussed in detail in chapter 4 (see chart 4-16).

55 Botha observes, in the analysis of BBS 9:1–9 (on women) and 9:10–16 (on men), that in Ben Sira's society, the division between "the God-fearing and the apostate" is one that "runs much deeper" than that "between male and female" ("Through a Woman," 32; mentioning work by McKeating and Smend).

56 Lincoln, *Discourse*, 137 n. 10 (p. 197).

of taxonomic precedence followed by restoration of 'the natural order' at the close of the play.[57]

1.4.2 A Greek Taxonomy of *Gender*

The schema of affinities in the Book of Ben Sira employs the binary male/ female through which privileges accrue to those who are classified as *male*. However, though that binary coding seems to pervade human cultures, it does not always occupy the same place in every system of signification. In particular, Ben Sira's taxonomic landscape is radically unlike the major Greek model of *gender* that the Hellenistic cultures inherited from Hellenic authors and philosophers—in particular, from Hesiod and Plato. Although the systems share elements, the arrangements of those elements produce different effects. For example, two taxonomic traits common to the "discourse of misogyny" are the identification of *woman* with *misfortune*, at an essential level, and woman's ontologically-secondary status.[58] These traits, present in "canonical Greek texts and notably in Hesiod,"[59] are present also in later Platonist thinkers such as Philo and Paul, but neither element is present in the Book of Ben Sira.

The hegemonic Greek discourse of *gender*, which Derrida identifies as the beginning of phallogocentrism, took shape in conjunction with a reordering of the signification of key terminology in Greek thought. According to Lincoln, in epic authors such as Hesiod and Homer, *logos* is considered feminine—it is the duplicitous speech assigned to Pandora—while *mythos* is hyper-masculine declarations like those of Achilles. After the time of Plato, the meanings and gender-assignments for the terms had reversed—the outcome of a discursive struggle. As Greek men of the dominant class found themselves unable

> [to] establish their dominance by force and a discourse of force (i.e., *mythos* in its epic sense), they adopted a discourse of crafty, well-wrought persuasion (i.e., *logos*). In this moment, they shifted the basis for their claim to preeminence, emphasizing their intellect, education, sophistication, and speech, instead of their birth, rank, weapons, and brawn.[60]

---

57 Anti-woman verses such as BBS 42:14 do not restore an underlying misogyny even though that verse occurs in the last unit about human females. See a further discussion in chapter 4.

58 Boyarin, *Carnal Israel*, 80.

59 Boyarin, *Carnal Israel*, 80. Boyarin mentions that the story of Pandora is central to the Greek discourse of *gender* (ibid., 78).

60 Lincoln, "Gendered Discourses," 12.

Ultimately, it was Plato's intervention that proved decisive and, by the time he was finished, the superiority of a sanitized and aggrandized *"logos"* over a trivialized and marginalized *"mythos"* had been secured.[61]

The pivot-point in this discursive choreography is the fact that *male* retains its unmarked status within the nexus of binary-terms that recombine around it. The historical reversal of value between the taxa of the binary mythos/logos demonstrates the inherent neutrality of the generic binary form, whose fundamental feature is its polarity.

Another binary is entangled in the mythos/logos reversal: the values of the binary nature/culture also reverse. When *mythos* is the unmarked taxon it causes *nature* to be unmarked also, as *natural* and *male* in relation to *logos* as *artificial* and *female*. This variant of the binary is demonstrably part of the epic gender-taxonomy of Homer and Hesiod, who link "culture" with "artifice." When Plato successfully stabilizes the reversed binary so that *logos* becomes unmarked, *culture* likewise becomes unmarked, as *civilization* in opposition to *mythos* as *nature*. These shifts of gender-linkage for mythos/logos and nature/culture demonstrate that the male/female binary is a central semantic device in the evolving Greek system, since the currently-valued condition always will be associated with the unmarked taxon *male*, whose ranking remains unchanged. The central role of the male/female binary combines with the centrality of *logos* in Plato's writings, forming the phallogocentric paradigm.

Foxhall declares that *gender* "is probably the most vigorous expression of meaning available to ancient Greek culture: its very pervasiveness attests its vitality. Consequently gender ... often serves as a metaphor for expressing other relationships. And it becomes a kind of lens through which Greeks perceived and thus defined the world around them."[62] The discursive lens of *gender* for ancient Greek culture is inscribed in Hesiod's story of Pandora, which had an etiological function in Greek society comparable to that of the early chapters of Genesis in Jewish and Christian societies. To speak of "a discourse of *gender* in ancient Greece" is to speak of Pandora, for she is the embodiment of that discourse. Pandora's story occurs in two works by Hesiod.[63] These stories tell how Zeus obtains revenge against humans for the theft of fire: He orders gods and goddesses to make a living statue of a young woman and to give her gifts according to their talents: Hephaestus forms the figure from clay and makes a golden headband decorated with lifelike monsters;

---

61   Lincoln, "Competing Discourses," 364.

62   Foxhall, "Household, Gender and Property," 23.

63   Hesiod, *Hesiod, the Homeric Hymns, and Homerica* (trans. Hugh G. Evelyn-White). The stories, with variations, are in *Theogony* (lines 561–616) and *Works and Days* (47–105).

Athena dresses her in "silvery" clothing and a veil; and other goddesses donate golden jewelry and garlands of flowers. The final gifts are from Hermes, who is ordered by Zeus "to put in her a shameless mind and a deceitful nature." Obediently, Hermes sets "lies and crafty words [λόγος] and a deceitful nature" within her and "puts speech in her" and names her "Pandora."[64] Pandora—the "All-endowed"—is now herself a 'gift,' and Hermes takes her to the man selected by Zeus to receive the "beautiful evil."[65] Too late, when he already has "the evil," the man understands. Pandora opens the storage jar that holds her gifts from the gods, and all the "evils" of the world fly out to torment people ever after. "For ere this the tribes of men lived on earth remote and free from evils [κάκη] and hard toil and heavy sicknesses which bring the Death-spirits upon men."[66]

A notably strange aspect of the story is the image of how this irresistible "gift" would appear to the wonder-struck gods and humans who beheld her. According to McClure, "[t]he spectacle of Pandora bedecked in nuptial garments—the elaborate gifts of clothing and jewelry given by the gods— makes her the concrete embodiment of feminine guile; she is both pure body and pure artifice."[67] Pandora is "both pure body and pure artifice"—*body* and *culture-as-artifice* being two marked taxa linked with the taxon *female*. Thus Pandora, the originary female Greek figure, functions as an empty billboard for the display of any taxa linked to *female*; this is especially evident with the taxon *evil* (κακός), mentioned many times with regard to Pandora.[68] Although the veil that covers Pandora in the *Theogony* could represent concealment, Loraux notes that "the woman has no interior to conceal. In short, in the *Theogony*, the first woman is her adornments—she has no body."[69] Another

---

64   The lines about Pandora's mind and speech are only in *Works and Days*, but *Theogony* has a longer section on ornaments. Her name, "the All-endowed," is explained in lines 81–82 as a reference to the fact that all the gods and goddesses each gave a gift.

65   The man is Epimetheus (Afterthought), whose brother Prometheus (Forethought) began the contest with Zeus, in the larger tale that includes the story of Pandora. This part of the story is only in *WD*, as is the section about the "storage jar."

66   The quote is from *WD* (90), but a version is present in both texts. "Death-spirits" is Keres (singular, Κήρ), Greek female spirits associated with violent death and death from disease.

67   McClure, *Spoken*, 63. Zeitlin ("Playing," 79 n.39) adds that Pandora is also woman-as-nature—"the physical, 'creaturely' side of life"—so that "[w]oman therefore embodies both extremes of nature and culture that together conspire to waste a man's substance and dry him up before his time."

68   There are seven instances in *WD*, referring to Pandora herself as "evil" or to the effects of her intrusion into the world of men; in *Th* there are six such instances.

69   Loraux, "On the Race of Women," 81. Note that if the lifelike golden creatures on her headband signify the disembodied Pandora, she then figures as an *animal* or *monster*.

way to phrase this is to say that there is no "Pandora" inside the apparel—she figures *absence* rather than *presence*. The image of Pandora is a perfect embodiment of the link between *female* and *absence* that is an entailment of the Platonic phallogocentric taxonomy.

The ubiquitousness of phallogocentrism—the enshrinement of the *phallus* as *logos*, "presence"—concerns contemporary theoreticians of *gender*. Ortner, speaking of the intersection of the binaries male/female and culture/nature, notes that "the two oppositions easily move into a relationship of mutual metaphorization."[70] When the two oppositions blend, Western phallogocentric thought-systems code the taxon *culture* as *male* and *nature* as *female*. "The logic that ... men get to be in the business of trying to transcend species-being, while women, seen as being mired in species-being, tend to drag men down" still seems "enormously widespread."[71] Butler voices similar concerns, that

> reason and mind are associated with masculinity and agency, while the body and nature are considered to be the mute facticity of the feminine, awaiting signification from an opposing masculine subject. ... The sexual politics that construct and maintain this distinction are effectively concealed by the discursive production of a nature and, indeed, a natural sex that postures as the unquestioned foundation of culture.[72]

Butler then carries the argument into structuralist theory, stating that "if the very designation of sex is political, then 'sex,' that designation supposed to be most in the raw, proves to be always already 'cooked,' and the central distinctions of structuralist anthropology appear to collapse."[73] Yet, as shown previously, the taxa *culture* and *nature* can be ordered as culture/nature (civilization/savagery) or as nature/culture ('natural'/artificial), but in both cases the unmarked taxon remains coded as *male*.

The concept of *phallogocentrism* has great explanatory power. Naming an invisible connection between the two binaries disrupts the seamless appearance of the taxonomy and can provide an entrance point for deconstructive analyses and, eventually, the possibility of recalibrating the taxonomy. DuBois, who uses the concept to analyze psychoanalytic theory, credits Derrida for pointing out that "Lacanian discourse, in its phallogocentrism, justifies a historically

---

70 Ortner, "So, *Is* Female to Male," 179.

71 Ortner, "So, *Is* Female to Male," 180.

72 Butler, *Gender Trouble*, 48. Butler prefaces this remark by citing anthropologists MacCormack and Strathern (*Nature, Culture, and Gender*).

73 Butler, *Gender Trouble*, 48.

dominant androcentrism."[74] She identifies another aspect related to the *mythos/logos* shift: "a transformation in the description of the female body … one that moves from metaphorical, analogical terms to a metonymic definition in the works of Aristotle."[75] The entailment of this move is that the Greek system has only one kind of person—a man—and that the category human consists of perfect examples, which are men, and defective ones, which are women.

As perfect examples of their kind, male humans are the only ones who can reproduce another creature of that category. Thus, according to Aristotle, the origin and quickening of the embryo is entirely from the male because the male has "something better and more divine in that it is the principle of movement for generated things, while the female serves as their matter."[76] Aristotle mobilizes standard phallogocentric binaries (spirit/matter; mobile/static; active/passive) but allows females a passive contribution. The other standard Greek taxonomy metonymizes females as containers for an entirely-male contribution: women are the oven that bakes the bread and—a standard metonymy—the earth that receives and nourishes a seed in whose production it had no part. The paradigmatic statement of woman-as-nurse is from Aeschylus's *Oresteia*, spoken by Apollo:

> The mother is no parent of that which is called
> her child, but only nurse of the new-planted seed
> that grows. The parent is he who mounts. A stranger she
> preserves a stranger's seed, if no god interfere.[77]

Though some Hellenic medical writers posit a female contribution to the embryo,[78] playwrights and philosophers seem to have ignored such theories in favor of the gender-discourse that limited women to an entirely supplemental role.

In contrast, though Jewish taxonomy is phallocentric in many ways, the embryology of the Book of Ben Sira places God, and not a male human, as the primary force in the fashioning of the embryo.

---

74 DuBois, *Sowing*, 16. She quotes Derrida ("Purveyor of Truth," 96–97).

75 DuBois, *Sowing*, 30.

76 Witt, "Form, Normativity and Gender," 123, citing Aristotle (from *Gen. An.* 732a2–10).

77 DuBois, *Sowing*, 33 (from *Eumenides* 658–61).

78 Dean-Jones (*Women's Bodies*, 149) cites the school of Hippocrates as believing women contribute in reproduction and the school of Aristotle as denying women a role, and mentions individuals who did, and did not, think women contribute to the embryo.

Chart 1-4a: Embryology in the Book of Ben Sira

BBS 50:22 (MS B)   עתה ברכו נא את ייי אלהי ישראל המפלא לעשות בארץ :
                                    המגדל אדם מרחם ויעשהו כרצונו :

Now, let us bless YYY the God of Israel—who does wondrously on the earth!
Who grows a human from the womb—and builds him according to His will.

For colon b, see עשה in *DCH* 6:586b "מַפְלָא לַעֲשׂוֹת 'he was making wonderful
to do,' i.e., 'doing wondrously' … Si 50:22." For colon d, see ibid., p. 587a
"'make, create, build, fashion'"; p. 588a, "OBJ 'human being' Si 50:22."

Moreover, a rabbinic text declares explicitly that the mother's contribution to
an embryo is equivalent to that of the father.[79]

Chart 1-4b: Embryology in b. Niddah *31a*

'וחכ"א אחד ברית זכר ואחד בריית נקבה וכו

תנו רבנן: שלשה שותפין יש באדם, הקב"ה ואביו ואמו. אביו מזריע הלובן, שממנו
עצמות וגידים וצפרנים, ומוח שבראשו, ולובן שבעין. אמו מזרעת אודם, שממנו עור
ובשר ושערות, ושחור שבעין. והקב"ה נותן בו רוח ונשמה וקלסתר פנים, וראיית העין,
ושמיעת האוזן, ודבור פה, והלוך רגלים, ובינה והשכל. וכין שהגיע זמנו להפטר מן
העולם - הקב'ה נוטל חלקו, וחלק אביו ואמו מניח לפניהם. אמר רב פפא, היינו דאמרי
אינשי : פוק מלחא - ושדי בשרא לכלבא.

THE SAGES SAY: THERE IS ONE CREATING, FOR THE MALE (EMBRYO)
AND FOR THE FEMALE, ETC. … Our Rabbis taught: There are three partners in a
human being—the Holy One (blessed be He) and his father and his mother. His father
from the seed/semen of white-matter, from which are bones and tendons and nails, and
the brain in his head, and the white of his eye. His mother from the seed/semen of red-
matter, from which are skin and flesh and hair, [and blood,] and the dark of the eye.
And the Holy One (blessed be He) gives him spirit and breath and beauty of face, and
the eye's seeing, and the ear's hearing, and the mouth's speech, and the feet's walking,
and understanding and intelligence. And when his time approaches, to depart from the
world, the Holy One (blessed be He) removes His portion, and the portion of his father
and his mother remains before them. Rav Pappa said, "It corresponds to what people say,
'Scatter the salt—and throw the flesh to the dog.'"

At the time the Babylonian Talmud was composed, the Greek motif of
woman-as-nurse was a prevalent paradigm for the mother's contribution to the
human embryo. Thus, the passage in *b. Niddah* 31a can be seen as a deliberate

---

79   The mishnah for this passage is part of the discussion of whether the "fashioning" of a female
      embryo takes longer than that of a male. The Sages maintain that the two take the same length
      of time.

renunciation of Greek embryology. The rabbis assign parallel contributions to
the two human "partners": each provides three components of the body-
structure, plus the brain or blood and a part of the eye.[80]

Furthermore, the rabbinic insistence on God as a third partner—who is the
sole source of all aspects of the person that distinguish life from death—can
signal a categorical renunciation of the taxonomy that produced the Greek
version of embryology. The description of God's repossession of the divine
contributions at the death of the person is superfluous to the discussion of
embryology and thus is available to be queried for additional meaning. It is
possible that the semantic maneuver of including a third taxon with the
male/female binary, and stressing its preeminent importance, calls into
question the independence or stability of that binary (a form of deconstruction?)
so long as God is neither male nor female, or else represents both. In any case,
the inclusion of God as a partner combines with the promotion of the woman's
role to reduce the role of the man, who in Greek embryology deposits a tiny,
pre-made, living human into the woman who then incubates it. In the rabbinic
model, the father (like the mother) contributes half the components of the
"flesh" and none of the immaterial qualities of a living creature. If all that the
rabbis intended for their model was to involve God as the giver-of-life, they
could have adapted the Greek model to say that God quickens the tiny homun-
culus in the man, which the man then deposits in the woman for incubation.

Though the use of rabbinic material requires careful caveats when one
makes statements about its constructions of *gender*, there is reason to use
rabbinic material in contrast with other thought-systems, because "the
distinctions between the patriarchal theories make a meaningful difference."[81]
One such "meaningful difference" between the Hellenic view of male/female
relations and that of a broad temporal range of Jewish writers is the degree of
antagonism expressed against women. "The fantasy of masculine *autarkeia*,
self-sufficiency, was a persistent theme in Greek culture. In Hesiod's myth …
[m]en were contented and sufficient unto themselves. In the fifth century, the
fantasy of single-sex, masculine culture appeared in the vehement wishes of
Euripides' Jason and Hippolytus."[82] Antagonism is a mild word for "[t]his

---

80 The brain probably was not considered the source of thought in the rabbinic era, at least not
    to the degree that modern medicine has that model. In the Hebrew Bible, the heart has the
    functions we associate with the brain. "Nervous system" would be a better understanding of
    "brain," in this context.

81 Boyarin (Torah Study," 521). Boyarin notes that it is not appropriate "to ask with respect to
    classical rabbinic culture whether or not a pre-given entity, the class of women, is or is not
    permitted to study the Torah" because "it is study of Torah as a gendered activity that
    produces the hierarchically ordered categories of men and women." (ibid., 520).

82 DuBois, *Sowing*, 172.

dream of a purely paternal heredity [that] never ceased to haunt the Greek imagination"[83] and that parallels "the dream of a world without women [which] exercised for the Greeks an equal fascination."[84]

Though the Jewish texts frame male/female relations in terms of various male-oriented paradigms of conflict—such as the rabbinic contrast between the wife as "house" and the synagogue as "house of study"—the conflicts women may represent for men are presented as conflicting loyalties. The major exception is Philo of Alexandria, whose view of women approaches the Greek fantasy of male *autarkeia*.

> But since no created thing is constant, and things mortal are necessarily liable to changes and reverses, it could not be but that the first man too should experience some ill fortune. And woman becomes for him the beginning of blameworthy life. For so long as he was by himself, as accorded with such solitude, he went on growing like to the world and like God, and receiving in his soul the impressions made by the nature of each, not all of these, but as many as one of mortal composition can find room for.[85]

Though the passage continues by saying that Adam was glad to see the woman when she appeared in the Garden, that is not a good thing in Philo's view because sex distracted Adam from his previous perfection—and that is exactly the point of Hesiod's passages about Pandora, that she is a "beautiful evil" (καλὸν κακὸν) whose creation heralds the race of women who spoil the idyllic world enjoyed by the men. In contrast to the Greek and Philonic longing for male *autarkeia*, the Hebrew text of Gen 2–4 states clearly that "It is not good that the (hu)man should be alone," and that the building of the woman is a positive step.[86]

The metonymic erasure that codes the *female* as a defective *male* persists as a component of Western thought systems. "The post-Platonic, metaphysical representation of woman sees her as a defective male, distinguished by absence and partiality. For both Aristotle and Lacan, the female body is defined

---

83 Vernant, "Hestia-Hermès," 19. "Ce rêve d'une hérédité purement paternelle n'a jamais cessé de hanter l'imagination grecque." Vernant identifies this trope as "the same dream that masquerades as scientific theory among physicians and philosophers," mentioning Aristotle. ("C'est le même rêve qui se déguise en théorie scientifique chez les médecins et les philosophes").

84 Arthur, "Dream," 97. Arthur introduces her statement with the quote from Vernant, linking the two Greek dreams that diminish or eliminate women.

85 Philo, "On the Creation," 121.

86 See chapter 5, "Human Female, Biblical Females," for similarities and differences between Eve's stories and those of Pandora.

in terms of metonymy. The female is the male, but lacking."[87] For example, the Aristotelian perception that women's genitals are formed like those of men, but inside the body rather than outside, took such powerful hold of the collective imagination that this theory prevailed beyond the time that observations from dissections refuted it—even beyond the sixteenth-century, anatomical drawings made from female cadavers show the same male-model configuration.[88]

Unlike the Platonic/Aristotelian model, the gender taxonomies operative in the Book of Ben Sira, the biblical book of Proverbs, and *b. Niddah* are built from a male/female binary that denotes real difference. *Female* is a category that exists independently and is, therefore, just as real as *male*. The Greek model, in contrast, uses a male/female binary that cannot denote real difference because only *male* exists independently. For the Rabbis, the "conceptualization of female bodies as different from male bodies is not rooted in the perception of the male body as normative—ontologically or biologically—and female bodies as substandard to the male body, as Aristotle would claim."[89]

Because there is no real *female* in the Greek binary but only a defective *male*, taxonomic slippage occurs through the binding of the two binaries male/female and presence/absence and the destabilizing effect of their incompletely combined form. Chart 1-5a, below, shows how the slippage occurs; arrows indicate semantic relationships and lines indicate a shared feature with no semantic relationship. In the diagram for the Book of Ben Sira, a generic binary "unmarked/marked" stands for any binary other than male/female.[90]

Chart 1-5a: The binary male/female in two gender-related taxonomies

BOOK OF BEN SIRA'S TAXONOMY   GREEK TAXONOMY

Male ⟷ **Female**   **Male** ◂┈┈┈┈▸ (Female)
⋮   ⋮   ▲   Absence
Unmarked ⟷ Marked   Presence ◂

87   DuBois, *Sowing*, 30.

88   See Laqueur, *Making Sex*, especially 79–96.

89   Fonrobert, *Menstrual Purity*, 44. Fonrobert identifies this taxonomic level of dissimilarity as "the foundation of [her] analysis of rabbinic thinking and discourse on women's bodies in the context of the impurity/purity system" (ibid., 43–44). She traces the rabbinic distinction of bodily difference to the different prepositional consonants used in Lev 15:2 and 19 for genital discharges, occurring *from* a male body and *in* a female body (ibid., 44–45).

90   The binary presence/absence is part of the diagram of the Greek system but is not used in the diagram of Ben Sira's system because it is less important there.

Because *female* is an incomplete category in the Greek taxonomy, the Greek system is not a collection of independent binaries. *Female* is partially absorbed into *absence*, so that the Greek pair male/female functions with presence/absence as a conglomeration that is somewhere between a binary and a quaternary—some fraction more than a trinary—and this invisible fold in the taxonomic plane causes slippage all across the system. The links between the unmarked and marked taxa of each binary weaken and new links form between all the unmarked taxa (likewise for marked taxa), with the result that the "unmarked" taxa relate to each other almost as much as any does to its "marked" partner. Chart 1-5b, below, is a larger-scale view of the two systems in chart 1-5a, showing the semantic warping around the combined male/female and presence/absence binaries in the Greek taxonomy.

Chart 1-5b: Semantic warping in the Greek taxonomy

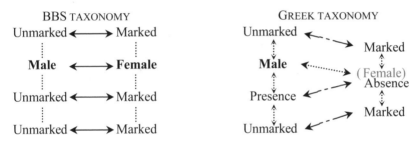

The "Greek taxonomy," above, is my view of a phallogocentric model that is present, in various permutations, in the writings of Hesiod and in those of Plato, Aristotle, and other Athenians. The "BBS taxonomy" is the religion-primary taxonomy (fig. 1-3a) derived from the schema of affinities and corroborated by relevant verses. In the Book of Ben Sira, the model is not phallogocentric because there is not an active presence/absence binary. Thus, the *female* taxon of the male/female binary is stable, disallowing a collapse of categories as in the Greek model. Taxonomic analyses foreground the relation of discourse to power because "[c]ategory creation itself is an act of power."[91] Phallogocentric systems are powerful, in part, because the invisible links between the unmarked taxa (and between the marked ones) interconnect the whole taxonomy and frustrate attempts to deconstruct any single binary.

It is noteworthy that the Book of Ben Sira is not organized according to the phallogocentrism of the Greek taxonomy. The default assumption would

---

91   Cornwall and Lindesfarne, "Gender, Power and Anthropology," 40.

be that Ben Sira shared the prevailing Platonic-Aristotelian taxonomic systems of his time, since they permeate the works of Philo and of early Christian authors. Moreover, the phallogocentric paradigm is also a foundation for Western philosophic systems from whose vantage point modern scholars analyze the ancient texts, thus reinforcing a sense of universality within the presumed Judeo-Christian inheritance. Thus, a significant part of demonstrating how the Book of Ben Sira constructs *gender* is to delineate how it differs from the default expectations. Two specific points of difference in the Book of Ben Sira are the status of the male/female binary—whose stability prevents conflation with presence/absence, and thus forestalls phallogocentrism—and the absence of the naturalizing use of the "head and body" metaphor, which is another model for constructing asymmetrical power relations. Other markers of difference are identified in later chapters, including those related to Ben Sira's situation as a colonial subject.

1.5 Parameters for *Gender*

For the project of analyzing *gender* in written sources, perfomative-gender models are a good match for the constraints and the liberties of a textual world because texts have relationships with each other, and with readers, but the overt constructedness of a text and the fixed boundaries of some of its parameters distance it from the infinite complexities of real people. The textual world of the Book of Ben Sira is a taxonomically-heterosexual system. Though I see elements of queerable strangeness—such as the High Priest wearing the garments of the female figure Wisdom, or vice-versa—the goal for this project is to describe the particular configuration(s) of heterosexual relations that I think are constituted in the Book of Ben Sira.

The foundational text for studies of gender issues in the Book of Ben Sira is Trenchard's *Ben Sira's View of Women*, published in 1982 and still in print.[92] An examination of the "initial data" led him to formulate "the following working hypothesis for this study: Ben Sira is personally negative toward women," and "to test the reasonability of this hypothesis in view of the evidence of the text."[93] After stating that the study meets the need to "settle

---

92   The book is a revision of his doctoral dissertation for the University of Chicago's department of New Testament and Early Christian Literature.

93   Trenchard, *Ben Sira's View*, 2. Trenchard nuances the formulation "personally negative toward women" by declaring that he prefers "to use this terminology rather than the expression misogynist, which contains connotations that cannot be determined or tested in a study of this nature" (ibid., 185 n. 12).

the issue of Ben Sira's view of women,"[94] he presents his conclusion that "Ben Sira exhibits a personal, negative bias against women."[95] Though Trenchard ascribes to personal bias what he sees as Ben Sira's negative views of women, some scholars consider that attitude a part of Ben Sira's sociolect.[96] Trenchard's investigative strategy is to assemble "all of Ben Sira's material related to woman into the five categories of good wife, mother (and widow), bad wife, adulteress (and prostitute), and daughter."[97] At this point, my strategy diverges conclusively from his, for I analyze through paired male/female categories such as father/mother, son/daughter, husband/wife, and friend/wife.[98]

Camp is the other scholar regularly quoted with regard to gender-issues in the Ben Sira texts.[99] Her views develop from a consistent application of feminist theory and social scientific methodologies concerned with *honor* and *shame*. Camp's outlook is coherent but intrinsically separate from mine because the two readings derive from different linguistic strands and depend on incommensurable methodologies; use of the "Mediterranean honor/shame theory" from cultural anthropology creates its own closed set of references that has little or no overlap with my use of tools such as taxonomic analysis, lexical studies, and postcolonial theory. When one accepts her premises, her conclusions stand as stated, but my divergence at the level of premises means our conclusions must differ, though her insights and mine coincide for particular passages.

The results of my analyses differ substantially from those of previous scholarship, including a more sanguine assessment of Ben Sira's views on a particular instance of gendered relations, those between wives and husbands. Some results of the analyses of specific passages of the Book of Ben Sira are

---

94 Trenchard, *Ben Sira's View*, 167.

95 Trenchard, *Ben Sira's View*, 173.

96 Among these are Archer ("'Evil Women,'" 243, 245); Skehan and Di Lella (*Wisdom*, 90–92); McKeating ("Jesus ben Sira," 85); and Tomes ("A Father's Anxieties," 73).

   A number of scholars conclude that the author of the Book of Ben Sira fears women and /or sex. The group includes Eron ("'That Women Have Mastery,'" 45) and Eisenbaum ("Sirach," 303). They, and others, ascribe to Ben Sira the view that women are sexually insatiable. This group includes Eron ("'That Women Have Mastery,'" 48, 51, 53); Eisenbaum ("Sirach," 302); McKeating ("Jesus ben Sira," 86); and Archer ("'Evil Women,'" 245).

97 Trenchard, *Ben Sira's View*, 5.

98 Davidson, in 1894, analyzed BBS in terms of matched discourses for female and male figures. He opens his article by stating that "[t]he judgment of Jesus-ben-Sira ... regarding women is popularly supposed to be very damnatory. This opinion is scarcely justified" ("Sirach's Judgment of Women," 402).

99 Camp has written a number of essays and articles on the Ben Sira texts; her book *Ben Sira and the Men Who Handle Books* became available too late for comment in this study.

given now in summary form so that readers may track the progress of the argumentation or envision where certain lines of inquiry will lead. With regard to *marriage*: marriage with an appropriate marriage-partner is a central human bond and a well-matched wife is a sage's most appropriate companion. Elements of the stories of Eve and Adam are used as a prototype for the ideal marriage. The sage's mutually-erotic relationships with the figure of Wisdom and the well-matched human wife share a semantic substrate that constitutes the wife as the human representative of Wisdom.

Chapter 2
Gender and Impersonal Speech

One function of the Book of Ben Sira is to produce images of correctly-Jewish masculinity, and in this sense it is thoroughly gender-focal. However, I am particularly interested in those portions of the text that construct *feminine* together with *masculine*. "Gender is not an attribute of individuals at all, but a relational category,"[1] and the taxonomic relationship is asymmetrical. As a default condition, the unmarked taxon *masculine* is constructed in relation to *feminine*—in other words, the boundary of the category *feminine* defines the shape of the category *masculine*, so that to be *masculine* is to be not-*feminine*.[2]

Can *female* or *feminine* ever be anything in itself, and not just the boundary that delineates *male* or *masculine*? Though masculinity usually is constituted as the inverse of femininity, the current study investigates possible sites in the text where the two categories are constructed in direct relation to each other—a condition I label "relational-gender." Gendered discourse has many gradations. At some sites it may be present only at a level of background noise and, if there are passages in which *gender* is incidental to the focal discourse(s), such units can be set aside from the group I analyze for gendered content. The objective is to identify a set of gender-focal passages and then to determine whether discourses of relational-gender occur in them.

Relational-gender could be a focal part of the discourse of any verse or passage that mentions "women" because "men" are an unmarked category for a male-oriented text such as the Book of Ben Sira. Yet, all passages that mention "women" need not be part of the same discursive continuum. Passages that might be gender-focal can be evaluated according to their types of *impersonal speech*—statements that are constrained to express a particular attitude that

---

1 Brod, "Studying Masculinities," 165. The article is a study of gender in "women's lives and men's lives."

2 For a phallogocentric taxonomy, the reciprocal statement that "*masculine* defines the shape of the category *feminine*" does not compute. The virulently asymmetrical nature of the power relations in the binary male/female, coupled with the exclusive nature of each taxon, entails that any admixture results in the degradation of the unmarked taxon. *Male* is always tainted by *female*, whereas *female* can be elevated by *male*, as in the positive value of the label γυναῖκα ἀνδρείαν, literally "a manly woman" (LXX Prov. 31:10).

may, or may not, match the writer's personal opinions. The schema of affinities features in this context, as do passages that include proverbial statements.

2.1 Ben Sira's Colonial Status

All discourses in the Book of Ben Sira are, potentially, inflected by the author's enforced participation in a colonial system. Texts produced in such a situation are available as sites for cryptic acts of literary resistance through choice of language, manipulations of a passage's genre, and the use of particular words that extend the semiotic range of the text. For the analysis of each passage, Ben Sira's colonial status intersects with the text's genre and form, and with its taxonomical system, as preeminent tools for interpretation; each component of analysis can modify the others, so that interpretations— though inevitably subjective—become more balanced.

The categories used to analyze Ben Sira's social location are also relevant starting-points for examining the texts. Some preliminary classifications for Ben Sira are that he was male and literate, that he lived in an urban setting (probably Jerusalem) during some span of the years between 220 and 150 BCE, and that he was a member of the ethnic group that produced the texts of the Hebrew Bible. The group's label for this era is "Judean" or "Jewish." Taken together, these data indicate several other categories relevant to texts by Ben Sira: as a literate male, he could be a scribe and as a male Jew he might be a sage. And, the geographical and temporal data combine with his ethnicity to situate Ben Sira as a member of a colonized group, subject to the Hellenistic empires.

The Book of Ben Sira advertises the author's skill as "a sage" (חכם) and his fitness as a teacher of sages; "scribe" (סופר)—the other job classification— appears only once in Hebrew (BBS 38:24). Ben Sira's roles require that he know Wisdom and be able to create texts.[3] Furthermore, a sage must be familiar with wisdom traditions and be able to engage in extemporaneous proverb-performance. A standard set of skills for one who claims "wisdom" could include the production of "song-poem, proverb, riddle, and figure," which are Solomon's areas of expertise: שיר מ[ש]ל חידה ומליצה (BBS 47:17, MS B).

A sage—in Ben Sira's Torah-centric description of that role—would be recognized as an important person within the Jewish world but less so among Greeks. The Jewish sage would be of little use to the Greek populace unless his status was so high within the Jewish sector that he was designated as a

---

3   See the chart AppLex-8, in the Appendix, for instances of the verb roots כתב and ספר as references to writing.

spokesman for the entire group, representing their interests to the Greek overlords, or acting perhaps in the role of a "diplomat or emissary."[4] As a majority opinion, "it has been presumed that Sira must have been a member of the Jewish upper class,"[5] but Reiterer thinks it more likely "that Sira came from the poorer class. Living in poor circumstances, he gained wisdom and then rose into the upper class, so that he had access to the powerful of his time."[6] Ben Sira's intended audience seems to be members of an intermediate Jewish class that could gain access to elite groups through training, or by patronage, in contrast to members of the underclass (who have little chance of access to elite groups by any means) or of the elite (who are born into the group and therefore need no "access").[7] Ben Sira's patrons would have had status at least as high as his own, with respect to birth and/or wealth. A youth born into an elite Jewish family would learn the manners of his class from inside and, if training in Greek language and manners were necessary, the family would hire a Greek tutor.[8] The subjects for which Ben Sira would be the best teacher would be topics pertaining to Jewish wisdom: "paradigms for existing in the world"[9]—and for surviving as a (wise) Jew in a Greek world.

2.1.1 Hellenistic Colonialism

Ben Sira's situation as a member of a colonized group profoundly affects issues of social status. Judah had been part of the Persian empire before the time of Alexander, but, by 300 BCE, the area that included Judah belonged to the Egyptian Ptolemaic dynasty that had claimed this part of Alexander's empire. "Greeks and Macedonians came as conquerors and settled as ruling

---

4 Perdue, *Proverbs*, 25.

5 Reiterer, "Review of Recent Research," 62, with reference to the 1906 work by Smend (*Die Weisheit*, 345–46) as the first in this line of thought.

6 Reiterer, "Review of Recent Research," 63, citing Tcherikover ("Jerusalem on the Eve," 148). Marttila (*Foreign Nations*, 2) comments that Ben Sira was not "on the highest level of the society," but that "the middle class did not exist in ancient Israel," and that it "remains obscure whether Ben Sira belonged to the upper-class since his birth or whether he made a social rise by having a chance to educate himself."

7 As Camp observes ("Understanding a Patriarchy," 14), a sage "requires standards for dealing with both" the rich and the poor, and "takes precautions against the hazards confronted in each direction." Horsley and Tiller ("Ben Sira," 80) point out that "the book contains enough cautionary and critical remarks about the wealthy and powerful to suggest that they or their children were not the audience."

8 Horsley (*Scribes, Visionaries*, 48) and Perdue (*Wisdom Literature*, 174) mention that some elite Jews (e.g., the Tobiads) probably had Greek tutors for their children.

9 Perdue, *Wisdom and Creation*, 286.

classes" in Judah, and the Jews were subject to them, politically and militarily.[10] Though it is not a foregrounded issue in his writing, Ben Sira's situation in a colonial system is a pervasive background for all he says and, more cogently, for *how* he says it.

One essential task of an empire is to forestall violent protest by attuning the minds of the subject peoples to the empire's values and away from their own—and *discourse* is the tool that orchestrates this process of mental displacement. *Discourse* combines with *power* to construct, maintain, and modify a varied range of social formations. Although force is necessary for conquest, discourse is indispensible for maintaining power, "to mystify the inevitable inequities of any social order and to win the consent of those over whom power is exercised, thereby obviating the need for the direct coercive use of force and transforming simple power into 'legitimate' authority."[11] Within empires, these processes play out through standardized sets of relations between colonizers and colonized. The categories of interrelation in this model are continuous from empire to empire, though specific instantiations of the categories vary. Ben Sira's situation does not parse well according to the classifications used to analyze the asymmetrical power relations within recent Euro-centric colonial systems.[12] For example, the particularities of categories such as *mimicry*,[13] developed in specific reference to relations within the British empire, are not all equally applicable to conditions in the Hellenistic empires. A full expression of *mimicry* involves self-presentation through a repertoire of (never exact) likenesses or 'copyings' in a colonial subject's choice of language, bodily demeanor, apparel, diet, companions, occupations, and pastimes. In the case of the British empire in India, for example, we can view drawings and photographs of how colonizers and

---

10   Gruen, *Heritage and Hellenism*, xiii.

11   Lincoln, *Discourse*, 4–5.

12   As Charles notes, "one simply cannot find direct correspondences between the different colonial and diasporic contexts present in literature of ancient times and modern examples of imperialist rule and migration situations" ("Hybridity and the *Letter of Aristeas*," 245). However, the *Letter* explicitly ingratiates itself with a Gentile audience, as when the writer declares that the Gentiles worship the same god as the Jews, but "'[t]heir name for him is Zeus and Jove'" (ibid., 248). Ben Sira's hybrid condition is negotiated through some strategies that parallel those of the *Letter*, but a fundamental difference of outlook—his messages are directed almost exclusively toward Jews—is indicated by his choice of Hebrew for the messages as well as by their content.

13   According to Bhabha, "[m]imicry is at once resemblance and menace," a condition in which "to be Anglicized is *emphatically* not to be English" (*Location of Culture*, 85, 86). Charles notes that in mimicry "there is ... the mixture of the familiar and the unfamiliar, the double articulation of appropriation and challenge, approval and mockery" ("Hybridity," 250).

colonized dressed and the postures they assumed, and literary evidence gives us their views of themselves and each other—we have a rich trove of data. In contrast, we know almost nothing about the appearance of Ben Sira: Did he have a beard? Did he wear Greek styles of clothing? We surmise that he attended Greek-style banquets, but did he follow Jewish dietary laws? The text is our only source for "Ben Sira," therefore the text must function as the entity performing mimetic acts: the text wears approximations of various Greek genres as its apparel but it speaks in cryptic forms that do not reach the ears of the colonizers.[14] It is careful about its manners at fashionable banquets, and wary of those in power; it hopes to be remembered forever among its "companions" while remaining inconspicuous to predatory elites.[15]

Ben Sira and his fellow Jews occupy a multi-axial range of responses to their Hellenistic milieu, so that acceptance of Hellenistic norms in one category, such as language, need not imply acceptance of any others such as religious practices. Moreover, the Hellenistic discourse is already an amalgam that includes Jewish influences. Ben Sira engages in a process of identity-formation that is neither acquiescence nor ignoring, but consists of concurrently claiming, rejecting, adapting, resignifying, and combining elements of both discourses, 'native' and 'colonial.'

2.1.2 Language and Resistance

The Ptolemaic empire and that of the Seleucids who replaced them c. 200 BCE added cultural imperialism to the economic and political imperialism the Jews had already experienced as Persian subjects. The Greeks, who "took their superiority for granted," felt no need to learn the languages of the colonized nations or their customs. [16] And, Greek superiority must posit the inferiority of non-Greeks. Since the time of the victories against Persia, βάρβαρος "not-Greek" had become a commonplace statement of contempt for other ethnicities,

---

14 Burkes (*God, Self, and Death*, 117) comments on the relationship between book and name: "The book is the carrier of the tradition and also the innovative defender of it; Ben Sira, the man and the book, themselves become part of the chain of historical continuity."

15 The members of "those in power" and "predatory elites" are not listed, but the categories would include Jews, as well as Greeks. See passages that warn against relationships between men of unequal status, such as "How shall a clay-pot befriend a kettle?—for when [the kettle] strikes it, it is broken" (BBS 13:2); see also BBS 8:1–4, 10–19; 10:6–7; 11:29–34; and 13:1–13, 14–23, many verses of which are in chart 2-6.

16 Gruen, *Heritage and Hellenism*, xiii.

whose people were figured as dull, stupid, cowardly, and fit to be slaves.[17] Throughout the empire, the "ability to speak and write Greek fluently and in the prevailing fashion was a requisite for advancement" in all areas of public life.[18] Aramaic was the other major language of the Hellenistic empires.

Ben Sira probably could write one or both of the languages that were in common use and, thus, Hebrew is not an obvious choice as his medium for communication. If the use of Hebrew was a *choice*—that is, it was not the only language Ben Sira could write fluently—what advantages might this language offer? The power of discourse is also available to members of subordinate groups, as a tool to "demystify, delegitimate, and deconstruct the established norms, institutions, and discourses that play a role in constructing their subordination."[19] As a member of the native elite who were the direct negotiators between the Greeks and their own people, Ben Sira occupied a social niche that is a standard element of colonial hierarchies. In this role, Ben Sira would experience the general ambivalence felt by the Greek colonizers for partially-assimilated subordinate groups, while his insistence on living according to the commands of Torah would exacerbate Greek contempt.

Indigenous elites, as intermediaries between colonizers and colonized, are "able to support or deconstruct the empire's cultural metanarrative."[20] Ben Sira's mastery of the Hebrew language makes him an excellent intermediary for the work of support or deconstruction because his use of Hebrew introduces the option of cryptic forms of speech through which he could both dismantle Hellenism's hegemonic discourse and selectively appropriate some of its elements. Cryptic speech is useful for a colonized group during intervals without overt oppression and necessary for survival when the political situation becomes tense. According to Calduch-Benages, Ben Sira expresses political views "in an allusive way in his work, so that it requires reading between the lines, and probably allows for considerable space for interpretation."[21] Chart 2-1, below, shows how negative views of the colonial situation could be expressed as part of a larger topic.

---

17 Long, "Concept of the Cosmopolitan," 52. Long notes that the Stoics, in particular, did not share in the wholesale vilification of non-Greeks and that the works of Homer are not xenophobic.

18 Bickerman, *Jews in the Greek Age*, 301.

19 Lincoln, *Discourse*, 5.

20 Perdue, "Book of Ben Sira and Hellenism," 3.

21 Calduch-Benages, "Fear for the Powerful," 88.

Chart 2-1: "The oppressed-man's cry for help" BBS 35:21–26 (MS B)

KEY→ Greek (gap in Hebrew text)

35:21 The oppressed-man's cry for help pierces the clouds
—and it shall not rest silent, until it will arrive.
It shall not give-way until God will inspect
—and the Righteous Judge will make judgment.

35:22 God, also, shall not delay
—and like a powerful-one, He will not be patient.
Until He will strike through, on account of the cruel-one
—and He will repay vengeance on the nations.

35:23 Till He shall dispossess the scepter of insolence
—and the staff of wickedness, surely, He will hew-down.

35:24 Till He shall repay to the person his actions
—and recompense of a human, according to his scheme(s).

35:25 Till He judges the quarrel of His people
—and He will cause them to rejoice in His deliverance.

35:26 His mercy is apt in a time of distress
—as thunderclouds, in a season of drought.

The passage opens with an oppressed (or "poor") man crying out for help,[22] and the sources of his distress are listed in terms of those whom God will judge and punish: the cruel, the insolent, and the wicked.[23] These targets can be among the Jews, but the mention of "the nations" and "the scepter of insolence" enlarges the discourse to include non-Jews such as the Greek-speaking overlords. The final verse in the group moves back from nations to individuals, as an ethnically-generic statement that closes off a brief (and prudently encapsulated) polemic.[24] Though *gender* is not a concern in BBS

---

22 The selected unit is part of a larger passage only partially extant in Hebrew (Sir 34:21–35:22; BBS 35:11–26). The full passage intertwines the themes of *proper sacrifice to God* and *justice to disadvantaged persons*. The section BBS 35:17–20 mentions an orphan and a widow whose distress is heard by God, but the Hebrew is defective in the section about the widow, so all that can be said with regard to *gender* is that a stock female figure is listed as having access to God. Bicola 35:22cd refers to "the nations," and may inaugurate the unitary theme of BBS 36:1–17, an explicit prayer for the destruction of nations that persecute "Israel" and the restoration of the people and "Jerusalem, the site of Your sabbaths."

23 In 35:22c, I chose the marginal מפני ("on account of/from before," given in *DCH* 5:227b) in preference to מתני ("loins of," given in the entry for אבזר in *DCH* 1:240a, 2b).

24 As Wright ("'Put the Nations,'" 128) observes, Ben Sira "appear[s] in some cases to cloak warnings about specific contemporary people or situations in the more universal language of

35:21–26, identifying the colonial components of other passages, such as those that mention *shame*, can clarify the semantic range of what is, and is not, considered gendered discourse in the Book of Ben Sira.

In his position as a sage, Ben Sira reframed the discourse of *identity* for Jews by presenting a compelling and vigorous reinterpretation of the traditions, formulated to counteract the Hellenistic narratives of superiority. The fact that Ben Sira wrote these statements in Hebrew enabled them to function as counter-hegemonic discourse because they were invisible—they would pass "under the radar" of Greek awareness.[25] Detailed analyses of other passages, later in this study, continue the discussion of colonial subtexts in the Book of Ben Sira.

2.2 The Production of "Impersonal Speech"

The most surprising result of the current study of *gender* in the Book of Ben Sira is the strong equivalence between comments about females and those about males.[26] Virulently-gendered passages are thus anomalies in the over-all discourse of *gender* in the extant Hebrew MSS.[27] The theoretic material in this section of the study traces my efforts to formulate categories through which to discuss these discordant passages; questions about the topics are framed in this chapter, and answers—if any—come later.

If all statements in the Book of Ben Sira are construed at face value, the discussion of anomalies ends here—but, what if there is not always a direct correspondence between the overt meaning of a statement and the viewpoint of the author? If a writer's work does not always—in all cases—reflect a personal opinion, then there is room for categories of "impersonal speech." I investigate genres, schemata, and proverbs as examples of impersonal speech and examine their effects on gender-focal texts and on those that are not gender-focal.

---

admonitions and proverbs." He notes of BBS/Sir 35:23, "it seems that Ben Sira's expectation that God will stand on the side of the oppressed has brought to his mind his own nation that is under the 'scepter of the unrighteous.'"(ibid., 134).

25 In response to my question on this topic, L. G. Perdue stated that not "many Greeks living in Israel would know Hebrew. ... However, this does allow a 'native' Jew who speaks Hebrew to communicate a message to those learned Jews he knew that would be a 'hidden transcript'" (personal communication by email, 9 Sept 2009).

26 See the chart 4-6 in chapter 4, "Human Females," for six instances of equivalent verses.

27 The passages are BBS/Sir 25:13–26:3, "From a woman is the beginning of sin, and because of her we all die," and BBS/Sir 42:9–14, "Better the wickedness of a man than a well-doing woman and a woman bringing shame to the point of reproach" (both NETS). A third loudly-gendered passage, Sir 26:5–12, is not extant in Hebrew.

2.2.1 Greek Genres Available to Ben Sira

Many statements in the Book of Ben Sira occur as elements of literary templates, such as genres, that modulate the semantic effect of the statements. Genres such as *praise* (the encomium) and *blame* (the invective) skew the meaning of individual statements in the passage by virtue of their nature as monovocal literature, so that meaning resides more at the level of the passage than at the level of a single statement. And, similar to the fixity entailed by certain genres, a form such as a proverb must be absolute. Due to these tight constraints, the semantic *content* in the Book of Ben Sira cannot be assessed apart from *genre* and *form*, a point I emphasize because interpretations of gender-issues in this text are especially vulnerable to confusion between genre/form and content.

A statement's genre and form are part of its context, contributing to the discursive process.[28] Thus, "different literary genres, within the same society, may be part of different discourses with their own views and vocabulary."[29] If such is the case, then a lexical study of a certain text would, ideally, include information on the generic and formal context for each item of vocabulary. Literary form and genre have intertwined roles as codifiers of meaning. One way in which genre and form can modulate the semantic range of statements is that their monovocal tendencies—deriving from the genres themselves, from forms such as the proverb, or from textual devices such as schemata— wipe out nuances of opinion and vestiges of personal presence, leaving a homogeneous and impersonal affect.

Elements that comprise a genre "operate within a set of structural relations that function meaningfully together *as a template or background schema*."[30] In classical Greece, instruction in rhetoric included rules for manipulating the

---

28 However, the assignment of particular genres and forms to written statements is as much an "issue of power" for interpreting the contexts of written works as the assigning of categories for viewing the contexts of human communities. See Osiek ("Women, Honor, and Context," 335) on "context" in anthropological studies.

29 Dieleman, "Fear of Women?," 10. The article analyzes "representations of women" in Egyptian demotic wisdom texts. I presume that Dieleman's range of meaning for "literary genres" approximates my range of meaning. However, my tools differ from those of Dieleman, who builds upon models of narratology by Bal and Greimas.

30 Wright, "Joining the Club," 297; emphasized in original. Wright's definition of genre includes the concept of the ICM (idealized cognitive model) that originated with George Lakoff (*Women, Fire and Dangerous Things: What Categories Reveal About the Mind*, Chicago: University of Chicago Press, 1987). I have used only part of his definition, since my study uses a closer level of magnification than does Wright in this essay where he seeks a comprehensive set of criteria for a wide-spread and varied class of texts.

elements of these genre-templates to produce specific effects on a listener (or reader). Knowledge of the rules of rhetoric was part of the cultural package that spread in the aftermath of Alexander's conquests, and by Ben Sira's era it is quite possible that a Jew familiar with the Greek language and linguistic tropes would know the basic outlines of classical instruction.

Several passages in the Book of Ben Sira are cited for their resemblance to encomia,[31] making that category a point of interest for scholars of Ben Sira. The Greek *encomium* is a rhetorical composition that praises an individual person or members of a particular category of persons. The paired categories of the encomium and its antithesis, the invective, were fundamental subjects for rhetorical instruction in classical Greece[32]—the link between the two is so emphatic that there is little chance the encomium would be taught without the invective, for the latter is built from the same elements as the former, but with reversed valuations. Thus, if Ben Sira could craft a Hebrew approximation of an encomium he would have had the skills necessary for the creation of an invective.

Aristotle's formulation of theories of rhetoric could provide a foundation for Judaean familiarity with the encomium and the invective.[33] He introduces the subject by declaring that "there are necessarily three kinds of rhetorical speeches, deliberative, forensic, and epideictic" and that "[t]he epideictic kind has for its subject praise or blame." He then enumerates the elements of these categories, *praise* and *blame*:

> 1.9 [1] We will next speak of virtue and vice, of the noble and the disgraceful, since they constitute the aim of one who praises and of one who blames. ... [5] The components of virtue are justice, courage, self-control, magnificence, magnanimity, liberality, gentleness, practical and speculative wisdom. ... [28] We must also assume, for the purpose of praise or blame, that qualities which closely resemble the real qualities are identical with them; for instance, that the cautious man is cold and designing, the simpleton good-natured, and the emotionless gentle. [29] And in each case we must adopt a term from qualities closely connected, always in the more favorable sense; for instance, the choleric and passionate man may be spoken

---

31   See Lee (*Studies*) for a full treatment of encomia in Greek rhetoric, and in BBS 44–50.

32   Russell ("Rhetoric and Criticism," 140) states that there was a "recognized sequence" of preliminary exercises, beginning with "exercises in the development of a single theme." Boys "began by writing animal fables, and then ... proceeded to anecdotes ... and maxims. ... The technique thus learned could then be used in a variety of more ambitious exercises involving composition on a rather larger scale: refutation and confirmation of arguments, ... encomium, invective, comparison."

33   *Praise* and *blame* (ἔπαινος and ψόγος) are a generalized grouping in Aristotle's paired categories while the encomium and invective (ἐγκώμιος and ὄνειδος) are particular subgroups (Liddell and Scott; *Greek-English Lexicon*, 604a).

of as frank and open, the arrogant as magnificent and dignified; those in excess as possessing the corresponding virtue, the fool-hardy as courageous, the recklessly extravagant as liberal. … [33] Now praise is language that sets forth greatness of virtue; hence it is necessary to show that a man's actions are virtuous. But encomium deals with achievements—all attendant circumstances, such as noble birth and education, merely conduce to persuasion … Hence we pronounce an encomium upon those who have achieved something. … [39] Amplification is with good reason ranked as one of the forms of praise, since it consists in superiority, and superiority is one of the things that are noble. That is why, if you cannot compare him with illustrious personages, you must compare him with ordinary persons, since superiority is thought to indicate virtue.[34]

The enumeration closes with the following statement:

Such are nearly all the materials of praise or blame (ἔπαινος and ψόγος), the things which those who praise or blame (ἐπαινέω and ψέγω) should keep in view, and the sources of encomia and invective (ἐγκώμιος and ὄνειδος); for when these are known their contraries are obvious, since blame (ψόγος) is derived from the contrary things.[35]

Aristotle's system has only one set of rules for praising and blaming—*blame* is the negative image of *praise*. Thus, since "blame (ψόγος) is derived from the contrary things," the above components of a speech of praise will provide those "contrary things" from which I compose the materials of a genre of *blame*, given below with its elements keyed by section-number to those for *praise*:

[1] ascriptions of vice and disgracefulness; [29] adopting a term from the more unfavorable sense, such that the frank and open man may be spoken of as choleric, the courageous as fool-hardy, the liberal as recklessly extravagant, etc.; [33] the necessity of showing a man's actions/achievements are instances of vice; [39] reduction as a form of blame, since it consists in inferiority, and inferiority is one of the things that are disgraceful. That is why, if you cannot compare him with infamous personages, you must compare him with ordinary beasts, since inferiority is thought to indicate vice.

The catalogue of *blame* can be applied to women at least as well as to men,[36] and the art of blaming women, which was perfected by Hesiod, became a

---

34 Aristotle, *Rhet.*, 1.3.3 and 1.9.1–39. All selections are from the translation by Freese (*Aristotle: The "Art" of Rhetoric*).

35 Aristotle, *Rhet.*, 1.9.41.

36 Consider Aristotle's statement that "Virtues and actions are nobler, when they proceed from those who are naturally worthier, for instance, from a man rather than from a woman" (*Rhet.*, 1.9.22).

distinct rhetorical/literary genre, the ψόγος γυναικῶν. Hesiod's depictions of
Pandora are not just one characterization among a range of classical passages—
the story of Pandora was immensely influential in Athenian self-definition, for
the qualities he assigned to Pandora he also assigned to all women, in tropes
that echo through several centuries of Greek literature and beyond. Fundamental
tropes of femaleness that originate with Hesiod include what McClure describes
as "two traditional elements of the ψόγος γυναικῶν: the idea of women as an
evil to men, a κακόν, and as a species distinct from them, the θῆλυ γένος."[37] A
third trope is the link between women and lies, made through Hesiod's use of
λόγος—in its early sense of "duplicitous speech"—to describe Pandora's mode
of speech as "lies and crafty words" (Hesiod *WD* 78).[38] Loraux emphasizes
that "the subsequent tradition did not modify Hesiod's account in any way:
from Semonides to Euripides, and from Amorgos to Athens, woman is Zeus's
creation, and the *genos gynaikon*, in its cohesion, threatens the unity of a
masculine society."[39] The *Anthologies* of Stobaeus[40] include an entire chapter
on the "Blame of Women," and here, "in a summary that ranges from Hesiod
to Euripides, including Hipponax and the comic writers, the Greek discourse
about women demonstrates its remarkable homogeneity."[41] There is, of course,
no equivalent discourse of a "Blame of Men" because *man*, as the unmarked
taxon in the binary man/woman, constitutes men as the default subject.

Though there are distinct differences between Ben Sira's model for
gender and the phallogocentric model of his Hellenistic milieu, these
differences in themselves do not automatically mean that he would contest
Greek *gender* tropes. However, the differences do mean that *gender* is available
to him as an arena for contesting the hegemony of Greek cultural models. Ben
Sira would have had a wide range of Greek literature from which to hear, if
not read, the tropes of the "blame of women." Together with the genre of
praise, in the encomium, the genre of *blame* would be part of the curriculum
offered by a teacher like Ben Sira, who would have had them in his repertoire.
The monovocal quality of *praise* and *blame* fit them as examples of "impersonal
speech," for "[t]he end of those who praise or blame is the honorable and
disgraceful; and they ... refer all other considerations to these."[42]

---

37   McClure, "Worst Husband," 383; with reference to Jason's speech in Eu. *Med.* 573–75.

38   McClure (*Spoken*, 26), who also notes that the figure of Pandora was "popularized in the
      fifth century by Sophocles in his satyr play *Pandora*."

39   Loraux, "On the Race of Women," 75.

40   The date for Stobaeus is c. 5th century CE.

41   Loraux, "On the Race of Women," 106.

42   Aristotle, *Rhetoric*, 1.3.5.

2.2.2 Schematic Figures in the Book of Ben Sira

Schematization can occur as the discursive product of fixed literary genres such as *praise* and *blame*, but schemata composed of interacting figures can function as literary devices that cross genre-limits. The previously-mentioned schema of affinities is a model whose figures become schematized in two passages, Sir 22:9–15 and BBS 25:13–26:3.[43] The group consists of two females and two males: אשה טובה, the "good wife"; אשה רעה, the "bad wife," חכם, the "sage"; and כסיל, the "fool." The "sage," as the central figure for the whole text, is also the center-point of the schema. All three of the other schematic figures relate only to him; they do not relate to each other. The "fool," the "good wife," and the "bad wife" qualify as schematic figures because they are each the subject of at least one sustained, unilateral account, the effect of which is to constitute a persona that is stylized and monolithic.[44] Other males and females have labels that characterize them by a particular activity, for example, the "adulterer/ess," "fierce-man," or "prostitute," and some females in the role of *wife* are mentioned with modifiers other than the all-encompassing "good" or "bad," such as the "the wife of your bosom" (BBS 9:1) and the "intelligent wife" (BBS 7:19; 25:8; 26:13; 40:23). Such figures are too specific to be units of a schema. Nor are intergenerational relationships part of the central unit of the model, though good/bad sons (and daughters) replicate the binary formulations.

'Real' characters have no place in a schema, and I emphasize the schematic nature of the four figures by formatting the translations of their labels with initial caps. Although "Sage" and "Fool" are acceptable translations, a literal translation of the females as the "Good Wife" and the "Bad Wife" is misleading because they are "good" and "bad" only in relation to their fitness as wives for a sage. Therefore, I use the titles "Right Wife" and "Wrong Wife" to emphasize the generic, contingent quality of their labels—that their identities are

---

43   For a detailed discussion of genre in BBS 25:13–26:3, see section 2.4.

44   The schematic formation of the "fool" is Sir 22:9–15; for the "bad wife" and the "good wife" it is the two sections of BBS 25:13–26:3.

The only other figures in the Book of Ben Sira who receive this sustained, genre-fueled, schematic development are Simeon the High Priest (BBS 50:1–21) and Wisdom (Sir 24). They are discussed in section 3.1 of chapter 3.

Although the Hebrew and Greek words for "wife" also mean "woman," the fundamental identity of the two schematic females is *wife*. For nine of the eleven instances of אשה in the schematic episodes of BBS 25:13–26:3 it is necessary to translate אשה as "wife." The exceptions are 25:21, which refers to a man planning to marry "a woman" for her beauty or wealth, and the proverbial statement in 25:24. Levison ("Is Eve to Blame?," 619) considers that, in Sir 25:16–26:18, fourteen of the twenty-one instances of γυνή clearly refer to a "wife."

designations for a group and are contingent on another character, the Sage.[45] Chart 2-2, below, shows the double-identity of the sage (Ben Sira): as a person, he interacts with the other realistic figures, human and non-human, and, as part of the schema, his persona "the Sage" interacts with the other schematic figures.[46]

Chart 2-2: The Sage's Two Identities

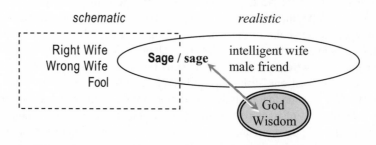

The schema of affinities reflects Ben Sira's view of *appropriate partners*. The basic principle of *appropriateness* is that likes should associate.[47] For his friends, the Sage should choose other sage-like men and avoid Fools and, for his spouse, the Sage should choose a woman who shares his qualities (piety, intelligence, and care in the use of speech) and should avoid marrying someone who has the opposite qualities. The following verses from MS C are examples of *appropriateness* in marriage:

25:8	Happy is he who has not fallen by the tongue —nor served one more dishonored than himself. Happy is the husband of an intelligent wife —he is not plowing like ox-with-ass.
25:19	There is little badness like a wife's badness (מעט רעה כרעת אשה) —may a sinner's lot befall her!
26:3	A good wife is a [good] share —may she be given in the portion of one fearing YYY.[48]

---

45   For a comparison of טוב and רע in Genesis 1–8 and in the Book of Ben Sira, see the chart AppLex-3 in section A.1.1 of the Appendix.

46   See the discussion of realistic human figures in chapter 4, "Human Females."

47   For examples of *appropriateness*, see BBS 12:13–13:26, especially BBS 13:14–20 (chart 5-3).

48   In the Hebrew MSS A, B, C, and E, the letters "YYY/ YY" translate "ייי/יי," multiples of the letter *yod* that represent the Tetragrammaton. MS M uses other words: אדני (twice), אליון (once).

In BBS 25:8d, the phrase "plowing like ox-with-ass," which alludes to the biblical prohibition against yoking together such dissimilar animals (Deut 22:10), serves as a metaphor for a mismatched marriage.[49] Thus, for the previous colon, "Happy is the husband of an intelligent wife," it is the "intelligent" husband who will be happily matched with an intelligent wife because they are the same 'species.' BBS 25:19 and 26:3 refer to other appropriate matches that would be like "ox-with-ox" or "ass-with-ass": the Wrong Wife with "a sinner" and the Right Wife with a "God-fearing" husband.

The female figure of the Wrong Wife and the male figure of the Fool are both constituted schematically by particular examples of the genre of *blame*— the Wrong Wife is schematized through the "blame of women" and the Fool by a formal invective applied to "fools." Sets of verses contrast the positive and negative schematic figures by gender: Sage and Fool are contrasted in chapters 21 and 22, and Right Wife and Wrong Wife in chapters 25 and 26. Chart 2-3, below, shows the pattern of comments about the schematic figures.[50]

---

49 In the verse from Deuteronomy it is the word יַחְדָּו , "as one," that permits the marriage trope. Deut 22:10 has לֹא־תַחֲרֹשׁ בְּשׁוֹר־וּבַחֲמֹר יַחְדָּו, and the Hebrew text of BBS 25:8d from Beentjes (*Book of Ben Sira in Hebrew*, 98) is וﬥו חורש כשור עם חמור. However, Ben-Hayyim (*Book of Ben Sira*, 24) gives only ...חורש כשור . Skehan and Di Lella (*Wisdom*, 340) give the truncated version and reconstruct the colon from Syriac, stating that the plowing activity is "something explicitly forbidden in the Law (Deut 22:10) ... the context clearly indicates, [it is] a statement about an undesirable marriage" (ibid., 342).

The Greek text of Sirach lacks 25:8d, and the three cola change the order of the Hebrew: "Happy is he who dwells with a sensible wife and who did not slip with the tongue and who did not become a slave to one unworthy of himself" (NETS).

50 Though all of chapters 21 and 22 are missing in Hebrew (and parts of 25 and 26), the Greek texts show clusters of related verses whose topics I presume would be present in the Hebrew.

Chart 2-3: Schematic figures of BBS/Sirach

Sir 21 and 22			BBS/Sir 25 and 26	
SAGE	FOOL		WRONG WIFE	RIGHT WIFE
21:11	—		—	25:1 (Sir.)
21:12	21:12		*[25:2–7]*	
	—		—	25:8
—	21:14		*[25: 9–12]*	
21:15	21:15		25:13	—
21:16	21:16		25:14–16 (Sir.)	—
21:17	—		25:17	—
—	21:18		25:18	—
—	21:19		25:19	—
21:20	21:20		25:20	—
21:21	—	Wrong Wife 9 cola BBS; 15 cola Sir.	25:21	—
21:22	21:22		25:22	—
21:23	21:23		25:23	—
21:24	21:24		25:24	—
21:25	21:25		25:25–26 (Sir.)	—
21:26	21:26		—	26:1–3
[21:27–22:8]			—	26:4 (Sir)
—	22: 9		*[26:5]*	
—	22:10		26:6 (Sir.)	—
—	22:11, 2x		26:7 (Sir.)	—
—	22:12		26:8 (Sir.)	—
—	22:13, 3x	Fool 10 cola Sir.	26:9 (Sir.)	—
—	22:14		*[remainder of chapter]*	
—	22:15			
22:16	—			
22:17	—			
22:18	22:18			
[remainder of chapter]				

The chart emphasizes the schematizing diatribes against the two negative figures, the Fool and the Wrong Wife, against a background of the textual range of the schematic discourse: an approximate total of twenty-six Greek cola for the males and twenty-three for the females. The Sage is present in both sets, as the figure in the Sage/Fool set and as the uxorial referent whose well-being or debilitation defines the Right Wife and Wrong Wife.

The schematic label for the Fool is כסיל, which occurs first in opposition to חכם, "sage/wise man" (BBS 20:7,13).[51] However, the semantic ranges of words related to "fool" extend from "stupid" (כסיל) through "ignorant," "untaught" and "lacking in sense" (כסיל and אויל /אולת and פותה) to "silly" (פותה).[52] The words closest to "naïve" seem to be אויל and פותה. The Fool in the Book of Ben Sira is not linked with "insolence" (זד) or "pride" (גאוה), qualities that are denounced repeatedly; nor is the Fool associated with the "wicked man" (רשע). The moral weight of this range parallels the mildness of רע in the Book of Ben Sira as "bad," with "wicked" expressed by the word רשע.

The verses against the Wrong Wife and those against the Fool have similar flavors of hyperbole—the cumulative impression is of exaggeration for rhetorical effect. As such, the passages resemble lists of proverbial statements that could be used, a verse at a time, as social currency. Chart 2-4, below, shows the two passages.[53] Both the Wrong Wife and the Fool annoy the authorial Sage, who advises his audience of male students to avoid both types (Wrong Wife, vv. 21, 26; Fool 13c–f). In each case, the wrong use of speech is the cause of irritation (Wrong Wife v. 20; Fool v. 13ab) and the effect on the Sage is debility (Wrong Wife, vv. 23, 24) or weariness (Fool, v. 13ef).

---

51 Although chapters 21 through 24 are entirely missing in Hebrew, the lack of כסיל until chapter 20 and its probable abundance in chapters 21 and 22 gives a sense of the uneven distribution of the word.

52 Three Greek words in Sirach translate the five instances of כסיל:—μωρός twice ("foolish, stupid," in Sir 20:13 and 42.8), ἄφρων twice ("foolish, ignorant," in Sir 20:7 and 31:30), and ἄπληστος once ("an immoderate man," in Sir 31:20). See the chart AppLex-6, in the Appendix, for the full list of words related to "fool." In Sir 20, μωρός and ἄφρων are the words, with μωρός for every likely instance in Sirach 21 and 22.

53 The Greek translations are from NETS, except that I translate μωρός in 22:9a, 10a, 11b, 11d, 12b, and 14b as "fool(ish)," ἄφρων in 13a as "lackwit," and ἀσύνετος in 13b and 15b as "stupid." These changes nudge the translation toward my view that it is a schematic passage, heralded by the opposition between the חכם, the Sage, and the כסיל, the Fool, in BBS 20:7, 13 (MS C). The schematic Fool passage in Prov 26:1–12 (chart 3-7) provides a Hebrew precedent for such a passage in BBS 22, though that chapter of BBS is not extant.

Chart 2-4: Passages about the Wrong Wife and the Fool

WRONG WIFE (SIR 25, NETS)	FOOL (SIR 22, MOSTLY NETS)
13 Any wound, and not wound of the heart, and any wickedness, and not wickedness of a woman.	**9** He who teaches a fool is one gluing together a potsherd, one rousing a sleeper out of a deep sleep.
16 I shall be content to live with lion and dragon, rather than to live with a wicked woman.	**10** He who recounts to a fool recounts to one who is drowsy, and at the conclusion he will say, "What is it?"
17 A woman's wickedness alters her appearance, and it darkens her face like a bear.	**11** Weep over a corpse, for he has left the light, and weep over a fool, for he has left understanding behind.
18 Among his neighbors her husband will recline, and involuntarily groan bitter things.	Weep sweetly over a corpse, because he died, but the life of the fool is a sorry plight beyond death.
19 Any evil is small touching a woman's evil; may a sinner's lot befall her.	**12** Mourning for a corpse is for seven days, but for a foolish and impious person, it's all the days of his life.
20 A sandy ascent for the feet of an elderly man, so is a garrulous woman to a quiet husband.	**13** Do not increase speech with a lackwit, and do not go to a stupid person.
21 Do not fall down upon a woman's beauty, and do not yearn after a woman.	keep away from him, lest you have trouble, and you will not be sullied by his shaking off.
23 Slack hands and weakened knees are from a woman who does not make her husband happy.	stay clear of him, and you will find rest, and you will never be wearied by his madness.
24 From woman's the beginning of sin, and because of her we all die.	**14** What'll be heavier than lead? And what name does he have but "Fool"?
25 Do not give water an outlet—nor freedom of speech to a wicked wife. **26** If she does not walk according to your hands, cut her off from your flesh.	**15** Sand and salt and a lump of iron are easier to bear than an unintelligent person.

The Greek translation of BBS 25 is used to match Sir 22, which is not extant in Hebrew. For the negative female and male figures, the level of invective seems functionally equivalent—the diatribes are constructed, in equally hyperbolic language, from the same or similar complaints. Therefore, the discursive functions of the Wrong Wife cannot be assessed separately from those of the Fool, to indicate Ben Sira's view of women, because the schema constitutes a female figure with the same language as a male figure. Thus, this is an instance of relational-gender. The schema of affinities conveys its message that the sage should marry, or befriend, certain kinds of people and avoid others, though the genre of *blame* limits the message's tone to the level of caricature.

Gender-focal discourse in the Book of Ben Sira is conducted in terms of the two sets of figures shown in chart 2-2, a "schematic" set and a "realistic" set. The passage about the schematic female figures (BBS 25:13–26:3) is gender-focal by reason of its genres, "blame/praise of women," but the schema is a taxonomy of the sage's affinities and antipathies—it is not a taxonomy of *gender*. The genre-driven, schematic nature of the passages about the Fool, the Wrong Wife, and the Right Wife removes these statements from the realm of personal authorial-opinions and renders the passages examples of "impersonal speech." And, any gendered-content I categorize as "impersonal speech" will be evaluated separately from that which will emerge from the later analyses of the "realistic" set of figures.

2.2.3 Proverbial Statements

The last type of "impersonal speech" of interest for this study is the *proverb*. What semantic and functional elements might proverbial statements in the Book of Ben Sira share with the literary form of *the proverb*? In the Book of Ben Sira, *the proverb* is present in two ways: in the implied oral performances and in the written instantiations. Ben Sira's comments on the proverb indicate that it is intended for use in speech as a response to a particular situation. In this setting, one function of the proverb—in its role as a unit of conversational commerce—is to provide an impersonal token of approval to the previous speaker without expressing the personal views of the proverb-speaker. The proverbial statements embedded in the Book of Ben Sira share some of the qualities of the performed proverb but receive meaning from their textual context, rather than from the proverb-evoking statement of a partner in dialogue.

"Bicola" are standard proverb-units examined by biblical scholars. In biblical bicola, the first colon often resembles a folklorist's standard proverb and the second colon explains or extends the meaning of the first. Seitel gives a provisional definition of proverbs as "short, traditional, 'out-of-context' statements used to further some social end."[54] The quality of being "out-of-context" allows proverbs—which often use animals or inanimate objects as characters—to match the context of many situations. This multivalent quality

---

54   Seitel, "Proverbs: A Social Use of Metaphor," 124; the folklorist cites English proverbs.

of the proverb "increases its value as a rhetorical tool."[55] An example from the Book of Ben Sira that fits these criteria is "How shall a clay-pot befriend a kettle?" (BBS 13:2a). However, the example is only the first half of the unit: "How shall a clay-pot befriend a kettle—for when [the kettle] strikes it, it is broken." The first colon is well-suited for oral use, but the full bicola-unit is too long for oral use—nor do proverbs explain themselves. The unit is suited for a written venue because the second colon—which explains, or decodes, the first—replaces the contextual clues that would be part of an oral performance. Therefore, when I speak of a "proverbial statement" in the Book of Ben Sira, I may refer to only one part of a bicola-unit.

The book of Proverbs declares that proverbs are "only fully meaningful if spoken 'in season,'" a concern also in the Book of Ben Sira where proverb performance is part of the correct and incorrect uses of speech.[56] Four literary forms mentioned in the Book of Ben Sira are related to proverbial statements and could encompass both spoken and written productions: משל, the "proverb" (used eight times);[57] שיח, the "discourse/meditation" (nine times); אומר, the "saying" (five times); and חידה, the "riddle" (twice).[58] The *proverb* and *discourse* are well represented and have clear affinities to oral transmission (in contrast to *riddle*), but the *saying* cannot be presumed to be, exclusively, a spoken form.[59] *Proverb* and *discourse* have both written versions and spoken (BBS 44:4–5).

For Ben Sira's use of proverbial statements, the most significant verses are BBS 50:27, and BBS 44:4 and 5 (all MS B), below.

---

55   Yankah, "Do Proverbs Contradict?," 10.

56   Camp, "Female Voice, Written Word," 102.

57   In the Hebrew Bible, the word מָשָׁל includes the *similitude* and the *by-word* in addition to the *proverb*. Due to the range of meanings, Skehan and Di Lella (*Wisdom*, 21) prefer to use the transliteration of מָשָׁל (*mashal*) instead of its common translation as "a proverb." However, *the similitude* and *the by-word* are distinct from proverbial speech because they are not performed. The meaning of מָשָׁל shifts in rabbinic literature to "parable."

58   Chart AppLex-7, in the Appendix, has each instance of משל, שיח, אומר, and חידה, and its context as an oral and/or written production. For evidence of writing, see the chart AppLex-9 for all instances of כתב and ספר in BBS. Three of the four instances of כתב indicate the activity of writing (once, by the author), but for ספר, six of the eight instances are "recount" (either written or oral), one is "counting" property, and the mention of "the scribe" in 38:24 is the single instance in which a word related to the root ספר indicates the activity of writing.

59   Six of the eight instances of *proverb* are oral and seven of the nine instances of *discourse*; two of the five instances of *saying* are inconclusive; and only one of the two instances of *riddle* is oral. The categories *proverb* and *saying* may overlap, and both might be formulated as verbal even when written. *Discourse* is probably a flexible category, for it can be paired with another category in the same verse: twice with *proverb* (BBS 6:35; 44:4) and once with *riddle* (BBS 8:8).

50:27   מוסר שכל ומושל אופנים   לשמעון בן ישוע בן אלעזר בן סירא :

            אשר ניבע בפתור לבן   ואשר הביע בתבונות :

Intelligent instruction and the timely telling-of-proverbs
—[belonging] to Simeon, son of Yeshua, son of Eleazar, son of Sira.[60]

That he has poured out, to explain to a son
—and that he has poured forth, with understanding.[61]

            חכמי שיח בספרתם ומושלים במשמרותם :

            חוקרי מזמור על חוק נושאי משל בכתב :

44:4cd   Wise-men of discourse, in their narration
—and proverb-tellers, in their "nails."

44:5   Searchers of psalm, by chord
—composers of proverb, in writing.

Verse 50:27 declares explicitly that Ben Sira's work encompasses the oral performance of proverbs. Oral proverb-usage would require two stages: first memorizing a collection of proverbs spoken or written by others (BBS 3:29, 6:35) and then choosing the appropriate unit from those stored in memory and speaking it properly (BBS 9:17, 44:4).[62]

The distinction between "proverb-tellers with their proverb-nails" (BBS 44:4d) and "composers of proverb in writing" (BBS 44:5) may reflect a conceptual division between speaking proverbs and incorporating them in a written text.[63] Both oral and written proverbs are acceptable, since each type of

---

60   The name "Simeon" (unattested in Greek versions) is the subject of debate. However, I consider it a legitimate part of the Hebrew texts, whatever its provenance. Reif ("Discovery," 1), among others, uses the personal name "Simeon" for Ben Sira, calling him "Simeon ben Jeshua ben Eleazar, better known simply as Ben Sira." Beentjes ("Canon and Scripture," 169) calls him "Simeon ben Jeshua ben Eliezer ben Sira" in referring to Ben Sira's identity. Reiterer ("Review of Recent Research," 52) gives a useful chart of Hebrew, Greek, and Syrian variants and comments that "[a]s there is no complete solution, there is no objection to the generally adopted term 'Ben Sira/Sirach.'" See the chart AppLex-12, "The name שמעון," in the Appendix.

61   The "pouring" does not indicate a literal, continuous stream of proverbs, either oral or written, because the telling-of-proverbs must be "timely" (colon 27a). If Ben Sira is like a canal, river, and sea that will "pour out" teachings (Sir 24:30–33), the metaphor emphasizes both his link with Wisdom, who has filled him to become her conduit/canal, and also the overflowing and expansive fullness of his own wisdom (see also BBS 32:4; Sir 18:29).

62   As the folklorist Mieder (*Proverbs: A Handbook*, 137) observes, familiarity "with a number of proverbs is one thing, knowing when and how to use them is quite another."

63   The use of "nails" (משמרות) is possibly a play on a verse in Qohelet: דִּבְרֵי חֲכָמִים כַּדָּרְבֹנוֹת וּכְמַשְׂמְרוֹת נְטוּעִים בַּעֲלֵי אֲסֻפּוֹת נִתְּנוּ מֵרֹעֶה אֶחָד : "The words of the wise are like goads, and like the 'nails' of masters of collections (of proverbs) given from one 'shepherd'" (Qoh 12:11).

proverb is juxtaposed with an approved activity. In BBS 44:4cd, oral proverbs—the spoken "nails"—are matched with the oral "narration" of sages; in 44:5, written proverbs are matched with (written) "psalms." The verb נשׂא (BBS 44:5b), here translated as "to compose," more literally means "to lift up," as in lifting the voice in song—an apt juxtaposition since both kinds of writing are also used in performance. Thus, the "writing" Ben Sira mentions is a legitimate form, though it can degenerate into a jumbled collection of proverbs of the sort that Camp contrasts with oral performance:

> Once proverbs are put in written collections, ... their vitality ebbs away. ... To the extent that form reveals meaning, a proverb collection is meaningless because formless. The timelessness they seem to assume constitutes a second problem ... [as] they take on the appearance of general moral principles. This combination of formlessness and timelessness ... either trivializes them as platitudes or inappropriately elevates them to doctrine.[64]

Written collections of proverbs have another element: the *impersonal* aspect of a performed proverb is lost when it is part of a written collection, so that it appears to be a personal opinion. However, I identify no such collections in the Book of Ben Sira.

The connection between proverbs and performance is a basic conceptual link in the Hebrew textual tradition.[65] Indeed, Crenshaw firmly believes that ancient Israel is among the many societies that have "used proverbial sayings for argument in circumstances as diverse as entertainment and legal decision-making."[66] And, in the Book of Ben Sira, the prevalence of topics related to *speech* prompts Di Lella's comment that "the book contains more material on the use and abuse of the tongue/lips/ mouth/palate (all organs of speech) than any other book of the Old Testament."[67] Ben Sira's self-identification as one who specializes in "the timely telling-of-proverbs" emphasizes the essential

---

On the question of whether Ben Sira could have been familiar with the text of Qohelet, Crenshaw mentions a date of "between 225 and 250" for the text (*Ecclesiates*, OTL [Philadelphia: Westminster, 1987] 5), which would put *Qohelet* about 50 to 70 years before the Book of Ben Sira. Another explanation is that both authors were familiar with a common figure of speech.

64 Camp, "Female Voice, Written Word," 103; regarding the book of Proverbs.

65 For Camp's work with proverbs, see "Female Voice, Written Word" and "Female Sage." For Fontaine's, see "Proof of the Pudding," "Proverb Performance," and *Traditional Sayings*.

66 Crenshaw, "Proverb in the Mouth of a Fool," 109.

67 Di Lella, "Use and Abuse of the Tongue," 33. Di Lella lists BBS/Sir 4:23–24; 14:1; 18:15–19; 19:5–17; 20:18–20; 22:27–23:1,7–15; 25:8; and 28:12–26. He also mentions that "'Death and life are in the power of the tongue'" (Prov 18:21) and other verses in Proverbs are precursors in these topics.

element of correct timing (BBS 50:27), as does his statement that a proverb "from the mouth of a foolish person will be rejected, for he will not tell it at its proper time" (Sir 18:29; 20:20 NETS). By definition, *performance* requires the presence of an audience, linking proverb performance with the "assumption of accountability to an audience for a display of communicative competence."[68] The composition of the audience would vary with the nature of the proverb-performance, and much of the literature on proverb performances, including literary creations of performances in Ben Sira's time and place, describes formal settings such as displays of rhetoric in a school, or witty 'table-talk' at a banquet.

Formal proverb-performance is so thoroughly typified by semantic fluidity that Yankah speaks of "the illusion of contradiction in proverbs," noting that "it is difficult to talk of contradiction between proverbs, since proverbs have more than one meaning."[69] However, groups of written proverbs often include contradictory statements, either as individual sayings or as contrasting themes. The performance of such proverbs in a specific context banishes the illusion of contradiction, since each member of an opposed pair would be spoken only in its proper context. Thus it is the *contexts* that are contradictory, because the complexities of life require a full range of proverbs to respond to every situation and a corresponding range of meanings to enable "impersonal speech." A sage such as Ben Sira who advertises his skills as a teacher needs a large repertoire of proverbs covering every viewpoint on a wide spectrum of subjects because the extent and range of his stockpile of proverbial statements shows the breadth of what he can teach. And, the need for a teacher is emphasized by the repeated message that to know the proverb is not enough: one must know when and how to use it.

Though the workings of classic proverbs illuminate some aspects of *the proverb* as a form of "impersonal speech," the model does not apply to the majority of gender-related proverbial statements in the Book of Ben Sira. These examples require a different model to delineate their use as "impersonal speech." I will approach the problem from another direction, starting from the fact that proverbial discourse is absolute.

The intrinsic absoluteness of the proverb can be deduced from the fact that proverbs formulated with qualifiers such as "some" or "may be" would sound absurd.[70] And, if a proverbial statement must always be absolute, then the all-or-nothing quality may, or may not, be related to authorial opinion. The

---

68 Yankah, "Risks," 133; the linguist cites Hymes ("Breakthrough into Performance," 18) and Bauman (*Verbal Art as Performance*, 11).

69 Yankah, "Do Proverbs Contradict?," 2, 10.

70 Yankah, "Do Proverbs Contradict?," 11–12.

proverb's absoluteness fits it for use in genres that share the trait, such as *blame* and *praise* in the passage about the schematic figures Wrong Wife and Right Wife (BBS 25:13–26:3).[71] Particular topics "like shame, women, or friends, ideally suit popular advice and homiletical contexts."[72] Proverbial statements about such figures typify my subcategory, the *proverb-token*, which could include many statements in the Book of Ben Sira. A proverb-token deals with generically-labeled human figures, often family members but also other groupings based on a single attribute, such as "rich man," "wicked man," or "godly man." The status of the proverb-token is analogous to that of the subway token: each kind represents both a specific unit of currency (conversational or monetary) and a specific, limited function (validating a previous statement or riding a subway).

A functional overlap between proverbs and relevant snippets of culturally canonical literature or songs, as spoken responses, means that "it is legitimate to speak of proverb-related literary forms "acting as [a] ... 'proverb.'"[73] All of these forms are brief and memorably phrased—and, they are established as opinions that originate in society-at-large rather than with the individual. Thus, if Person B quotes a proverbial statement by Ben Sira as a response to a remark by Person A, what matters is that the quote can be recognized as originating outside Person B.

In the situations I imagine, the proffering of a proverb-token has no underlying message—it is purely 'social noise,' but it is extremely functional in this guise. For example, in a situation where several men are talking, and Man A makes a personal comment or revelation about his marriage, Man B has a range of potential responses. If his goal is to demonstrate his friendly attitude toward Man A and, concurrently, to maintain an impersonal stance toward the revelation Man A has just made, Man B can quote an appropriate proverbial statement from Ben Sira about wives. On the topic of wives or friends, and on the topics of other family members (sons and daughters, but not parents or in-laws) or social contacts (wicked men, rich men, poor men, greedy men, etc.) the Book of Ben Sira has an apt proverb-token for many such interactions. And—here is my major point—Man B may or may not agree with the sentiment expressed in the proverb he uses, because the only

---

71   BBS 25:1–26:3 is analyzed in the following section of this chapter. See also section 1.4.1 of chapter 1.

72   Wright, "*B. Sanhedrin* 100b," 48. Wright notes that "[t]hose who used such proverbs certainly molded them to specific uses or adapted them to differing circumstances, separated out of their original context," and they memorized a repertoire of these proverbs to cite as needed.

73   Obeng, "Proverb as a Mitigating and Politeness Strategy," 535. The linguist speaks of a case in which a reference to the outcome of an Akan folktale functions as a proverb.

required agreement is between Man A's statement and the content of the proverb-token. The concept of *audience* in such a social interaction would be fulfilled by Man A, who accepts the proffered proverb as an adequate summation of his statement or else rejects it. Thus, the proverb-token carries no message that requires decoding—it functions purely as a token, a kind of "social currency" that reinforces the relationship between A and B on an impersonal social level.

The classic proverb and the proverb-token share these qualities: both are formulated as absolutes; both achieve impersonality by being ascribed to cultural wisdom; and both must be performed with delicate artistry in order to deliver the appropriate utterance at the right moment.[74] Chart 2-5, below, shows how the proverb-token differs from the ideal model. The proverb-token has fundamental differences, particularly in having a single context and carrying no coded message.

Chart 2-5: Proverb-tokens vs. the classic model of the proverb

	CONTEXTUAL?	CODED?	AUDIENCE?	ACTANTS?
PROVERB TOKEN	- "in context" (specific)	- no (social noise)	- dialogue	- people
CLASSIC PROVERB	- "out of context" (multivalent)	- yes (unstated goal)	- many or few	- animals or things

The proverb-token is an impersonal marker that gives no indication of the speaker's opinion of the proverb-token's content—it relates only to the content of a previous statement made by another speaker. In an oral setting, this previous statement that elicits the proverb is evident, but in a written text

---

74 Proverb performance differs from Austin's category of "performative utterances" because "[t]he uttering of the words is," for Austin, a "leading incident in the performance of the act ... the performance of which is also the object of the utterance" (Austin, *How to Do Things*, 6, 8). For proverb performance, the "object of the utterance" is never the performance—the enactment—of the proverb. In Austin's model each specific, formulaic utterance brings about its own specific result as a one-to-one relationship, whereas performance of a token-proverb is always a "many to one" relationship because a successful performance with *any* token-proverb has exactly the same result: it validates the previous speaker's right to speak the sentiments she or he has just expressed but neither approves nor disapproves of the sentiments themselves. Thus instead of changing some condition of reality as does a performative speech-act in Austin's model, the proverb-token's performative function is "[to] steady social reality" (Y. Sherwood, personal communication by email, 5 August 2010). Nor does the classic proverb fit Austin's description of a "performative utterance," because it operates as a "many to many" relationship in which what is said must be interpreted, and a performative cannot be ambiguous.

such as the Book of Ben Sira the eliciting-statement is absent. Thus, the context that the eliciting-statement provided is also absent in written forms, and must be compiled from the surrounding discourse of the proverb's poetic unit. And, for all kinds of proverbs, the apparent message might be modified or even negated by its context, which includes the messages of surrounding statements and the genre of the passage.[75] Because proverbs (including proverb-tokens) are a type of "impersonal speech," they should be evaluated as a separate category in assessing the "weight" of Ben Sira's opinions on any topic, including *gender*.

2.3 Colonial Contexts for Some Gender-Incidental Passages

For the Book of Ben Sira, proverb-function impinges on another topic—the agonistic behavior patterns whose presence would be predicted by the Greek/ Hellenistic model for masculinity. The use of proverbs, as an impersonal means of conveying problematic information and opinions, maintains mutual respect and discourages confrontational behavior. However, Hellenistic values for masculinity are often posited for Jews of Ben Sira's era, based on a schema from cultural anthropology. According to this theory, most cultural groups in the Mediterranean area have shared a similar set of values in which *honor* and *shame* function as a central binary pair.[76] A number of biblical scholars have used the Mediterranean honor/shame theory convincingly, to map certain interactions between characters in the New Testament. However, my results for the Book of Ben Sira do not align with the values presumed by the Mediterranean honor/shame theory, though the prevalence of interpretations focused through the lens of that model constrains my own analysis in terms of *honor* and *shame*. The Mediterranean honor/shame theory is seldom mentioned in the analyses that follow, but readers may map my remarks onto those concepts by means of the terms "agonistic," "limited good," and "negative male shame." This key derives from the following set of discursive elements I identify as criteria for a diagnosis of "Mediterranean" thought-patterns and behaviors:

---

75 Written proverbs that lack such contextual information (e.g., a list of contradictory proverbs) are "undefined" with regard to authorial opinion.

76 Pitt-Rivers and Peristiany introduced the theories in the 1960's and they, and others, have nuanced and particularized some of the original claims. See, for example, Peristiany and Pitt-Rivers, eds., *Honor and Grace in Anthropology*; Pilch, *Social Scientific Models* and "'Beat His Ribs'"; Moxnes, "Honor and Shame" (1993; 1996); and Malina, *New Testament World*.

1) *agonistic behavior*, with extremes of competition between men for recognition,

2) *perceptions of "limited good"* in which one man gains the honor of another, and

3) intersections of gender with "honor" and "shame," especially where there are *negative values of shame for males* and positive values for females.[77]

Those who work with concepts of *honor* and *shame* register a range of opinions. For example, Wikan concludes that "the apparently binary nature of 'honour' and 'shame' is deceptive. They are poorly matched at a conceptual level. ... And, at least in some empirical cases, their local glosses are not treated as binary at all."[78] The Book of Ben Sira is a textual "empirical case" in which *honor* and *shame* do not form a binary relation—the opposites are *honor* (כָּבוֹד) and *dishonor* (קָלוֹן), with *shame* (בֹּשֶׁת) operating independently. Although the Mediterranean honor/shame model links *shame* with gendered discourse, many instances of "shame" in the Book of Ben Sira are gender-incidental.[79]

2.3.1 Speech and Shame in Ben Sira's Colonial Context

Aristotle formulates agonistic values in terms of "noble" actions and attitudes, as in his statement that "to take vengeance on one's enemies is nobler than to come to terms with them; for to retaliate is just, and that which is just is noble; and further, a courageous man ought not to allow himself to be beaten."[80] In contrast, Ben Sira's statement that "a fierce soul will destroy its possessors—and the joy of one-who-hates will overtake them" (BBS 6:3)[81] is one of many that are antithetical to an agonistic worldview.[82] For Ben Sira, honorable behavior—associated with a positive value of *shame* for men—includes "care

---

77   (1) Moxnes, "Honor and Shame" 1996: 20–21; (2) Malina, *The New Testament World*, 33; (3) Moxnes, "Honor and Shame" 1993: 169.

78   Wikan, "Shame and Honour," 649. Wikan's remarks are from a summary of the results of her work in Cairo and of a study in the Omani town of Sohar.

79   See the chart AppLex-9 for concepts related to *honor* in the Book of Ben Sira.

80   Aristotle, *Rhet.* 1.9.24.

81   "Fierce soul" translates נפש עצה and "one-who-hates" is שׂונא, literal translations that posit "possessor" and "hater" as the same person. However, Corley (*Ben Sira on Friendship*, 44) translates נפש עצה as "strong desire" and שׂונא as "an enemy," presumably interpreting the enemy as a separate person.

82   The Greek binary noble/base has no direct equivalent in ancient Hebrew texts, which assign the highest ranking to a person who behaves in accord with divine law rather than one who claims aristocratic parents. The hereditary Jewish priestly-class, which decided what the divine law requires, did not have Aristotle's connotations of 'nobility.'

of the neighbor,"[83] and he clearly marks human speech as a decisive factor in maintaining honorable relationships.[84] Chart 2-6, below, shows relevant comments about *speech* in the Book of Ben Sira, and about *mutual respect*.

Chart 2-6: Speech *and* mutual respect *in BBS (MSS: A is default, B̲, C)*

4:7	Endear yourself to the congregation—and to those with more power, bend the head.
4:8	Incline your ear to a poor man—and return him a greeting, with humility.

4:23	Do not withhold a word forever—do not conceal your wisdom.
4:24	For in speaking, wisdom is known—and understanding in answer of the tongue.

5:10	Be supported by your knowledge—and your word will be afterwards.
5:11	Be one who hastens to listen—and with patience, return a response.
5:12	If you have a reply, answer your companion—and if not, your hand over your mouth.
5:13	Honor and dishonor in the hand of one who speaks-impetuously—and the tongue of a human is his downfall.
5:14	Do not be called "master-of two-tongues"—and by your tongue do not slander a companion.

6:3	For a fierce soul will destroy its possessors—and the joy of one-who-hates will overtake them.
6:4	Pleasant speech will multiply friend(s)—and gracious words, well-wishers.
	[NOTE: In a literal translation, "speech" is "palate," and "word" is "lip."]

8:3	Do not argue with a man of unbridled-tongue—and do not give wood upon fire.
8:4	Do not joke with a foolish-man—lest he will despise generous-men.

8:8	Do not leave the discourses of wise-men—and teach yourself their riddles.
8:9	For from it, you will learn instruction—to stand firm in the presence of chiefs.
	Do not reject the tradition of grey-haired-men—that they have heard from their fathers.
	For from it you may take intelligence—to return a response at the right time.

8:16	With a master-of-anger do not "butt heads"—and do not be expansive with him on a journey.
	For blood is trivial in his eyes—and without a deliverer, he will destroy you.

8:17	Do not consult with a naïve-man—for he is not able to conceal your secret.

---

83   Krammer, "Schamm im Zusammenhang mit Freundschaft," 199. Krammer closes the summary of her analysis of the *shame* passages with the statement that "behaviors that expose the neighbor and/or disappoint him, impair or destroy the relationship. Ben Sira warns against these behaviors, for which one should be ashamed, and at the same time he calls out for care of the neighbor."

84   Exalting the power of speech must also exalt the status of the sage as one who can control this source of power, yet other occupations also provide people with metaphors.

9:14 As is your strength, answer your companion—and take counsel with wise-men.

9:15 Let your conversation be with a discerning-man—and all your counsel, their insights.

9:17 A straightforward-man will be unceasing with the hands' wisdoms—and a teller-of-proverbs, making his people wise.

9:18 One who speaks impetuously is dreaded, in the testimony of a man of unbridled-tongue—and an utterance will be changed by his mouth.

10:6 For every transgression do not repay evil to a companion—and do not walk on a path of pride.

10:7 Hateful to the Lord and to men is pride—and to both of them, oppression is sinfulness.

10:8 Kingship goes round from nation to nation—on account of the violence of pride.

13:20 Humility is the abomination of the proud—and the poor, abomination of the rich.

25:8 Happy is the one who has not fallen by the tongue—nor served one more dishonored than himself.

32:18 A wise man will not conceal wisdom—and a mocker will not guard his tongue.

36:19 The palate examines flavors of word/thing—and the heart understands flavors of lies.

37:18 Good and evil, and life and death—and the ruler of them, completely—the tongue.

The verses in chart 2-6 demonstrate that the agonistic behaviors of the "master-of-anger" and of men who are "proud," "insolent," "mockers," "haters," "fierce," or "cruel" are disparaged. Recommended behaviors in the Book of Ben Sira are non-agonistic, and BBS 10:6 is the epitome of this teaching: "For every transgression do not repay evil to a companion—and do not walk on a path of pride." The quality of "humility" is praised (BBS 3:17; 4:8; 10:28; 13:20)—it is a trait for which God chose Moses (BBS 45:4).[85] "Humility" is linked with "honor," as are other behaviors such as "kindliness" and "non-violence" (BBS 10:23, 28; 44:1–7).[86] Furthermore, the acquisition of honor is repeatedly linked with Wisdom and/or God—semantic connections that indicate a perception of "*un*limited good" (BBS 4:13; 6:31; 10:20, 24; 37:26; 44:22; 51:17) and, thus, no emphasis on the scarceness of resources and the need for fierce competition to gain them.

The topic of *shame* is relevant to the current study as an intersection of *gender* and colonialism. Ben Sira's colonial status situates *shame* in the context of maintaining a viable group-identity under the constraints of asymmetrical power relations. His frequent references to "shame"—as a positive value for men—could involve both the knowledge that the Greeks would attribute

---

85   The praise of Moses for his humility spans biblical and rabbinic literature (Hebrew Bible, Num 12:2–4; Mishnah, *m. Avot* 6:1; Talmud, *b. Avodah Zara* 20b).

86   See the chart AppLex-10, in the Appendix, for a list of words linked with "honor.."

unethical behavior by any Jew to all Jews[87] and a resolve to define *shame* by Jewish, rather than Hellenistic, standards. What proportion of the poetic units about *shame* in the Book of Ben Sira are gender-focal? Three units of text focus explicitly on the topic of *shame*: BBS 4:20–28, BBS 41:15c–42:1d, and BBS 42:1e–8. In the charts that follow, each of the thirty-three bicola are assigned to a category: **G** for gender-focal, **T** for behavior toward others, **B** for business, and **M** for miscellaneous righteous behavior. Chart 2-7, below, shows the first poetic unit. The letters "YYY" translate three of the letter yod (') that are used in BBS to represent the four-letter name of God.

Chart 2-7: "My son, in a time of tumult" BBS 4:20–28 (MSS A, C)

CATEGORIES → **G**ender; **T**oward others; **B**usiness; **M**isc. good behavior.

4:20	My son, in a time of tumult, watch and be wary of evil —and do not be ashamed for yourself.	**M**
4:21	For there is shame that is a burden of guilt —and there is shame that is honor and grace.	**M**
4:22	Do not favor yourself —and do not be tripped by your stumbling-blocks.	**M**
4:23	Do not withhold a word forever —do not conceal your wisdom.	**M**
4:24	For in speaking, wisdom is known —and understanding in the answer of the tongue.	**M**
4:25	Do not be obstinate with God —and to God, humble-yourself.	**T**
4:26	Do not be ashamed to turn from guilt —and do not stand against a torrent.	**M**
4:27	Do not 'fetter' yourself to an impious-fool —and do not act defiantly before rulers.	**T**
	Do not remain with an unjust judge —for you will be judged by his disposition, with him.	**T**
4:28	Until death, strive for righteousness —and YYY will fight for you.	**M**

The first two verses declare that the context for the admonitions on *shame* is "a time of tumult"—a fitting phrase for the years before the Maccabean

---

87 In situations where Jews interacted negatively with Greeks (e.g., if a Jewish merchant used false weights), the *shame* would be ascribed to the group as well as the individual.

uprising and perhaps a code for "living as subjects of a foreign power." The second colon of v. 27 would be useful advice in any society where acting "defiantly before rulers" provokes severe responses—in this case, responses from the rulers of colonized Judea. All the verses in this passage envisage the image of a proper Jewish male, but no verse is gender-focal.

Charts 2-8 and 2-9, below, show the remaining passages, the double poem BBS 41:15c–42:1d and 42:1e–8.[88]

---

88   The Hebrew for chart 2-8 is from three MSS and for chart 2-9, two MSS. See the fully-annotated versions in the Appendix, as charts A2-8 and A2-9.

Chart 2-8: "Listen, children ..." BBS 41:15c–42:1d (MSS B, C, M→ no v. 20)

CATEGORIES → **G**ender; **T**oward others; **B**usiness; **M**isc. good behavior.

41:15c	Listen, children, to an instruction on shame —and be abased according to my judgment.	**M**
41:16	Not every shame is fit to retain —and not every abasement, to be chosen.	**M**
41:17	Be ashamed before father and mother, for recklessness —before prince and chief, for deceit.	**T**
41:18	Before lord and lady, concerning a lie —before assembly and people, concerning a transgression.	**T**
	Before partner and companion, concerning treachery —and in the place you sojourn, concerning theft.	**T**
41:19	For breaking stipulation and covenant —and reclining to dine, concerning fighting.	**M**
	For holding-back from granting a request —and for turning away the face of your kin.	**M**
41:21	For keeping quiet at the allotment of a share —and for 'not hearing' one who greets you.	**M**
	For regarding a woman/wife —and for looking at a stranger-woman.	**G**
41:22	For occupying yourself with your female servant —and for 'rising up' upon her bed.	**G**
	Before a friend, concerning disgraceful words —and after a gift, reproaching.	**T**
42:1	For repeating a word you will hear —and for making bare each word of counsel.	**M**
	And you will become modest, one who feels shame truly —and find grace in the eyes of all the living.	**M**

- For v. 1c, MS M has ת[4] בייש בוש באמת (see above) and MS B has והיית בוש באמת ("and you will become one-who-feels-shame truly").

In chart 2-8, the "prince and chief" of BBS 41:17b and the "lord and lady" in colon 18a could be either Jewish or gentile. However, those cola are sandwiched between thoroughly Jewish groups: "mother and father" (colon 17a) and the "assembly and people" (colon 18b). The "stranger-woman" in colon 21d could also be a member of the colonizing group. Bicola 41:21cd and 22ab are clearly instances of gender-focal situations, and are discussed after the charts.

The two poetic units are semantically linked. The first passage (chart 2-8) opens with the announcement that the addressee is to "feel shame according to" the author's judgment. Then follows a catalogue of actions and inactions for which a man should feel shame—in the sense of guilt for doing wrong or for not doing what is right—and the people concerned in each case. The theme of *shame* continues with a reversal of meaning in the second passage (chart 2-9) that announces a list of practices and attitudes for which one should not "be put to shame."

Chart 2-9: "However, for these matters ..." BBS 42:1e–8 (MSS B, M)

CATEGORIES → **G**ender; **T**oward others; **B**usiness; **M**isc. good behavior.

42:1e	However, for these matters do not be put to shame —and do not show partiality, and sin.	**M**
42:2	Concerning the Torah of the Most High, and statute —and concerning a judgment to acquit a wicked-man.	**M**
42:3	Concerning a reckoning of a partner and a path —and concerning an allotment of inheritance and property.	**B**
42:4	Concerning accuracies of scales and a balance —and concerning cleansing of measure and weight.	**B**
	Concerning acquiring, between much to little —and concerning the price of something sold by a vendor.	**B**
42:5	[?] *{Greek is about discipline of children}* —and a bad servant and who limps because of beatings.	**T**
42:6	Concerning the Wrong Wife, a seal —and a place of many hands, a key.	**G**
42:7	Concerning a place where you deposit, an accountant —and for giving and taking, everything in writing.	**B**
42:8	Concerning instruction of the naïve-man and the Fool —and the grey-haired stumbler, occupied with whoring.	**G**
	And you will become truly enlightened —and a man who is humble before all the living.	**M**

- For אל תבוש in v. 1e, translating as "do not be ashamed" makes sense only if a positive value is assumed for each "concern," such as "[fulfilling] the Torah" in v. 2a, "a [just] reckoning" in v. 3a, and "[maintaining] accuracies" in v. 4a. Translating the Qal stem of בוש as "be put to shame" (*DCH* 2:130b) covers the ambiguous phrasing of vv. 2–4.
- In 42:6a, MS B has אשה רעה "a bad wife/woman" (Wrong Wife), but the margin has אשה טפשה "a stupid wife/woman." MS M has a ten-space gap.

Comments in BBS 42:1e–8 focus on business concerns, which are absent from the other two *shame* passages. Note that both sections of BBS 41:15c–42:8 close by stating that modest behavior[89] is the goal for the passage's exhortations—BBS 42:1cd notes public approval of such a man and BBS 42:8cd mentions the man's demeanor toward others. The emphasis on humility as an ideal is another indication of non-agonistic values.

Of the thirty-three bicola in the set of passages about *shame*, I identify four as gender-focal (G). Eight bicola concern treatment of others (T), four bicola concern business ethics or money matters (B), and the remaining seventeen list miscellaneous examples of righteous behavior (M), including four on the power of speech (BBS 4:23, 24; BBS 41:22cd; BBS 42:1). These are the four gender-related bicola:

41:21cd	For regarding [...a woman/wife ...] —and for looking at a stranger-woman.
41:22ab	For occupying yourself with your female servant —and for 'rising up' upon her bed.
42:6ab	Concerning the Wrong Wife, a seal —and a place of many hands, a key.
42:8ab	Concerning instruction of the naïve-man and the Fool —and the grey-haired stumbler, occupied with whoring.

Bicola 41:21cd is similar to BBS 9:3–9, part of a poetic unit that lists a group of women whom Ben Sira considers sexually off-limits.[90] Bicola 41:22ab introduces a type not listed in BBS 9:3–9, the "female servant," who in large segments of Greco-Roman society had little or no control of her body.[91] Ben Sira's statement that a female slave/servant was not sexually available to her owner/employer would have been disputed by many male Jews as well as by

---

89 See BBS 10:6–8 and 13:20 in chart 2-6 for the opposite of "modest" behavior: "pride." The word "modest" (בייש) in BBS 42:1c is used for a woman in BBS 26:15.

90 See the analysis in chapter 4, "Human Females."

91 Osiek and MacDonald (*Woman's Place*, 104) comment that a number of ancient Roman authors "advocate the marital fidelity of husbands, ... but it is doubtful whether sex with one's own slaves is included." Westbrook ("Female Slave," 237) applies legal principles from Old Assyrian and other Near Eastern law codes to the stories of the Hebrew Bible. He presumes sexual use of a female slave, stating that "the owner's interest in her sexuality was protected against interference by outsiders through the rules of property law ... [and] offspring of the slave, even when fathered by her owner, were in principle subject to the rules of property law, like the fruits of any asset."

male Gentiles.[92] Both verses contribute to an important set of themes in the Book of Ben Sira: the delightfulness and sanctity of sexual relations between appropriately-compatible marriage partners and the concomitant destructiveness of such relations either with an incompatible spouse or outside marriage. The fourth bicola, BBS 42:8ab, pertains to that topic and, like the others, points to the man's behavior with no comment concerning the women. The third bicola, 42:6ab, is the only negative reference to a female figure, and that is the schematic figure, the Wrong Wife, who reappears in this poetic unit with her negative male counterpart, the Fool (v. 8).[93] Note that the four gender-focal verses are evenly divided between the two parts of the double-unit (charts 2-8 and 2-9) and occur, in both cases, in the third section of the poetic unit. Thus, interactions with women are considered from both focal perspectives: treatment of others (BBS 41:15c–42:1d) and business/financial concerns (BBC 42:1e–8).

For these major passages on the theme of *shame*, gender-focal bicola units occur half as often as the units that concern treatment of other people (and God), and are about one-eighth of the total number of bicola. Therefore the semantic range of *shame* for these passages is not focally linked with *gender*. Of the seven other bicola in the Book of Ben Sira with relevant instances of "shame,"[94] the only example of gender-focal discourse is the incomplete phrase "כי בעדה [5] בושת" (BBS 25:22a, MS C), completed by the colon "a wife providing [?] her lord-husband." The poetic unit is analyzed later in this chapter.

2.3.2 "Praise of the Fathers": Genre in a Colonial Context

One strategy for selecting a limited set of gender-focal passages is to define a boundary condition by excluding any passages with a vestigial level of gendered content. Excluded passages would include units that make no

---

92   About BBS 41:22, Osiek and MacDonald (*Woman's Place*, 106) note that it "seems to have been altered from Hebrew to the Septuagint in the direction of justifying sex with one's own slave" because "Lucian and Origen read *autēs* for *autou*, so that the prohibition is against the female slave of another man's wife" (ibid.). Balla (*Ben Sira on Family*, 155) also mentions the change in the Greek text.

93   The major appearance of the schematic figures is discussed in section 2.2.2.

94   As a basic lexical sampling, I only consider words from the root בוש. The other verses are: "you will not feel ashamed" linked to trusting in Wisdom (BBS 15:4b, MS A) or God (BBS 32:24b, MSS B, E, F), and miscellaneous instances: "shame was created for a thief" (BBS 5:14a, MS A); "do not be ashamed of an aged person" (BBS 8:6a, MS A); "one annihilates his soul/self by means of shame" (BBS 20:22a, MS C); and "before shame, [grace] excels" (BBS 32:10, MS B).

reference to *femaleness* as an abstract category, as female human characters, or as the female figure Wisdom. Such passages are not sites of gender-focal discourse and are set outside the boundary of the target group unless the exclusion of *femaleness* could reflect gender-bias. The long sequence known as "Praise of the Fathers/Ancestors" could be such an exception because the absence of female characters from the author's summary of biblical events and personages (chapters 44 to 49) could result from an implicit gender-bias.

"Praise of the Fathers" consists of two lists: an introductory poetic unit (BBS 44:1–15) that includes a list of occupations and a long catalogue of biblical figures (BBS 44:16–50:21).[95] The elements of each list represent choices from a larger group, the remainder of which are not part of the list. Therefore the question arises: by what criterion or criteria could these particular figures be chosen and others rejected? If the biblical figures in the catalogue-list are chosen because they are the most important characters, then the absence of female biblical characters leads to the conclusion that the author ignores them because they are less significant than the male characters.[96] However, if the all-male roster is the outcome of an inherent trait such as the unit's genre, then the selection process could occur at the level of choosing the genre, rather than the level of choosing which characters to include.

"Praise" opens with the announcement that the whole production is in the literary form of an "encomium/eulogy"[97] and continues with a fifteen verse prologue comprised of a series of praiseworthy occupations and a segue linking the list of occupations with the catalogue of biblical characters that follows the introduction. I analyze the list of occupations in detail because it is interesting not only from the perspective of gender-discourse but also because

---

95 The designation "biblical" includes the possibility that sources available to the author of "Praise" could have included multiple versions of what we know as canonical texts, of apocryphal and pseudepigraphical materials, of written and/or oral stories, and of novels

96 Brown ("Sinners, Idol-Worshippers and Fools," 188–90, here 190) speaks of "Ben Sira's defeminization of Israel's history." Egger-Wenzel ("Absence," 313) states that biblical women are of "minor importance" in Ben Sira's "collective memory." Kugel (*Traditions*, 12) calls BBS 44–49 "a review of the Bible's major figures," which might imply that *importance* is the criterion for selection.

97 The Hebrew noun שֶׁבַח designates formal praise, as in a eulogy (*DCH* 8:230b). See Lee's book that considers the encomiastic qualities of BBS 44–50 (*Studies*). Perdue (*Wisdom Literature*, 257) speaks of chapters 44 through 50 as an "encomium, a literary form that was originally a eulogy"; Corley ("Sirach 44:1–15," 152) comments that "Ben Sira was surely aware of the cultural phenomenon of the encomium."

it provides another example of Ben Sira's response as a colonized subject. Chart 2-10, below, shows the list of occupations: [98]

Chart 2-10: BBS 44:1–6 (MSS B, M) from "Praise of the Fathers"

KEY→ *political roles*; 'sage' roles.

44:1   An encomium, of the fathers of ancient-time:
       Let me praise men of piety/kindliness/disgrace חסד
       —our fathers in their generations.
44:2   Abundant honor has the Most High apportioned
       —and they became great, from days of ancient-time.
44:3   *Governors* of the earth, in their reign
       —and *men of renown*, in their might.
       Counselors, in their understanding   BIBLICAL ROLES
       —and those 'seeing' all, in their prophecy.
44:4   *Chiefs of nations*, in their discretion
       —and *princes*, in their decrees.

       Wise-men of discourse, in their narration
       —and proverb-tellers, in their 'nails.'
44:5   Searchers of psalm, by chord   BIBLICAL / COLONIAL ROLES
       —composers of proverb, in writing.
44:6   *Men of valor* and supporters of strength
       —and tranquil-men, on their dwelling place.

OCCUPATIONS

The arrangement of the occupations can be read as two sets of roles. The first set is political roles: reigning governors, mighty men-of-renown, counselors, chiefs of nations, and princes (cola 3a–4b, except 3d).[99] A set of sapiential roles follows: wise-men, proverb-tellers, psalmists, composers of proverbs, and tranquil-men (cola 4c–6b, except 6a). Although verses 1 and 2 introduce the list with reference to "ancient-time," I suggest that the set of political roles are temporally distinct from the set of sapiential roles, with both sets corresponding to exemplary figures in biblical stories but only the latter set having any relevance for Jews in Ben Sira's time. [100] By placing the whole list

---

98   MS M lacks 44:1a and 3ab. There are gaps, mostly minor, at the ends of cola 44:1ab, 2b, 3d, 4abd, 5b, and 6b. Otherwise, MSS M and B agree for 44:1–6 with minor differences of spelling, except that MS B has במחקרותם (with their searching-out) in 4b and חוק (statute) in 5a.

99   Verses 3d and 6a are "out of place," each belonging to the other's set.

100 Mack (*Wisdom and the Hebrew Epic*, 105) notes that "the listing is strangely disproportionate in its emphasis upon those engaged in scholarly and literary activities."

under the rubric of "abundant honor" apportioned to the "fathers" by God, Ben Sira constitutes sapiential expertise as having existed—*"from days of ancient-time"*—at the same status-level as political power and, thereby, denies that any loss of honor has occurred to the people through their loss of political and economic independence.[101] Thus, as Perdue observes, "Ben Sira's narrative presentation of Jewish history uses the Greek encomium as a strategy of discourse"[102] and constructs Jewish history in a manner that "deconstructs the empire's understanding of military, cultural, and moral superiority."[103] The passage BBS 44:1–6 is one of several instances in which Ben Sira demonstrates familiarity with a Greek literary genre while crafting it to carry a counter-Hellenistic subtext.[104]

Returning to the question of criteria for choosing the biblical characters who appear in "Praise"—why, among all the missing female figures, are those who rescued the Israelites from their enemies absent from the catalogue? Why do not Deborah and Jael, for example, appear in the catalogue as Israel's defenders? Women are not absent by an authorial accident or oversight—some coherent reason must dictate such a wholesale absence. My answer is that the exclusion occurs at the level of genre, not at that of authorial choice.[105] The Greek genre of *praise* precludes a combination of female and male subjects—an encomium can accommodate men *or* women, but not a

---

Perdue ("Ben Sira and the Prophets," 142–43) observes that "Ben Sira himself could be described with many of the same accolades, a fact that was probably intentional in his writing" and that, "[i]interestingly enough, the priests, who are described later ... are not mentioned in this introduction." The lack of priests in BBS 44:1–6 could dovetail with Reiterer's claim for a political subtext in the passage about Aaron (BBS 45:6–22): "Although partially expressed in coded language, it is clear that Ben Sira regards Aaron ... primarily as a political representative ... Aaron's appearance is similar to that of a king, since his function includes power and competence to make political decisions" ("Aaron's Polyvalent Role," 47; citing Wright, "Use and Interpretation" and "Ben Sira on Kings").

101 The fore-grounded claims to a tradition that has existed "from days of ancient-time" challenge Greek claims of cultural preeminence based on the antiquity of Greek traditions.

102 Perdue, *Wisdom and Creation*, 287, noting "how Ben Sira took a Hellenistic form and imbued it with the spirit and substance of Jewish history, religion, and wisdom."

103 Perdue, "Book of Ben Sira and Hellenism," 16.

104 Passages relevant to Ben Sira's colonial situation are BBS 4:20–28 (chart 2-7); BBS 25:13–24 and 26:1–3 (chart 2-11); BBS 35:21–26 (chart 2-1); BBS 42:9–14 (chart 4-16); and BBS 44:1–6 (chart 2-10).

105 Here, I distinguish between a text's literary template (*genre*) and its *content*. For similar argumentation, see Wieringen ("Why Some Women Were Included," 291–300), who states that "the genealogical *genre* itself may well provide a strong criterion for the inclusion or exclusion of certain names" (ibid, 296). I thank L. G. Perdue for asking the question about Deborah and Jael.

mixed group.[106] For example, in Sirach 21 and 22 *praise* for the Sage combines with a solid block of *blame* for the Fool, while in chapters 25 and 26 *praise* for the Right Wife combines with *blame* for the Wrong Wife. Thus, a single passage can mix categories of genre, but not of gender.[107]

Gender need not be a foregrounded discursive preoccupation in the passage even though there are always gendered background-codes such as the operative one in this case, which mandates separate discursive vehicles for females and males even when both groups fill the same role, such as obtaining a military victory. Another such code dictates that Ben Sira's imagined audience of future sages can only be male. Female characters are absent not because they are the rejects from the lists of important roles and characters but because the genre of *praise*, in a composition patterned on "the encomium," disallows combinations of female characters with males.

2.4 Genre in a Gender-Focal Passage: BBS 25:13–26:3

The passage BBS 25:13–26:3 approximates the forms of a pair of Greek genres: an invective in BBS 25:13–24, followed by an encomium in BBS 26:1–3.[108] In the passage of *blame*—one of three notorious sites that have extremely negative comments about women[109]—the schematic figure of the Wrong Wife is constituted with invective phrases that repeat combinations of אשה with רע or רעה. The actual phrase אשה רעה, "a bad wife," does not occur in BBS 25, though it is possible that our only Hebrew source, the anthological MS C, omits at least one of the three "evil wife" verses present in Sirach.[110] The semantic range of the words for "bad/evil/wicked" in the Greek translations is closer to the use of רע(ה) in the early chapters of Genesis, as "evil/wicked(ness)," than to the use of רע(ה) in the Book of Ben Sira as

---

106 Most encomia are about men, but "[i]n the early Hellenistic period Charon of Carthage wrote a four-volume compilation entitled *Biographies of Famous Women*" (McInerney, "Plutarch's Manly Women," 326; citing "Charon of Carthage, *Bioi endoxôn gunaikôn* [= *FHG* IV 360]"). The Sophist Gorgias' *Encomium of Helen*, written c. 425 BCE, is not a good example because it is an 'impossible topic' and thus a showpiece for the author's prowess.

107 See chart 2-3 for an outline of the units, together.

108 In the analysis that follows, I present the results as *possible*, the middle range on the scale from *probable* (very likely) to *conjectural* (suspended judgment, either likely or unlikely).

109 The other two sites are BBS 42:9–14 (chart 4-16, in chapter 4) and Sir 26:12 (not extant in Hebrew). BBS 25:24 is analyzed separately in section 5.2 of chapter 5.

110 In BBS 25:13, "wife" is inferred from context. For 25:19, Ben-Hayyim (*Book of Ben Sira*, 25, 98) has רעת, which matches the other instances, though Beentjes (*Book of Ben Sira in Hebrew*, 98) has רעה. For 42:6, a margin-note replaces רעה with טפשה, "stupid."

"bad(ness)," "misfortune," or "unpleasant(ness)."[111] Chart 2-11, below, has my literal translations of both Hebrew and Greek.[112]

Chart 2-11: "Any wound, but not like a heart's wound" BBS/Sir 25:13–26:3

BOOK OF BEN SIRA (MS C)	25:#	SIRACH (GREEK)
Any wound, but not like a heart's wound— any badness, but not like badness of a wife.	**13**	Any blow, but not a heart's blow— and any evil, but not a wife's evilness.
[No Hebrew equivalent.]	**14**	Any attack, but not an attack of haters—and any vengeance, but not vengeance of enemies.
	15	There is not a head above a serpent's head—and there is not a wrath above an enemy's wrath.
	16	I would prefer to dwell-with a lion and a dragon—than to dwell-with an evil wife.
Wife-badness darkens the appearance of a husband—and englooms his countenance like a bear.	**17**	A wife's evilness changes her appearance—and darkens her countenance like a bear.
Her husband dwells among bad-things—and without his 'taste,' he bemoans himself.	**18**	Her husband sits among the neighbors —and he cannot help sighing bitterly.
There is little badness like a wife's badness—a sinner's lot befall her!	**19**	Trivial is any badness to a wife's badness—a sinner's lot fall upon her!
Like a hard ascent for an old man— talkative wife for diminished husband.	**20**	A sandy ascent for an elder's feet— thus talkative wife for quiet husband.
Do not fall for a woman's beauty— and do not hasten to what is hers.	**21**	Do not attach yourself to the beauty of a woman—and do not yearn for a woman.
For in the assembly [?] shame— a wife sustaining [?] her husband.	**22**	Anger, shamelessness, great disgrace— whenever a wife supplies her husband.

---

111 For a full discussion of these words, see section A.1.1 of the Appendix, which includes the chart AppLex-1, for definitions of the Hebrew and Greek words, and the chart AppLex-2 for the words in BBS 25:13–24.

112 In Sir 25:15a, it seems likely that "head" translated רוש, which also means "venom" or "poison"; also, the Hebrew word רעים in colon 18a (translated here as "bad-things," from the root רעע) may have been read as "companions/neighbors," from the root רעה. In BBS 25:18b, the word טעם is translated as "'taste'" because the English word can include "discernment" and also allows sexual connotations, as in Prov 30:20. See *DCH* 3:372b "'taste; discernment; decree' ... Si 25:18 'he sighs without his discernment.'"

[No Hebrew equivalent.]	**23** Downcast heart and sullen countenance and a heart's blow—an evil wife.
Slackness of hands, weakness of knees—**23** wife who won't make her husband happy.	Restless hands, palsied knees—she who does not welcome her husband.
From a woman, the start of iniquity—and **24** because of her, we waste away, all alike.	From a woman, the beginning of sin—and because of her we all die.
[No Hebrew equivalent.]	**25** Do not give to water an outlet —nor give free speech to an evil wife.
	26 If she does not go beneath your hands —cut her off from your flesh.

A good wife—happy her husband— **26:1** and the number of his days is doubled.	A good wife—happy her husband— and number of his days is double.
A "valorous wife" fattens her husband **2** —and his years [?] she'll make joyful.	A "strong wife" rejoices her husband —and he will fulfill his years in peace.
A good wife is a good gift (מנה)— **3** and in the portion (חלק) of one- fearing-YYY, may she be given.	A good wife is a good portion (μερίς) —in the portion (μερίς) of one- fearing-the Lord she will be given.

The intense condensation of the *bad wife* motif in chapter 25 corresponds to the attributes of a specific genre—the Greek "blame of women." McClure speaks of the ψόγος γυναικῶν ("invective against women"), a traditional literary trope that "may have been a very early feature of the ancient Greek literary tradition."[113]

> By the time of tragedy, the invective against women, whether understood as a ψόγος γυναικῶν modeled on Hesiod and the earlier tradition, or simply as a form of κακῶς λέγειν (slander), is a literary commonplace epitomized in a fragment from Euripides' *Aeolus*, "Whoever stops slandering women will be called a wretch and a fool" (...Eur. frag. 36 N²).[114]

If the ψόγος γυναικῶν is "modeled on Hesiod," then Hesiod's passages about Pandora are the prototype for the genre.

How well does BBS 25:13–24 fit the template of a ψόγος, a composition of *blame*? Aristotle, after listing the elements of *praise*, for an encomium, notes that "when these are known their contraries are obvious, since *blame*

---

113 McClure, "'Worst Husband,'" here 374, 377. For the interchangeability of the labels "blame" and "invective," see Aristotle's comments (section 2.2.1).

114 McClure, "'Worst Husband,'" 377–78. For Hesiod's presentations of Pandora, see section 1.4.2 of chapter 1.

(ψόγος) is derived from the contrary things."[115] The qualities of the Wrong Wife correspond closely to Aristotle's list of the elements of an encomium, in their reversed form as *blame*:[116]

REVERSAL OF ENCOMIUM	WRONG WIFE IN BBS/SIR 25:13–24
[1] ascriptions of vice and disgracefulness;	(Sir 25:13) wife's "evilness" is worst of all evilness; (BBS/Sir 25:19) all other badness trivial to "wife's badness." (BBS/Sir 25:19) appropriate wife for sinner.
[29] adopting a term from the more unfavorable sense, such that the frank and open man may be spoken of as choleric, the courageous as fool-hardy, the liberal as recklessly extravagant, etc.;	Wife is said to debilitate the husband, but annoyance is a more likely description of his suffering.
[33] necessity of showing a man's actions/ achievements are instances of vice;	Wife accomplishes the gradual debilitation of the husband.
[39] reduction as a form of blame, since it consists in inferiority, and inferiority is one of the things that are disgraceful. That is why, if you cannot compare him with infamous personages, you must compare him with ordinary beasts, since inferiority is thought to indicate vice.	(Sir 25:16–17) Wife is worse than a lion and a dragon, and looks like a bear.

The cumulative effect of these reversals is that the tone of BBS/Sirach 25:13–24 is massively intensified, so that every image contributes to the total effect of a caricature. The range of meaning for רע(ה) (between "bad" and "evil") would allow an intensification of sources of annoyance such as talkativeness to the level of moral evils.[117]

In the brief passage BBS 26:1–3, values for the Right Wife match Aristotle's criteria for an encomium, reversing the values of the elements that constituted the Wrong Wife in the preceding verses. The Right Wife "fattens" the husband and doubles his life-span, is "valorous," and is a fitting partner for a man who "fears God;" the Wrong Wife debilitates the husband, is worse than fearsome beasts, and is a fitting partner for a sinner. Moreover, the label "valorous wife" links the Right Wife to the "valorous wife" of Prov 31:10–31, who is the subject of an alphabetic acrostic—an elaborate poem of *praise*.[118]

---

115 Aristotle, *Rhet.*, 1.9.41.
116 The reversed forms of Aristotle's encomium are my composition, given in section 2.2.1.
117 For a discussion of טוב and רע, see section A.1.1 of the Appendix.
118 See section 5.2 of chapter 5.

The weight of scholarly opinion that classifies "Praise of the Fathers" (BBS 44–50) as "patterned on Greek models" validates efforts to designate similar passages as examples of the genre of *praise*—approximations of encomia.[119] And, if one or more passages in Ben Sira's book are acknowledged to be similar to encomia, then it is reasonable to extend the labeling activities to passages in the form of the encomium's rhetorical inverse, the invective. As Collins states, "[w]hile the study of a genre inevitably involves a diachronic, historical dimension ..., its identification and definition are independent of historical considerations. A genre is identified by the recognizable similarity among a number of texts. Similarity does not necessarily imply historical relationships."[120] Thus, on the basis of recognizable similarities to Aristotle's definition of rhetorical *praise* and *blame*, sections of the Book of Ben Sira can be identified with these genres. Arguments in favor of Ben Sira's familiarity with Greek literary forms can strengthen the identification, but are not required as proof.

In addition to the effects of its genres, the passage BBS 25:13–26:3 provides another impersonal device: proverbial statements. The passage offers a collection of statements about "bad wives" and "good wives," available for oral use as the occasion arises. The proverbial qualities of 25:19 and 25:24, in particular, contribute to the passage's monolithic effect.

The poetic unit BBS 25:13 to 26:3 is one of two that are atypical for extant gender-focal passages in the Book of Ben Sira. I have classified it as an example of "impersonal speech," specifically a production that is governed by the monovocal genres of *blame* and *praise*. Ben Sira uses passages of *blame* against women (here) and against male "fools" (Sir 22:9–15) and of *praise* for women (here) and for heroic, male, role-models (BBS 44:1–6) because these were recognizable standards of Greek rhetoric. By crafting 'set-pieces' in these styles, Ben Sira advertises himself as a teacher who can equip his students to participate in a social world organized according to Greek principles.

Thematic issues are involved, as well as those of genre. *Appropriate marriage* is a major theme in the discourse of *gender* in the Book of Ben Sira and BBS 25:13–26:3 is structured by that theme, with the "good" wife assigned to a sage-figure and the "bad" wife to a "sinner." However, BBS

---

119 For example, Gammie ("Paraenetic Literature," 62) states that "[n]ot only is the Book of Sirach framed with texts which approximate the Greek encomia, its most significant division is marked by a hymn in praise of wisdom (Sirach 24) and this work contains the largest encomium in Israelite, sapiential literature which is patterned on Greek models—the so-called 'Praise of the Fathers' (Sirach 44-50)."

120 Collins, "Towards the Morphology," 1.

25:24 does not fit the *appropriate marriage* theme—its negativity is of a different order of magnitude, escalating the level of blame by generalizing it beyond a contrast of types to a universal condemnation. The semantic weight of this one verse skews interpretations of the poetic unit as a whole—and the verse receives an appropriately-thorough analysis, later, that situates it within a context for its poetic unit.[121]

Literary conventions that constrain the content of a passage as "impersonal speech" are useful lenses for examining texts to assess types and degrees of gendered content. The other atypical gender-focal passage, BBS 42:9–14, has a share of "impersonal speech" from the presence of proverbial statements, but is not subject to large-scale generic or schematic impersonalities, as is BBS 25:13–26:3. I have chosen a group of seventeen gender-focal passages for detailed analysis, listed below with chart-numbers.[122] These units are chosen for a combination of reasons that includes the arguments made thus far, my subjective evaluations, and previous usage by other scholars. In later chapters, these units are grouped according to topic—Wisdom in chapter 3, human females in chapters 4 and 5, and biblical allusions in chapter 5—and are analyzed for relational-gender content.

BBS #'s	Chart	BBS #'s	Chart	BBS #'s	Chart
4:11–19	→ 3-1	Sir 23:16–21	→ 4-13	36:18–26	→ 5-6
6:18–31	→ 3-2	Sir 23:22–27	→ 4-13	37:16–26	→ 5-7
7:18–26	→ 4-8	25:13–26:3	→ 2-11	40:18–27	→ 5-9
9:1–9	→ 4-9	(Sir 22:9–15	→ 2-4)	42:9–14	→ 4-16
9:10–16	→ 4-10	26:13–17	→ 5-11	51:13–30	→ 3-5
14:20–15:8	→ 3-4	33:20–30	→ 4-5		

---

121 See section 5.2 of chapter 5.

122 The structural pattern for each poetic unit is given in chart 1-1, and a list of all translated passages on the first page of the Source Index.

Chapter 3
Divine Female(s)

Three female figures are the focus of this study of *gender* in the Book of Ben Sira: Wisdom, Eve (by allusion), and a human female whom I label as the "intelligent wife." The discourses of these three overlap, and I investigate the figures separately and together. For all the figures, the analyses cover any topic only insofar as it relates to *gender*. Thus, the question of how close Wisdom's identity is to that of God is not an object of inquiry in itself, but only with regard to how that identity would affect the sage's erotic relationship with Wisdom. A similar disengagement from theology applies to human characters. Theological inferences are applicable only insofar as they impinge on *gender*, as in comparing the context of "one who fears God" for a woman and for a man. In the analyses that follow, my assessments of individual results vary greatly, and I label the resulting evaluations—explicitly—on a scale from *probable* (very likely) through *possible* (less likely) to *conjectural* (suspended judgment, could be either likely or unlikely).

3.1 Wisdom

The lack of a Hebrew version of Sirach 1 and 24, the major passages about Wisdom, hampers even the current, limited analysis. However, the extant Hebrew manuscripts have four passages about Wisdom that I identify as poetic units—BBS 4:11–19; 6:18–31; 14:20–15:8; and 51:13–30—and these, with a few additions from Sirach, are adequate for the current project. It would be helpful to have the Hebrew for the beginning of the Book of Ben Sira because the passage should provide strong evidence for some particular relationship between YYY—Ben Sira's typographic label for the hidden name of God—and the female figure Wisdom. The Greek translation states that "all wisdom is from the Lord, and with him it/she exists forever" (NETS), and the next verses speak more of w/Wisdom before opening the theme of *fearing-God*. A semantic range for "w/Wisdom" (חָכְמָה) includes "skill" in technical work and also "prudence" and "insight" as well as the name of the female personification, Wisdom. The choice between "wisdom" and "Wisdom" is not always clear, except in the case shown in chart 3-1, below, which uses an

unambiguous label for Wisdom: חכמות.[1] This instance, in BBS 4:11, is the
first reference to w/Wisdom after chapter 1. The poetic unit includes her first
speech.

Chart 3-1: "Wisdom has taught her sons" BBS 4:11–19 (MS A)

4:11	Wisdom has taught her sons —and she has exhorted all who perceive her.
4:12	Those who love her love life —and those who seek her will obtain favor from YYY.
4:13	And those holding her will find honor from YYY —and they will be graced with the blessing of YYY.
4:14	Those who serve the Holy One are serving her —and God loves those who desire her.
4:15	"One who hearkens to me will be judged true—and one who listens to me will encamp in the innermost-chambers of the house. *[no v. 16]*
4:17	For when he has made himself known, I will walk with him —and face-to-face he will choose us by tests.
4:18	And till the time his heart is filled with me, I will return, I will lead us —and I will reveal to him my secret-place.
4:19	If he deviates then I will reach out to him —and I will warn him, on forbidden-things. If he deviates from following me, I will reject him —and I will deliver him to marauders."

In the first half of the unit, Wisdom is closely linked with God through a
sequence of multiple repetitions of "YYY" (three times) and the other labels
"Holy One" and "God"[2]—all in the space of three bicola (BBS 4:12–14). The
sequence culminates in a formulation—"[t]hose who serve the Holy One are
serving her" (BBS 4:14a)—that establishes a strong though unquantifiable
identity between Wisdom and God.[3]

The second half of the poetic unit is Wisdom's speech to those who seek
her. "House" (colon 15b) can stand for the Temple in Jerusalem, which is

---

1   See *DCH* 3:224a for חכמות. See *DCH* 3:222a, for a semantic range for "w/Wisdom."

2   The translation of colon 14b is an open question, but there is some form of a name for God.
    See chart A3-1, the fully annotated version of this poetic unit, in the Appendix.

3   Di Lella (Skehan and Di Lella, *Wisdom*, 171) comments on the Greek version that "a
    remarkable affirmation is made in v 14a: to serve Wisdom is to serve God himself" but the
    Hebrew is even more remarkable: to serve God is to serve Wisdom herself.

Wisdom's dwelling (Sir 24:11).[4] Thus, the phrase "the innermost-chambers of the house" (חדרי מבית) can stand for the Holy of Holies. In v. 18, Wisdom's "secret-place" can denote the "innermost-chambers," but can also have a secondary meaning as "vagina"; an erotic overtone is present in these verses but not to the degree of subsequent poetic units.

Chart 3-2, below, shows BBS 6:18–31, the next poetic unit about Wisdom. In this unit, Wisdom is presented through a rubric of *agriculture*, by means of four bicola-units of related images: v. 19a–d has "plowing," "reaping," "produce," and "fruit," while vv. 20 and 21 turn to Wisdom's effect on those who reject her, for whom she is "like a carried stone"—a negative agricultural image of the work necessary to prepare a field. The "produce" of Wisdom—for those who persevere in seeking her—is that the symbols of the arduous search are transformed into a splendid array of sartorial emblems. Scholars note numerous similarities in the descriptions of Wisdom's regalia in this passage and that of the high priest Simeon in BBS 50, but interpretations of these similarities vary. [5]

---

4   For a further meaning of "house," see Baker's discussion of the rabbinic metonymy of "woman/wife" and "house" (*Rebuilding the House*, 52, 54–56, esp. 56). She speaks of "'woman' or the female body itself termed '*bayit*,' an entity at once fully place *and* person." While the full-blown rabbinic metonymy is not operative in BBS, a precursor is possible.

5   To Himmelfarb ("Wisdom of the Scribe," 97), "Simon appears… almost as Wisdom's double." Among those who construe the parallels between Wisdom and the high priest as displacement/usurpation are Camp ("Honor and Shame," 184, 186; "Storied Space," 76) and McKinlay (*Gendering*, 139, 151–159).

Chart 3-2: "... you will reach Wisdom" BBS 6:18–31 (MSS A, C, 2Q18; Sirach (NETS))

6:18ab	**Child, from your youth welcome education, and until gray hairs you will find wisdom.**
6:18b	...you will reach Wisdom. *[18b, top of III recto]*

6:19	Like one who plows and like one who reaps, approach her —and hope for her produce to become abundant. For in her service you will scarcely work —and quickly, you will eat her fruit.
6:20	To a foolish-man, she is 'rough going' —and one lacking heart will not hold her.
6:21	Like a carried stone she will be to him —and he will not delay to cast her off.
6:22	For "the discipline" המוסר is like her name, thus it is —and she is not straightforward to many. *[6:23-25 not in Hebrew. BBS 27:5,6 inserted here—out of context]*

6:26	Bow down your neck and accept her —and do not cut off her guidance.
6:27	Investigate and search out, seek and find —and be attached to her, and do not let (her) fall.
6:28	For in the end, you will find her repose —and it/she will be changed for you, into pleasure.
6:29	And her net will become for you a site of strength —and her ropes, garments of fine-gold.
6:30	A yoke of gold is her yoke —and her fetters, a cord of blue-purple. *["fetter" מוסרה]*

6:31	As garments of honor you will wear her —and as a crown of glory you will encircle her (round you).

Wisdom and Simeon the High Priest have a significant set of shared attributes that includes plants, jewels, and raiment, and both are found in the precincts of the Temple. They are each the subject of an encomium: Wisdom in Sir 24 (Greek only) and Simeon in BBS 50:1–21. The presence of both in encomia could constitute them as schematic figures—but, is there the sort of relationship that could combine them in a schema? Simeon is not labeled as a "sage" (one who seeks w/Wisdom); the word "sage" (חכם) does not appear in his portion of chapter 50, nor does "Wisdom/wisdom" (חכמה). Furthermore, the set of shared attributes is not exclusive to Wisdom and the High Priest Simeon. Chart 3-3, below, shows the elements shared by Wisdom, all high-priests, and the "family" of the sage.

Chart 3-3: Wisdom, the high-priest, and the sage: Who has what?

	WISDOM	HIGH-PRIESTS: AARON AND SIMEON		SAGE AND WIFE, "SONS"
GARMENT:	for sage, her ropes = garments of fine gold (6:29); fetters = blue-purple thread (6:30),	wears garments with gold + blue-purple thread (45:8–10)		Sage wears Wisdom as garments of honor (6:31) (+ items in 6:29, 30), + golden yoke (6:30)
CROWN:	—	crown of pure-gold (45:12); crown of sons (50:12); garments of honor and of glory (50:11)		Sage wears Wisdom as crown of glory (6:31)
PERFUME:	incense in tent (*Sir 24:15*)	incense as duty (45:16); burns incense (50:9)		"Sons" = fragrant (*Sir 39:14*)
H./HOLIES:	tabernacle (*S. 24:10*); inner chambers of house (4:15)	דביר (45:9); אהל and בית הפרכת (50:5)		Wife in chosen דביר (26:16); sage in (4:15)
SUN:	—	= sun on Temple (50:7)		Wife = sun in the heights (26:16)
MOON:	—	= full moon (50:6)		Sage filled with thoughts = full moon (*Sir 39:12*)
WATER:	rivers from Eden (*Sir 24:25,26*)	spring of water (50:8)	Sage = stream from W. (*S. 24:30*); "sons" = rose by water (*S. 39:13*)	
TREE:	= cedar, cypress, palm (*S. 24:13,14*); olive (*Sir 24:14*)	Aaron's sons = palm, cypress, olive, cedar (50:10,12)		Sage has garden + flower-beds (*Sir 24:31*)
FLOWER:	rose (*Sir 24:14*)	roses, lilies (50:8)		"Sons" = rose, lily (*Sir 39:13, 14*)

Each item a high-priest shares with Wisdom is shared also by a sage-figure: the sage, the sage's wife, or his fictive sons. Even if the repetition of similar elements is the result of a literary convention such as a sequence of laudatory comparisons in an encomium, the comparisons in that genre are not assigned randomly. I approach the similarities in terms of their distribution among a larger group than Wisdom and Simeon.

Aaron is part of the group because the apparel in question originates with the description of the high priest's garments in Exod 28. The vestments include items of gold and of blue and purple fabric, plus a turban (מִצְנֶפֶת).

Ben Sira summarizes the biblical list in his description of Aaron (BBS 45:8–12), adding a "crown (עֲטָרָה) of gold" upon the turban.[6] Simeon inherits from Aaron in general terms, but does not have the crown of gold. Instead, the priests gathered around Simeon function for him as "a crown of (Aaron's) sons." However, the figure of Wisdom in the Book of Ben Sira has some of the exact accoutrements described for Aaron in Exodus. Wisdom's "cord of blue-purple" is the פתיל תכלת that holds the high priest's breastplate and attaches the piece of gold on his turban (Exod 28:28,37; 39:21,31), but it is also the "cord of blue-purple" that God commands Moses to tell the people to attach to the fringes (צִיצָת) of their garments, in their generations, to remind them of the commandments of the Torah (Num 15:38–39).[7] Thus, the blue-purple cord is not only a priestly device but is also a token commanded for all (male) Israelites as a symbol of obedience to Torah, which in this case may indicate the identification of Wisdom with Torah (BBS 15:1).[8]

The sage is the defining figure for the third group that I consider with Wisdom and the high-priests: the sage and his wife and his fictive sons. No explanation of the semiotic relations between Wisdom and the high-priest(s) is feasible unless it accounts for the sage-group's ownership of the same apparel, location, celestial objects and botanical items. Receiving and wearing garments that are the insignia of a particular office constitute a performative claim to that role, as investiture—thus, the parallel language used for the "enrobings" of the sage and the high-priest indicates parallel investitures. The "one who reaches Wisdom" (BBS 6:18b) is authorized to perform the role of *sage*, just as Simeon has been authorized to perform the role of *high priest*. Simeon "wears" Aaron as a crown that signifies both his claim to the office of high-priest and the father-to-son inheritance-model of the priesthood. In perfect replication and significant contrast, Ben Sira wears the same substances and colors, yet they are robed upon him symbolically as Wisdom herself, and he "wears" Wisdom as his crown, signifying both his right to the title of sage and the form of inheritance, by teaching rather than birth.[9] The co-equal status of

---

6   The only other biblical reference to a priestly crown is Zech 6:11, in which the prophet is told to make crowns of silver and gold and place one on the head of the high priest Joshua. Any parallel would apply to Simeon, not Moses, because the high priest Joshua is another post-exilic personage who rebuilds the Temple.

7   Di Lella (Skehan and Di Lella, *Wisdom*, 194) notes the link with Num 15:39.

8   Snaith ("Biblical Quotations," 9–10) notes that "Ben Sira is using a quotation [Num 15:39] to point out the close link he felt between Wisdom and the requirements of the Torah."

9   Ben Sira's students relation to him replicates his with Wisdom, in that they will model themselves on him—wrapping his persona around themselves, so to speak, as a "garment of glory." Wright ("Ben Sira on the Sage as Exemplar," 181) states that "the sage sets himself up as one who must be emulated, identified with," and that "the student ... can embody

the two roles is evident because the phrases "garments of honor, garments of glory" that apply to Simeon's clothing (BBS 50:11) also apply to the sage, for whom Wisdom is his "garments of honor" and a "crown of glory" (BBS 6:31).

By the time Ben Sira goes out into the world from chapter 24, with "teaching like prophecy" (Sir 24:33), he has been invested by Wisdom with the vestments mentioned in chapter 6, the golden yoke and golden garments, the blue-purple cord, and the crown of glory that is Wisdom herself. In this case, when he names himself as "Simeon" in 50:27, he positions himself as an equal to the Simeon who has just presided in the Temple, with both Simeons ministering to God, for the people: one through the temple-service and the other through "teachings like prophecy." Camp identifies these two stages of development, noting that "significantly, just as Ben Sira's paean to personified Wisdom in chapter 24 concludes with reference to the prophetic quality of his own teaching, so also his hymn to Simeon in chapter 50 segues into self-authorization for his own text."[10] In the latter case, Ben Sira describes Simeon giving the priestly blessing (BBS 50:20–21), then shifts to "a self-naming and the assurance that those who concern themselves with the matters in his book will also find blessing" (BBS 50:27–29).[11]

Though without the Hebrew original of Sir 24 no definite statement about those passages is possible in the current study, I suggest that the sequence of symbolic investments begins not in the Book of Ben Sira but in the Hebrew Bible, when God sends Wisdom into the world and when God bestows the office of High Priest on Aaron. Wisdom and the high-priest are both in the Temple, and both have similar garb, but Simeon inherits from Aaron and Simeon ben Sira inherits from Wisdom. It is semantically difficult for the

---

Wisdom only inasmuch as he regards the sage as the exemplar to be emulated." Perdue (*Wisdom and Creation*, 288) notes that "Ben Sira regards wisdom as more than an intellectual activity. ... the sage attempts to embody the moral life," and that "through this embodiment of cosmic wisdom, the sages both realize and constitute world order"; with note "see Marböck, *Weisheit im Wandel*." Di Lella (Skehan and Di Lella, *Wisdom*, 195) comments on the inheritance Ben Sira provides, that "[t]he wise, because of their fidelity to the Law will enjoy the splendor of royalty and the glory of the high priesthood."

10   Camp, "Storied Space," 71. Camp states that Ben Sira "claims for himself a divinely authorized space that is the equivalent of the priest's" (ibid., 78) by his mention of his "house of instruction," which she investigates in conjunction with the high-priest's "house," the Temple. Gilbert ("Review," 324) also notes a semantic continuum between the high priest and Ben Sira, stating his opinion "that, at the time of Ben Sira, sacred history does not end with Simon, but with the wisdom master and his disciples."

11   Camp, "Storied Space," 71, 77. My deductions from these patterns differ from hers, but reading her formulation of the sequence of events prompted the idea of a parallel between the two Simeons by linking it to chapter 24. Camp uses the Greek text for 50:27, which does not have the name "Simeon."

potency of Wisdom to pass from her to Simeon the high-priest because the other players—Aaron, and Ben Sira and his wife and "sons"—share in all the markers that would be passed in a simple case of supersession. Ben Sira expands the categories of people authorized to share Wisdom's markers and, by this tactic, expands the range of those who may interpret Torah. The legitimating function is noted in Wright's observation that "since the person who single-mindedly pursues Wisdom can possess her, Ben Sira not only authorizes his own teaching, he also legitimates the entire enterprise of the sage," and in Perdue's comment that Ben Sira's claim to divine inspiration "could legitimate as authoritative his interpretation of Scripture and the authority of his own writings," making it possible for later sages "to assert the same position."[12]

The third poetic unit about Wisdom is BBS 14:20–15:8 (chart 3-4, below), which follows the preceding unit after several scattered references to "wisdom." In BBS 14:20b, "understanding" (תבונה) appears as a grammatically-parallel counterpoint to "wisdom" (חכמה) in colon a. Both w/Wisdom and u/Understanding can be read either as personified figures or as abstract concepts.[13] However, if תבונה functions as a semantic motif that orchestrates this poetic unit, then colon 20b can be read as a literal injunction: "pay attention to [the word] 'understanding.'" What happens to the word "understanding"? In colon 21b, תבונה multiplies into two related words, ובתבונתיה יתבונן: a plural form of the noun "understanding" combined with a verbal form of its root, בין. The superfluities of the formulation can signal a site of wordplay—perhaps the word תַּבְנִית, which is "a pattern (for construction), plan, design (of tabernacle and its furnishings)," from the root בנה ("to build").[14] Wordplay between colon 21b's תבונתיה and its hypothetical companion תבניתיה would give a conjectural translation of BBS 14:21 as "Who sets his heart upon her paths—and he will consider her designs/plans." By this translation, the pairing of "paths" with "designs/plans" matches the semantic closeness of "wisdom" and "understanding" in 14:20 The word תבנית

---

12 Wright, "Biblical Interpretation," 369, after noting that the "discourse of chapter 24 provides a ... comprehensive strategy for conferring authority on Ben Sira's instruction"; Perdue, "Ben Sira and the Prophets," 134, introducing chapter 24 and other passages.

13 In Prov 8:1, חכמה and תבונה are mentioned as separate personifications—Wisdom and Understanding—but the verbs used thereafter are feminine singular, implying that these are two names (or aspects) of one figure, Wisdom.

14 See *DCH* 8:586a–588a and 590a–591a for definitions of תְּבוּאָה, תְּבוּנָה, and תַּבְנִית. For BBS 50:9a, the incomplete word ת[1]בֹּ[1]ת (Beentjes, *Book of Ben Sira in Hebrew*, 89) is filled in by Ben-Hayyim (*Book of Ben Sira*, 303a) as תֹבֹנֹית; the word is used in conjunction with the golden vessels to which the high-priest Simeon is compared.

would also function as a segue to the architectural motifs that follow—the "entrances," "window," "house," "wall," and "tent" in BBS 14:22–25.

Chart 3-4: "Happy the person who will meditate on Wisdom" BBS 14:20–15:8 (MSS A, B)

14:20	Happy the person who will meditate on Wisdom —and he will pay attention to understanding.
14:21	Who sets his heart upon her paths —and he will consider her understandings. *[or "her designs/plans."]*
14:22	To go forth after her, searching —and all her entrances he will observe-jealously.
14:23	Who looks down through her window —and because of her openings he can listen carefully.
14:24	Who encamps roundabout her house —and brings his tent-cords to her wall.
14:25	And spreads out his tent near her —and he will dwell, a good dwelling.
14:26	And he has established his nest in her foliage —and in her branches he will lodge.
14:27	And takes refuge in her shade from parching heat —and in her abodes he will dwell.
15:1	For one who fears YYY will do this —and one holding to Torah will attain to her.
15:2	And she will meet him like a mother —and like the wife of his youth she will accept him.
15:3	And she will feed him with bread-of-intelligence —and water-of-understanding she will give him to drink.
15:4	And he will lean upon her, and will not stumble —and he will trust in her, and will not be ashamed.
15:5	And she will exalt him more than his companion(s) —and she will open his mouth among the congregation.
15:6	He will find gladness and joy —and she will cause him to possess an everlasting name.
15:7	Untruthful men will not attain to her —and insolent men will not see her.
15:8	She is far from scoffers —and deceitful men will not remember her.

The hypothetical rubric of *architecture* functions here—as does the explicit rubric of *agriculture* in the previous poetic unit, BBS 6:18–31 (chart 3-2)— organizing the content of the second section of its unit. The word תבונה reappears in the third section of the poetic unit, in BBS 15:3b as Wisdom's gift of the "water-of-understanding," being some of the "understandings" from BBS 14:21b.[15]

Several motifs that develop over the course of the four poetic units for Wisdom are the need to seek diligently in order to "find" Wisdom and the rewards of persevering to find her. For example, the exhortation in BBS 6:27a (chart 3-2) to "[i]nvestigate and search out, seek and find" expands into a detailed plan of search in BBS 14:22–27 (chart 3-4). As the seeker comes close to Wisdom's house, Wisdom herself becomes the architecture, in her likeness of a tree[16] in whom the seeker will "establish a nest," "lodge," and "take refuge." For a final consummation of the seeker's approach to Wisdom, he will dwell (with her) in her "abodes."[17] The word מְעוֹנָה used in v. 27 indicates a non-human habitation, the "abode" of God and of Wisdom, but also the "lair" of wild animals—a fitting domicile for the seeker, who has already transformed himself to become a nesting bird.

The first half of the poetic unit (vv. 20–27) presents Wisdom through images that carry the possibility of erotic overtones. A general category of "all her entrances" (v. 22), which describes the seeker's means of visual and aural access to information about Wisdom, includes the word פתחיה "her openings" (v. 23). Words related to "openings" or "doors" can refer to the assiduity of a student seeking instruction[18] but can also be metaphors for the vagina.[19] It is interesting that the seeker behaves toward Wisdom much as the "defamer" behaves toward people (BBS 11:30, chart 4-15a), with an approach that could be described as "lurking" or "stalking." However, the units about Wisdom form a series, and Wisdom has invited the seeker in BBS 4:15b, "one who

---

15 Or, even some of her "produce," a tenuous link between תבואה "produce" in BBS 6:19b and תבונה "understanding" in BBS 14:20–21.

16 See Sir 24:13–14 and 16, in which Wisdom likens herself to different trees. Sources of knowledge are commonly associated with "trees," e.g., the "Tree of the Knowledge of Good and Evil" in Genesis and its partner, the "Tree of Life"—which becomes a metonymy for the Torah (and for Wisdom as Torah?).

17 Balla (*Ben Sira on Family*, 192) comments that "Sir 14:27b further confirms that the person no longer lives just close to wisdom but *in* her home as her lover or spouse."

18 The student is told to "hollow out the threshold" of the house of a prospective teacher of proverbial-wisdom and "seek him early" in the day (BBS 6:36, MS A).

19 One example of such a double meaning is Wisdom's speech in Prov 8:34: אַשְׁרֵי אָדָם שׁ[i]מֵעַ לִי לִשְׁקֹד עַל־דַּלְתֹתַי יוֹם | יוֹם לִשְׁמֹר מְזוּזֹת פְּתָחָי "Happy is the man who hearkens to me—to be wakeful at my doors day-by-day—guarding the doorposts of my opening."

listens (אזן) to me will encamp (חנה) in the innermost-chambers of the house."
Thus, "listen carefully" (יצת) in v. 23 can fulfill "to listen" in BBS 4:15, and
the seeker does "encamp" (חנה) around Wisdom's house in v. 24.

In the second half of the poetic unit, the theme changes and Wisdom
appears as a mother-figure. The only glimmer of erotic possibilities for this
section is BBS 15:2b, in which Wisdom will "accept/embrace [him] like the
wife of [his] youth." The two halves of the poetic unit are linked by BBS 15:1,
which points to the preceding verses as the activities that will lead to the
situations that follow.

The fourth and last of the poetic units about Wisdom, BBS 51:13–30b, is
the last unit of Ben Sira's book. In Qumran manuscript 11QPs[a], the poem in
the Book of Ben Sira is in the form of an acrostic, while those verses in Cairo
manuscript MS B appear to be a partially-preserved acrostic form. Chart 3-5,
below, gives my translation from the Hebrew of BBS 51:13–30g, the entire
closing-section of the Book of Ben Sira. The part of the unit that has erotic
content is BBS 51:13–21. The Qumran text 11QPs[a] is the default for vv. 13–
20b because that portion is well-preserved, and MS B is the default for the
remaining bicola because this portion is damaged or lacking in 11QPs[a]. The
sources for this passage are unusually complex.[20]

Though the erotic section that is the target for the current study occupies
only the first half of the passage, the entire passage is important for context—
it is also a beautiful poem (in Hebrew, if not in my translation), and deserves
to appear in its entirety and to be discussed as a whole, at least briefly. The
acrostic part of the passage is verses 13 through 29, with bicola 30ab, and the
rest of v. 30 is a closing for the whole book. In the first half of the passage
(vv. 13–21, which I parse as four sets of three bicola) the author speaks about
his relationship with Wisdom; in the second half (vv. 22–30ab, parsed as two
more sets of three bicola and a final set of four) the author speaks of YYY and
Wisdom, addressing sons or students as "you" (pl.). The poetic unit closes in
bicola 30ab with the author bequeathing, to these students, the promise that
God will give them their "reward, in His time," just as God gave to him his
"words' reward" (colon 22a). And, though the rest of v. 30 is not part of the

---

20 See chart A3-5 in the Appendix for a fully-annotated version of the passage. The last verse
    (v. 30) is controversial because it gives the author a different name than does Sirach. Some
    scholars consider this passage (and other parts of chapter 51) to be addition(s) to the original
    text. However, Gilbert ("Review," 324) considers 51:1–12 and 13–30 "the final part of the
    Praise of the Lord, which started in Sir 42:15." See J. A. Sanders, Muraoka, and Skehan and
    Di Lella for an overview of this discussion. By my understanding of the *gender* discourse of
    the Book of Ben Sira, BBS 51:13–30 is the culmination of a motif that opens in the early
    chapters, and is an intrinsic part of the discourse(s) as a whole.

poetic unit, these cola that begin with "Blessed be YYY forever" (BBS 51:30cd) participate in the overall pattern by fulfilling the author's announcement that he will "praise" God (colon 22b).[21]

Chart 3-5: "I was a young man, before I wandered" BBS 51:13–30

51:13	אני	I was a young man, before I had wandered about —and I sought her.
14	באה	She came to me in her form —and until the end-of-time I will study her.
15	גם	Likewise, when blossom diminishes with the ripening of grapes —they will rejoice a heart.
	דרכה	My foot advanced on level ground —for from my youth I have known her.
16	הטיתי	I inclined my ear just a little —and abundantly I found knowledge.
17	ועלה	And she was an ascent for me —to my teacher I will give my splendor.
18	זמותי	I have planned so that I may be joyful —for I have been zealous in pleasing, and I will not turn back.
19	חריתי	I kindled my desire for her —and my face I have not turned away.
20	טרתי	I have kept my desire with her —and at her exaltation I will not be slack.
	ידי	My hand has opened her gates —and I will be surrounded by her, and I will regard her. *[no "כ"]*
20fe	לב	And a heart I gained by her, from her beginning —and in purity I found (Wisdom/the heart).
21	מעי	My belly is 'fired up' like an oven, in regarding her —in order that thus I gained her, a good gain.
22	נתן	YYY gave to me my words' reward *[literally, "my lips' reward"]* —and with (the speech of) my tongue I will praise Him.
23	סכלים	"Confused-ones! Turn to me —and lodge in my house-of-study.
24	עד	How long will you lack some of these things, and these? —and your soul will be very thirsty.

---

21   Liesen's comment on Sir 19:20–29 ("'With All Your Heart,'" 212) is relevant also for this passage that links Wisdom and teaching with praise of God (BBS 51:22–30). Liesen states that, for Ben Sira, praise of God "is practically equivalent to true wisdom and he thinks it can be learned from a wise and sensible person, like himself."

25	פי	I have opened my mouth and I have spoken, concerning her —'Gain for yourselves Wisdom, without money.
	צואריכם	Bring your necks within her yoke —and her burden will lift up your souls.
26	קרובה	She is close to those who seek her —and one who gives himself finds her.'
27	ראו	See with your eyes! For I was a young-one —and I persisted with her and I found her.
28	שמעו	Hear many-things that were taught me in my youth —and silver and gold you will gain with me.
29	תשמח	My soul rejoices, because of my academy —and you will not be ashamed, because of my song.
30	—	Your works are made with righteousness —and He gives you your reward, in His time."
	—	Blessed be YYY forever —and exalt His name to generation and generation!
	—	Thus far, the words of Simeon son of Yeshua, who is called "son of Sira."
	—	The wisdom of Simeon son of Yeshua son of Eleazar son of Sira.
	—	Let the name of YYY be blessed, from now until forever!

At several points in the poetic unit, a comment refers back to a previous verse. Between the two halves of the unit, "for I was a young-one ... and I found her" (v. 27) and "hear many-things taught me in my youth" (v. 28) refer back to the first verse, "I was a young man ... and I sought her," and to "I inclined my ear ... and ... found knowledge" (v. 16). Within the second half of the unit, "YYY gave to me ... reward" (v. 22) is echoed by "(if) your works are made with righteousness, (then) He gives you your reward" (v. 30).

Images in BBS 51:13–21 are both passionate and tender. The unit begins with the image of a relationship whose "ripening" is a greater source of rejoicing than its early, "blossom" stage.[22] The pattern unfolds as a gradual intensification of the speaker's relationship with the female figure Wisdom, in terms of "an ascent" (17a) that culminates in his activity "at her exaltation" (20b). Language of "acquiring/gaining" a wife that is used of human marriage is used here (21b), and carries into a reading of 22a as God "giving" Wisdom, who is שכר שפתותי—both "reward" (שָׂכָר) for the author's words and "mead"

---

22 Rabinowitz ("Qumran Hebrew Original," 177) notes the pattern of progression from blossom to fruit as "the quest for wisdom throughout life," but he rejects erotic interpretations of the passage.

(שֵׁכָר) for his lips. The passage BBS 51:13–21 recapitulates some of the vocabulary from previous units. Ben Sira, as a student-sage, encircled wisdom around his head as a crown (BBS 6:31), now Wisdom "surrounds" him in sexual union (BBS 51:20d).[23] Angel notes the mutuality of the relationship:

> Much as the sexual imagery speaks clearly of a man making love to a woman, it also speaks of a woman making love to a man. It is true that this comes from a male author and thus from his world of fantasy, but in this fantasy world, Wisdom is not so much an object of his desire as a lover in a mutual quest for sexual pleasure.[24]

The erotic undercurrent is complete in this passage, with almost every bicola capable of yielding a level of erotic discourse. I wish my translation could convey both levels: the passionate desire for wisdom and its equally passionate counterpart in the images of love-making between Ben Sira and Wisdom. The delicacy of the erotic allusions is better served by not translating them with clinical accuracy and, perhaps, a single translation better preserves the balance between the two semantic levels.

The LXX translation of the poetic unit BBS 51:13–21 downplays erotic elements that are present in the extant Hebrew MSS—both MS B and 11QPs[a] are erotic poems and the Greek versions do not fully transmit this quality. The Greek translation (Sir 51:13–21) diverges consistently, replacing the erotic language of the Hebrew texts with comments that are non-celebratory as well as non-erotic.[25] For example, "my face I have not turned away" (BBS 51:19, MS 11QPs[a]) is translated as "in the performance of the law I was exacting" (Sir 51:19); "my hand has opened her gates" (BBS 51:20c, MS B) becomes "I spread out my hands on high" (Sir 51:19c); and "I will be surrounded by her, and I will regard her" (BBS 51:20d, MS B) becomes "I thought about ignorance of her" (Sir 51:19d, all NETS).

The basic survey of erotic overtones in BBS/Sir 51:13–29 is the work of J. A. Sanders, who published a commentary on the Psalms Scroll in 1965, with infrared photographs of the text.[26] At the beginning of a detailed analysis of the verses, he comments: "One suspects that the *mots à double entente* are intentional and that in those instances the two meanings were understood

---

23 I translate ולה אחדר as "and by her I will be surrounded" (20d) though it can also mean "and I will penetrate her deeply" (see the Notes in chart A3-5, in the Appendix) because vagina-centric possibilities require explicit mention, as the marked term in a penis/vagina binary.

24 Angel, "From Wild Men," 158.

25 See the chart AppLex-13, in the Appendix, for translations of both Hebrew and Greek for verses where the Greek diverges significantly. Angel ("From Wild Men," 157) considers a few phrases in the Greek version to have erotic overtones, but fewer than the Hebrew.

26 J. A. Sanders, *Psalms Scroll*.

together."[27] Responses to Sanders' suggestions for double readings cover a wide spectrum of opinion.[28] Muraoka has given the fullest response to the suggestions; the chart below gives words identified as definite, or likely, double meanings.

BBS 51:#		J. A. SANDERS *Psalms Scroll*, 81–82	MURAOKA "Sir 51,13–30," 170–173
15c	רגלי	"Euphemism?"	"cannot denote *penis*"
17	הודי	"'my manhood'"	"[my] honour"
18	ואשחקה	"'make sport'"	—
18	בטוב	"'for pleasure'"	—
19	חריתי נפשי	"'I kindled my desire'"	"'I kindled my desire'"
20b	וברומיה	"'her heights'"	"'her exaltation, i.e., orgasm'"
20c	ידי	"Euphemism?"	"euphemistic use"

Muraoka concludes—after asking why the Greek version differs from the Hebrew—that though the passage shares some elements with the Song of Songs, "the affinity stops there" because Ben Sira's central concern was "a search after Wisdom and deep devotion to it, only he saw an extremely close analogy between this religious, ethical zeal and a man's intimate association and physical union with his female companion." [29] By my reading of the texts, Ben Sira's central concern with Wisdom has an additional dimension that *does* have strong affinities with the Song of Songs, because the semantic ranges

---

27 J. A. Sanders, *Psalms Scroll*, 81.

28 Those who agree with Sanders include Muraoka ("Sir. 51, 13–30," 170), who wonders if the translator took offence at "the sensuous allusions in it and set about producing a decent, censored version of the poem?"; Martone ("Ben Sira Manuscripts," 87), stating about 11QPsᵃ that "there can be little doubt that we can explain the differences between the Greek and the Qumran text as an attempt on the part of the Greek translator to avoid too explicit terms to be found in the Hebrew text"; Camp ("Storied Space," 77), who calls the passage "an arguably erotic—or at least eroticized—autobiographical poem"; Wright ("Wisdom and Women," 242), who observes that "there seems no doubt that some eroticism is intended"; Winston ("Sage as Mystic," 390), noting "an artful use of erotic imagery"; and Deutsch ("Sirach 51 Acrostic," 406), who says Ben Sira "uses erotic language to describe his response to [Wisdom] in 51:13–22." Collins (*Jewish Wisdom*, 53) remains a neutral observer, though he acknowledges that "the Greek translation eliminated the erotic overtones." Those unconvinced by Sanders include Di Lella (Skehan and Di Lella, *Wisdom*, 578), who interprets the ardor as a sage's enthusiasm—"he never relented in his burning desire for wisdom" and Rabinowitz ("Qumran Hebrew Original," 174), who declares that the "'erotic' interpretation ... is fundamentally (and grossly) mistaken."

29 Muraoka, "Sir. 51, 13-30," 173–74.

for Wisdom and the sage's "intelligent wife" overlap and include vocabulary shared with Song.[30]

3.1.1 Wisdom and God

Wisdom, as depicted in the Book of Ben Sira, occupies a semantic range that overlaps with the range depicted for God. The ramifications of this possible overlap intrigue theologians, but the overlap intrigues me now because the sage (Ben Sira himself in chapter 51) is sexually intimate with Wisdom. Because two major poetic units about Wisdom are missing in Hebrew, my comments on the topic remain tentative. Chart 3-6, below, shows the verses I consider useful for assessing the relationship between Wisdom and God. Hebrew texts for the full poetic units are given in the Appendix, charts A3-1, A3-4, and A5-1.

Chart 3-6: Verses that associate Wisdom with God

4:12	אהביה אהבו חיים	Those who love her love life—and
	ומבקשיה יפיקו רצון מייי :	those who seek her will obtain favor from YYY.
4:13	ותמכיה ימצאו כבוד מייי	And those holding her will find honor from YYY
	ויחנו בברכת יי :	—and they'll be graced with the blessing of YYY.
4:14	משרתי קדש משרתיה	Those who serve the Holy One are serving her
	ואלהו במא ויהא	—and (?) those who desire her.
4:15	שומע לי ישפט אמת	"One who hearkens to me will be judged true
	ומאזין לי ייחן בחדרי מבית :	—and one who listens to me will dwell in the house's inner chambers."
14:25	ונוטה אהלו על ידה	And spreads out his tent near her
	ושכן שכן טוב :	—and he will dwell, a good dwelling.
14:26	וישים קנו בעופיה	And he has established his nest in her foliage
	ובענפיה יתלונן :	—and in her branches he will lodge.
14:27	וחוסה בצלה מחרב	And takes refuge in her shelter from parching heat
	ובמעונותיה ישכן :	—and in her abodes he will dwell.
15:17c	כי ל[3] חכמת יי	For abundant is w/Wisdom of YYY
	אל בגבורה ומביט לכל :	—God-in-power, and beholding all.
15:18	ספקה חכמת יי	Overflowing is w/Wisdom of YYY
	אמיץ גבורות וחוזה כל :	—firm of powers and perceiving everything.

---

30 See chapter 5 for discussions of similarities between Wisdom and the "intelligent wife," as well as vocabulary shared with Song.

Colon BBS 4:14a comes closest to including interchangeability as an element of the relation between Wisdom and God.[31] And, the startling direction of identity is that "those who serve the Holy One are serving her." The designation chosen for God is significant: קדש is an indirect identifier or a label, but not a name. To say "those who serve YYY are serving her" would be too explicit a declaration of identity; the preceding triple use of "YYY" emphasizes the change to קדש but also links the two designations for God.

A word in 14:27 refers to God's habitation: מְעוֹנָה is "God's abode" as well as that of Wisdom.[32] The pericope BBS 14:25–27 continues the topic of Wisdom's dwelling-place from the reference in BBS 4:15: חדרי מבית, the "innermost-chambers of the house," which can be the Holy of Holies in the Temple. The biblical account of the building of the Holy of Holies (1 Kgs 6:16) states: וַיִּבֶן לוֹ מִבַּיִת לִדְבִיר לְקֹדֶשׁ הַקֳּדָשִׁים "... and he built/furnished the interior of it as an innermost-chamber, as the Holy of Holies." The word דביר occurs in BBS 26:16, as the author's wife's place, where they meet. Yet, לִדְבִיר לְקֹדֶשׁ הַקֳּדָשִׁים can also mean "as an innermost chamber for the Holy-One-of-holy-ones," perhaps a reference to this chamber as the "dwelling place" of God above the throne with the two intertwined cherubim, a motif that is part of the Shekhinah traditions.[33] The constellation of references to Wisdom's cohabitation with God indicates intimacy between the two, though it need not imply they are coextensive.

Although Wisdom in the Book of Ben Sira could be considered a hypostatic being, in the sense of "acting like a being separate from God,"[34] I see Wisdom in terms of the figure's overlap with God, rather than separation. Ben Sira's statement that "those who serve the Holy One are serving her"

---

31 In colon 14b, no group of letters is a recognizable Hebrew word or phrase. See chart A3-1 in the Appendix for two possible interpretations.

32 See *DCH* 5:390a.

33 This is applicable if a tradition reported in the Babylonian Talmud dates back to Ben Sira's time. It is stated in *b. Yoma* 54a that the two cherubim, whose images form God's "throne" in the Holy of Holies, are intertwined in sexual union: אמר רב קטינא: בשעה שהיו ישראל עולין לרגל מגללין להם את הפרוכת, ומראין להם את הכרובים שהיו מעורים זה בזה, ... ואומרים להן: ראו חבתכם לפני המקום. "R. Kattina said: whenever Israel came up for a festival, the curtain was rolled up for them; and the cherubim—that were intertwined this one with that one—were shown to them ...," and that this image is כחבת זכר ונקב "like the love of male and female." See also the next section in this chapter.

34 Charlesworth, "Lady Wisdom," 94, n. 128. "I am convinced that early Jews, beginning in the second century B.C.E., were not satisfied only with the concept of personification, since they often portrayed Wisdom, like the highest of the archangels, as acting like a being separate from God; that is, she was a hypostatic being."

(BBS 4:14) brings Wisdom-in-BBS in line with Wisdom-in-Proverbs, of whom Murphy makes this explicit declaration:

> Is she an aspect of Israel's God? Instead of speaking about "attribute," should one not recognize a gender designation, by analogy? Thus she would be the "feminine" in God, who created human beings in the divine image when he "created them male and female" (Gen 1:27b).[35]

As a result of analyzing the Hebrew texts of Ben Sira, I think it quite likely that his formulation of the relationship between יהוה (YHWH) and Wisdom is the relationship behind God's words in Gen 1:26a: "Let Us make them in Our image." However, that is a meaning that could only be stated indirectly, as it is in Genesis and, perhaps, in BBS 4:14 (using קדש, "the Holy One").

For the current purpose, all that is necessary is to demonstrate *some degree* of overlap in the semantic ranges for Wisdom and God. To the degree that these overlap, to that same degree Ben Sira presents his intimate relationship with God as sexual union—he represents himself as sexually intimate with God. The theme of *union with God* is not unusual in religious texts, but this instance would be unusual in Jewish and Christian sources because God would be represented as *female*.[36] The reverberations of this theological earthquake may seem less important to others than to me, for whom it is an astounding discursive maneuver on the part of Ben Sira. To the degree that Ben Sira believes that Wisdom is (in some way) God, to that degree he breaks the hermeneutical sequence that allows mirror-image interpretations in which a male God creates (male) humans in "His own image."

3.1.2 Personified-Wisdom in Later Texts

The presence of a female figure with divine attributes—Wisdom—became problematic for later writers who made use of the Hebrew and Greek biblical texts. The Rabbis solved the problem by equating W/wisdom with Torah and by shifting many aspects of Wisdom to a new female figure, the Shekhinah. The name שְׁכִינָה means "She-who-dwells,"[37] and she is the immanent aspect

---

35 Murphy, *Proverbs*, 280. See also the discussion of the Shekhinah, in section 3.1.2.

36 The gender-taxonomy of BBS is part of a Western, heterosexual gender-model. Yet, within that universe, a man's choice of a female God-image is uncommon if not anomalous, and I seek to map the territory of this particular discourse of *heterosexuality*.

37 The Shekhinah tradition is built upon biblical verses that connect God's activities with words from the root שכן, "to dwell," all interpreted as the Shekhinah's presence.

of God, the "Divine Presence."[38] In rabbinic literature,[39] the Shekhinah is figured (more or less) as the female counterpart of the male-aspect of God and also as the one who blesses human sexual relations, but she is not figured as sexually involved with humans, as is Wisdom in the Book of Ben Sira and in Proverbs.

Though a "Shekhinah-motif" is not explicitly present in either the Book of Ben Sira or Proverbs, both have places to attach such a motif. In Proverbs, Wisdom declares "I have dwelt" (Prov 8:12). And, if BBS 24 has שכן,[40] it would be a step in the direction of later Shekhinah troping that links this figure to the Temple.[41] Other elements of Wisdom's speech in chapter 24 parallel aspects of the Shekhinah. In particular, Wisdom's association with the "pillar of cloud" (Sir 24:4) parallels later associations of the Shekhinah as God's Presence with the Israelites in the desert, as the "pillar of cloud." References to the Shekhinah appear in rabbinic literature as early as the Mishnah:

רבי חלפתא בן דוסא ... אומר עשרה שיושבין ועוסקין בתורה. שכינה
שרויה ביניהם. שהאמר (תהלים פב). אלהים נצב בעבת אל.

R. Halafta ben Dosa ... said, "Ten who sit together and occupy themselves with Torah—the Shekhinah abides among them, as it is said, 'God stands in the congregation of God'" (m. Avot 3:6, citing Ps 82:1).

---

38 Murphy ("Personification of Wisdom," 227) concludes that Wisdom in Sirach 24 "was apparently the presence of God ... dwelling in the 'tent'"—words that I associate with the figure of the Shekhinah—and again, "[w]e are dealing with a theology of presence," but Perdue (*Wisdom and Creation*, 288) considers that, throughout BBS, Wisdom's function "represents both the transcendence and the immanence of God" because she is "the imaginative incarnation of the words that came from the mouth of God."

39 Jastrow (*Dictionary*, 1573b) lists instances in *b. Yoma* 9b; *b. Berakhot* 6a; *b. Shabbat* 12b; *b. Pesahim* 117a; *b. Megillah* 29a; and *b. Bava Batra* 25a. Other instances are in *b. Sotah* and *b. Rosh HaShanah*. Also, there may be a link in *b. Sotah* 11a between the Shekhinah and Wisdom, made through a complex interplay between verses that include "And his sister stationed herself afar" (Ex 2:4) and "Say to Wisdom, 'You are my sister'" (Prov 7:4).

40 In Sir 24:4 Wisdom declares that she "dwelt in the heights" and her throne was "a pillar of cloud;" in 24:8, that God caused her "tabernacle" to rest where she would "dwell" (both Greek words translated as "dwell" are from the verb κατασκηνόω). "Dwelling," the "tabernacle," and the "pillar of cloud" are all associated with the Shekhinah. See Perdue (*Wisdom Literature*, 244); McKinlay (*Gendering*, 137); and Di Lella, who cites Philo as identifying Wisdom with the "pillar of cloud" in Exodus (*Wisdom*, 332; citing Philo, *Quis. Rer. Div. Heres.*, 42).

41 Use of the root שכן would allow Ben Sira to allude to a Shekhinah figure, or for later readers of Ben Sira to interpret his words as such an allusion. Though the Book of Ben Sira lacks Prov 8:12's direct association of Wisdom with שכן, there are two cases similar to Prov 1:33, where the verb applies to the one seeking Wisdom, who "will dwell-in a good dwelling" (BBS 14:25, chart 3-4) and "will dwell" in Wisdom's habitations (ibid, v. 27).

The unexplicated mention of the Shekhinah in this mishnah indicates that traditions for this figure were already well-developed in the era of the Mishnah.[42]

The Rabbis, following canonical Hebrew texts that included some form of the Book of Ben Sira,[43] shifted aspects of Wisdom—with some of the erotic imagery—to the Shekhinah.[44] The shifting of attributes away from Wisdom may be a rabbinic response to the Christian discourse that links Jesus with Sophia. Early Christians who used the Septuagint (including Sirach) shifted non-erotic aspects of Wisdom to Jesus.[45] As a male figure, Wisdom could be accommodated in the Trinity. These oversimplified descriptions of rabbinic and Christian discourses trace the paths of a Hebrew-centered trajectory from the Hebrew Bible through the Book of Ben Sira to rabbinic literature and mystical texts and—with increasing divergence over time—a Greek-centered trajectory from the biblical books of the Septuagint, through Sirach, to the New Testament (including identifications of Jesus with Sophia).

Popular Jewish stories about the Shekhinah and Christian stories about Mary, Jesus' mother, present both females in terms of their wisdom, compassion, and close relationships with God. The figure of Wisdom, as constituted in the Book of Ben Sira, consists of both "discipline/instruction" and "delight," but the figure has no explicit associations with "compassion." The identification of Wisdom with Torah necessitates the aspect of discipline, which is not a component of the Shekhinah.[46]

---

42   The full proof-text (Ps 82:1) is : אֱלֹהִים נִצָּב בַּעֲדַת־אֵל בְּקֶרֶב אֱלֹהִים יִשְׁפֹּט "God stands in the congregation of God, among the divine-ones He will give judgment." In the mishnah's use of the biblical verse, the 'heavenly-court' becomes a human congregation, and also the Shekhinah is explicitly declared to be God. The mishnah continues with proofs that the Shekhinah's presence is true for five persons, then three, then two, and finally, one. See also *m. Avot* 3:2.

43   The argumentation in *b. Sanhedrin* 100b constitutes BBS as a non-scriptural canonical text. An exhaustive discussion by Leiman (*Canonization of Hebrew Scripture*, 100) of the expression ספר המטמא את הידים is the basis for my taxonomy of four rabbinic categories of texts: those that "defile the hands," which are divinely-inspired biblical texts ("biblical" texts are both inspired *and* canonical); "semi-biblical" texts, which are uninspired yet canonical; books for casual reading (e.g., Homer); and "outside books." BBS belongs in the category of semi-biblical texts. See also Ellis, "Negotiating."

44   Penchansky notes that the Rabbis see Wisdom "as the Shekinah ... The Christians change her gender and she becomes the Christ" ("Is Hokmah," 85).

45   Modern scholars who implicitly or explicitly link Jesus with Sophia in speaking about BBS/Sirach include Deutsch ("Wisdom in Matthew"), Edwards (*Jesus the Wisdom of God*), Pistone ("Blessing of the Sage"), and Schroer (*Wisdom Has Built Her House*).

46   In BBS, both Wisdom and God have the double-nature. God is "compassionate" in BBS— רבים רחמי אלהים "abundant is the compassion of God" (BBS 3:20, MS A)—but also, כי רחמים ואף עמו "for compassion and anger are with Him" (BBS 8:6, MSS A, C; BBS 16:11, MS A).

3.2 Why Is the "Strange Woman" Not in the Book of Ben Sira?

The taxonomic systems that I describe for the Book of Ben Sira include four schematic human figures and one semi-divine female figure, Wisdom. However, in the similar system of Proverbs,[47] Wisdom has a counterpart—the "strange woman." Given the strong, *gender*-related parallels between the Book of Ben Sira and Proverbs,[48] it is likely that Ben Sira was familiar with some version of what we have as the book of Proverbs and, to some degree, modeled his work on it. If there is such a relation between the two texts, then the question of why Strange Woman is not part of the Book of Ben Sira is germane to the discursive construction of *gender* in that text.

Strange Woman personifies, at a super-human level, the linked categories *female* and *evil*. Therefore, if Proverb's Wisdom and Strange Woman are taxonomically balanced as positive and negative quasi-divine females, and if the relevant taxonomies of Proverbs and the Book of Ben Sira are parallel with the exception of Strange Woman, then what happens to Strange Woman's portion of gendered negativity when Ben Sira reformulates the system without her? Do her qualities accrue to a human female figure in the Book of Ben Sira?[49] Though Proverbs has no fully-developed equivalent to the four-figure schema of affinities in the Book of Ben Sira,[50] all the elements of the schema are present in Proverbs, to different degrees.

3.2.1 Schematic Human Figures in Proverbs

As in the Book of Ben Sira, the sage figure in Proverbs is the hub of schematic interactions and, of the three other members of Ben Sira's affinity-schema (Right Wife, Fool, and Wrong Wife), the Fool and the Right Wife have the closest counterparts in Proverbs. The pattern of presentation for the Fool is similar in the two texts: chapter(s) with verses that contrast the Sage and the Fool (Prov 17; BBS/Sir 20, 21), followed by a distinctly schematic

---

47 The current discussion of the book of Proverbs is conducted entirely in terms I derive from the Book of Ben Sira and is, therefore, a lop-sided analysis of Proverbs itself.

48 For example, both texts close with an acrostic poem to a female figure.

49 Camp ("Honor and Shame," 179, 182) states that, in Ben Sira, "[t]he real possibility" of women's evil, "defined repeatedly as sexually transmitted shame, has moved from the streets of Proverbs into the heart of the man's home." Thus, the negative qualities projected on Strange Woman in Proverbs are inherited by the Wrong Wife in BBS, making her a more immediate, domestic threat to the husband.

50 The affinity-schema and its taxonomy are discussed in section 1.4.1 of chapter 1, and section 2.2.2 of chapter 2.

passage of comments about the Fool (Prov 26; Sir 22). For both texts, the foolish-behavior labels "fool" (כְּסִיל), "foolish-man" (אֱוִיל), and "folly" (אִוֶּלֶת) cover much the same semantic range, though they are not necessarily interchangeable. A separate but associated category is gormless-behavior, whose labels "naïve" (פותה or פְּתִי), and "lacking heart" (חֲסַר־לֵב) have a rather neutral status between "sage" and "fool." For both texts, words and labels associated with the opposed pair "sage" and "fool" are not the same as those linked with the other major pair, "righteous-man" (צַדִּיק) and "wicked-man" (רָשָׁע). The chart below gives the schematizing passage for the Fool in Proverbs.

Chart 3-7: Schematic "Fool" verses in Proverbs 26:1–12

26:1 כְּסִיל Like snow in summer and like rain in the harvest—thus honor is
            not fitting for a fool.   *[Verse 2 has no reference to a "fool."]*

3 כְּסִילִים Whip for the horse, bridle for the ass—and rod for the back of fools.

4 כְּסִיל אִוֶּלֶת Do not answer a fool according to his folly—lest you, yourself,
                 be comparable to him.

5 כְּסִיל אִוֶּלֶת Answer a fool according to his folly—lest, in his eyes, he
                 become a sage.

6 כְּסִיל [Cutting off feet, drinking violence]—one sending a message by a
           fool's hand.

7 כְּסִילִים Hanging down, legs of a lame-one—and proverb in the mouth of fools.

8 כְּסִיל Like one binding a stone in a sling—thus one giving honor to a fool.

9 כְּסִילִים Thorn came to the hand of a drunkard—and proverb to the mouth of
            fools.

10 כְּסִיל An archer who wounds all—and one who hires a fool or passers-by.

11 כְּסִיל אִוֶּלֶת Like dog who returns to his vomit—fool who repeats his folly.

12 כְּסִיל You see a man who is a sage in his own eyes? More hope for a fool
            than for him.

In Prov 26:1–12, the solid block of hyperbolic rhetoric devoted to a single character, indicates the creation of a schematic persona in that passage. Though the similar passage in Sirach is not extant in Hebrew, this passage in Proverbs demonstrates a precedent for such a diatribe and the hyperbolic tone of the Greek of Sirach 22 (chart 2-4) is comparable with this passage in Proverbs.

The labels for the schematic female figures in the Book of Ben Sira (אשה טובה, "good wife," and אשה רעה, "bad wife") never occur in Proverbs.[51]

---

51   I translate אשת רע in Prov 6:24 as "wife of a neighbor" in parallel with אשת רעהו, "wife of
     his neighbor," in v. 29.

Thus, if similar figures appear in that text they have other labels. The positive (human) female in Proverbs is the "valorous wife," whose schematic passage is the acrostic encomium in Prov 31:10–31. She is present in BBS 26:2 as the prototype for the Right Wife,[52] thus identifying a clear inheritance from Proverbs to the Book of Ben Sira. However, Proverbs has no passage about a negative human female that matches the schematic intensity of the poem about the "valorous wife." The only candidate in Proverbs is the figure labeled the "contentious wife" (אשת מדינים).[53] Though she is mentioned only five times, in isolated passages, the content of the verses is similar to several about the Wrong Wife.

Chart 3-8: Wrong Wife in BBS/Sirach and Contentious Wife in Proverbs

WRONG WIFE IN BBS	CONTENTIOUS WIFE IN PROVERBS	
25:20 Like a hard ascent for an old man—a talkative wife for a diminished man.	19:13	Ruin for a father, the son is a fool—and constant dripping [of water], the contentions of a wife.
	27:15	Constant dripping on a day of rain—and a contentious wife is equivalent.
25:16 (Sir.) I'd prefer to dwell with a lion and a dragon—than dwell with an evil wife.	21:9, 25:24	Better to dwell upon a corner of the roof —than a contentious wife and a shared house.
	21:19	Better to dwell in a wilderness—than with a contentious and provoking wife.

The examples from BBS/Sirach parallel those from Proverbs in two topics: the wife's verbal behavior that debilitates her husband and the husband's wish not to dwell with her. Similarities of topic and of the repeated use of a particular label for the wife—רע and πονηρία in BBS/Sirach and מִדְיָן in Proverbs—justify including the "contentious wife" in a schematic taxonomy for Proverbs, in the role occupied by the Wrong Wife in the schema of the Book of Ben Sira. Thus, a schema of human figures in Proverbs could consist of the Sage, the Valorous Wife, the Fool, and the Contentious Wife.

Though Proverbs can be parsed in terms of the schematic taxonomy of the Book of Ben Sira, the system in Proverbs is less evenly developed and thus is

---

52   See the analysis of BBS 25:13–26:3 in chapter 2, and BBS 26:1–3 in chapter 5.

53   The word "contentious" (מדין or מדון) is used for a woman five times, of which two are repetitions (Prov 19:13/27:15; Prov 21:9/25:24; Prov 21:19); for a man seven times, with reference to men who are duplicitous (Prov 6:14, 16:28), wrathful (Prov 15:18), a scorner (Prov 22:10), contentious (Prov 26:21), greedy (Prov 28:25), and angry (Prov 29:22).

more of an outline, or proto-schema. All schematic figures are, by definition, monotonic—gaining attention by the strident repetition of their one note—but the Contentious Wife, in particular, is given little space in relation to the Fool and the Valorous Wife. The schema of affinities in the Book of Ben Sira is more developed than the proto-schema in Proverbs: the greater symmetry of the Sage's relations with the other figures clarifies the taxonomy's identity as a schema of partnerships that are appropriate for the Sage, in marriage and in friendship. The set of figures in Proverbs could be an outline available for amplification and reworking by the author of the Book of Ben Sira, but are not a direct import. Another human-female character in Proverbs is of interest for the study of *gender* in the Book of Ben Sira—she is the "wife of your youth" in Prov 5:15–23, whose poem has elements in common with those of Ben Sira's "intelligent wife."[54]

3.2.2 Non-Human Figures in Proverbs

In addition to the schematic taxonomy of four human figures, the book of Proverbs uses two female non-human personifications: Wisdom and Strange Woman. These figures dominate the first nine chapters of Proverbs, and the schematic human characters are found later: the Fool in chapters 17 and 26, the Contentious Wife (sparsely, with repetitions) in chapters 19 to 27, and the Valorous Wife closing the book with a passage the equal of those for Wisdom. The Sage figure appears throughout the text of Proverbs.

One explanation for the absence of a figure like Strange Woman in the Book of Ben Sira is that her role is subsumed in that of the Wrong Wife, thus accounting for the expanded role of that negative human figure in the Book of Ben Sira. However, the semantic range for Strange Woman centers on sexual transgressions such as adultery—a type of charge not leveled at the Wrong Wife.[55] Another explanation focuses on Strange Woman's discursive link with death and with Sheol, the habitat of the dead (Prov 5:5; 7:26–27). The motif of *Sheol* begins in Proverbs 1:10–12, where a father warns his son against blood-thirsty "sinners" (חַטָּאִים) who entice young men to join them, saying, "Come with us! Let us lie in ambush, for blood; let us lie in wait for

---

54   See chart 4-12b in chapter 4 for the poem from Proverbs, and a comparison with BBS.

55   None of the sexually-transgressive women in BBS, nor the adulteress in Sir 23:22–27, are instances of the Wrong Wife. The Wrong Wife—being a schematic figure—exists only when the Hebrew label (ה)רע (Greek: κακός or πονηρός) is applied to a wife/woman, which does not occur with the adulteress or the other characters.

the innocent, without cause. Let us swallow them up, alive, like Sheol."[56] The motif continues in chapters 5 and 7 with the passages about the Strange Woman: "her feet go down to death; her steps take hold of Sheol" (Prov 5:5) and "her house is the way to Sheol, going down to the chambers of death" (Prov 7:27). When Wisdom speaks of herself in chapter 8, the speech emphasizes her close relationship to YHWH, and in chapter 9 Wisdom has the last word in the interplay with the Strange Woman (Prov 9:10–11, 13–18):

Chart 3-9: The Foolish Woman in Proverbs 9:10–18

9:10 [Wisdom speaks:] "The beginning of wisdom is fear of the Lord
—and knowledge of holy-things, insight.

9:11 For by me your days shall be multiplied
—and the years of your life shall be increased.

9:13 A foolish woman/wife is noisy
—she is naïve, and knows nothing.

9:14 And she sits at the door of her house
—on a seat in the high places of the city,

9:15 To call to those who pass by on the road
—those going straightforward on their ways:

9:16 'Whoever is naïve, let him turn aside here
—and he who lacks heart.' And she says to him,

9:17 'Stolen waters are sweet
—and bread in secret is pleasant.'

9:18 And he does not know that the dead are there
—her guests are in the depths of Sheol."

In the discourse of Prov 9:10–18, Wisdom's speech demotes Strange Woman to human status by applying Strange Woman's motifs to the "foolish woman" (אֵשֶׁת כְּסִילוּת). Indeed, it is only by the label given in v. 13 that the reader knows that vv. 14 through 18 apply to the "foolish woman" and not Strange Woman. Camp points out the similarities between the three female figures: all three call out to men and "invite the listener to their respective houses (the Strange Woman or Folly's in 7.15-20 and 9.14-16; Wisdom's in 8.34 and 9.1-6)" and "both Wisdom and Folly offer bread ... at their banquets (9.5, 17)."[57] Prov 9:18 is, literally, the "last word" on the topic of Strange Woman and

---

56 Aletti ("Seduction et Parole," 129) notes that the female adulteress in Prov 7:18, like the male sinners, calls out to the hapless youth, "Come!".

57 Camp, *Wise, Strange and Holy*, 76.

Wisdom since it is the last verse of "the concluding poem of the introductory chapters."[58] The final phrase, "her guests are in the depths of Sheol," firmly anchors the discursive identification of the foolish-woman with Strange Woman. However, Strange Woman cannot remain in the signifying system of Proverbs. If female-gendered Wisdom is, to some degree, co-extensive with a (presumably) male-gendered God, then, to preserve taxonomic parallelism, there cannot be a semi-divine, negative female figure because that figure would have to correspond to some divine, negative male figure. Therefore, Strange Woman must cease to be more than human.

With regard to any transference of a negative female figure's role in Proverbs to the Wrong Wife in the Book of Ben Sira, there could be a development from the Contentious Wife because both figures share expertise in debilitating their husbands and neither figure is accused of sexual misconduct.[59] It is evident from the chart of the Contentious Wife's few verses (chart 3-8) that she does not share the adulterous tendencies of Strange Woman and the foolish-woman. Therefore, it is the Contentious Wife, rather than the foolish-woman and/or Strange Woman, whose persona could contribute to the formation of the Wrong Wife in the Book of Ben Sira. And, more significantly, if the figure of Strange Woman transforms into the foolish-woman and disappears at the end of Proverbs 9, then there is no need to explain why Strange Woman is not part of the Book of Ben Sira; she did not disappear between Proverbs and the Book of Ben Sira, but between chapters 9 and 10 of Proverbs.

All of the above speculations on the book of Proverbs are considered conjectural, on the scale that evaluates results as *probable* (very likely), *possible* (less likely), or *conjectural* (suspended judgment, could be either likely or unlikely). Like the later speculations about the identity of the "woman/wife" who brings sin and death (BBS/Sir 25:24), those about Proverbs are included only because their contexts demand an answer.

---

58 Camp, *Wise, Strange and Holy*, 16.

59 One "wicked wife" passage in Sirach mentions πορνεία γυναικὸς, "whoredom of a wife" (Sir 26:5–9, v. 9), but there are pervasive uncertainties about the total number of negative verses about women in chapter 26 of Sirach. Of the two Greek passages, Sir 26:6–12 and 19–27, the latter is present only in the Greek II MSS and the Syriac version. Though Skehan and Di Lella (*Wisdom*, 346) say that "the presumption [for vv. 19–27] is that the verses were composed in Hebrew," I disagree and conclude, from the extent of the problems, that a substantial number of these non-Hebrew negative-female verses are probably accretions. These verses remain—for my methodologies—open questions.

Chapter 4
Human Females

Only a partial world is visible to the reader of the Book of Ben Sira because there are no interactions among females, neither between Wisdom and human females, nor among the female humans—the mothers, daughters, sisters, and others.[1] In a homosocial society such as that of Ben Sira,[2] where most women would interact with other women on a daily basis, we can see what is, literally, only half of this divided society because the author is excluded from many of the social interactions of his female relatives and their friends and neighbors. Another aspect of this homosocial framework is the limit on available categories for interaction between women and men. Specifically, there are no categories for a female friend of a man, married or unmarried, or for a male friend of a woman. This taxonomic sparseness combines with the male-oriented perspective of the model to produce extreme differentiation between categories of women: the small, socially-available group consisting of a man's wife (probably one) and his close female relatives contrasts with the large, unavailable group that includes all the rest of adult female humanity. There is also a category of females who are sexually available to a man but not socially-available, consisting of prostitutes and, in some cases, female slaves.

The narrowness of the range of contacts between women and men in an extremely homosocial society does not necessarily entail a correspondingly narrow range in the quality of those contacts. Attitudes toward the 'opposite' group would include ranges of antipathy, indifference, and approval similar to those in other social arrangements. A more salient predictor of attitudes—at least, of those attitudes expressed publically—would be the explicitness of the discourse that authorizes the homosocial behaviors. A fully-naturalized discourse allows greater latitude for interpretation than a discourse that explains its premises. Thus, if separate social interactions for women and men are a universal and unspoken part of the social order, then, for those relationships that are permitted, a man or woman could express either positive or negative feelings toward the other group and could choose the companionship of either

---

1   The only hint is the incidental mention of jealousy in 9:1-9 and 37:11.

2   "Homosocial" is used for a spectrum of social arrangements, not a "yes-or-no" proposition.

group. In contrast, if the separation is said to be necessitated by women's inferiority, then a man would be socially constrained to not express a preference for his wife's companionship. Classical Greece and Second Temple Judaism operate with different taxonomies of *gender*, but both qualify as homosocial societies. The upcoming analyses of passages from the Book of Ben Sira demonstrate that the author's view of relations between spouses fits a social model that permits a man's public expression (in an indirect manner) of his passionate regard for his wife and his valuation of her companionship as equal to, or better than, that of his closest male associates. For classical Greek literature, such concepts would be unthinkable.

4.1 Male/Female Pairs

Five female figures that have been identified as the range of female experience in the Book of Ben Sira are "the good wife; the mother or widow; the bad wife; the adulteress or prostitute; and the daughter."[3] For a number of reasons, this set of categories and mine are incommensurate. The fundamental difference is that I use male/female pairs rather than exclusively female figures. Several paired—or, at least, comparable—categories in the Book of Ben Sira that cross the gender gap are father/mother, son/daughter, and male-friend/wife. The functioning of these pairs provides a basis for discussions of the husband/ wife pair that is the focus of my study. Relationships within the family are the primary inter-gender links in a homosocial paradigm. Spouses are included as family to the extent that a woman would move into the husband's living arrangements. The male-friend/wife pairing is the exception to the "family" rule, and it is not a pairing of those who interact but a virtual pairing of the functions of the two roles. And, as always, the categories are all constructed from the viewpoint of the male and, particularly, of the "wise" male.

4.1.1 "Father" and "Mother"; "Son" and "Daughter"; "Brother" (and Sister)

The Book of Ben Sira contains frequent admonitions to "my son," thereby creating a fictional fatherhood for the author,[4] and Wisdom "has taught her sons" (BBS 4:11), creating a fictional motherhood for that figure. However,

---

3   Corley, "Intertextual Study of Proverbs and Ben Sira," 169–170; citing Trenchard (*Ben Sira's View of Women*, 5).

4   See Wright, "From Generation to Generation" and "Ben Sira on the Sage as Exemplar." See also Newsom, "Wisdom and the Discourse of Patriarchal Wisdom."

the fictive sons are instructed in how to treat their actual parents and how to raise their own children—a training that is part of the "instruction/discipline" to be "accepted" in youth so that their lives in old-age will be satisfying and praiseworthy.

Chart 4-1, below, shows the only sustained treatment of parents in the Book of Ben Sira. The first five bicola, not extant in Hebrew, are translated from Sirach.

Chart 4-1: "... honors his mother" Sir 3:1–6 (NETS), BBS 3:6b–16 (MSS A, C)

Sir 3:1	Listen to a father's reproof, children and act accordingly so that you may be safe.
Sir 3:2	For the Lord has glorified father over children, and [H]e has confirmed a mother's judgment over sons.
Sir 3:3/4	He who honors father will atone for sins, and like one who lays up treasure is he who glorifies his mother.
Sir 3:5	He who honors father will be gladdened by children, and in the day of his prayer, he will be heard.
Sir 3:6	He who glorifies father will prolong his days, and he who listens to the Lord will give rest to his mother.
BBS 3:6b	...honors his mother.
BBS 3:8	My son, honor your father in speech and in deeds —in order that he will bring you near all blessings.
BBS 3:9	A father's blessing will found a root —but a mother's curse will uproot a plant.
BBS 3:10	Do not honor yourself with the dishonor of your father —for it is not an honor to you.
BBS 3:11	His father's honor is a man's honor —and he who curses his mother multiplies sin.
BBS 3:12	My son, strengthen yourself with your father's honor —and do not forsake him all the days of your life.
BBS 3:13	Even if his intellect should fail, forsaking him —yet do not humiliate him all the days of his life.
BBS 3:14	The righteousness of a father will not be blotted out —and it will change sin *[MS A marg. = "it will be planted"]*.
BBS 3:15	In the day of anguish it will be remembered for you —like heat upon frost, to abolish your guilts.
BBS 3:16	For one who acts proudly despises his father —and provokes his Creator, who curses his mother.

Though the son in BBS/Sir 3:1–16 replicates the father in a way that is not true for his relation to the mother, the Hebrew text clearly indicates that equal honor is due to fathers and to mothers.[5] Moreover, the Greek text in v. 2 declares that God ordains that sons are subject to a mother's discipline, in parallel with God's ranking the father above his children. Again, I stress that interactions between females are invisible; in this case, they are not visible because the discourse answers questions about how a son relates to his parents, but not about the functions of mothers. Relations between females are not nonexistent—such relations are just invisible because, even though there are categories for female roles, a thoroughly male-oriented taxonomy has no links between those categories.

A female category that does not exist in the Book of Ben Sira is that of the sister.[6] Ben-Hayyim lists nine entries for אח ("brother"), but none for אחות ("sister"). The first "brother" verse is BBS 7:12, "Do not devise violence against a brother, and thus upon a companion and associate, at the same time." Equating the familial role of brother [7] with the chosen-associate roles implies that the close relationship may continue throughout life. In later verses, "brother" is juxtaposed (colon-a/colon-b) with "friend" (BBS 7:18) and with "companion" (BBS 14:14). "Brother" appears in verses adjacent to those that feature the "intelligent wife" (BBS 7:18, 19; BBS/Sir 40:23, 24) and thus is one of the sage's male-companions viewed in context with the sage's (appropriate) wife.

The lack of any "sister" in the Book of Ben Sira means that the categories of son and daughter are not in relation to each other, but only to father (and to mother, in the case of the son). The Greek text of Ben Sira mentions daughters in five passages: Sir 7:24–25; 22:3–5; 26:10–12; 36:21; and 42:9–14. Of these, the verses in chapters 22 and 26 are not extant in Hebrew, BBS 42:9–14 is the subject of a later section of this chapter, and BBS 7:23–25 and 36:21 appear below and also in discussions of the full poetic units.[8]

The three bicola-units of BBS 7:23–25, below in chart 4-2, mention both sons and daughters:

---

5   Collins, "Marriage, Divorce, and Family," 141. Collins states that the parallel between a
     father's blessing and a mother's curse (Sir 3:9) suggests that "both blessing and curse are
     effective on the part of both parents" (ibid.).

6   Reiterer ("Review of Recent Research," 71) notes, without further comment, that "there are
     no rules about relations between brothers and sisters" in BBS/Sirach.

7   The term "brother" can include kinsmen such as cousins, or be applied to colleagues.

8   See chart 4-8 for BBS 7:18–26, charts 5-6 and 5-8 for BBS 36:18–26, and chart 4-16 for
     BBS 42:9–14.

Chart 4-2: Sons and daughters in BBS/Sir 7:23–25

BBS 7:23–25 (MSS A, MS C)	#	SIR 7:23–25 (NETS)
Your sons, discipline/instruct them—and accept wives for them, in their youth.	**7:23**	Do you have children? Educate them, and bend their neck from youth.
Your sons, protect their body Your daughters, protect their body—and do not shine your face upon them.	**7:24**	Do you have daughters? give heed to their body, and do not brighten your face towards them. *[i.e., "do not be indulgent to them"]*
Marry a daughter and a duty fulfills—and unite her to a discerning fellow.	**7:25**	Give a daughter in marriage, and you will have completed a great task, and present her to an understanding man.

The father has a duty to arrange marriages for sons (v. 23) and for daughters (vv. 24, 25). In the case of the daughter, the bridegroom is to be chosen for his discernment, or intelligence, presumably so he will be "well-yoked" with her as an appropriate match.[9] Verse 24 is structurally parallel to v. 23, with "discipline/instruction" for sons matched by "protect their body" for daughters, both items being forms of parental control. Fathers are not to be indulgent to daughters (v. 24) or to sons (v. 24, MS C; BBS 30:11, chart 4-3).

The Hebrew of BBS 7:25a sounds like a proverbial statement— הוצא בת עסק ויצא—a translation like "Daughter's wed, duty's fled" is possible. Though the Greek translation lacks proverbial crispness, it follows the meaning of the Hebrew verse, unlike Sir 36:21, below, which follows the pattern of the Hebrew but uses entirely different terms. The pattern for both the Hebrew and the Greek of 36:21 is "Any W, an X will Y—but there is a Z that is better than another Z." The unexpected words "wild-beast" and "blow" are semantically appropriate in the coherent poetic unit (BBS 36:18–26), and "daughter" is not mentioned.

BBS 36:21 (MS B)	#	SIR 36:21 (V. 26 IN NETS)
Any wind-fall, a wild beast will eat—but there is a "blow" that will be more pleasant than a blow.	**36:21**	A woman will accept any male, but there exists a daughter better than a daughter.

The verse BBS/Sir 36:21 is an extreme instance of a divergent Greek text. The situation for BBS/Sir 7:23 is similar but with a less dramatic difference—the

---

9   Though "daughters" in MS A v. 24 is a structural parallel that is attested in Greek, the
     presence of "sons" in MS C v. 24 matches the m. pl. possessive pronouns, "their/them."

Greek lacks mention of finding wives for the sons, thus unbalancing the gendered content (unless "bend their neck" in Sir 7:23b matches "accept wives for them" in BBS by alluding to a marriage yoke motif).

All the remaining extant passages concerning children are about sons, but the poetic unit dedicated to the subject of sons, BBS/Sir 30:1–13, is only partially extant in Hebrew.[10] Chart 4-3, below, shows the Hebrew verses.

Chart 4-3: "Do not give him rulership in his youth" BBS 30:11–13 (MS B)

30:11   Do not give him rulership in his youth
         —and do not show favor, ruining him.
30:12   You will meet with hostility like a viper against a living thing.
         —crush his strength while he is still a youth.
         Bend down his head in his youth
         —and tear apart his strength/loins like he was a little-one.
         Why will he show stubbornness and rebel against you?
         —and disappointment is born to you.
30:13   Discipline your son and make his yoke heavy
         —lest, in his folly, he will exalt himself.

This thematically-problematic passage is also difficult to translate. For instance, literal usage for the verb בקע ("tear apart") in colon 12b includes fatal dismemberment by wild beasts, a range of meaning that is unexpected if the intended meaning is to "'strike' loins, i.e., beat child" (*DCH* 2:249a), since other verbs such as נכה have a narrower range of meaning.[11]

The Book of Ben Sira is written at a time between the famous message in Genesis, "Be fruitful and multiply," and the later rabbinic interpretation that a male Jew must have children—yet, the Book of Ben Sira does not encourage procreation.[12] The passage BBS 16:1–4, translated below in chart 4-4, definitely favors quality in offspring rather than quantity.

---

10 Sir 30:1 opens with Ὁ ἀγαπῶν τὸν υἱὸν αὐτοῦ ἐνδελεχίσει μάστιγας αὐτῷ, "He who loves his son will persist in whipping him" (NETS), but no Hebrew is extant for 30:1.

    For a discussion of this passage in a "Mediterranean" context, see Pilch ("'Beat His Ribs'"). Pilch speaks of "'traditional Mediterranean culture'" and relies on the Greek text, Sirach, thus combining a theoretical framework and a text that are not my current choices for interpreting Ben Sira.

11 See the annotated version of the passage in the Appendix, chart A4-3, for detailed information on this verse and others.

12 Collins ("Marriage, Divorce, and Family," 127) notes that "Ben Sira does not mention procreation as the purpose for marriage."

Chart 4-4: "Do not yearn for… worthless youths" BBS 16:1–4 (MSS A, B)

16:1 Do not yearn for the appearance of worthless youths
      —and do not rejoice in unjust sons.
16:2 Moreover, if they multiply, do not seek for them
      —if they have not the fear-of-YYY.
16:3 Do not have confidence in their living—and do not trust in their deceits,
      For there will not be a good end for them.
      For better is one who does the divine-will, than a thousand
      —and to die childless, than someone with many unjust sons,
      and posterity that is insolent.
16:4 From one childless-person who fears-YYY, a city will be established
      —and from a clan of traitors, it will be devastated.

Several points in the preceding charts are useful for comparing recommended treatment of females and with that for males:

- *honor* is due from a son to both parents (BBS 3:6–16);
- the father arranges marriages for sons and daughters, and the sons' marrying "in their youth" implies sexual restraint for males (BBS 7:23), just as "protect their bodies" explicitly expects such restraint from females (BBS 7:25);
- for both sons and daughters, the father is advised not to "show favor" to them—an indication that fathers *were* inclined, in both cases, to "show favor" (for sons see BBS 30:11b, and for daughters, BBS 7:24a); and
- having children is not portrayed as a primary value for women or for men since having no progeny is better than having impious ones.

However, an unmentioned item is also intriguing: although the text recommends beating sons to make them obedient, no female is mentioned as an appropriate target of physical violence. Even if the society expects children and wives to be so submissive that a word is enough to compel obedience—and, thus, that a man who beat his child or his wife in public would lose face—in a book of advice on properly-gendered behavior, if it is appropriate to advise beating a son to ensure obedience, then it is appropriate to advise beating a wife or daughter *if* that is socially acceptable. Yet, though beating a son is mentioned as a commonplace, nowhere in the Book of Ben Sira is physical violence against females mentioned or implied.

4.1.2 "Friend (Male)" and "Wife"

In the passage BBS 33:20–30, shown below in chart 4-5, solid lines between bicola on the chart mark semantic divisions in the poetic unit. The first two sections cover categories of people who might "rule over" the life of the sage:

son, wife, friend, and companion; the last two sections are those over whose lives the sage rules: animal and slave. For both situations, the author advises moderation (v. 30).

Chart 4-5: "Son and wife, friend and companion" BBS 33:20–30 (MS E)

33:20	Son and wife, friend and companion —do not cause to rule over your life.
33:21	While you are still alive and breath is in you —do not allow any [?] to have power over you.
	Do not give that which belongs to you to another —to return to entreat [?].
33:22	For it is better that your sons entreat your favor/face —than that you accept, at the power/hand of your sons.
33:23	In all your deeds, be excellent —and do not put a stain on your honor.
33:24	At the time your days are a small number —at the day of death, cause to inherit [?].
33:25	Fodder and whip and burden for an ass —and chastisement in labor for a servant/slave.
33:26	Cause your servant/slave to work, so he does not seek repose —and if his head is lifted, he will betray.
33:27	Cause your servant/slave to work, so he does not rebel —for badness/evil increases [?].
33:28	[?] a rod holding him —concerning a bad servant/slave, [?]. *[no space on MS for v. 29]*
33:30	Do not act-excessively against any human —and without judgment, [?].

The division in BBS 33:20a between "son and wife" and "friend and companion" separates family (financially dependent on the sage) from well-known outsiders (independent). Yet, of the four categories, the son is the only one mentioned in the following section, vv. 21–24. Are all four categories equally excluded from "ruling over" the adult male—in the sense that his parents and God are the only ones so entitled—or do the son and wife constitute a group disqualified by 'natural,' taxonomic inferiority? The matched exclusions of "son and wife" and "friend and companion" limit the degree to which the exclusion of the wife can be due to a perceived gender-based inferiority. In this case, the four categories are present because they represent the people to whom a man might willingly give "rulership" over himself.

Chart 4-6, below, is a collection of verses that show equivalent statements about females and males.[13] Statements that use semantically-equal commentary to relate the actions or status of a female to those of a male, or that use the same vocabulary for both groups, are significant parallels because the presumed default is that there would be little equivalence.[14] Such parallels are evidence for my category of "relational-gender"—that is, for how the author of the Book of Ben Sira constructs *femininity* in relation to *masculinity*.

Chart 4-6: Some equivalent comments for females and males in BBS

FEMALES	MALES
26:15 (C) חן ע[3] אשה ביישת {[2] [ל]ע}	42:1cd (M) [4]תֹ ביישׁ באמת ומצא חן בעיני כל חי
Grace upon [grace], a *modest* wife—	And you will become truly *modest* —and find *grace* in the eyes of all the living.
ואין משקל לצרורת פה :	לאוהב אמונה אין מחיר ואין משקל לטובתו : (A) 6:14
and there is *no weighing* for one who is 'close-mouthed.'	For a faithful friend there is no price —and there is *no weighing* for his goodness.
26:3 (C) {אשה [1]וטֹבה מנה [3]]ת[ה[ובֹ} {ובחלק ירא ייי תנת[1]]תנתֹן{	6:15 (A) צרור חיים אוהב אמונה ירא אל ישיגם
A good wife is a good gift—and as portion of *one-fearing-YYY*, may she be given.	A faithful friend binds up life— *one-fearing-God* will reach them.
36:24 (B) קנה אשה ראשית קנין עזר ומבצר ועמוד משען :	6:6 (A) קנית אוהב בנסין קנהו ואל תמהר לבטח עליו :
Gaining a wife is the beginning of *gain* —help, and citadel, and pillar of support.	*To gain* a friend—by means of a trial, *gain* him—and do not rush to place trust upon him.
7:19 (A) אל תמאס אשה משכלת וטובת חן מפנינים :	7:18 (A) אל תמיר אוהב במחיר ואח תלוי בזהב אופיר :
Do not *reject* an intelligent wife—and a good-one, grace more than *pearls*.	Do not *exchange* a friend for a price— or lend a brother for the *gold* of Ophir.

---

13 See charts 2-6, 2-7; 2-8; 2-11; 4-8; 4-16; 5-6; and 5-11 for the verses in context.

14 Camp ("Female Sage," 194–95) notes four specific points on which she disagrees with Trenchard's assessments (*Ben Sira's View of Women*, 26–27, 38, 205 n. 187), among which she points out the significance of the phrase אשה משכלת whose "contexts suggest … her ability to provide well for her husband and household" and the fact that "as far as the wife's silence is concerned, verbal control, humility, and restraint are virtues of the wise *man* as well (Sir 1:21, 22; 3:17–19; 18:18–20), so this only says that the sage holds women to similar standards."

25:20 (C)　　　כמעלה חזק לאיש ישיש אשת לשון לאיש מך Like a hard ascent for an old man—*a woman of unbridled-tongue* for a diminished man!	8:3a (A)　　　　אל תינץ עם איש לשון Do not argue with *a man of unbridled-tongue*
	9:18a (A)　　　ביטה נורא בעד איש לשון An impetuous speaker is dreaded, in the testimony of *a man of unbridled-tongue*.
42:14 (M)　　　　טוב רע איש מטיב אשה ובת מפחדת מכול חרפה "Better the evil of a man than the goodness of a woman"—but a daughter who is *afraid-before-God* is better than any taunt.	4:20 (A)　　בני עת המון שמר ופחד מרע ואל נפשך אל תבוש : My son, in a time of tumult: watch and be *afraid-before-God*, (to avoid) evil—and do not be ashamed for your soul/self.
	37:12 (B,D)　　אך אם איש מפחד תמיד אשר תדע שומר מצוה Be always with a man who's *afraid-before-God* —so you'll understand keeping a commandment.

In the chart, each of the ten italicized references to a female is matched by at least one reference to a male: positive instances match the sage (BBS 42:1), the sage's friend (BBS 6:6,14,15; 7:18; 37:12), or the sage's "son" (4:20), and the negative instance matches men who are not friends of the sage (BBS 8:3; 9:18). In the second row, the "faithful friend" and the "good wife" (Right Wife) are both appropriate associates for a man who "fears-God." The third row has the verb-root קנה ("to gain, acquire"). The fourth row shows the verse-sequence BBS 7:18 and 7:19, both of which caution against abandoning a close associate and compare the associate's worth to that of gold and gems, v. 18 speaking about the sage's friend/brother and v. 19 about the sage's wife.[15] The second, third, and fourth rows all apply words associated with commerce to male figures and, because a parallel system of "financial imagery" is used for females, parallel conclusions are appropriate: for instance, a man's wife cannot be his *possession* unless his male-friends are also his *possessions*. The verses in the fifth row show the use of the phrase "a ___ of (unbridled) tongue," once for a woman and twice for men. In the last row, the root פחד is used for a daughter and for a son or friend of the sage.

There are multiple sources of distinction for BBS 26:15, the first verse in the Females section of chart 4-6. The word ביישת in colon 15a, translated as "modest," is the counterpart of a word for male modesty; it is listed in *DCH*

15　Corley ("Friendship," 68) comments on the verses about the male friend, to stress that "Ben Sira uses financial imagery to express the value of a faithful friend" because "friends are more valuable than wealth," mentioning BBS 6:14–17 and 7:18.

2:15Ia as "בַּיִשׁ 'decorous,'" used here in BBS 26:15 and BBS 42:1c. "Modest/decorous" behavior is linked with "grace" (חן) in both 26:15 and 42:1cd, and another verse also links "grace" with a positive form of "shame": "before hail, lightning will flash—and before shame, grace" (BBS 32:10). The quintessential declaration for positive-shame again links "shame" with "grace," in BBS 4:21: "For there is shame that is the burden of guilt, and there is shame that is honor and grace."

Ben Sira's situation as a colonial subject affects his statements about *shame*, but the vocabulary in chart 4-6 opens another aspect of the topic: in the Book of Ben Sira, is *shame* figured as a positive or a negative value for males? The Mediterranean honor/shame theory predicts positive values of *shame* for females and negative values for males.[16] However, the motif of בייש in the Book of Ben Sira—being modest or decorous—constitutes *shame* as a positive value for both women and men. Chart 4-6 shows specific instances of *shame* with positive connotations for a male and for a female, including the explicit mention of בייש andביישת (BBS 26:15 and 42:1cd) and the parallel condemnations of indecorous behavior such as that of the woman or man "of unbridled tongue" (BBS 25:20, 8:3, and 9:18).

"Before Ben Sira's time," as Kister observes, there had developed "a convention of wisdom literature according to which 'shame' and 'being shamefaced, bashful' are right and recommendable."[17] A shared ethos of modest male behavior links the Book of Ben Sira with rabbinic texts. The Babylonian Talmud uses the masculine form ביישן in the discussion of appropriate rabbinic male behavior (*b. Nedarim* 20a): מיכן אמרו: סימן יפה באדם שהוא ביישן "hence they said: it is a goodly sign in a person that he is shamefaced."[18] The opposite of "shamefacedness" is "insolence," a trait I associate with agonistic interactions between males (such as the "men of unbridled-tongue"). The verse BBS 10:6 (MS A) typifies the preference in the Book of Ben Sira for non-agonistic male behavior: כל פשע אל תשלֵם רע לריע ואל תהלך בדרך גאוה [1] :, "For any transgression do not repay badness/evil to a companion—and do not walk on a path of insolence." *Shame* is thus a positive value for males and for females.

Parallels in the descriptions of the "wife" and the "friend" are strong evidence for the discursive construction of the two categories as functionally parallel. The parallels I present are more than incidental similarities; the concurrent references (BBS 6:14–15; 7:18–19) and multiple links from a single verse (esp. BBS 26:15) form a network of semantic equivalences—or at

---

16 See section 2.3.1 of chapter 2.

17 Kister, "Some Notes," 168. Jastrow (*Dictionary*, 161) gives "bashful, chaste, bashful man" for בייש, and ביישת is the feminine form.

18 *Judaic Classics Library*, Version 2.2, with my translation.

least, comparabilities—for the behavior and status of females and that of males. The examples in chart 4-6 are part of the counterweight against which the few discordant verses are to be evaluated.

4.2 Passages concerning the "Intelligent Wife"

Thus far, my only defined subcategory for the "woman/wife" (אשה) in the Book of Ben Sira is the *schematic* wife.[19] Since there are only two of these and they occupy a narrow expanse of text—the figures Right Wife and Wrong Wife in BBS 25:13–26:3 and BBS 42:1–8—it is time to consider the human adult-females mentioned in the rest of the Book of Ben Sira and identify *non-schematic* women/wives. The schematic female figures were identified by the repeated use of the words "bad" and "good" that modify "wife/woman" and were labeled accordingly. Now, following the same strategy, I identify the modifier "intelligent" that is used consistently with "wife/woman" in a range of gender-focal contexts and use this word as a label for a category of human females: the "intelligent wife/woman."[20] Book of Ben Sira 7:19 (see charts 4-7 and 4-8) is the first of four verses that refer to an "intelligent wife/woman." Because there is no cluster of monovocal development, the "intelligent wife" cannot be a schematic figure.[21] The use of the label in a range of important gender-focal contexts indicates its status as a major category and its presence in three chapters indicates its sustained usefulness to the author.

Chart 4-7: The "intelligent wife"

7:19 (A)	אל תמאס אשה משכלת	Do not reject an intelligent wife
	וטובת חן מפנינים :	—and a good-one is grace more than pearls.
25:8 (C)	אשרי בעל אשה משכלת	Happy is the husband of an intelligent wife
	ולא חורש כשור עם חמור	—he is not "plowing like ox-with-ass."
26:13 (C, Ben-H.)	אשה[3] יב[2] (מטיב)	Grace of a wife 'pleases' her lord-husband
	בעלה [4] ידשן שכלה	—and her intelligence will fatten [?].
40:23 (B, Sir.)	ת[9] ינהגו	Friend and companion will lead your steps
	ומשניהם אשה משכלת:	—more than both, an intelligent wife.

---

19   See section 2.2.2 of chapter 2.

20   See the chart AppLex-14, in the Appendix, for a complete list of modifiers for אשה. Of thirteen relevant modifiers, eleven occur once and only משכלת more than twice.

21   The major schematic-female passage, BBS 25:13–26:3, occurs between two verses on the "intelligent wife" (vv. 25:8 and 26:13), separated by many verses not extant in Hebrew.

Not only do all the verses emphasize the desirability of an intelligent wife, but BBS 25:8 is the verse that constitutes the thematic metaphor of *appropriate marriage* and BBS 40:23 values the intelligent wife more than a man's male associates.[22] These verses direct my choice of "intelligent wife" as a label for the non-schematic female figure in the Book of Ben Sira who is as close to a 'real' woman as the sage figure is to a 'real' man.

What is the semantic range for "intelligence" in the Book of Ben Sira?[23] From the references to "accepting/taking intelligence,"[24] "intelligence" is not only *inherent intellectual capacity* but also forms of behavior and/or practice that set "intelligence" together with "wisdom" and "understanding of a thing/word" as the members of a category.[25] "Intelligence" is associated with speech (BBS 13:22; 16:24) and forms part of Ben Sira's self-portrait of his activities as a sage: מוסר שכל ומושל אופנים "Intelligent instruction and the timely telling-of-proverbs" (BBS 50:27).

Book of Ben Sira 7:18–26 introduces the "intelligent wife" in parallel with the "friend."[26] The full poetic unit is shown in chart 4-8, below. Subjects of the unit shift from the sage's friend or brother and his wife, in the introduction, to his slave and animal in the first middle-section and his son and daughter in the second middle-section, closing with a return to the wife.

---

22 See Spatafora ("Intelligent or Sensible") for a discussion of Sir 25:8.

23 Forms of שכל occur as a label for a wife four times, for a slave twice (BBS 7:21; 10:25), and once for a poor man (דל, BBS 10:23). See BBS 13:22, where the poor-man's intelligent words are disregarded while the rich-man's ugly speech is made beautiful by his hangers-on. Solomon is mentioned as "intelligent" (47:12, as "a son," where the usage could be ironic). The general use of שכל is in admonitions to associate with men who are intelligent. Other instances are: chiefs (שרים, BBS 10:3), rich man (sarcastically in BBS 13:23); aged men (BBS 8:9); behavior at feasts (BBS 32:2–3); and the comment that intelligence is not missing from God's mouth (BBS 42:20).

24 Ben Sira exhorts his students to "hearken to me and accept/take my intelligence—and place my words upon the heart" (BBS 16:24); also, a violent man will not "accept/take intelligence" (BBS 32:18, B^m).

25 The group of these three items is "from YYY" (BBS 11:14), and Wisdom offers her followers "bread-of-intelligence and water-of-understanding" (BBS 15:3).

26 Verses 23 to 25 appeared previously in chart 4-2, and vv. 18 and 19 in chart 4-6.

Chart 4-8: "Do not exchange a friend for a price" BBS 7:18–26 (MSS A, C)

7:18	Do not exchange a friend for a price
	—and lend a brother for the gold of Ophir.
7:19	Do not reject an intelligent woman/wife
	—and a good-one is grace more than pearls.
7:20	Do not treat badly a slave serving honestly
	—and thus a hireling giving his self.
7:21	An intelligent slave—cherish like a self
	—do not withhold from him freedom.
7:22	Your animal—inspect with your eyes
	—and if it is faithful, maintain it.
7:23	Your sons—discipline/instruct them
	—and accept wives for them, in their youth.
7:24	Your daughters—protect their body
	—and do not show favor *["be overindulgent"]* to them.
7:25	Marry a daughter and a duty fulfills
	—but unite her to a discerning fellow.
7:26	Your wife—do not abhor her
	—or, hating her, do not trust her.

The father is expected to find spouses for both the son and the daughter, and colon 25b qualifies 25a by asserting that the husband should be a good match for a sage's daughter: the "discerning-man" is a type Ben Sira recommends as an appropriate friend for a sage (BBS 9:15). Thus, the desired outcome of the marriage includes the well-being of the daughter, as well as the production of another "sage's family."

The poetic unit's divisions orchestrate meaning at the structural level, and the inclusion of the male-friend and the brother in the group precludes an assumption that the entire group represents those whose lives are controlled by the male addressee. The sage's male friend and the sage's intelligent wife are paired as a semantic category because, in each case, the reader is admonished not to exchange/reject the person, who is more valuable than treasure. The semantic congruence of the two verses (BBS 7:18, 19) matches their physical juxtaposition. In the sets of paired units that follow, the first set (BBS 9:1–9 and 10–18) expands the motif of a man's exchanging his closest long-term companions—the "friend" and the "wife"—for new ones.

4.2.1 First Set of Paired Poetic Units

Adultery, in the Hebrew Bible, means that a married woman has sexual relations with any man other than her husband, or that a man has intercourse with the wife of another man. This definition leaves all sexual relations between a man and an unmarried woman outside the parameters for *adultery*. A married man could, therefore, have sexual relations with prostitutes and not be committing adultery. Such is the situation envisaged in the poetic unit BBS 9:1–9, and I suggest that the author disapproves of such liaisons for the effect they have on the man's relationship with his wife. If this is the author's viewpoint, it marks a distinct break with the tradition from the Hebrew Bible.[27]

Several charts, below, show BBS 9:1–16 divided into a pair of poetic units that, together, form a balanced composition on the virtue of a man's loyalty towards the closest non-kinship-based interactions of his life: his wife and his male friends. Botha and Corley note the similarities between the two passages.[28]

---

27 See chart 4-12a for a comparison of *adultery* in BBS 9:1–9 and in Prov 6:23–35.

28 Botha ("Through the Figure," 23) states that "[v]erses 1–16 can … be described as a poem on social interaction", with vv. 1–9 on men's interactions with women and vv. 10–16 on their interactions with other men, and that there are "similarities between these two sets of directives. Both sets dwell on relations which can be described as intimate (the wife; the close friend). … Both sets warn against people with questionable morality (prostitutes; evil and arrogant men)." He gives a chart of shared vocabulary in the two poetic units, including: 9:1a "Be not jealous" and 9:11a "Do not be envious"; 9:3a "Do not approach" and 9:13c "if you do approach" (added on my chart 4-11); 9:3b "into her snares" and 9:13f "over a net"; and 9:4a (3c) "Do not keep company" and 9:14b "consult … with the wise" (ibid., 30). Corley (*Ben Sira's Teaching*, 94) cites Botha's chart, but translates 9:3c "do not confide" and 9:14b "confide." Corley (ibid., 84) describes BBS 9:1–16 as "a pericope concerning two kinds of relationships: with women (vv. 1–9) and with male friends (vv. 10–16)" and notes that the "same sequence of women (9:1–9) followed by friends (9:10–16) also occurs in 36:26–37:6, where 36:26–31 discusses women and 37:1–6 deals with friends" (ibid.). I interpret these pairings (using BBS 37:16–26 rather than 37:1–6) as strong evidence that the female and male roles are functionally parallel, and view Sir 23:16–21 and 23:22–27 as another such pair of poetic units.

Chart 4-9: "Do not make jealous the wife of your bosom" BBS 9:1–9 (MS A)

9:1   Do not make jealous the wife of your bosom
       —lest she learn evil concerning you.

9:2   Do not allow yourself to acquire a woman
       —to 'attain to' her upon your 'high places.'

9:3   Do not approach a stranger-woman
       —lest you fall into her nets.
       With a prostitute do not 'take counsel'
       —lest you be captured in her traps.

9:4   With singers-of-satires do not sleep
       —lest they burn you with their 'mouths.'

9:5   Do not observe an unmarried girl,
       —lest you be ensnared by her fines.

9:6   Do not give yourself to a prostitute
       —lest you besiege your inheritance.

9:7   To befool your eyes with her appearance
       —and to 'play the fool' behind her house.

9:8   Avert your eyes from a graceful-woman
       —and do not regard beauty that is not yours.
       Through a woman/wife, many will be destroyed
       —and thus with fire she will set her lovers ablaze.

9:9   With a mistress-of-the-house do not 'taste'
       —and do not recline-at-table with her, intoxicated.
       Lest you turn aside to her your heart
       —and in blood turn aside to destruction.

The notoriously obscure bicola 9:1 and 9:2 that introduce the wife-unit are translated with reference to the first two bicola of the friend-unit, BBS 9:10ab and 10cd. Colon 10a is about rejecting a long-term associate, and the man in colon 10c is the intended replacement.

Chart 4-10: "Do not reject an old friend" BBS 9:10–16 (MS A)

9:10	Do not reject an old friend —for a new one will not be known to you. New wine, new friend —and you will drink it after it is grown old.
9:11	Do not be envious/jealous of a wicked man —for you do not know what is 'his day.'
9:12	Do not [??] with insolence leading to success —remember that at the time of death he will not be held guiltless.
9:13	Be far from a man who has the power to kill —and you will not fear the terrors of death. And if you have approached you must not trespass —lest he will take your breath! Know that among snares you will step —and you will walk about upon fowling-nets.
9:14	As is your strength, answer your companion —and take counsel with wise-men.
9:15	With a discerning-man be your conversation —and all your counsel, their insights.
9:16	Men of righteousness are your table-companions —and your glory is in the fear-of-God.

If the pattern of BBS 9:10 serves as a template for the translation of BBS 9:1 and 2, then colon 1a concerns rejecting a wife (long-term associate) and the woman in colon 2a is the intended replacement.[29] Colon 2a is difficult to translate because the verb תקנא—from the root קנה ("to acquire, gain")—is spelled as though it were from קנא ("be jealous"), the root in 9:1a.[30] Verse 2 has another tricky phrase, in colon b: להדריכה על במותיך, translated as "to attain to her upon your high places." Here, the verb "attain to" includes sexual connotations comparable to those elsewhere in the Book of Ben Sira.[31]

---

29 The choice to translate אשה in BBS 9:1a as "wife" and in BBS 9:2a as "woman" results from my interpretation that vv. 1 and 2 refer to different women.

30 For the Hebrew text of these poetic units, with fully annotated translations, see charts A4-9 and A4-10 in the Appendix.

31 See two poetic units about Wisdom: chart 3-4 (BBS 14:20–15:8), in which the verb דרך is used, and chart 3-5 (BBS 51:13–30), in which the "attaining to" is implied by sexualized images at the culmination of the author's "advance" (דרכה) toward Wisdom.

The vocabulary of the phrase about "high-places" echoes biblical usage rather than that of everyday life, but how does the biblical trope function here? Under biblical law, a married man could legitimately have had sexual relations with some of the women in the list of BBS 9:3–9, including prostitutes. Therefore, a man might have argued that he was permitted such liaisons, saying "I have a right to do this because it's not *adultery*," thus taking a 'high-hand' by declaring himself to be in accord with biblical law. "High places" might be chosen as the allusion because "high places" are acceptable in the early stories of the Tanakh but are denounced in later ones. This would enable Ben Sira to claim, as a parallel, that the Torah allows a married man to have liaisons with some unmarried women, but that such behavior no longer is acceptable.

In BBS 9:1–9, the sexual "acquiring" in colon 2a and "attaining to" in 2b will be the cause of the "jealousy" in colon 1a. The overall meaning is that marriage is the only appropriate venue for "acquiring a woman" and, therefore, the examples on the list that follows are instances of inappropriate "acquiring." The word for "mouth"(פה) in v. 4 can have a secondary meaning of "vagina," making a double meaning because the satirical words of the singer may "scorch" the man, but sexual contact could result in his "getting burned" by the dangerous situation.[32] Another example of the use of terms related to eating as metaphors for sexual activity occurs in colon 9a, with the verb טעם ("to taste"). A later passage in Sirach (not extant in Hebrew) makes an explicit metaphor, "To a sexually promiscuous person all bread is sweet" (Sir 23:17 NETS). The most important biblical precedent for "eating" as "sexual activity" and "mouth" as "vagina" is Prov 30:20, where the adulteress "ate and wiped her mouth, and said 'I have not committed iniquity'" (אָכְלָה וּמָחֲתָה פִיהָ וְאָמְרָה לֹא־פָעַלְתִּי אָוֶן :).[33]

The chart below shows both halves of BBS 9:1–16, arranged for comparison.

---

32 See the use in BBS 26:15 (chart 5-11), which is an acknowledged instance in which פה has the double meaning "mouth/vagina." See chart 4-12a for a parallel in Proverbs 6:27 for figuratively 'being burned' by a dangerous situation.

33 Rabbinic literature continues the trope. See, for example, Satlow, *Tasting the Dish.*

Chart 4-11: Comparison of BBS 9:1–9 and BBS 9:10–16

BBS 9:1–9	BBS 9:10–16
1 Do not *make jealous* the <u>wife of your bosom</u>—lest she learn evil concerning you.	**10** Do not reject an <u>old friend</u>—for a new one will not be known to you.
2 Do not allow yourself to acquire a <u>woman</u>—to 'attain to' her upon your 'high places.'	New wine, <u>new friend</u>—and you will drink it after it is grown old.
3 Do not **approach** a stranger-woman—lest you fall into her **nets**.	**11** Do not *be envious/jealous* of a wicked man—for you do not know what is 'his day.'
With a prostitute do not 'take **counsel**'—lest you be captured in her **traps**.	**12** Do not [?] with insolence leading to success—remember: at the time of death, he will not be held guiltless.
4 With singers-of-satires do not sleep—lest they burn you with their 'mouths.'	**13** Be far from a man who has power to kill—and do not fear the terrors of death.
5 Do not observe an unmarried girl,—lest you be **ensnared** by her fines.	And if you **have approached**, do not trespass—lest he will take your breath!
6 Do not give yourself to a prostitute—lest you besiege your inheritance.	Know that among **snares** you will step—and you will walk about on fowling-**nets**.
7 To befool your eyes with her appearance—and to 'play the fool' behind her house.	**14** As is your strength, answer your companion—and **take counsel** with wise-men.
8 Avert your eyes from a graceful woman—and do not regard beauty that is not yours.	**15** With a discerning-man be your conversation—and all your counsel, their insights.
Through a woman many will be destroyed—and thus with fire she will set her lovers ablaze.	**16** Men of righteousness are בעלי לחמך 'masters of your bread'—and your glory is in the fear-of-God.
9 With a בעלה **mistress**-of-house do not 'taste'—and do not recline with her, intoxicated.[34]	
Lest you turn aside to her your heart—and in blood turn aside to destruction.	

---

34   A reference to the husband occurs in BBS 9:9b if עמו is translated as written, "with *him*." The translation "with her" is based on the lack of a male referent for "him," which would leave "master-of-house" to be inferred from the given "mistress-of-house."

The poetic units in chart 4-11 share a set of vocabulary—"make/be jealous," "approach," "take counsel," "mistress/master"—and a series of words related to "being ensnared," such as "nets," "traps," "snares," and "fowling-nets." In the chart, the first verse of each unit names one of the sage's closest relationships: his wife or his long-time friend, who are both at risk of being replaced. The next verse names a potential replacement: the "(other) woman" or the "new friend." Thus, the second verse closes the introduction and also functions as a generic model for the series of bad choices that follows. The middle section lists dangerous figures who could be examples of the replacements mentioned in the second verse of the opening; in both cases, snares and nets await the unwary. The closing sections tell how to avoid the dangerous figures who provoke bloodshed: associate with people who share your values. Therefore, if a man has a congenial wife he should "regard beauty" that *is* appropriate to him (v. 8) and if he has a faithful friend he should "answer to" him (v. 14). Though the wife is not mentioned explicitly after 9:1, colon 9c evokes the image of the wife because the heart being "turned aside" *to* the adulteress would have been "turned aside" *from* the wife. And, the last colon of the final verse of the friend-unit could apply to both its own unit and that of the wife since a man who glories in "the fear-of-God" would act appropriately with spouse and with friends.

The legal codes of the Hebrew Bible identify *adultery* for a woman only if she is married and for a man only if his female-partner is married. There is no sense—in the legal codes—of marriage as a mutual agreement to restrict one's sexual boundaries within the contracting parties. The only pertinent agreement is a tacit one between husbands, who are obligated to respect each other's exclusive right of sexual access to his own wife (or wives). In chart 4-12a, below, BBS 9:1–9 is presented next to a passage from Proverbs that illustrates this biblical view of *adultery*.[35]

---

35   J. T. Sanders (*Ben Sira and Demotic Wisdom*, 36) notes the similar vocabulary of BBS 9:2–9 and Prov 6:20–7:5, especially Prov 6:25–26.

Chart 4-12a: Differences between adultery-passages in BBS and in Proverbs

BBS 9:1–9	PROV 6:23–34
1 Do not make **jealous** the wife of your bosom—lest she learn evil about you.	**23** For the commandment's a lamp...
...[verse less pertinent]...	**24** To keep you from woman-of-badness—from smoothness of tongue
3 Do not draw near a **stranger-woman**—lest you fall in her nets.	of an **alien-woman**.
With a prostitute do not 'take counsel' —lest **you be captured** in her traps.	**25** Do not desire her beauty in your heart—and do not let her **captivate you** with her eyelids.
4 With singers-of-satires do not sleep— lest **they burn you** with their 'mouths.'	**26** For a prostitute's price is a loaf of bread—but wife-of-man hunts a soul.
...[verses less pertinent]...	**27** Can a man carry fire in his bosom, and his clothes not **be burned**?
8c Through a woman many will be destroyed—and thus **with fire** she will set her lovers **ablaze**.	*...[verses less pertinent]...*
9 With a mistress-of-house do not 'taste'—and do not recline with her, intoxicated.	**33** Wound and dishonor he will find —and his reproach will not be wiped away.
Lest you turn aside to her your heart— and in blood turn aside to **destruction**.	**34** For **jealousy** is the wrath of a male—and he won't spare, on the **day of vengeance**.

Though the two passages share several phrases and concepts, there are significant differences. In Prov 6:26a, sexual relations with a harlot are accounted as 'small change,' in contrast to BBS 9:6, where the prostitute has the power to "besiege" the man's inheritance. Proverbs 6:26b shifts to the "wife of (another) man," who lures the speaker to break his (implicit) contract with her husband. The passage from the Book of Ben Sira has five female characters, that from Proverbs has three. The married-woman in Proverbs takes on the attributes of the extra females in the Book of Ben Sira as she burns the man, like the "singer of satires" in BBS 9:4. The husband's jealous rage is a prominent feature of the passage from Proverbs, a jealousy so great that no amount of gifts will appease him. It is clear in this passage that the speaker's wife is not part of the equation; the only participants are the speaker, the adulteress, and her husband— and the adulteress has a minor role.

However, another passage from Proverbs expresses "concern for husbands remaining sexually faithful to their wives, as well as vice versa"[36] Proverbs 5:15–23, below in chart 4-12b, discusses men's sexual activities and also

---

36 Camp, "Woman Wisdom and the Strange Woman," 92.

includes a man's wife as part of the equation. In the passage from Proverbs, cola 19bc clearly state that a man should maintain an erotic sexual relationship with his wife, as Ben Sira recommends in BBS 40:19d and 20b, and should "be infatuated" with "her loving" rather than being "infatuated with a stranger-woman" mentioned in the next colon. In BBS 9:1–9, the "stranger-woman" is listed with the prostitute and other sexually-available women whom the married man should avoid—for example, BBS 9:3cd advises the man not to associate with a prostitute lest he "be captured," a phrase that occurs also in the passage from Proverbs. Both Prov 5:21 and Sir 23:19 mention—in the context of a man's adultery—that "the eyes of YHWH/the Lord" observe all the acts of a person and, as is evident in the discussion of the next set of paired poetic units (Sir 23:16–27), the adultery is an offense against God.

Chart 4-12b: Similarities of adultery-passages in BBS and Proverbs

#	PROVERBS 5:15–23, WITH INSETS FROM BBS AND SIR (NETS)	
15	Drink waters from your (own) 'well'—and flowing-waters from your 'cistern.'	
16	Shall you let your 'springs' overflow outside—a stream of waters in the plaza?	
17	Let them be for you, yours alone—and not for strangers along with you.	
18	Let your 'fountain' be blessed—and find joy from the wife of your youth,	
19	a loving doe and graceful wild goat. דַּדֶּיהָ יְרַוֻּךָ בְכָל־עֵת בְּאַהֲבָתָהּ תִּשְׁגֶּה תָמִיד: Let her breasts satisfy you at all times —be infatuated with **her loving**, always.	**BBS 40:19d** ומשניהם אשה נחשקת — more than both, a wife who's desired. **40:20b** ומשניהם אהבת דודים: —more than both, **she who loves love-making**.
20	Why will you be infatuated, my son, with a stranger-woman —and embrace the bosom of an alien-woman?	
21	For the paths of a man are before **the eyes of YHWH**— and He examines all his tracks.	**Sir 23:19** … [the adulterer] does not realize that **the eyes of the Lord** … look upon all the ways of human beings …
22	His iniquities will **capture** the wicked-man—and he will be held fast by the ropes of his sins.	**BBS 9:3cd** With a prostitute do not 'take counsel'—lest you **be captured** in her traps.
23	He, himself, will die for lack of discipline —and be infatuated by the magnitude of his folly.	

In contrast to the emphasis on the punishment of the adulterer by his paramour's husband in Prov 6:25–35, in Prov 5:15–23 the offended husband is entirely absent and in BBS 9:1–9 that figure is present only insofar as the "blood" and "destruction" in 9:9d might portend his revenge. Thus, Prov

5:15–23 provides a biblical precedent for interpreting BBS 9:1–9 as an instance in which the biblical definition of *adultery* for a woman—sexual union with any man except her spouse—is applied to a man's relationships with women. A married man should celebrate an erotic sexual relationship with his wife and should also forgo other partners.

4.2.2 Second Set of Paired Poetic Units

Though the last passage on *adultery* in the Book of Ben Sira is not extant in Hebrew, I include it because it is another pair of male-protagonist/female-protagonist units and its theme repeats that of the previously-discussed paired unit, BBS 9:1–16. The double-unit Sir 23:16–27 opens with a statement about three kinds of offenders. The adulterer, identified in v. 18, is the last of the enumerated types. The central portions of the unit concern the adulterer (vv. 17–21) and the adulteress (vv. 22–26), and the unit closes with general comments.[37] Chart 4-13, below, shows the unit with the "adulterer" and "adulteress" sections formatted side by side to emphasize the parallel terminology. If the Hebrew of Sir 23:18 matches the Greek, it is an explicit statement that an adulterer "sins" against his own marriage: "There is a person who transgresses against his bed, saying in his soul, "Who will see me?"" (NETS).[38]

---

37 The choice of demarcations for the poetic unit depends on whether vv. 17 and 26 fit with the central portions or the end portions, the opening and closing. Verses 17 and 26 can both function as segues between the verses that precede and follow them. The segue function is especially clear for v. 26, which refers back through mention of the adulteress and refers forward through the verb "she will leave behind," which reverses in the following verse as "those left behind."

38 Loader (*Sexuality and the Jesus Tradition*, 34) comments: "Sirach can … speak of adultery as sinning against one's marriage bed (23:18), which must carry some sense of betrayal of one's female spouse"; cited by Balla (*Ben Sira on Family*, 133), who states that "[h]ere the man is criticized for being unfaithful to his own marriage." She adds the comment that "[t]his is remarkable since usually a married adulterous man commits an offence against the woman's husband and not against his own wife" (ibid., 225).

Chart 4-13: "A person who transgresses against his bed" Sir 23:16–27 (NETS)

S**IR** 23:16-21 (LEFT), 23:22-27 (RIGHT)

16 Two kinds multiply sins, and **a third will bring on wrath**. A hot temperament like a burning fire will never be quenched until it is consumed; a person who is sexually promiscuous with the body of his flesh will never cease until a fire burns out.

17 To a sexually promiscuous person all 'bread' is sweet; he will never grow weary until he dies.

18 There is a person **who transgresses against his bed**, saying in his soul, "Who will see me? Darkness surrounds me, and the walls will hide me, and no one will see me. Why am I discreet? *The Most High* will never remember my sins."

22 So also a **woman when she leaves her husband** and presents an heir by another.

19 And people's eyes are his fear, and he was unaware that *the eyes of the Lord* are ten thousand times brighter than the sun, as they look upon all the ways of human beings and as they look into obscure parts. **20** Before all things were created, they were known to him, and also after they were completed.

23 Now, first, she disobeyed the law of *the Most High*, and second, she committed a wrong against her husband, and third, she committed adultery by an illicit act and presented children by another man.

21 This one will be punished in the streets of the city, and when he did not suspect it, **he will be seized**.

24 She herself shall be brought out into an assembly, and there will be a visitation on her children. **25** Her children will not spread out into a root, and her branches will not bear fruit.

NOTE: In v. 18, ἄνθρωπος can be "man," not "person." See Muraoka (*Greek-Eng. Lexicon*, 37-38), that ἄνθρωπος translates אִישׁ in the LXX, for Gen 2:24.

26 She will leave behind her memory for a curse, and her reproach will not be blotted out.

27 And those who are left behind will know that nothing is better than *fear of the Lord*, and nothing sweeter than to heed *commandments of the Lord*.

This passage is not extant in Hebrew. Therefore, although the concept that these poems are "paired" is demonstrated by parallels in the Greek text, the claim that in the Book of Ben Sira the adulterer offends against his own wife can be no more than a possibility since it depends on the verse about "his bed." However, such a value would not be anomalous in the Book of Ben Sira since the paired-poems on discarding a wife or an old friend also point toward a husband's adultery as an offense against his wife, equivalent to forsaking a true friend for newcomers (BBS 9:1–9, 10–16). The language of these paired sets of poetical units reflects the biblical standard—the adulteress of chapter 23 is the only subject in the four units who explicitly "has disobeyed the law of the Most High." The actions of the married man who has sexual relations with unmarried women are not against "the law," nor are those of the man who rejects an old friend in favor of new ones—this is part of the equivalence of the two poetic units in chapter 9. Both actions are offences against God, but neither is covered by a biblical commandment. Sir 23:27, the final verse of that pair of units, provides a closing judgment; colon 27a applies "the fear of the Lord" as a standard for behavior—as it is in BBS 9:16, the final bicola of those paired units—and colon 27b adds "the commandments of the Lord" as a standard for the adulteress.

The Book of Ben Sira presents a restrictive code of male sexual behavior, in which the ideal for men becomes closer to that for women—not identical ideals, just closer than the biblical model exemplified in Prov 6:23–35.[39] The passage Prov 5:15–23, however, does provide a biblical precedent. The two paired sets of male-and-female poetic units in the Book of Ben Sira, with a third set discussed in chapter 5, are my primary examples of coherent and sustained discursive constructions of relational-gender.

4.3 Interlude for Wordplay

The limits of "wordplay," like those for "context," are everything and nothing. And, for Hebrew works such as the Book of Ben Sira that are written without vowels, the number of possible permutations is exceedingly large. My strategy for cataloging different kinds of wordplay—similar to the development of the poetic-unit pattern to standardize forays into complex literary compositions— is to devise the categories according to examples I identify in the text, rather than conforming the text to formal theories. The basic division of types is between small-scale wordplay that involves one or two elements and large-scale compositions in which a series of multivalent words can be read so as to produce and sustain two separate versions. Small-scale types include words that are spelled alike but derive from different verb-roots and the words by which Ben Sira alludes to other texts, such as the early chapters of Genesis. Certain Hebrew words and word-pairs seem to be particularly 'punnable.' For example, there are words with different or even opposite meanings, such as

---

39 In addition to the passages on *adultery* in the Book of Ben Sira, another instance of a restriction for males is the prohibition against "rising up" upon the bed of a female servant (BBS 41:22).

חסד meaning both "loving-kindness" and "disgrace."[40] The meaning of חסד as "disgrace" is present in BBS 41:22c (MSS B^m, M), "[Be ashamed] before a friend, concerning disgraceful words" (מאהב על דברי חסד).[41] A fruitful arrangement for punning is word-pairs whose forms may be spelled the same in unvocalized Hebrew, but which derive from different verb-roots, such as רעה ("1. to pasture animals; 2. to be a companion; 3. to take delight in") and רעע ("1. to be bad; 2. to break something"). Both verb-roots are used in BBS 10:6: כל פשע אל תשלֵים רע לריע[1] "For every transgression do not repay *evil* to a *companion*."

On the basis of my translations from the Book of Ben Sira, I expect that elaborate wordplay abounds in those texts, an expectation supported by the notion that Ben Sira's "love of puns leads to their extensive use."[42] In the current study, descriptions of certain passages of the Book of Ben Sira as "wordplay" are my interpretations (or those of my contemporaries) and the degree to which these interpretations align with the intentions of the author(s) is an open question. The better I can document my perceptions of semantic patterns that appear in multiple passages, the greater the likelihood that some flavor of the author's style is documented, also.

The remainder of this chapter is geared—from several directions—toward an analysis of BBS 42:9–14, the poetic unit that closes with the statement "better the badness of a man than the goodness of a woman." I identify BBS 42:9–14 as a possible site of large-scale wordplay that yields two separate translations for a series of verses. The other possible site of large-scale wordplay is BBS/Sir 38:24–34, the poetic unit that begins, "the wisdom of the scribe increases wisdom" (BBS 38:24a). That passage has been interpreted as an expression of contempt—or at least distaste—for manual labor, and thus a confirmation of Ben Sira's elite social location.[43] However, my double translation of the passage precludes a simple conclusion about the author's opinions of the merits of various occupations.

---

40   *DCH* 3:281a,b lists חסד as "disgrace" for Lev 20:17, Prov 14:34, and BBS 41:22.

41   Both meanings of חסד may be present at the beginning of the passage called "Praise of the Fathers" (chart 2-10), where the author announces his intention to praise men of חסד. However, a number of the characters are denounced, as has been noted by Brown ("Sinners, Idol-Worshippers and Fools") and others.

42   Kister, "Genizah Manuscripts," 39.

43   Opinions differ. For example, Horsley (*Scribes, Visionaries*, 55) states that "as an intellectual with an apparently comfortable living, [Ben Sira] looks down on those who work with their hands." Di Lella (Skehan and Di Lella, *Wisdom*, 449–450) notes that we should not conclude that Ben Sira "distained all manual labor; his teaching in 7:15, 22, clearly indicates that the wise should also work with their hands. In fact, later rabbis did just that."

Chart 4-14, below, shows part of the only portion of Sir 38:24–34 that is extant in Hebrew, vv. 24–25c.[44] Though the text becomes increasingly corrupt after v. 25c, the intact verses 24 to 25c establish the opening of a doubled translation in which Version 2 more or less parallels the Greek text's contrast between a scribe and a cattle-herd, and Version 1 opens with the sage/teacher figured as a cattle-herd and his students as the cattle. Such a pattern would continue through vv. 25d and 26, perhaps shifting at v. 27 to the sage as artificer and wisdom (or his students) as his "jeweled" product. The rest of the images from the Greek text[45]—the smith and the potter—could also have such metaphoric doubles, but after verse 27 the Hebrew is lacking. Note that the first bicola-unit acts as an introduction for the specific instances that follow, which is the same structure shown in charts 4-8 to 4-10. In this case, only the first half of the poetic-unit pattern is present: a single bicola for the Introduction and four bicola for Topic 1. Verse 24 includes the only instance of the word "scribe" (סופר) in extant versions of the Book of Ben Sira.

---

44   The Hebrew is shown, with simplified formatting, in this version of the chart. Also, Ben-Hayyim's versions are omitted here. The Hebrew in my sources differs slightly because Ben-Hayyim guesses some letters that Beentjes leaves blank, but the differences are not significant. For a fully-annotated version of all the extant verses of BBS 38:24–27, see chart A4-14 in the Appendix. See also section 2.2.3 of chapter 2.

45   Below is a translation from the Greek of Sir 38:24–27 (NETS):
   24 A scribe's wisdom is in the opportunity for leisure, and he who does less business, it is he who will become wise. **25** How shall he who takes hold of a plow and boasts in the shaft of a goad become wise, when he drives cattle and is engaged in their tasks and his talk is about the offspring of bulls? **26** He will give his heart to producing furrows, and his sleeplessness is regarding fodder for heifers. **27** So every artisan and master-artisan, who keeps going by night as by day, those who cut signets of seals, and his patience is to diversify ornamentation; he will give his heart to making a painting lifelike, and his sleeplessness is to complete the work.

Chart 4-14: Double translation of a poetic fragment BBS 38:24–25c

BOTH VERSIONS

חכמת סופר תרבה חכמה

24 The wisdom of the scribe increases "wisdom"

וחסר עסק הוא יתחכם :

—but/and one lacking business, he will make himself wise.

VERSION 1: "TEACHER"		VERSION 2: "CATTLE-HERD"
25 How can he make himself wise, who maintains teaching	מה יתחכם תומך מלמד	**25** How can he make himself wise, who holds a [cattle] goad
—and boast, who tests בחן a trembling-one רעד?	ומתפאר בחנית מרעיד :	—and boast, a trembling-one with a spear חנית?
With a companion he will go forward, and he will return with a song	באלוף ינהג {וישובב בשיר} בّשור [לשדד] יّשובב	With an ox he will drive forward, he will turn about [to harrow] with a song
???	NOTE: the last four extant cola are too damaged to provide a useful translation. See chart A4-14 in the Appendix.	???

In colon 24a, *teaching* is a subtext, since the scribe "increases wisdom" both by making copies of wisdom texts and by teaching, so that his students are another kind of product that increases wisdom.[46] As a semantic key for the whole poem, 24a allows the reading of later verses in terms of *teaching*. Thus, the word מלמד in colon 25a, which scholars commonly translate as "a cattle-goad," needs a second translation as its ordinary meaning, "one who teaches."[47] The use of מלמד as "teacher" is attested elsewhere in the Book of Ben Sira (BBS 51:17b), proving that Ben Sira used the word in that sense.[48] Yet, מלמד is read as "goad" only in BBS 38:25 and once in the Hebrew Bible, where it appears in combined form with the word "cattle."[49] It is not likely that a writer who puns as much as Ben Sira, and who has, obliquely, brought *teaching* into the discourse, would use the word מלמד without reference to "a teacher."

---

46 I thank L. G. Perdue for pointing out that the students, also, are the scribe's product.

47 Rabbinic literature connects the two usages, in a similar interpretation: "it is called *malmed*, because it trains the cow" (Jastrow, *Dictionary*, 793, from *y. Sanhedrin* 28a).

48 BBS 51:17a is extant in two manuscripts: MS B "and to/for my teacher I will give a song of thanks" (ולמלמדי אתן הודאה) and 11QPs[a] "to/for my teacher I will give my splendor" (למלמדי אתן הודי). Also, "Wisdom has taught her sons" (חכמות למדה בניה, BBS 4:11).

49 The word count is from *DCH* 5: 328b, and the other instance is Judges 3:31 "… and he slew 600 Philistines with a cattle-goad …" (וַיַּךְ אֶת־פְּלִשְׁתִּים 600 אִישׁ בְּמַלְמַד הַבָּקָר).

The components of the bicola BBS 38:24 can be related in two ways: in Version 2 the scribe can "increase wisdom" and also "lack business," and therefore can become wise; in Version 1 the cola are antithetical, so that the scribe who "increases wisdom" is also the one in 25a who is kept from making himself wise because he is very busy teaching. Book of Ben Sira 38:25ab asks how a man who has certain occupations "can make himself wise" and colon 25c begins to answer the question. If the reflexive form is read literally, the answer could be that he will not make himself wise; rather, he will seek wisdom "with a close-companion"—perhaps Wisdom herself?

If a text were composed to have a double translation such as I propose here, an entailment would follow—the production of some of the doubled phrases would result in unexpected or strained vocabulary that would not be the most natural choice for either meaning but would suffice for both. In this case, 'improvements' and emendations by later editors would often flatten these awkward phrases into monovocal normality. The alternative reading of BBS/Sir 38:24–34 is conjectural. It can be no more than a *possibility* since the full unit of text is not available in Hebrew, and the extant Hebrew has gaps in many cola. However, the 'normal' translations are not straightforward either, but are based on emendations that match the Greek versions. To the degree that BBS 38:24–27 allows a double reading based on metaphors of a teacher as a cattle-drover, jeweler, etc., the passage becomes enigmatic as a comment on the place of those occupations in Ben Sira's social hierarchy, with respect to the occupation of the scribe.[50]

The scribe and the herdsman/artisan might both make themselves wise, in different sorts of wisdom(s). Ben Sira declares this attitude in BBS 9:17 MS A, below:

בחכמי ידים יחשך יושר ומוש[1] עמׄז חכם :

A straightforward-man will be unceasing with the hands' wisdoms
—and a teller-of-proverbs, making his people wise.[51]

Yet, we still do not know whether Ben Sira ranks "wisdom(s)" in a hierarchy that privileges the sage/scribe. The juxtaposition of the occupations of scribe and cattle-herd, in the double-reading, makes at least some degree of equiva-

---

50 Another complication is that the "ox-goad" passage is followed by a linked, parallel passage that extols the role of the one "who thinks about the law of the Most High" (Sir 38:34d, NETS), but what the links might be in full Hebrew versions of both units is unknown.

51 The translation of BBS 9:17b considers BBS 44:4c, "proverb-tellers" (מושלים), and BBS 37:20a, "there is a wise-man who will make his people wise" (יש חכם לעמו יחכם). An alternate translation for BBS 9:17b is "and a wise-man, telling-a-proverb [to] his people."

lence between them, whatever the purpose of the juxtaposition.[52] The poetic unit can also function as an ironic echo of texts such as the Egyptian "Satire of the Trades"[53] by saying that the scribe, also, is not at leisure. In any case, the unit's function in this study is to provide a structural precedent for the other double-translation (BBS 42:9–14), which shares the pattern of a semantically-single opening that delineates the parameters of the discourse, then a split into two separate sets of meanings, triggered by multivalent words.

4.4 Two Poems in One Gender-Focal Passage: BBS 42:9–14

The poetic unit BBS 42:9–14 handles themes of *gender*, *shame*, and *speech* through the topic of a father's worries about his daughter. This unit is of disproportionate significance in evaluating the discourse of *gender* both by reason of its position as the last poetic unit on human females and because it closes with one of the pericopes cited most often as evidence of the author's negative view of women.[54] The poetic unit's status as the last of its type means that it is, literally, the 'last word' on the subject of human females. And, it is also the last word on *shame* because BBS 42:9–14 is the closing segment in a chain of units about *shame*: 4:20–28, 41:15c–42:1d, 42:1e–8, and 42:9–14.

The theme of *shame* begins in the poetic unit BBS 4:20–28 with an announcement of the double nature of shame: "For there is shame that is a burden of guilt—and there is shame that is honor and grace" (v. 21).[55] I will analyze BBS 42:9–14 as the embodiment of this doubleness of shame; the preceding units BBS 4:20–28, 41:15c–42:1d, and 42:1e–8 develop the rubric of doubleness explicitly, but BBS 42:9–14 *enacts* the doubleness. The unit BBS 4:20–28 also introduces another major element of the doubled discourse of *shame*—the use of "the tongue"—which develops fully in BBS 5:9–16 with the declaration that "honor and dishonor are in the hand of one who speaks

---

52 Owens ("'Come, Let Us Be Wise,'" 236) notes that Ben Sira "embraces the practical wisdom that can be found both in the life of the mind and in the work of one's hands."

53 Rollston ("Ben Sira 38:24–39:11," 132 nn. 6, 7) summarizes previous scholarship and remarks that both BBS and the Egyptian text could be a "motivational tool" for scribal students (ibid., 139). To Perdue (*Sword and the Stylus*, 267), "it seems quite possible that Ben Sira was familiar with this Egyptian text" because it and other Egyptian works were well-known in his era. Di Lella (Skehan and Di Lella, *Wisdom*, 449–450) notes the relation of Sir 38:24–34 to the Egyptian "Satire of the Trades," but states that Ben Sira "removed from his own composition all traces of ridicule."

54 For example, McKinlay (*Gendering Wisdom the Host*, 175) states that 42:13–14 "rivals 25:24 as the work's strongest negative comment on women."

55 See chart 2-7, and the annotated version in chart A2-7, in the Appendix.

impetuously, and the tongue of a human is his downfall (v. 13)."[56] One component of "dishonorable" speech is malicious gossip, whose mode of operation is described in BBS 11:29–31, below. Comments on malicious gossip in BBS 11:29–31 parallel those on the topic of *slander* in BBS 42:9–14, making these verses an important benchmark for interpretations of 42:9–14, in which *slander* is the key to the doubled translations.

Chart 4-15a: "Do not bring every man to a house" BBS 11:29–31 (MS A)

11:29   Do not bring every man to a house
         —and (this is) how the wounds of a defamer multiply!

11:29c–11:30f → incomplete and/or less pertinent to the topic of slander.

11:30g   The defamer lurks like a bear near a house of scoffers
         —and like a spy he will see vulnerability/nakedness.

11:31   Good to bad, a whisperer will pervert
         —and against your delights he will send treachery.

The skulking figure of the male "defamer" and "whisperer" lurks near houses in order to slander the inhabitants.[57] The comparison of this figure with a bear is apt (11:30g) because a bear lurks near human habitations to forage through the garbage for tasty tidbits to eat and creates havoc in the process, just as the slanderer seeks the best morsels of 'garbage' to spread about, creating havoc in the lives of the victims.

Another treatment of *slander* [58] occurs in BBS 51:2, in the author's prayer of thanksgiving for deliverance from various dangers.

Chart 4-15b: "Let me declare Your name" BBS 51:1–2 (MS B)

51:1   Let me declare Your name, Refuge-of-Life
        —for You have ransomed my soul from death.

51:2   You have spared my flesh from the pit-of-destruction
        —and from the hand of Sheol You have delivered my foot.

---

56   See chart 2-6 for thirty-two bicola in BBS that relate to the topic of *speech*, and the chart AppLex-10, in the Appendix, for verses about *slander*.

57   In vv. 29b and 30g, the word רוכל (m. s. participle of the root רכל) is translated as "gossiper," or "defamer," but in this instance the level of harm to the victims seems equivalent to that for "slander" in BBS 42:9–14 and 51:2.

58   The word translated as "slander" in BBS 51:2 is דבה, as in BBS 42:9–14.

> You have rescued me from the slander of the people,
> —from the spreading of slander-of-the-tongue,
> and from the judgment of the spreaders of false-report.

The writer of BBS 51:1–2 speaks as one who has, himself, been slandered. In such a case, the discussions of *death* in relation to *slander* would be more than abstract moral speculations because the sage expects his reputation, his "good name," to live on after his death, and slander would destroy that hope.

In the Book of Ben Sira, the theme of *speech* provides criteria for assessing different kinds of people, and the judgments align with the two kinds of בשת ("shame"). Honorable-shame, ביש, refers to modest or decorous conduct, including speech, and guilty-shame—often בשת paired with חרפה ("reproach")—describes behavior that is immodest, either "unchaste" or "arrogant." BBS 41:15c opens the concluding ruminations about *shame* by describing what follows as an "instruction on shame." The "instruction" has two parts: a unit with examples of "shame that is fit to retain" (BBS 41:15c–42:1d) and a unit that lists situations for which a man should "not feel ashamed" (BBS 42:1e–8).[59] Thus, the doubleness of *shame* has been carried through from BBS 4:20–28 into the units that immediately precede the passage about the father and daughter. *Gender* and *speech* feature prominently in the list of "shame that is fit to retain" but only tangentially in the situations for which shame is not appropriate. However, two schematic figures reappear in the latter unit: the Wrong Wife (אשה רעה) and the Fool (כסיל).[60]

42:1e　However, for these do not be put to shame …

42:6　Concerning the Wrong Wife, a seal—and a place of many hands, a key.

42:7　Concerning a place where you deposit, an accountant
　　　　—and for giving and taking, everything in writing.

42:8　Concerning instruction of the naïve-one and the Fool
　　　　—and the grey-haired stumbler, occupied with whoring.

The need for "a seal" with regard to the Wrong Wife (v. 6) makes sense in light of BBS 7:26, "Your wife—do not abhor her—or, hating her, do not trust

---

59　See charts 2-8 and 2-9, in chapter 2.

60　The Wrong Wife ("a bad/evil wife") is from MS B; MS B^m has אשה טפשה ("a stupid wife"); MS M has a gap. The female figures I describe as "schematic" appear in BBS 25:13–26:3, given in chart 2-11 of chapter 2. The annotated version of the Hebrew text is chart A2-11, in the Appendix.

her" (chart 4-8). The passage above closes with a bicola similar to the closing of the "appropriate shame" portion of the paired units: the man who follows all the advice about shame will become "truly modest" and be favored by "all the living" (42:1cd) and will also become "truly enlightened" and be humble "before all the living" (42:8cd).

Between these explicit discussions about *shame* and the major change to the theme of "the works of God" in 42:15 is the gender-focal poetic unit about the father and daughter (BBS 42:9–14). The father has numerous potential sources of worry as his daughter grows up and marries a congenial man or a man who neglects her. However, an invisible part of the interpersonal dynamics is that the father is responsible for choosing the daughter's husband because it is his duty to "unite her to a discerning fellow."[61] And, given Ben Sira's estimate of marriage as a crucial human bond, it is reasonable that the father would worry about making such a momentous choice. This passage mentions "shame" (colon 11d), but also participates in the discourse of *shame* by embodying the double nature of that theme through multivalent language: in addition to the standard translation of the pericope as examples of *immodest* behaviors by the daughter, I present a second translation that produces *modest* behavior. Chart 4-16, below, shows the poetic unit. The first half has a single translation (vv. 9a–11b) and the second half splits into two separate translations made from the same multivalent Hebrew text (vv. 11c–13b).[62] For vv. 11cd–13, the right-hand column is the standard, direct translation that yields *immodest* behaviors; the left-hand column is my translation geared toward *modest* ones. The two translations merge in v. 14, the final verse. For all of chart 4-16, note that the typographic changes show related words, although the same typographic elements are used in the charts in the Appendix to show manuscript sources.

---

61   See BBS 7:18–26 in chart 4-8. The Hebrew is אל גבר נבון חברה.

62   For Hebrew texts and full notes, see chart A4-16 in the Appendix. The text in chart 4-16 is a composite translation because the three extant versions are often incomplete, incoherent, and/or contradictory. The first half of the unit also shows little coherence between the MSS because the six "X, lest Y" cola appear in different sequences even if they show the same vocabulary, in the same combinations. The convoluted margin notes of MS B comprise a third text, with MSS M and B.

*Chart 4-16: "A daughter is a deceptive treasure to a father" BBS 42:9–14
(MSS B, M)*

KEY: No typographic key and no default; MS B, MS B^m, and MS M are combined.

BOTH VERSIONS

9ab	A **daughter** is a ▊deceptive treasure▊ to a father —and anxiety about her will disperse slumber.
9cd	As a girl, lest **she** will reject —and as a maiden, lest **she** be profaned.
10ab	As a maiden, lest **she** be seduced —in the house of a *lord-husband*, lest **she** be <u>forgotten</u>.
10cd	In the house of her father, lest **she** "propagate" —and in the house of a *man-husband*, lest **she** be barren.
11ab	**Slander** concerning a **daughter**, make firm one who guards —lest [?] a rotting name.

Left margin labels (top to bottom): KEY · DAUGHTER'S GUILT OR INNOCENCE · SLANDER APPEARS · SLANDER ENTERS · SLANDER IN HOUSE · SLANDER DEPARTS · JUDGMENT

"SLANDER" VERSION ↙ ↘ "DAUGHTER" VERSION

"SLANDER" VERSION		"DAUGHTER" VERSION
Slander of a city and an assembly of the people —and **it** will cause you shame, in the congregation of the gate.	11cd	**Slander** of a city and an assembly of the people —and **she** will cause you shame, in the congregation of the gate.
Let there not be a lattice —a place **it** will attack —and "a house looking out brings in the neighborhood."	11ef	Let there not be a lattice in a place **she** will sojourn, —and "a house looking out brings in the neighborhood."
For any (slander), <u>remember</u> —do not let **it** break through —and in a house of <u>men-who-forget</u>, do not take counsel.	12	For any male, do not permit **her** form —and in a house of women, do not let **her** take counsel.
For "from a garment goes forth a moth" —and from a woman, the female-companion of a woman.	13	For "from a garment goes forth a moth" —and from a woman, the evil of a woman.

↘ 14, BOTH VERSIONS ↙

"Better the evil of a man than the goodness of a woman"
—but a **daughter** who is afraid-before-God is better than any **taunt**.

The phrase "deceptive treasure" (מטמון שקר, the literal translation is "treasure-falsehood") in the first bicola is a contradiction that presages the coming split: is the daughter an *immodest* "falsehood" or "lie" (שקר), or is she a *modest* "treasure" (מטמון)? Three bicola follow, each with two possible worries that could cause the father's anxiety.[63] In the translation, I have assembled the scattered elements into combinations of guilty daughter (*immodest*) and innocent daughter (*modest*) scenarios:

#	DAUGHTER'S STATUS	WORRY FOR FATHER	VERDICT
9c	- child or unbetrothed	"will reject" = reject marriage? God?	- guilty
9d	- betrothed	"be profaned" = be raped	- innocent
10a	- betrothed	"be seduced" = be seduced	- guilty
10b	- married (wrong man)	"be forgotten" = unloved, neglected	- innocent
10c	- un/betrothed	"'propagate'" = become pregnant	- guilty
10d	- married (right man)	"be barren" = loved, cannot conceive	- innocent

Two words for "husband," בעל and איש, are translated differently in cola 10b and 10d to distinguish between them. The term בעל ("lord" or "master") is the usual term for "husband" in the Book of Ben Sira, so that איש ("man" or "husband") is notable.[64] The use of איש may hearken back to the relationship between Eve and Adam in chapters 2 and 3 of Genesis, to imply an appropriate marriage.[65]

The last bicola before the semantic doubling speaks of "slander concerning a daughter," naming the two actants in the divided story-line. For the divided section of the unit, feminine grammatical forms are translated twice: once with reference to the noun דִּבָּה ("slander") and once with reference to בַּת ("daughter"). The translation as "daughter" is analyzed later in conjunction with archaeological and anthropological evidence, but the translation itself is self-explanatory in terms of a (presumed) need to sequester young women to ensure that they are chaste before marriage, both in reputation and in practice.

In the version translated for "slander," some other words have alternative roots or meanings. For example, the masculine singular imperative of "to remember" has the same consonants as the noun "a male," and the masculine

---

63 The Hebrew for these verses exists in several permutations, none of which are definitive. See chart A4-16, in the Appendix.

64 See BBS 25:8,18, 22, 23; 26:1, 2, 13; 42:10b for בעל; see BBS 36:26; 42:10d for איש.

65 In chart 5-6, see BBS 36:23 ("And further, if she has healing speech—'her man' אשה is not among the 'sons-of-Adam'"), which parallels אשה in Gen 3:6. See chapter 5 for a discussion of Ben Sira's use of the biblical character Eve.

plural participle "(men) who forget" is the same as "women." The semantic pair "remember" and "forget" in bicola 12ab of the "slander" version recalls colon 10b, in which the daughter married to a "lord-husband" is unloved and "forgotten."

A *house* motif also links the two halves of the unit: the houses of the father and the two kinds of husband are balanced with a generic house in which the daughter lives. In BBS 42:11ef, the personification Slander moves from public spaces to the "lattice" of the house, to listen to the occupants.[66] The house is vulnerable not only to Slander, but also to "the neighborhood" in the form of a "female-companion" who visits the wife (colon 13b). Once a tale-bearer is admitted to the house, both conversation and conduct are fodder for gossip.

In BBS 42:12, Slander is inside the house of people like the inappropriate husband in colon 10b who "forgets" the daughter after marriage. In order to prevent Slander from spying-around, the reader is advised not to converse on private matters in such a place. Slander exits in the next verse in the form of a female-companion of the wife (colon 13b), a member of the "neighborhood" (colon 11f). If the locale is the house of the husband who "forgets," then the daughter/wife's companions who visit could leave with plenty to report—an action likened to a moth's leaving a garment. The female-companion's going out is moth-like because she will go elsewhere to deposit her "eggs" of information that give birth to slander. In terms of *gender*, it is significant that a male figure is named in BBS 11:29–31 as the one who lurks near houses in order to defame the inhabitants. As a female/male parallel, the woman in BBS 42:13 is figured as a moth and the man in BBS 11:30 as a bear, but both are occupied with the same task: gathering information and spreading it, as a weapon. The "slander" and "daughter" versions coalesce for the last verse, BBS 42:14:

BBS 42:14 (MS M)   טוב רע איש מטיב {מטוב} אשה ובת מפחדת מכול חרפה

"Better the evil of a man/husband
   than the goodness of a woman/wife"
—but/and a daughter who is afraid-before-God,
[better] than any taunt/reproach.

---

66   Any opening in an outside wall would be too small for someone to enter or exit and too high for a passer-by to peer in. These small openings would probably be latticed; someone inside could see out but outsiders could not see in, yet could hear conversations in the house.

The word מפחדת ("one (f.) who is afraid-before-God") in colon-b is a positive value for Ben Sira, whose highest praise is for those who "fear-God."[67] In 42:14b (MS M), the use of מפחדת is parallel to the use of מפחד in BBS 4:20 (MS A) and 37:12 (MSS B, D), with regard to males.[68]

The word חרפה in 14b, which is usually translated as "reproach" and linked with "shame," is interpreted here as its other meaning, "a 'reproach,' or 'taunt' of an enemy."[69] The use of חרפה as "taunt" in the closing colon recalls "slander" in cola 11a and 11c, and links back to שקר, "falsehood" or "lie," in the key-phrase "deceptive treasure" (מטמון שקר) that opens the poetic unit. Hellenistic gender models presume a discourse of female *shame*, but that is not the case for חרפה in BBS 42:14b, which is the only one of the seventeen (extant) instances of חרפה in the Book of Ben Sira that concerns females.

In the version from MS M, colon 14a ("better the evil of a man than the goodness of a woman") is nonsense because it contradicts all Ben Sira's other statements about good and bad behavior—statements that apply equally to women and to men. If colon-a of v. 14 is the pattern "X is better than Y," then colon-b should match it, as some form of a "better than" statement in which the presence of טוב ("good") at the beginning of colon-b is presumed and the מ־ in מכול indicates "more than (any)," for a combined meaning "better than any."[70] I suggest that colon-b is a variant of the pattern "and Z is better than either X or Y." In this case, however, colon-b ("and a daughter who is afraid-before-God is better than any taunt") negates colon 14a if "any taunt" is self-referential—i.e., if the "taunt" is colon 14a, with its predecessor, v. 13.

Both BBS 42:13 and 14a read like proverbial statements.[71] As an example of the kinds of proverbial statements mentioned in chapter 2, BBS 42:13a would be a classic proverb because the actants are an insect and a garment and the proverb can be applied to a range of situations—it is colon-b that 'spells out' the message that would have been inferred by an audience in a spoken performance. In contrast, BBS 42:14a would be a proverb-token because it must fit a specific, narrow range of scenarios and has specific classes of persons as actants, a man and a woman; colon 14a has no function except as social-noise.

---

67   Goering (*Wisdom's Root*, 232 n.150) lists 42:14b as an instance of "the verbal use of פחד as practicing piety."

68   See chart 4-6 for verses that use the same vocabulary for males and females.

69   See *DCH* 3:321a "חרפה 1."

70   However, *DCH* reads the מ־ as a preposition. See *DCH* 3:321b for חרפה "PREP:מן ... of cause, 'at,' + פחד 'be in dread' Si 42:14 (M)," also *DCH* 6:674a: "חרף 'taunt,'" plus מן, "on account of."

71   Camp speaks of colon 13a as "a proverb" ("Understanding," 35).

The author's use of proverbial statements need not translate into any directly discernable opinion of their content. In the case of a seemingly-nonsensical statement such as BBS 42:14a, colon-b should provide the decoding key—and it does. A self-reference to colon-a as the "taunt (of an enemy)" destabilizes a literal interpretation of the whole poetic unit. Such an interpretation is further destabilized by reading the poetic unit in conjunction with information about the living conditions of women in Ben Sira's era.

4.4.1 Archaeology, Anthropology, and Texts

The rubric of *social networking* unfolds an area of gendered social interaction that is visible in ancient texts—if at all—only in incidental phrases at the edges of discourse, not at focal topics. One of these edges of discourse could be BBS 42:9–14. I will present enough archaeological information and related commentary to support the idea that, in the "Anxious Father" passage, we have glimpses of a world that includes women. The gender-hierarchy of the social structure is more complex in societies where women "network intensively" because women look not "to the world of men for their honor, but to other women and with other criteria than those of the male world."[72] Concepts such as 'female networking' and 'homosociality' highlight the fact that several gender-hierarchies can be operative in the same place at the same time and, thus, offer alternatives to 'patriarchy' as tools for analyzing issues of *gender* and *status*.[73]

Anthropological archaeology and ethnography have begun to foreground *gender* as an essential parameter of research, focusing on textual and material evidence about what Meyers describes as the "social reality of women's lives" in the ancient world.[74] She notes that a woman in a patrilocal society such as

---

72   Osiek, "Women, Honor, and Context," 327 (mentioning work by Rogers, "Gender in Southwestern France") and 332 (mentioning work by Kennedy, "Women's Friendships on Crete," and Wikan, "Shame and Honour").

73   'Patriarchy' is of limited value as a conceptual tool. Meyers ("Contesting the Notion of Patriarchy," 87) notes that the concept originates in the work of William Robertson Smith, who based his image of biblical patriarchy on "Western male observations of nineteenth-century Arab tribal life as well as on classical models," and Smith's depiction of Israelite society passed into common usage through the work of Julius Wellhausen and his contemporaries. Butler (*Gender Trouble*, 45-46) also comments on the overuse of the concept, noting that "the very notion of 'patriarchy' has threatened to become a universalizing concept that overrides or reduces distinct articulations of gender asymmetry in different cultural contexts." Elsewhere, Butler warns against seeing patriarchy "as inevitable or as primary, more primary in fact than other operations of differential power" ("Question of Social Transformation," 212).

74   Meyers, "Contesting the Notion of Patriarchy," 84.

ancient Israel would have had two sets of social bonds—with her birth family and with the family in which she would live after marriage—while her husband "usually remained with his natal family and consequently had only one set of connections." The double linkages of these women could have been instrumental in facilitating "interfamily and intercommunity cooperation."[75] Women's connections in their communities had social benefits, but also economic ones that included "informal networks" for the production and distribution of goods such as bread and textiles.[76]

In Israelite/Jewish contexts, the production of bread and textiles are two areas of activity that are discursively associated, almost exclusively, with females—though not exclusively female in actual practice.[77] Bread production changed in the Persian era due to technological innovations in the processing of grain into flour.[78] The grinding implements and those used for the stages of production from flour to bread were located "in or near households, in interior or exterior workspaces."[79] Archaeological data that reconstruct "room function as opposed to room configuration"[80] identify "the positioning of the implements and the installations used in bread production, a female task, [which] shows that women from several households would have worked together."[81] The water for mixing with flour to make bread was "as likely to be carried from a community well, aqueduct, or fountain, or from a nearby spring or stream, as to come from a cistern or rain barrel in a courtyard."[82]

---

75 Meyers, "Contesting the Notion of Patriarchy," 93. The patrilocal residence pattern fits better with a scattered population, and the matri-core pattern with an urban setting. The point is that in both situations women have opportunities to build networks.

76 Meyers, "Contesting the Notion of Patriarchy," 92. On the basis of "archaeological remains" of an Iron Age dwelling at Tel Halif, Hardin ("Understanding," 83), also, had identified "textile production" and "bread making" as women's activities.

77 Meyers, "Material Remains," 430–34. See also Meyers ("From Field Crops to Food," 67–84) and Peskowitz (*Spinning*).

78 In the new kind of mill, grain "was poured through a slot in a mobile upper stone that was moved over a lower stone using an attached wooden rod" (Ebeling and Rowan, "Archaeology of the Daily Grind," 115). The labor required to operate these mills is within the range of women's strength (C. Osiek, in a written communication [9/19/2010], notes that a woman in the 1974 Greek film *Kypseli* is "shown operating exactly that kind of mill"). If, as Frankel notes ("Olynthus Mill," 107), "milling houses may have operated in Judah during the Iron Age," it is even more likely they would have operated in Hellenistic times, thus allowing some households to buy pre-ground flour.

79 Meyers, "From Field Crops to Food," 71.

80 Meyers, "Engendering," 189.

81 Meyers, "Contesting the Notion of Patriarchy," 92.

82 Baker, *Rebuilding the House*, 38.

The other female-identified set of crafts is textile production.[83] Ancient
Greek and Hebrew texts, iconography, and physical signifiers such as grave
goods associate women—to the point of metonymy—with the spindle.[84] Few
textiles survive from the Hellenistic era, but spindle-whorls and loom-weights
are found at Iron Age, and later, sites, in quantities that could indicate "an
active cottage weaving industry."[85] The loom of Ben Sira's time was the
warp-weighted loom. Although such looms were not portable, women might
spin with a spindle while visiting the houses of those who were weaving.[86]

Osiek declares that economic activities by women are "precisely where
female power is most likely to have been exercised" and, in Meyers' succinct
equation, "gender-associated artifacts signify gender-associated economic
activities, which in turn signify gender-linked power."[87] Women's "wage-
producing labor" is also visible from another direction: "the corners and niches
of rabbinic writing."[88] Peskowitz lists the following instances in which Jewish
women "engaged in a waged economy": selling textiles, bread, calves, clothing,
and olives; baking bread, preparing oils and wines, grinding grain at millstones,
spinning yarn, weaving yarn into cloth; organizing egg-hatching enterprises;
and manufacturing wool and flax products.[89] The list by Baker is similar—
"women as shopkeepers, as wool, linen, or livestock vendors; as bread or olive
sellers" as well as dealing in "fowl, and eggs"[90] Though this evidence is from
Roman Palestine rather than Ben Sira's era, I presume some continuity, in part
because the list includes the activities mentioned for the "valorous wife" in
Prov 31:10–31, such as acquiring a field (v. 16), making cloth and selling it
(colon 24a), and dealing with a merchant to distribute her textiles (colon 24b).
Authorial attitudes towards the women's activities might change—from praise
in Proverbs to degrees of disapproval in rabbinic texts—but the activities they
report seem continuous, as is some form of authorial re-use of earlier materials,

---

83   Meyers, "Contesting the Notion of Patriarchy," 93.

84   For counter-examples of the motif, see David's curse against Joab (2 Sam 3:29) and the
     giantess who tries to kill David with a spindle (*b. Sanhedrin* 95a).

85   Hardin, "Understanding," 80, with regard to Tel Halif.

86   In warp-weighted looms, a group of (vertical) warp threads, attached to a board at the top, is
     weighted with a piece of clay or other material attached at the bottom, to maintain tension.
     Weaving proceeds from top to bottom, as each new horizontal strand is pushed up against
     the body of the cloth.

87   Osiek, "Women, Honor, and Context," 334; Meyers, "From Field Crops to Food," 76.

88   Peskowitz, *Spinning*, 64.

89   Peskowitz, *Spinning*, 64. The examples are as given, but condensed into one list. I omit the
     category of "glassmakers," since glassmaking is not well attested for Ben Sira's time.

90   Baker, *Rebuilding the House*, 80, 85–86; she mentions (pp. 81–82) that she expands on
     Peskowitz's concept of "'decommodification' of 'women's work,'" citing *Spinning*, n.p..

of Proverbs by Ben Sira and of the Book of Ben Sira by both Talmuds.[91] This is the background against which I consider Sir 28:15, available only in Greek (mostly NETS).

> (v. 14) A 'third tongue' has shaken many …
> and demolished strong cities and overturned the houses of nobles.
>
> v. 15   γλῶσσα τρίτη γυναῖκας ἀνδρείας ἐξέβαλεν
> καὶ ἐστέρησεν αὐτὰς τῶν πόνων αὐτῶν.
> A 'third tongue' has cast out valorous women
> and deprived them of their labors.

Sirach 28:15 could be an instance in which Ben Sira views women without regard to their relationship with men. The concept of female social networking and the extensive list of women's commercial activities, combined with the use of the phrase that evokes the Valorous Wife whose activities are listed in Prov 31:10–31, [92] gives the image of women facing economic loss due to slander ("a third tongue"). A rift between the wife and husband [93] could cause the "driving out" in Sir 28:15, but it is also reasonable to read v. 15 as a woman's being driven from access to textile workshops or other marketing venues available through her female-network,[94] and thus being deprived of income from her labors.

---

91   I use material related to earlier (biblical) and later (rabbinic) eras to highlight topics in the Book of Ben Sira that seem semantically continuous with those texts.

92   The Greek of Sir 28:15— γυναῖκας ἀνδρείας— is the equivalent of BBS/Sir 26:2 and the LXX of Proverbs 31:10.

93   Di Lella (*Wisdom*, 365) states that ἐξέβαλεν means "drive out … because their husbands will divorce them on the basis of false allegations reported to them," and that τῶν πόνων αὐτῶν means to be deprived of "the 'fruit,' i.e., the acceptance, praise, and gratitude, which the virtuous woman has a right to enjoy because she has been a good wife and mother," citing Prov 31:10–31. Calduch-Benages ("Cut Her Away," 92, n. 56) speaks of the victims of such slander (literally, "the third tongue"), stating that "the third tongue refers to a 'third person,' who interferes maliciously with the life of a couple in order to disrupt the harmony between husband and wife." She concludes that "the cause of the divorce has nothing at all to do with the woman, but has everything to do with a terrible weapon, … slander."

94   Meyers, "Material Remains," 433. The following statement by Meyers could apply to later eras: "even if some Iron II textile production was 'industrial,' it still may have been a female enterprise."

4.4.2 Reading a Text Together With External Evidence: BBS 42:11–14

How might BBS 42:11–14 be read with regard to female social networks? The translation that links a "female neighbor" with the production of "slander" relates well to a situation in which women move about—among spaces in their own dwellings, the dwellings of others, and communal areas—for various tasks. The two strands of translation for BBS 42:11c–13 are designated by the feminine singular noun that is read as the referent for the feminine grammatical forms: "daughter" for the expected translation and "slander" for the alternate. In the case of BBS 42:11ef, the "daughter" version is often interpreted as a directive to seclude the daughter and keep her away from the company of married women.[95] However, the thought that a girl or young woman would not hear the conversations of adult women in her home makes no sense in view of what we know of the intergenerational nature of most households and the communal nature of much of the work that took place. Most families needed the help of children, boys *and* girls, in running errands and doing the simplest parts of the labors that occupied the adults—this was also how children learned what they needed to know to run their own households in later life. Elite women and non-elite were expected to work with textiles, one of the primary venues for female-networked activities. Furthermore, most domiciles did not have the facilities for sequestering daughters, even if that had been desirable. The salient feature of dwelling units in ancient Galilee, according to Baker, is

> the apparent cheek-by-jowl connectedness of the dwelling practices represented by these domestic structures, with several "living groups" evidently occupying an enclosure [with multiple interconnected chambers]. … "Houses" like these were structurally integrated with one another in a fashion that bespeaks relationality far more than seclusion or isolation, "society" much more than "privacy." Hence, architecturally, many of these excavated houses were "social," in that they were shared by undetermined numbers of people of varying relationship to one another.[96]

---

95 For example, Di Lella states that the daughter "should not be allowed the company of married women" (*Wisdom*, 483); Camp ("Understanding," 35) interprets BBS/Sir 42:11 as instructions to the father "not to allow windows in her [the daughter's] room, lest she display her beauty before men; and not to let her talk with married women, lest she learn about sexuality"; and McKinlay follows with the comment that "[t]he solution is to keep the daughter away from windows and even from the company of older women: in other words, to shut her up" (*Gendering Wisdom the Host*, 165; citing Gilbert, "Ben Sira et la femme," 439).

96 Baker, *Rebuilding the House*, 36–37. Marttila (*Foreign Nations*, 19 and 19, n. 57) states that "[a]rchaeological findings from Hellenistic Palestine are scarce," though the situation "becomes better" for the Maccabean period. Though very little archaeological evidence remains for Jerusalem in Ben Sira's time, I presume similarities of social usage—and of

Thus, the protection of a daughter's chastity would have been more a factor of the constant surveillance that is intrinsic to populous living-situations than a factor of isolation.[97]

In a homosocially-organized society, the spousal relationship is a major conduit for transferring information between the groups.[98] Wives, more than husbands, can control the flow of information because women in these social systems "obtain information that is unavailable to men and that may often be critical for forging supra-household political connections."[99] A woman's double allegiance—to her birth family and to her husband's family—would give her a wide range of contacts. Since the texts we see are the products of male imaginings, stories about women talking together can indicate male nervousness about a female-world that is open to them through their wives, who tell or withhold information from that network as they see fit.[100] For the "slander" version of the passage, it is the neglectful son-in-law's house that is the site of the invasion by slander. The slander in BBS 42:9–14 can be envisioned as coming out of the son-in-law's house (like a moth from a garment) in the person of a "female companion" of the daughter/wife who returns to her own home and tells her husband, who then tells his own social network.[101] Likewise, the behavior of the male "defamer" in BBS 11:30g fits the homosocial pattern whereby a man must "lurk like a bear" outside the house, instead of entering. Thus, both women and men are responsible for producing slander, though they are portrayed as gathering the raw material for it in gender-specific ways. What groups could be the slanderers in 42:9–14?

---

architectural design, or unplanned sprawl—for these later dwellings in Galilee. The poorer sections of a city or town would probably be less affected by Hellenistic influences on the use of domestic space.

97   For a complete discussion on issues of *surveillance*, see "anopticons" and "panopticons" in Baker, *Rebuilding the House*, 42–47, 59–70, 74.

98   Mothers could give information to sons, also, but "wives" figure in these passages.

99   Meyers, "From Field Crops to Food," 77.

100 For an example of selective reporting from modern societies, see Wikan, "Shame and Honour," 639–40. See also Osiek ("Women, Honor, and Context," 331–32) for comments on studies of two societies in which male control of female sexuality is a paramount value, yet women, in their own networks, will ignore the adulterous activities of one among them who is a true friend, "kind, gentle, understanding, sympathetic" and above all, able to keep confidences (ibid., citing Kennedy, "Women's Friendships on Crete," and Wikan, "Shame and Honour").

101 In the context of the close relationships between the women who work together, this woman's behavior would be dishonorable—a betrayal of her female-network affiliations. In a parallel for betrayal between men, Corley (*Ben Sira's Teaching*, 23) comments that Sir 27:16–21 "considers the harm done to friendship by the disclosure of secrets, which typically occurs behind the closed doors of one's home."

Would they be Jewish, since they have access to the house, or Hellenistic, since the "taunts" are reminiscent of Greek invective? Specific information about daily life in Ben Sira's world is sparse—probably, most of his "neighbors" are Jews, but there might well be visitors from different neighborhoods.

On the basis of archaeological and textual evidence presented here, the concept of secluded Jewish females sequestered in separate living-quarters is not a viable concept for the second century BCE. Whatever separations were maintained were more fluid, involving spaces, and times of day, and social surveillance rather than windowless walls. Even in Palestinian rabbinic texts the "walls" are absent. Baker reports that "there are no halakhic traditions remotely associated with domestic seclusion of women or the construction of 'men's quarters' and 'women's quarters' in houses, and no terminology or unambiguous images associated with such practices in the aggadic tradi-tions."[102] Unless a relaxation of constraints on female activity occurred between the writing of the Book of Ben Sira and the early rabbinic texts, the over-all situation in Ben Sira's time would be no more constraining than in the time of the Palestinian rabbis. However, some classical Greek domestic architecture did enforce female-seclusion by the division of space, with an ἀνδρών ("apartment for males") between the entrance and the women's areas.[103]

It is interesting to ask how the "daughter" version of BBS 42:12 would sound to Ben Sira's contemporaries if we presume that fully-functional female networks were the norm in his time and were operating in "relational" domestic spaces: "For any male, do not permit a daughter's form—and in a house of women/wives, let her not take counsel." While colon 12a might sound farfetched, colon 12b would register as an absurdity in a homosocial society where "women/wives" and females of all ages were precisely the group with whom a daughter spent many hours of every day. The discordance generated by 12b could trigger a search for other meanings, starting with the fact that v. 12 has three words that can supply alternative translations: זכר means both "a male" and "to remember"; תאר can mean both "a form" and "to break through"; and נשים means both "women/wives" and "those (m.) who forget."[104] In addition, the verb תסתיד ("to take counsel") can be either a feminine third-person

---

102 Baker, *Rebuilding the House*, 19.

103 See Walker, "Women and Housing in Classical Greece," and Whitley, *Archaeology of Ancient Greece*.

104 Kister ("Genizah Manuscripts," 42, on BBS 38:17) gives an example of a pair of double-translations, though the verse is not related to *gender*. He notes that מרר can mean both "flow" and "bitter," and חמם both "lament" and "warm."

singular form or a masculine second-person singular. In the previous bicola, 11cd, "slander" is as capable of "causing shame in the congregation of the gate" as is the daughter's behavior that is the topic of the slander. The substitution of "slander" as the referent in colon 11d can be repeated for vv. 11ef and 12, other verses with feminine grammatical forms. For such a re-reading of BBS 42:9–14, the self-referential aspect of "taunts" in colon 14b completes the cumulative destabilization of literal readings.

The strangeness of BBS 42:14a is even more apparent in its context than in isolation, since the next verse opens a new thematic section.[105]

42:14 (MS M)   טוב רע איש מטיב אשה ובת מפחדת מכול חרפה

"Better the evil of a man than the goodness of a woman"
—but a daughter who is afraid-before-God is better than any taunt.

42:15 (MS M)   אזכרה נא מעשי אל וזה חזיתי ואשננה

Let me remember the works of God
—and that which I have perceived, let me teach incisively / repeat.

The juxtaposition of v. 14 with v. 15 is jarring, and should provoke questions about that text. Why are there so few such questions? As Sherwood says about the uncritical belief in prophetic literature as a "mirror" of its times, "[i]f the prophet says that the people are sleeping with she-goats then they are sleeping with she-goats"[106]—likewise, if the sage says that the evil of a man is better than the goodness of a woman then that is his opinion of women. However, the statement in BBS 42:14a makes sense only if readers take the statement itself as evidence that Ben Sira upholds a different standard of piety for women than for men. It is the very grotesquery of BBS 42:14a that allows colon 14b to undermine and explode the statement, since 14a—dropped blatantly into the text without the context necessary for a proverb-token—is the epitome of a gendered taunt.

Though BBS 42:15 shifts to a new topic, its language can create close links to the "slander" translation for vv. 10–12, through connections formed

---

105 Camp ("Honor and Shame in Ben Sira," 184) interprets the juxtaposition of the "magnificent hymn to God as creator" with "verses on the danger to men of women's shame" as an indication that "the shame of women" is a threat whose "cosmic force … is signified [by the location of] the bitter invectives"; citing "Understanding," 35–36.

106 Sherwood, "Prophetic Scatology," 184. The reference concerns "traditional biblical criticism" in the style of the sixteenth century, by which "*A Mirror for Magistrates* … becomes a kind of *Mirror for Israelites*." The prophetic mirror is thought to reflect its world—"a society that is singularly mouldering, rotten and out of joint" (ibid.)—just as the sapiential mirror faithfully reflects its society in all the details of its rampant misogyny.

by repeated vocabulary and associations. "Remember" in colon 15a recalls "remember" and "forget" in v. 12, but shifts the object of memory to "the works of God" in creating the world.[107] These "works" would include God's activity as the matchmaker who arranges Adam's union with Eve, a union that functions in the Book of Ben Sira as the prototype for a major *gender*-related theme—the "gaining" of an appropriate wife by a man who "fears God" (BBS 26:3 and 36:24).[108] Colon 15b has several elements that can allude to *slander*. The verb שנן that means "to teach incisively" provides the word שְׁנִינָה, "a sharp word, taunt,"[109] and is related to שנה "to repeat." A paraphrased translation— "this I have seen, and I will repeat"—is, itself, a description of slander, but here the "repeating" is a righteous act.

To resume the evaluation of BBS 42:9–14 as a final comment on the doubleness of *shame*—the interpretation of this poetic unit as the embodiment of such a concept is based on the immediately-preceding passages that explicitly develop the concept of two kinds of shame, an honorable shame and another that is dishonorable. For BBS 42:9–14, the double nature of *shame* materializes through contrasts between innocent and guilty behaviors by the daughter, in the list of the father's worries about misfortunes that could involve her (vv. 9 and 10). These options are fairly consistent in the Hebrew texts and, though their sequence varies, they do resolve into a subset of misfortunes in which the daughter is blameless and ones in which she is guilty of causing the misfortune. Thus, when "shame" appears in v. 11cd, the two possible outcomes have already been prepared.

The focus of all the passages on *shame* is the formation of a Jewish-male mindset that can judge behaviors according to Ben Sira's interpretation of Torah. The daughter is presented not so much as a treatise on female-shame, but more as an ultimate 'test case' in reaching Torah-approved judgments. By my interpretation/translation of the passage (chart 4-16), slander against an *innocent* daughter would be another example for which the man "should not feel shame" (BBS 42:1e–8). If "slander concerning a daughter" in 11a includes all six of the father's worries in vv. 9 and 10, then the daughter could be slandered whether or not her behavior is at fault. In that case, "any taunt" in colon 14b includes both categories—taunts against daughter-as-wrongdoer and those against daughter-as-victim. I interpret colon 14b to mean that the *innocent* daughter, who is "afraid-before-God," is approved by Ben Sira even

---

107 Colon 15c notes that God made His works באמר \ באומר "by (means of) speech," or "speaking," a clear reference to Genesis 1, where God speaks and creation occurs.

108 See chapter 5, "Human Female, Biblical Females," for a discussion of Eve.

109 See *DCH* 8:514a "שְׁנִינָה" and 514b "שנן I 'sharpen' Pi. 2. 'teach incisively' (unless שנן II 'repeat') Si 42:15 (Bᵐ, M)"; MS B has "recount."

if she is slandered, since she is judged to be "better than any taunt."[110] Such an opinion would contradict Hellenistic honor/shame models that consider a woman's guardian to be shamed by slander against her even when she is innocent, because her reputation affects her guardian's reputation.

In the Book of Ben Sira, the topic of *shame* moves from units BBS 41:15c–42:1d and 42:1e–8 into the *gender* unit, BBS 42:9–14, where it is completed along with the topic of *speech*, discussed in terms of *slander*. The final transition—to the cosmic unit, BBS 42:15–25 and 43:1–33—shifts from the sharp taunts of *slander* to the sharply incisive teachings of Ben Sira, forming a reasoned sequence of transitions between overlapping themes, rather than abrupt shifts or contrasts. The complexities I propose for BBS 42:9–14 are fitting for a passage that stands at such a prominent position in the sequence of discourses in the Book of Ben Sira. The poetic unit BBS 42:9–14 completes and encapsulates the discourse of *shame* as it intersects with that of *gender*, but, if the figure of Wisdom shares semantic elements with female humans, then the discourse of *gender* is complete only with the close of the acrostic poem to Wisdom (BBS 51:13–30) that closes the book.[111]

How do I evaluate these analyses of BBS 42:9–14? For the translation, I think the number of coherently-multivalent words means it is *probable* that this is a site of elaborate wordplay, and some sort of semantic split based on "daughter" and "slander" is *possible*. In summary, the translation of BBS 42:9–14 and its interpretations have explanatory power and offer a solid alternative to a literal reading of the passage.

---

110 In BBS 42:11d, והובישתך is translated as "*may/might/could* cause you shame" if slander is the subject, because the daughter may be innocent; it is translated "*will* cause you shame" if the daughter is the subject, because she is guilty in that scenario.

111 See chart 5-13 in chapter 5 for elements shared by Wisdom and the human wife.

Chapter 5
Human Female, Biblical Females

In addition to the long passage in BBS 44–49 that recounts Israel's history through the naming of a set of male characters from the Hebrew Bible, the Book of Ben Sira has other references to biblical stories and characters. None of these scattered references are in the form of explicit citations. The clearest examples are those that name a character, but often the references operate by means of allusions based on rare and evocative vocabulary.

5.1 Citation by Allusion: Genesis 1–4 in BBS

Though scholars have identified phrases in the Book of Ben Sira as allusions to most books that became part of the Masoretic canon, in this portion of the study I am only concerned with possible connections to two of these books: Genesis (chapters 1–4) and the Song of Songs. Allusions to Genesis are presented first because they are clearer and more developed than those to the Song of Songs. Not that the allusions to Genesis are always explicit—as Gilbert comments, "at times Ben Sira made incidental use of an expression from Genesis 1–11 without necessarily and clearly referring to its original context."[1] Yet, such minor imprecision does not interfere with Wright's assessment that "it is virtually impossible to escape the conclusion that Ben Sira knew some form of the accounts" in the first chapters of Genesis. [2] I amplify such speculations and extend their range in the direction of *gender*. A number of passages in the Book of Ben Sira refer to the first chapters of Genesis by speaking of God's acts of creation, a topic popular with many writers of that era. Chart 5-1, below, shows the poetic unit BBS 15:11–20, which has a clear reference to the creation-theme in v. 14.

---

1   Gilbert, "Ben Sira, Reader of Genesis 1–11," 90.
2   Wright, "Biblical Interpretation," 378.

Chart 5-1: "Do not say 'my transgression'" BBS 15:11–20 (MSS A, B)

15:11	Do not say "My transgression is from God" —for that which He hates, you shall not do. Do not say "What have I committed? —for that which He hates, I would not do."
15:12	Lest you will say "He, Himself, caused me to stumble" —for He has no delight in violent men.
15:13	YYY hates evil and abomination —and He will not allow it to happen to those who fear Him.
15:14	He—from the beginning—created a human —and He gave to him the power of his inclination.
15:15	If you choose, you shall keep commandment(s) —and Understanding is to do His will.
15:16	Before you are displayed water and fire —whichever you shall choose, reach out your hand.
15:17	Before a human, life and death —that which he shall choose will be given to him. For abundant is the wisdom of YYY —God-in-power, and beholding all.
15:18	Overflowing is the wisdom of YYY —firm of powers, and perceiving everything.
15:19	The eyes of God see His works —and He, Himself, will find out every action of humankind.
15:20	He did not command humankind to sin —and He did not teach lies to false men. And He does not have mercy upon those who make falsehood —and upon those who reveal a secret.

In BBS 15:11–20, the author combines a reference to the creation of the human in Gen 1:27 with יצר from Gen 6:5 and 8:21 (colon 14b) and the binary choices between Fire/Water and Life/Death from Deut 30:15–20 (vv. 16, 17). Ben Sira achieves a "transformation of meaning" through these juxtapositions. By shifting the "inclination" from the Flood story to creation itself, he disassociates its negative meaning so that "the יצר as a neutral capacity is the ability with which God endows all since the creation."[3] In other words, there

---

3   Levison, "Portraits of Adam," 35. Gilbert ("God, Sin and Mercy," 120) agrees that יצר is neutral in this case, meaning "simply 'inclination' or 'deliberation.'" Aitken ("Divine Will and Providence," 289) comments that "it is clear that the presence of the verb יצר "to

is no post-creation lapse into a 'sinful' state. Though humans are inclined to certain behaviors, Ben Sira "vigorously affirms free will. There is no place here for a theory of original sin."[4]

The first sustained treatment of the theme of *creation* in Genesis is Sir 17:1–8 (not extant in Hebrew), shown in chart 5-2, below. The right-hand column in the chart gives the verses in Genesis to which each colon of Sirach could allude—in a case such as this, with so many possible allusions clustered together, I presume that most would be in the Hebrew text and that Ben Sira intended at least some of the phrases as allusions.[5]

Chart 5-2: "The Lord created a human being" Sir 17:1–8 (NETS)

17:1	The Lord created a human being out of earth,	← Gen 2:7
	and he returned him into it again.	← Gen 3:19
17:2	He gave them days in number and a fixed time,	—
	and he gave them authority over the things upon it.	← Gen 1:26,28
17:3	He clothed them in a strength like himself,	← Gen 3:21
	and in his image he made them.	← Gen 1:26–28
17:4	He placed the fear of him upon all flesh,	← Gen 9:2
[17:5]	even to have dominion over beasts and birds.	← Gen 1:26, 28
17:6	Deliberation and a tongue and eyes,	—
	ears and a heart for thinking he gave them.	—
17:7	With knowledge of understanding he filled them,	← Gen 3:6
	and good things and bad he showed to them.	← Gen 3
	(ἀγαθὰ καὶ κακὰ ὑπέδειξεν αὐτοῖς)	
17:8	He put the fear of him upon their hearts,	—
	to show them the majesty of his works. (δεῖξαι)	—

---

fashion" in Genesis (2:7, 8 19) instigated the belief that the inclination (first mentioned in Genesis 6:5) was instilled in mankind during creation." Perdue (*Wisdom Literature*, 240, 398 n. 117) notes the significance of the יצר in rabbinic literature.

BBS 15:14b ויתנהו ביד יצרו can be translated by my choice ("He gave to him the power of his inclination"), to emphasize the statements in vv. 15–17 that the power of choice is with the human, or translated to emphasize that "from the moment of his origin, man was 'given' over to the power of his yetser" (Gilbert, "God, Sin and Mercy," 119–120).

4 Collins, "Before the Fall," 299.

5 See Perdue (*Wisdom Literature*, 238–40) and others for comments on the allusions. All talk of "allusions" presumes, of course, that the author of BBS had a Hebrew version of Genesis that was close to our MT text. The Greek text can only show that the translator saw allusions in the Hebrew. Because this passage is not gender-focal, I did not check the vocabulary against the LXX of Genesis.

If the Hebrew of BBS 17:7 matches the Greek translation, then the conjunction of "good and evil" with "knowledge," as gifts given by God, would disassociate both Eve and Adam from blame for disobedience to God. Kugel comments that "Adam had always been intended for mortality, his very creation from the earth embodying his intended end after the 'numbered days and time.'"[6]

BBS 33:10, though damaged, is another clear reference to Genesis 2: "and from dust Adam/a human was formed" (: לי חמר: ומן עפר נוצר אדם[8]). This verse is part of a poetic unit whose closing bicola introduce Ben Sira's taxonomic "principle of the bipolar division of reality."[7] BBS 11:14a-h, below, has some of the binaries.[8]

> Good things and bad, life and death, poverty and wealth—it is from YYY.
> Wisdom and intelligence, and understanding a word—it is from YYY.
> Sin and straight paths—it is from YYY.
> Confusion and [?] is formed for transgressors
> —and [for] those-doing-bad-actions, badness, with them.[9]

The *taxonomy of pairs* is a foundation for Ben Sira's view of the importance of having appropriate partners in all choice-based human associations. In particular, references to marriage (which can include allusions to Eve) are orchestrated through this theme of *appropriate partners*. The passage BBS 13:14–20, below, opens with a general expression of the theme as it applies to all creatures (vv. 14, 15). Verse 17 moves into the non-gender-focal topic of the oppression of the poor by the wealthy. The poetic unit continues through 13:23 or 24, giving specific examples of the mistreatment of the poor by the rich and specific instances of the social ratification of these unjust practices. Each verse of BBS 13:17–19 juxtaposes antagonistic types of animals, then decodes the animal types as an indictment of social injustice.[10] The

---

6 Kugel, *Traditions*, 127. Perdue (*Wisdom Literature*, 239) notes that "[u]nlike the negative implications of 'knowledge of good and evil'" in Genesis, for Ben Sira, "wisdom is freely given and does not bear the onus of rebellion against divine rule."

7 Perdue, *Wisdom and Creation*, 274.

8 See also chart 1-2 (BBS 33:14–15; 42:24–25), in chapter 1.

9 The Hebrew of colon 14h can also be read "and [for] companions, companionship with them" (ומרעים רעה עמם), since the preceding bicola combines a negative value ("sin") and a positive ("straight paths") in the first colon. The readings are not mutually exclusive.

10 Calduch-Benages ("Animal Imagery," 64) notes that all "the ferocious animals are identified with the rich man" and "much weaker and peaceful animals" with the poor man. Corley ("Friendship," 68) comments that Ben Sira suggests "true friendship between rich and poor is impossible to achieve; the rich become predators, while the poor remain victims."

"exploitation ... is chillingly captured" in colon 19b,[11] where the poor are a renewable "pasture" for the rich, who 'graze' at will like cattle in a pasture, leaving the poor just enough to sustain themselves and perpetuate the cycle. This passage is an especially strong argument for Ben Sira's personal experience of poverty, most likely in his early life.[12]

Chart 5-3: "Each creature loves its kind" BBS 13:14–20 (MS A)

13:14 Each creature loves **its kind**
    —and every **human**, his **likeness**.

13:15 Each creature's **kind** is beside it
    —and with **his kind** a human will be allied.

13:17 How can a wolf be allied with a lamb? [מה יחובר זאב אל כבש]
    thus a wicked-man, with a righteous-man
    —and thus a rich-man, with a man who is deprived.

13:18 How is there peace, of a hyena to a dog? [מאיש שלום צבוע אל כלב]
    —whence is peace, of a rich-man to a beggar? [מאין שלום עשיר אל רש :]

13:19 Asses of the wilderness are food for lions [מאכל ארי פראי מדבר]
    —thus the poor are the pasture of the rich. [כן מרעית עשיר דלים :]

13:20 Humility is an abomination to the proud
    —and poverty, an abomination to the rich.

NOTE: - Reading מאיש in 13:18a as מה יש ("how is there"). Alternative: מאיש as מאין in 18b; see *DCH* 1:220 " מַאַיִן in nom. cl., 'whence is?' ... 'peace' Sir 13:18."

Repeated use of the word מין, "kind (species)," can allude to Genesis 1 as the prototype for the notion of appropriate groupings. Gen 1:20–25 recounts how God creates living beings "in their kinds" and v. 26 states God's intention to create "the human ... as Our likeness." Gen 5:3 adds that Adam "begot [a son] in his likeness." The combination of מין and אדם and דומה, "kind" and "human" and "likeness," forms a substantial link with the first chapters of Genesis. The investigation of Eve begins, now, with the analysis of an alleged allusion for which the Hebrew text does *not* match Genesis.

---

11   Gregory, *Like an Everlasting Signet Ring*, 70.
12   Reiterer, "Review of Recent Research," 63.

5.2 Eve and the "Woman" in BBS 25:24

Two verses in the extant Hebrew of the Book of Ben Sira are commonly cited in discussions of Ben Sira's 'negative attitude toward women.' Poetic units for both verses have appeared in previous chapters—BBS 42:9–14 in chart 4-16 (colon 14a is "Better the evil of a man than the goodness of a woman"), and BBS 25:13–26:3 in charts 2-11 and 2-12. The analysis of BBS 25:24 occurs here because it is part of the investigation of the role of Eve in the Book of Ben Sira, and both the Hebrew and the Greek versions are part of the discussion.

BBS מאשה תחלת עון ובגללה גוענו יחד
    From a woman is the start of iniquity/guilt
    —and because of her, we waste away, all alike.

Sirach ἀπὸ γυναικὸς ἀρχὴ ἁμαρτίας, καὶ δι'αὐτὴν ἀποθνῄσκομεν πάντες.
    From a woman is the beginning of sin—and because of her we all die.

The female figure in Sir 25:24 is Eve, according to Saint Augustine, who used this Greek bicola as one of two prooftexts for the existence of a concept in Jewish writings that would be analogous to his formulation of "original sin."[13] Yet, the link between Eve and the origin of mortality is a tenuous one in BBS/Sirach, given verses such as BBS 40:4, which implies that humans were never intended for immortality because death "is the portion for all flesh, from God."[14] On the basis of contextual analyses of the Greek and Hebrew texts, several modern scholars have contested the identification of Eve as the female figure in Sir 25:24. The major dissenter is Levison, who states that "Sirach

---

13   The other text is Psalm 51:7 (JPS numbering). In *Contra Iulianum*, Augustine combines Sirach/Ecc 25:24 (and 22:13, about fools) with 40:1—"Hard work is created for every human and a heavy yoke on the sons of Adam, from the day of coming forth from a mother's womb till the day of returning to the mother of all" (*Against Julian*, 113 and 389)—to constitute the concept of *original sin*, posited as an inherited result of Eve's sin of disobedience that taints every person, but is nullified by baptism. Jesus' mother Mary becomes a counter-analogy to Eve as part of the reversal signified by baptism.

14   Collins, "Before the Fall," 296–97, citing Kugel (*Traditions of the Bible*, 127, that "Adam had always been intended for mortality"); Collins mentions Sir 17:1–2 (not extant in Hebrew) with BBS 41:4 (extant in MSS B and M). MS B has חלק כל בשר מאל and MS M has [7] זה קץ כל בשר. Wright ("Biblical Interpretation," 379) comments that, "[f]or Ben Sira, ... death was part of God's divine intention all along, whether humans obeyed or not." Levison ("Is Eve to Blame?," 618) declares that "the attribution of death to Eve conflicts with Ben Sira's view of the origin of death" because mortality was part of God's plan for all creatures "since the beginning," citing Sir 14:16; 16:26–17:10 and 41:3b, 4a.

25:24 refers not to Eve but to the evil wife."[15] Those who are more cautious comment on the verse as a special case within the allusions to the early chapters of Genesis. For example, Collins mentions that "Sirach 25:24 ... is anomalous in the context of Ben Sira. The viewpoint it expresses becomes standard in later tradition. ... In light of this tradition, most scholars assume that Ben Sira is referring to Eve in Sirach 25:24."[16]

Scholars have assumed, also, that the identification of the "woman" as Eve would apply to the source text, the Book of Ben Sira. However, though the language of Sir 25:24 fits that for Eve in the LXX, the vocabulary of BBS 25:24 does not match the language for Eve in the MT. Neither עָוֹן, "iniquity," nor גּוע, "waste away," can allude to Eve through the language of Genesis.[17] Therefore, the two texts BBS 25:24 and Sir 25:24 do not have the same capacity to generate allusions to Eve.

Eve cannot be the target of the allusion in BBS 25:24, but the question of identity remains—what other figure could be the "woman"? The verse is part of the poetic unit that features the Wrong Wife and Right Wife (BBS 25:13–26:3). The suggestion that the "woman" is the "evil wife" (Wrong Wife) works at a contextual level,[18] but 25:24 targets an iconic figure who is part of a culturally-recognizable story of the origin of sickness and/or death. On the basis of strong parallels between Hesiod's language for Pandora and Ben Sira's for the Wrong Wife,[19] I conjecture that the "woman" in BBS 25:24

---

15 Levison, "Is Eve to Blame?," 622. Gilbert ("Ben Sira et la femme," 434, n. 23), quotes the Hebrew text, BBS 25:24, "par la femme, le commencement de la faute et à cause d'elle nous périssons tout uniment," a translation that seems to follow the nuances of "iniquity" (rather than "sin") by rendering עָוֹן as "la faute" rather than "le pêche" and the nuances of "expire" (rather than "die") by rendering גּוע as "périr" rather than "mourir." He links the verse with Gen 3, but comments that the death can be "the death of the home" rather than human mortality: "Il nous semble que le verset doit aussi être interprété à la lumiere de son contexte: quand le mal vient de l'épouse, c'est la mort du foyer!" (ibid., 435, n. 23).

16 Collins, "Before the Fall," 297. Kvam, et al. (*Eve and Adam*, 49; BBS/Sirach from *NRSV*), note that 25:16–26 "makes a causal connection between woman, sin, and death. Whether or not the 'woman' to which the author refers is Eve, or the 'evil wife' of the surrounding verses, or even the 'daughters of men' of Genesis 6:1-4, however, is not clear."

17 A complete analysis of BBS 25:24 is given in section A.1.2 of the Appendix.

18 Levison ("Is Eve to Blame?," 618) states that if verse 25:24 refers to Eve then it "interrupts its immediate context, which deals with the drastic effects the evil wife produces in her husband." Balla (*Ben Sira on Family*, 94), with reference to Levison, states that it is "conceivable that this verse is practical advice from one husband, who had much to do with wicked wives in his life, to other husbands or unmarried young men."

19 Both Hesiod and Ben Sira contrast a good wife with a bad wife, but Hesiod's "good wife" is only a half-benefit. Hesiod states that a man who "takes a good wife suited to his mind, evil continually contends with good; [610] for whoever obtains the baneful kind, lives always

could be the Greek figure Pandora, and that a conflation of Eve with Pandora may have affected the Greek translation, in Sirach.[20]

Because the elements of Eve's stories so easily conflate with those of Pandora, that character is also part of the investigation of Eve's role in the Book of Ben Sira. As demonstrated in a previous chapter, Pandora figures in a Greek gender-taxonomy that differs from the model underlying the Book of Ben Sira and, in the classical Greek discourse of *gender*, she stands in metonymic relation to the category of "woman."[21] In her Hesiodic incarnations, Pandora (dis)embodies *female* in the Greek phallogocentric taxonomy, as pure *absence* in contrast to male *presence*. Though the biblical figure Eve has a similarly metonymic status as "woman," her story has different semantic repercussions. Chart 5-4a, below, shows my arrangement of similar elements, and whether the female figure is viewed as positive (+) or negative (-).

Chart 5-4a: Parallel elements in the stories of Eve and Pandora

	HEBREW BIBLE'S EVE	?	?	HESIOD'S PANDORA
MALE EXISTS ALONE, NO FEMALE	In Gen 2, man is alone. God says "Not-good for the human to be alone."	+	−	Race of men live alone, pleasantly, until Pandora is first of "the race of women."
WOMAN IS CRAFTED BY GOD(S)	God "builds" a woman from side of the (hu)man, whom God had formed from earth.	+	−	Gods/goddesses contribute to the creation and adornment of Pandora, the "beautiful evil," give her attributes like "deceit."
WOMAN IS CRAFTED FOR A CERTAIN MAN	"Not good" that human is alone; then search for a companion; then God builds the woman.	+	−	Previous story of Prometheus tricking Zeus—Pandora is Zeus's revenge, being made for P's brother, Epimetheus.

---

with unceasing grief in his spirit and heart within him; and this evil cannot be healed" (Hesiod *Theog.* 607–612). In contrast, Ben Sira's Right Wife has no such admixture in which "evil continually contends with good." Each schematic wife-figure in the Book of Ben Sira is purely a single value.

20 For a full treatment of BBS/Sir 25:24, including the proposal of Pandora as the female figure in Sir 25:24, see Ellis, "Is Eve the 'Woman' in Sir 25:24?" For other comparisons between Eve and Pandora, see Bremmer, "Pandora or the Creation of a Greek Eve"; Headlam, "Prometheus, and the Garden of Eden"; Kübel, "Eva, Pandora und Enkidus 'Dirne'"; Lachs, "The Pandora-Eve Motif in Rabbinic Literature"; Phipps, "Eve and Pandora Contrasted"; Schmitt and Vernant, *Eve et Pandora*); Séchan, "Pandora, l'Ève grecque"; and Türck, *Pandora und Eva.*

21 For the full discussion of Hesiod's Pandora, see section 1.4.2 of chapter 1. See also section 5.2 in chapter 5.

GOD BRINGS WOMAN TO MAN	God brings the woman to the man; he 'recognizes' her with a joyful poem.	+	–	Hermes leads Pandora to Epimetheus, who foolishly accepts her.
WOMAN'S ACT CAUSES HUMANS TO SUFFER IN FUTURE	Both man and woman eat the fruit, but woman is first. Both she and he will have harder lives, as will future humans.	–	–	Pandora opens the container she brought from Olympus and releases all the miseries of mortals: sickness, old age, etc. Only men will suffer.

Given the extreme parallelism of story-elements in chart 5-4a, the surprising result from chart 5-4b is that the discursive purposes for that set of elements are absolute opposites.

Chart 5-4b: Opposed elements in the stories of Eve and Pandora

	HEBREW BIBLE'S EVE	?	?	HESIOD'S PANDORA
WHY WOMAN IS MADE	Woman created as "opposite balance" for man.	+	–	Woman is created as a punishment for humans/men.
WOMAN AS ACTANT	Woman speaks and thinks; desires to be wise (Gen 3:6).	+	–	Woman is hard-wired to lie and deceive—has "shameless mind."
WOMAN'S DESIRABLE QUALITIES	At first sight, the man says "this one, now, bone of my bone and flesh of my flesh." He recognizes the woman herself.	+	–	At first sight, gods and humans are stunned by the wealth of ornaments that cover the (absent) woman like a cocoon.
EVALUATION OF THE PARTNERSHIP	"Two shall become as one flesh," though women and men both get hard "labor."	+	–	Women are "drones," parasites who consume men's goods and contribute nothing.

Pandora clearly figures *absence* and complete difference-from male humans, while Eve—acknowledged as an intimate relation by the male human—is portrayed thinking and speaking. Eve's value is positive, and Pandora's is negative. The extreme parallelism of the elements I have chosen from the two stories make Eve and Pandora interchangeable at the level of narrative, allowing the negative associations of Pandora to be mapped onto Eve with the result that the two become semantically equivalent.

Verse 25:24 is the last line of a poetic unit in the genre of *blame*, on the effects of the Wrong Wife on a Sage-husband.[22] The verse about the Right Wife's effect on a Sage-husband, which immediately follows 25:24, begins the contrasting genre of *praise*. In BBS 25:13–26:3, the Wrong Wife and Right Wife are well-matched opposites. A trope of *debilitation* connects the two passages—the Wrong Wife causes the husband to "waste away" and the Right Wife "fattens" him. [23] Since the two wife-figures are a balanced pair, the Wrong Wife's prototype from outside BBS should be balanced by a prototype for the Right Wife, sharing the same tropes. The passage below names, explicitly, the Right Wife's prototype: she is the "valorous wife" from Prov. 31:10.[24] Ben Sira's precise allusion to the "valorous wife" reproduces the classic Hebrew phrase of Proverbs 31:10: אשת חיל and אֵשֶׁת־חַיִל. The Greek of Sirach, likewise, matches the LXX of Proverbs: γυνὴ ἀνδρεία and γυναῖκα ἀνδρεῖαν.[25]

Chart 5-5: Hebrew and Greek versions of BBS/Sir 26:1–3 (MS C)

BOOK OF BEN SIRA (MS C)	26:#	SIRACH (NETS)
A good wife—happy is her husband —and number of his days, doubled.	1	Happy is the husband of a good wife, and doubled is the number of his days.
A valorous wife fattens her husband —and [his] years ... she will rejoice.	2	A courageous wife gladdens her husband, and he will fulfill his years in peace.
A good wife is a good gift (מנה)— and may she be given in the portion (חלק) of one-fearing-YYY.	3	A good wife is a good portion (μερίς), she will be given as a portion (μερίς) to the one who fears the Lord.

22 The discussion of genres occurs in section 2.2.1 of chapter 2, and the full poetic unit for BBS 25:24 is given in chart 2-11 (BBS 25:13–26:3), in section 2.4.

23 Camp ("Understanding," 24) objects to the usual English translations as reflections of the romantic views of current Western society rather than the social realities of Ben Sira's time. For example, she states that the translation of 26:1a as "A good wife – happy is her husband" obscures the public context of male status, and that a better translation of אשרי, μακάριος than "happy" is "'congratulations to her husband!' ... The point is not that he feels internally happy but that he has attained an honor worthy of societal notice" (ibid.).

24 See McCreesh ("Wisdom as Wife") for a detailed analysis of the relation between Wisdom and the "valorous wife" in Proverbs. Corley ("Intertextual Study," 170) calls the acrostic poem in Prov. 10-31 "the classic portrayal of the 'capable wife' or 'woman of worth.'" The other two instances of אשת חיל in the Tanakh are in Prov. 12:4, "A 'valorous wife' is the crown of her husband—and like rot in his bones, a deceiving/ shameful one," and Ruth 3:11, "...every 'gate' of my people knows that you are a 'valorous wife.'"

25 Corley ("Intertextual Study," 170) translates the Greek literally, as "manly wife," though he translates the Hebrew as the less-heroic "capable wife."

The stories of Eve and Pandora are similar enough to posit some form of semantic overlap, whether from a widespread multicultural motif that includes the story-elements shown in chart 5-4a, or from the oral transmission of particular texts—Hesiod's stories—that became emblematic within a culture that later established itself as the hegemonic center of a colonial system. With regard to Ben Sira's colonial status, his decision to write in Hebrew is a significant act in itself because the inherent ambiguity of the unvowelled language allows a full range of ideological tinkering with the text.

My suggestion of Pandora as the "woman" in BBS 25:24 is purely conjectural—presented here because the context of the verse demands an identifiable figure—but an identification of the "woman" as a Greek cultural icon introduces the possibility of cross-cultural commentary. The passage about wives in BBS 25 and 26 can be read as an example of the discursive deployment of sentiment evocation, in a colonial context, "to evoke the specific sentiments out of which social borders are constructed."[26] If Pandora can be the figure alluded to in BBS 25:24 as a prototype for the Wrong Wife, and the "valorous wife" in 26:2 for the Right Wife, then an opposition is created between a Greek figure and a Hebrew figure, opening the possibility of a cryptic commentary. By adopting the allegorical practice of using female figures as emblems of nations or institutions, Ben Sira could embody "their tradition" and "our tradition" through the use of Pandora and the "valorous wife."[27] An entailment to this semantic device would be that the "husband"—the Jewish male toward whom the discourse is directed—will flourish if he chooses the Right Wife/Judaism and languish if he chooses the Wrong Wife/Hellenism. The conjectural digression closes, now, and the discussion of Eve resumes.

5.3 The "Intelligent Wife" and Eve

In the time of Ben Sira, the early chapters of Genesis were a fruitful source of metaphysical speculation and the inspiration for numerous written compositions. The location of the texts as the beginning of the Torah and their function as stories of 'beginnings' give them a prominent role in "the formation of religious ideals."[28] The current study focuses on "religious ideals" that relate

---

26 Lincoln, *Discourse*, 9.

27 The labels "Hellenism" and "Judaism" are implied, though anachronistic.

28 Collins, "Marriage, Divorce, and Family," 127. Collins notes that the stories of Genesis 2–3 were "conducive to an ideal of monogamy" though the effect was "on the formation of religious ideals, if not always on practice."

to *gender*, specifically to Ben Sira's discourse(s) about marriage, because there is a long history of interpretation that codifies the union of Adam and Eve as a divinely-mandated model of *marriage*. The presence of this model in the Book of Ben Sira is another argument against the character Eve as "the woman" in BBS 25:24, since she is fully-constituted here—though by indirect means—as a positive model, and is thus unavailable for a negative allusion. Any allusions that link Genesis 1–4 with a "wife/woman" apply to the figure labeled as the "intelligent wife."

5.3.1 Third Set of Paired Poetic Units, Part 1: Female

Chart 5-6, below, shows BBS 36:18–26, the female-portion of the third and last set of paired poetic units. It is also the passage in which I identify the most allusions to Eve, though the label "intelligent" is not used for the "wife." The notes at the end of the chart list particular allusions.

Chart 5-6: "Any food the throat eats" BBS 36:18–26 (MSS B, C, D)

36:18	Any **food**, the throat eats —but there is 'eating' that will be more delightful than food. [?] —but there is a beautiful wife/woman.
36:19	The palate examines flavors of a thing —and the heart understands 'flavors' of a lie.
36:20	A deceived heart will give **pain** —and a faithful man will restore it for himself.
36:21	Any wind-fall, **wildlife** will eat —but there is a 'blow' that will be more delightful than a blow.
36:22	Form of a **wife** and face causing-light —and upon all that **greatly-delights** the eye, (heart) will grow strong.
36:23	And further, if she has healing speech —**her man** is not among the sons-of-**Adam**.
36:24	**Gaining** a wife is the **beginning of gain** —**help**, and citadel, and pillar of support.
36:25	Without a wall, an orchard will be burned —and without a wife, **weak and wandering**.
36:26	Who will trust an army's marauder —leaping about from city to city?
	Thus is a man who has no 'nest' —settling where he will be-at-nightfall.

Possible parallels with Gen 1–4 (for details, see chart A5-6 in the Appendix):
- BBS 36:18a ‖ Gen 3:6, eating the fruit.
- BBS 36:20a ‖ Gen 3:16,17, עִצָּבוֹן as "pain, toil."
- BBS 36:21a ‖ Gen 3:1, חיה "wildlife/a wild beast" as an allusion to the serpent, חַיַּת הַשָּׂדֶה.
- BBS 36:22b ‖ Gen 2:9, where the trees are **delightful to the eye.**
- BBS 36:23 ‖ Gen 3:6, the dagesh in the ה of אשה, "her man," reproduces the pointing in Gen 3:6, where Eve ate the fruit and "gave it to **her man** with her, and he ate." Ben Sira makes no reference to "sin" or "death."
- BBS 36:24a ‖ Gen 4:1, קנה ("gaining") used by Eve to explain Cain's name. Ben Sira's words קנה אשה are very similar to Eve's קניתי איש "I have gained a man/husband."
- BBS 36:24a ‖ Gen 1:1, the word ראשית in first verse of Genesis.
- For 36:24b ‖ Gen 2:18, 20, עזר "a help;" Adam's future companion is described as עזר כנגדו "a help as his opposite."
- BBS 36: 25 ‖ Gen 4:12,14, נע ונד "weak [trembling] and wandering" occurs only these two times in the Hebrew Bible: God's cursing of Cain and Cain's reiteration of the curse.

For my reading of the passage, the shift in topic to the "wife" in v. 22 is made through colon 21b, in which the "'blow' that is more pleasant than a blow" is the equivalent of a *coup de foudre* (love at first sight, literally "a blow/bolt of lightning")—though in this case it would be the sudden sight of one's beloved spouse—which "greatly-delights the eye" and causes the heart "to grow strong."

Though the "intelligent wife" is not named in this poetic unit, I interpret the unit together with BBS 40:18–27 (chart 5-9), which names her and alludes to Eve. Any single parallel between BBS 36:18–26 and Gen 2 to 4 can be a coincidence, but the aggregate effect demonstrated in chart 5-6 cannot be dismissed as random similarities: there are eleven strong parallels in the twenty cola.[29] As Zakovitch notes, shared expressions "which are not otherwise common in the Bible" are an example of "firm evidence" for "a relation between the two narratives."[30] I suggest that Ben Sira has combined elements of several Genesis-stories—the Garden of Eden, the Eating of the Fruit, and

---

29 Gilbert ("Ben Sira, Reader of Genesis 1-11," 90) offers examples, such as עזר alluding to Gen 2:18 (BBS 36:24b) and נע ונד for Gen 4:12, 14 (BBS 36:25b). Collins ("Marriage, Divorce, and Family," 127) mentions Sir 36:24 as an allusion to Gen 2:20. Trenchard (*Ben Sira's View*, 24) notes the allusion to Cain through נע ונד, as do Di Lella (*Wisdom*, 431), Wright (*No Small Difference*, 148), and Balla (*Ben Sira on Family*, 78).

30 Zakovitch, "Through the Looking Glass," 140, with regard to relations between biblical texts, though I consider it applicable to the use of Genesis in BBS.

Cain's Punishment—into one description of marriage that uses the early chapters of Genesis as an ideal. Ignoring the explicit topic of disobedience in Genesis 3, Ben Sira uses the distinctive word אשה ("her husband") from Gen 3:6 to craft a joyful image of marriage.[31] Similarly, ignoring the Cain story's aspects of murder, guilt, and punishment, he appropriates distinctive vocabulary from that story to build an image of men living lawless and aimless lives, like Cain, unless they are married.[32]

The Greek text of Sirach is a close match for the Hebrew of BBS 36:18–26 for all verses except v. 21, which is wildly divergent, and v. 24, which is precisely parallel. Verse 21 in Sirach declares that "A woman will accept any male, but there exists a daughter better than a daughter." Sirach 36:24 states that "He who **acquires** a wife makes a **beginning** of a **possession**—a **helper corresponding to him** and a pillar of rest," reproducing the Greek versions of words from the LXX of Genesis as the Hebrew reproduces the MT.[33]

5.3.2 Third Set of Paired Poetic Units, Part 2: Male

The passage BBS 36:18–26 is the female portion of the last pair that I identify as matched female and male poetic units. The first pair (BBS 9:1–9 and 10–16) and second pair (Sir 23:16–27) are sequential, but the male portion of this last pair has two possible sites. The adjacent unit seems like a perfect match because the subject is the male friend, making the same combination of wife/ friend as that in chapter 9, and both units have a structural pattern of two bicola in which the first colon of each begins with כל ("all/every") and the second with אך ("but").[34] However, the discussion of the male friend, which begins in terms of friends who betray their friendships, wanders over eighteen bicola and loses energy as it expands, making it a poor semantic partner for the wife-poem, which is entirely positive about the female character and maintains that tone through ten (or eleven) succinct bicola. My choice for the male-

---

31   The phrase in BBS 36:23a that I translate as "if she has healing speech" (literally, "healing-of-tongue") seems related to other statements about "the tongue"—that it can wound, and has power over life and death, good and evil. The recommendations for control of one's "tongue" apply to both women and men.

32   The lack of a Fall and Fratricide in Ben Sira's view of Genesis places him outside Derrida's category of "Western metaphysics" that refers to "all texts based on the idea of a pure first term (such as 'goodness' or 'purity') and a secondary derivation or corruption (such as 'impurity' or 'evil')" (Sherwood, *Prostitute and the Prophet*, 252). This is a fine example of how two taxonomies with the same binary elements (good/evil) may deploy them differently.

33   Vocabulary is: LXX Gen 4:1 (κτάομαι); 1:1 (ἀρχῇ / ἐνάρχομαι); and 2:18,20 (βοηθός).

34   The "all X … but Y" verses are BBS 36:18,21; 37:1,7.

poem to match BBS 36:18–26 is the passage that follows the friend-unit. This poetic unit, BBS 37:16–26, concerns different kinds of wise men, or sages, and matches BBS 36:18–26 in its length and in the tight focus of its theme.

Chart 5-7: "The source of every deed" BBS 37:16–26 (MSS B, C, D)

37:16	The source of every deed is a word —before every act is a plan.
37:17	The root of guidance is the heart —four branches spring up:
37:18	Good and evil, death and life —and the sender of them, completely, is the tongue.
37:19	There is a wise-man making many wise —and for his own self, he is foolish.
37:20 *(no 21)*	And there is a wise-man rejected for his words —and from any 'food,' pleasure is withheld.
37:22	And there is a wise-man who is wise for his own self —and the rewards of his knowledge are upon his person.
37:23	And there is a wise-man who will make his people wise —the reward of his knowledge is in their persons.
37:24	A wise-man will have his fill of pleasure for his own self —and all who see him, they will call him happy.
37:25	The life of humankind is a number of days —and the life of Yeshurun, days without number.
37:26	A wise-man of the people will inherit honor —and his name endures in everlasting life.

BBS 36:18–26, the "wife unit," shows two outcomes for males: those with a wife are happy and those without a wife are "weak and wandering." There is no female presence in BBS 37:16–26, but here, also, there are two outcomes for the male figures. In this case, some sages have hard lives through their own fault or through rejection by others, while some sages are successful and/or content whether they labor for themselves only or for the benefit of their "people." Chart 5-8, below, shows the passages together. The opening section of each poetic unit in chart 5-8 mentions "the heart" as the source of a person's understanding. For the middle sections of both units, the eighth bicola reverses the value of the fifth: thus, the heart "growing strong" in 36:22 is countered in v. 25 by "weak and wandering," while "pleasure is withheld" from a sage in 37:20 and in v. 24 a sage has "his fill of pleasure." The semantic trajectory in the sage-poem is from *misfortune* to *fortune*, reversing

the movement in the wife-poem, which went from *fortune* (with wife) to *misfortune* (without wife).

Chart 5-8: BBS 36:18–26 and BBS 37:16–26

THE "INTELLIGENT WIFE" OF SAGE	THE SAGE
36:18 Any *food*, the throat eats—but there is '**eating**' that will be more delightful than food.	37:16 The source of every deed is a word—before every act, a plan.
36:19 The palate examines flavors of a thing—and *the heart* understands 'flavors' of a lie.	37:17 The root of guidance is *the heart*—four branches spring up:
36:20 A deceived heart will give pain —and a faithful man will restore it for himself.	37:18 Good and evil, death and life —and the sender of them, completely, is **the tongue**.
36:21 Any wind-fall, wildlife will eat —but there is a 'blow' that will be more delightful than a blow.	37:19 There is a wise-man making many wise—and for his own self, he is foolish.
36:22 Form of a wife and face causing-light—and upon all that **greatly-delights** the eye, (the heart) will grow strong.	37:20 And there is a wise-man **rejected for his words**—and from any '*food*,' **pleasure** is withheld.
36:23 And further, if she has **a healing tongue**—her man is not among the "sons-of-Adam."	37:22 And there is wise-man who is wise for his own self—and rewards of his knowledge are on his person.
36:24 Gaining a wife is beginning of gain—help, and citadel, and pillar of support.	37:23 And there is a wise-man who will make his people wise—reward of his knowledge is in their persons.
36:25 Without a wall, an orchard will be burned—and without a wife, weak and wandering.	37:24 A wise-man will have his fill of **pleasure** for his own self—and all who see him will call him happy.
36:26 Who will trust an army's marauder—leaping about from city to city?	37:25 The life of humankind is a number of days—and the life of Yeshurun, days without number.
36:26c Thus is a man who has no 'nest'—settling where he will be-at-nightfall.	37:26 A wise-man of the people will inherit honor—and his name endures in everlasting life.

The topic of *speech* is an important link between the two units, in the word לשון, "speech," literally "the tongue" (BBS 36:23 and 37:18). Though there is no explicit reference to a wife in BBS 37:16–26, the previously-mentioned *fortune/misfortune* structure can itself be an implicit reference to the fact that it is the wife as "help, and citadel, and pillar of support" with her "healing speech/tongue" (BBS 36:24, 23) who helps to reverse the misfortune of the wise-man who is "rejected for his words" (BBS 37:20). "Delights" or "pleasures" are another link; BBS 36:18–26 and 37:16–26 use different vocabulary, but the associations are within the same semantic range. The word תענוג ("a pleasure")[35] in BBS 37:20 and 24 can allude to Song 7:7, "How beautiful and how delightful, love, with pleasures" (מַה־יָּפִית וּמַה־נָּעַמְתְּ אַהֲבָה בַּתַּעֲנוּגִים :).[36] The verse from Song of Songs provides a link between יפה ("beautiful") and תנעם ("be delightful") in vv. 18 and 21 of the wife-poem and תענוג ("pleasure") in vv. 20 and 24 of the sage-poem.[37]

The two poetic units shown in chart 5-8 give the most complete treatments of the central pair of non-schematic figures: the sage (whose viewpoint is the only source) and the sage's spouse, whom I designate as the "intelligent wife." Note that the words that build the image of the "intelligent wife"—in every one of the six verses in the center of her poem—echo the vocabulary of the early chapters of Genesis. However, the two poetic units can be read together as a wife-unit and a husband-unit (as above) or as two units about men: unsuccessful men in chapter 36 and successful men in chapter 37. The pivot for assessment is whether the wife in BBS 36:18–26 is equally present with the man—though seen from his viewpoint—or is mentioned only as an accessory, like an amulet that brings him good fortune.

5.4 The "Intelligent Wife" and Wisdom—and Eve

The poetic unit BBS 40:18–27 (chart 5-9, below) connects Wisdom with the "intelligent wife" and Eve indirectly, through allusive language and a progression of references that lead to the fear-of-God, and to Eden. Vocabulary of this unit is shared with Wisdom's poem in BBS 14:20–15:8 (chart 5-13), making a strong link between Wisdom and the "intelligent wife."

---

35 Ben Sira uses תענוג twelve times with a range that includes "luxury" and "delicacies (of food)." According to *DCH* 8:660ab "תענוג," the general meaning is "delight, pleasure" (the word is used five times in the Hebrew Bible, but twelve times in BBS).

36 See *DCH* 1:141a-b " 'love' … as term of address for beloved woman, Ca 7:7." See also Bloch and Bloch (*Song of Songs*, 204), who translate אַהֲבָה as an address to Love as an "abstract concept."

37 Alter ("Afterword" to Bloch and Bloch, *Song of Songs*, 130) states that תענוג is "associated with gratification of the senses." In the poetic unit BBS 37:16–26, "food" can have multiple meanings including visual pleasure and sustenance from love, as well as tasty comestibles.

Chart 5-9: BBS 40:18–27 "A life of abundance" (MSS B, M, Sirach*)*

40:18	A life of abundance and reward is sweet —and more than both, finding treasure.
40:19	Child and city establish a name —and more than both, finding Wisdom.
	Bearing and planting cause a name to blossom —and more than both, a wife who is desired.
40:20	Wine and mead cause a heart to exult —and more than both, she who loves love-making.
40:21	Flute and harp cause a song to blend —and more than both, speech that is clear.
40:22	Grace and beauty cause an eye to delight —and more than both, flowers of the field.
40:23	Friend and companion lead your steps —and more than both, an intelligent wife (אשה משכלת).
40:24	Brother and help reduce distress —and more than both, alms that rescue.
40:25	Gold and silver make a foot steady —and more than both, excellent council.
40:26	Valor and strength uphold a heart —and more than both, the fear-of-God.
	There is no want in the fear-of-YYY —and nothing to seek with it as support.
40:27	The fear-of-God is like an Eden of blessing —and its bridal-canopy is over all glory.

The poetic unit is a verse-by-verse progression. Thus, "**finding** treasure" (colon 18b) is fulfilled by "**finding** Wisdom" (19b) while "establish a **name**" (19a) becomes "cause a **name** to blossom" (19c), which introduces the "wife who is desired," and "loves love-making," and has "a clear tongue/speech" (cola 19d–21). I pause at this point in the sequence to emphasize that the progression[38] constitutes a semantic overlap between the female figure Wisdom

---

38   See Di Lella's comment (*Wisdom*, 472) that "the 'finding a treasure' of 40:18b is to be understood as a parallel to 'finding wisdom' in 40:19b." See also Gregory (*Like an Everlasting Signet Ring*, 30), who notes that "the 'treasure' that is superior to the comfort of wealth is to be understood metaphorically as wisdom." I extend the parallel from w/Wisdom to the wife through the repetition of colon 19a's "name" in 19c.

and the non-schematic "intelligent wife."[39] Furthermore, colon 19a can link this poem with Genesis because "child and city will establish a name" could refer to Cain, who founds a city and names it after his son, Enoch (Gen 4:17), although finding Wisdom perpetuates the sage's "name" better than children.

Together, cola BBS 40:19c and 20b depict a reciprocal relationship of love and sexual desire: colon 19c concerns the man/husband's desire for the woman/wife and 20b, the woman's desire for the man.[40] Colon 21b adds another element to the portrait of the wife: her clear voice or speech, and then colon 22b gives a surprising close to the section about the wife by naming "flowers of the field" as the item that exceeds (her?) "grace and beauty" in causing "an eye to delight." This step can indicate that Ben Sira ranks the "grace and beauty" of his wife-figure as less important than the preceding qualities of lovingness and clear speech, and rounds off the section with what can be either the fruition of the "blossoming" in 40:19 or else an indirect reference to the beauty of the works of God.[41]

The next section, vv. 23–26, concerns the male speaker's 'support system': the human, financial, and spiritual resources available to him. Colon 23b names the "intelligent wife" as the first of these resources; indeed, Ben Sira "asserts the superiority of a wife over all other friends."[42] Financial resources appear in 40:24, but in colon 25a the value of "excellent counsel" exceeds that of "gold and silver," moving the discourse out of material considerations and into the realm of the abstract qualities "valor and strength," which are themselves exceeded by "the fear-of-God." The closing section expands the concept of the fear-of-God/YYY, through which the discourse

---

39   The translation of חכמה with an initial cap as the female figure Wisdom is supported by parallels between Wisdom and the "intelligent wife" that are shown in chart 5-13.

40   Bloch and Bloch (*Song of Songs*, 137) declare that "the plural *dodim* is a comprehensive term for lovemaking, that is, kisses and caresses as well as intercourse. ... The word 'love' in most translations is too general and evasive." Collins ("Marriage, Divorce, and Family," 136) states that the Song of Songs is, without doubt, "a celebration of sexual love (dodim)." See also Diamond ("Nahmanides and Rashi," 209, n. 37) who states that Nachmanides translates עת דודים as "'*at the time of love*,'" meaning "the time at which a woman desires sex." Greenberg (*Ezekiel 1–20*, 277) declares that "*dodim* is specifically sexual lovemaking (Ezek 23:17; cf. Prov 7:16; Song 4:10; 7:13)."

41   See Sir 17:8 (chart 5-2) in which God shows humans "the splendor of His works."

42   Corley, *Ben Sira's Teaching*, 8 n. 28.

enters the Garden of Eden.[43] The fear-of-God covers "all glory/honor" as a bridal canopy, and the Edenic model of marriage is complete.[44]

Though Eve is not named, her presence is evoked by the mention of Eden and also by the label for the "intelligent wife." If an "intelligent" woman/wife is in Eden, then the woman is in the role of Eve because when Eve evaluates all she has seen and heard, before deciding to eat the fruit, her reasoning concludes—as its ultimate justification— with the statement that the tree is desirable "to make one intelligent/wise" (Gen 3:6 וְנֶחְמָד הָעֵץ לְהַשְׂכִּל).[45]

The "intelligent wife" is modeled with reference to Eve through the allusions in BBS 36:18–26 and BBS 40:18–27, and in the latter unit her semantic field overlaps with that of the female figure Wisdom. Given these two links to the "intelligent wife," and the lack of any sense that there was a disastrous event in the Garden of Eden when Eve ate the fruit and gave it to "her man, with her," I speculate that Ben Sira's conceptual model included some semantic equation to the effect that "Eve's giving Adam the fruit is giving him wisdom." An entailment to such an equation would be that one role of the "intelligent wife" is to emulate Eve and Wisdom by providing "wisdom" for "her man," thus rescuing him from the condition of a wifeless wanderer (BBS 36:25). Though playing with such semantic equations does not translate into real-life equations of greater gender-parity in the distribution of power, the semantic or taxonomical equations can differentiate between various "flavors" of the unequal distribution of power.

5.5 (Potentially) Erotic Passages in the Book of Ben Sira

In the Book of Ben Sira, the union of Adam and Eve in Genesis provides the model for an ideal of *marriage*. The idea that "it is not good for the (hu)man to be alone" (Gen 2:18) is expanded through the figure of Cain, whom God condemns to be "weak and wandering" (Gen 4:12), yet—after he marries—he founds a city and his children invent pastoralism, music, and metalsmithing.

---

43   See Di Lella (*Wisdom*, 473), "'a paradise [or Eden, cf. Gen 2:8–17; 3:23–24; Ezek 28:13] of blessings.'"

44   Kugel (*Traditions*, 117) notes that ועל כל כבוד חפתה in BBS 40:27b is almost identical to Is 4:5, עַל־כָּל־כָּבוֹד חֻפָּה, and connects this with early interpretations that Eve and Adam were covered with glory in Eden. If this is so, then Ben Sira may imply that the fear-of-God restores this covering to married lovers such as those in BBS 40:19–20.

45   See שׂכל in *DCH* 8:151a "the tree was desirable to make (one) wise" and 153b for the noun שֵׂכֶל as "intelligence." Chart 4-7 shows all the "intelligent wife" verses (BBS 7:19; 25:8; 26:13; 40:23).

At the human level, then, the theme of *marriage* is built through images from Genesis 2–4; however, the full semantic range of *marriage* develops through the portrayal of erotic relationships between the sage and Wisdom and between the sage and the "intelligent wife."

5.5.1 Erotic Images for Wisdom

Though major passages about Wisdom are not extant in Hebrew, the available passages suffice to demonstrate that an erotic undertone exists in the depictions of her. Chart 5-10, below, gives the major passages for Wisdom that I identify as "erotic." The erotic undertones in the three passages—displayed sequentially in the chart—become clearer as the sequence progresses. [46]

Chart 5-10: Erotic passages about Wisdom

4:15 (MS A)	"One who hearkens to me will be judged true—and who listens to me will encamp in the **innermost-chambers** of the house.
4:18	… And till the time his heart is filled with me, I will return, I will lead us—and I will reveal to him **my secret-place**."
6:26 (MS A)	Bow down your neck and accept her —and do not cut off her guidance.
6:27	Investigate and search out, seek and find —and be attached to her, and do not let her fall.
6:28	For in the end, you will find her repose —and **she will be changed for you, into pleasure**.
6:29	And her net will become for you a site of strength —and her ropes, garments of fine-gold.
6:30	A yoke of gold is her yoke —and her fetters, a cord of blue-purple.
6:31	As garments of honor you will wear her —and **as a crown of glory you will encircle her** round you.

---

46 Balla (*Ben Sira on Family*, 217 and 80) states that in BBS 51, the ultimate poem in the series, "an openness on sexual issues, including intercourse, female nakedness, and orgasm, is found along with lines about praising God. … This is certainly one of the most revolutionary characteristics of Ben Sira's erotically highly-charged poem"—but she states elsewhere that "[i]n general there is relatively little reflecting positive attitudes to sexuality in relation to a real feminine person, compared to the detailed, erotic comments that characterize the poems about wisdom."

14:22	To go forth after her, searching
(MS A)	—and all her **entrances** he will observe-jealously.
14:23	Who looks down through her window
	—and because of her **openings** he can listen carefully.
14:24	Who encamps roundabout her house
	—and brings his tent-cords to her wall.
14:25	And spreads out his tent near her
	—and he will dwell, a good dwelling.
14:26	And he has established his nest in her foliage
	—and in her branches he will lodge.
14:27	And takes refuge in her shade from parching heat
	—and in her abodes he will dwell.

51:18	I have planned so that I may be joyful
(11QPs[a])	—for I have been **zealous in pleasing**, and I will not turn back.
51:19	**I kindled my desire for her**
	—and my face I have not turned away.
51:20	**I have kept my desire with her**
	—and **at her exaltation I will not be slack**.
51:20cd	**My hand has opened her gates**
(MS B)	—and **I will be surrounded** by her, and I will regard her.
51:20fe	And a heart I gained by her, from her beginning
	—and in purity I found (Wisdom / the heart).
51:21	**My belly is 'fired up' like an oven**, in regarding her
	—in order that thus I gained her, a good gain.
51:22	YYY gave to me, mead for my lips
	—and with the speech of my tongue I will praise Him.

BBS 4:15 and 18, "'one who listens to me will encamp in the innermost-chambers of the house … and I will reveal to him my secret-place,'" are the first indication of an eroticized Wisdom: the motif of "the inner chamber," which can be the Holy of Holies in the Temple. Wisdom's "secret-place" can also be her personal "inner chamber"—her vagina or womb. The passage from BBS 6 introduces a different motif, that of the woman "encircling" the man. That phrase occurs as the ultimate element of a sequence in which Ben Sira clothes himself, metaphorically, with Wisdom's emblems and then with Wisdom herself.[47] Ben Sira is yoked to Wisdom by "encircling" her around

---

47   See charts 3-2 and 3-3 in chapter 3.

himself as a crown. He has "bowed down" his neck and "accepted her" (6:26), and now her yoke around him is "a yoke of gold" (6:30). In MS B of BBS 51:17 he declares "her yoke was an honor to me" and he tells prospective students to "put on the yoke" (51:25). The fact that Ben Sira is wearing the yoke of Wisdom—and uses another yoke-metaphor for appropriate marriage—means that his use of plowing metaphors has more ramifications than simple sexual overtones because he is not the one guiding the plow but is, himself, under Wisdom's yoke or else is under a double-yoke with the "intelligent wife."[48] Furthermore, his references to "plowing" are not equivalent to those of Greek physiologists who likened the process of human reproduction to plowing and dropping seed into the earth to be incubated there.[49]

"Entrances" are the motif for the passage from BBS 14. Her "entrances" become her "openings," leading to the author's "dwelling" with Wisdom, "in her abodes." The final passage, BBS 51, merges the motifs of "encircling" and "the inner chamber" (חדר) through the use of the verb form (אחדר) in v. 20, "I will be surrounded by her." The erotic aspects of this passage are evident,[50] and I survey them later in the chapter, in conjunction with passages about the "intelligent wife."

5.5.2 Erotic Images for the "Intelligent Wife"

The "intelligent wife" receives her label from four verses, including BBS 26:13 in chart 5-11, below.[51] The passage BBS 26:13–17 does not comprise a full poetic unit because the only Hebrew MS is MS C, a florilegium in which chapter 26 is sparsely represented: only BBS 26:1–3 and these four bicola. Though these verses might be part of a larger unit with chapter 25, I expect that they are part of a separate discursive strand that does not participate in the genres of *blame* and *praise* that orchestrate BBS 25:13–26:3. One contrast between BBS 26:1–3 and BBS 26:13–17 is the erotic tone of the latter.

---

48 The basis for the marriage-yoke metaphor is Deut 22:10 (see section 2.2.2 of chapter 2). The "marriage-yoke" is a double-yoke—two creatures are yoked together and the pair is driven/ guided by a third. There could also be one creature in a single-yoke, being driven/guided by a second; this would be the Wisdom reference, which denotes *service* rather than *marriage*.

49 For a discussion of Greek and Jewish metaphors for reproduction, see section 1.4.2 of chapter 1.

50 The fully-annotated poetic unit is chart A3-5, in the Appendix.

51 Chart 4-7, in chapter 4, has all instances of "intelligent wife."

Chart 5-11: "Grace of a wife pleases her husband" BBS 26:13–17 (MS C, Sir.)

26:13   [Grace of] a wife 'pleases' her lord-husband
(no 14) —and her intelligence will fatten [his ?].
26:15   Grace [upon grace], a modest wife
         —and there is no weighing for one who is 'close-mouthed.'
26:16   Sun rising in the heights of the heavens
         —beautiful a wife in the chosen holy-of-holies.
26:17   Lamp burning upon the holy candlesticks
         —splendor of face upon tallness of stature.

The Hifil form of the verb טוב in BBS 26:13a is translated as "'pleases,'" with quotes to indicate a second meaning of sexual 'pleasing' as in 51:18. For this passage, BBS 26:15b provides the definitely eroticizable element: the word פה, "mouth," which in this case also means "vagina."[52] The secondary reading of פה in BBS 26:13 as "vagina" allows scope for interpreting לצרורת, the partner of פה, with a semantic range that is equally erotic. My translation of the phrase צרורת פה as "one who is 'close-mouthed.'" is a paraphrase of the literal translation: "she who is 'narrowed' of mouth." Di Lella interprets צרורת as "chaste" vagina, presumably meaning that the wife is not an adulteress, and I add to this another meaning for צרורת פה: having a "tight," meaning "well-muscled," vagina.

For the whole bicola BBS 26:15, the word ביישת in 15a means "decorous" and, as a description of the wife (like בייש is used of a man in BBS 42:1), it accords with the delicacy of the presentation of the erotic phrase in colon 15b. My analysis emphasizes the erotic aspects because that is the topic here, but the translation as "she who is close-mouthed" emphasizes decorous behavior in speech—including keeping confidences—and also in sexuality. The erotic translation coexists as a double reading.

Another possible site for a double-meaning is the "lamp" in v. 17 because "the candle often figures as a symbolical representation of female sexuality (recall the form of ancient ceramic candles)."[53] I do not use the word "euphe-

---

52   Di Lella ("Review: *Ben Sira's View*," 332–33) translates as "'restricted (or shut-up) of mouth' … The 'mouth' here is a euphemism for the vagina (cf. 26:12d)." Camp ("Honor and Shame," 179-80 states that "the double entendre of 26:15b"(ואין משקל לצרורת פה) defines shame in two ways, noting a literal reading in which the "'binding up' or 'narrowing' of her mouth most obviously refers to the desirability of wifely silence, the first meaning of proper shame" and citing from Skehan and Di Lella (*Wisdom*, 345, 350) that "mouth" also can have another meaning as "vagina."

53   Hasan-Rokem, *Tales of the Neighborhood*, 67 (with regard to a story about R. Meir); citing Nacht (*Simle Isha*, 67 n. 19).

mism" for examples like these because that can imply that the author has masked something distasteful with a 'better' word. In the case of Ben Sira, I think he follows a tradition in which sex (in marriage) has a sacred aspect that obliges delicacy in the choice of words—consider that even the Song of Songs, an exuberently erotic document, does not read like a medical treatise or like slang.

BBS 26:16–17 locates the scene for an amorous encounter in what is probably a domestic space but shifts the encounter to the level of religious observance by naming the location as the "chosen holy-of-holies."[54] By placing the sage's human wife in the innermost chamber of the Temple and constituting her as the physical equivalent of its architectural components, the author traces her outline with that of Wisdom, the other female who dwells in the Temple. Although a concurrent link between the sage and the high-priest could be imagined,[55] I think the equivalences are more likely made through unions of a divine female/male pair and a human pair. Thus, as female (Wisdom) and male (YYY?) aspects of God unite in the Holy of Holies of the Temple, so the "intelligent wife" and the sage unite in their own "chosen holy-of-holies."

Chart 5-12, below, gives the major passages about the "intelligent wife" with erotic content, as a summary of that discourse before examining these passages together with similar passages about Wisdom.

---

54 Camp ("Honor and Shame," 180) remarks that דביר in the Hebrew Bible "always refers to the holy of holies of the Temple. In its only other appearance in Ben Sira (45:9), דביר refers at least to the Temple precincts, if not to its inner chamber." She also notes (ibid., 181, n. 24) that בחור can be both "chosen" and "a young man." Balla (*Ben Sira on Family*, 62) gives "in the chosen shrine," noting that Trenchard (*Ben Sira's Views*, 189–90 n.21) "sees it as corrupt together with the other variant: 'in the shrine of a young man.'" Kister ("Genizah Manuscripts," 41–42) does not interpret דביר as the Holy of Holies, though "[t]he possibility of such a bold and strange figure cannot be totally excluded." Nevertheless, דביר is not the only Temple-reference, and Wisdom can be a woman whose house is the Holy of Holies.

55 The link is suggested by the direct shift from Simeon the high-priest to Simeon the sage in BBS 50:27. However, the equation has a problematic entailment because the Holy of Holies is accessible to only one man, the high-priest, but Wisdom is accessible to all Jewish men.

Chart 5-12: Erotic passages about the "intelligent wife"

26:13	Grace of a wife **'pleases' her lord-husband** —and her intelligence will fatten [his ?].
26:15	Grace upon grace, a modest wife —and there is no weighing for one who is **'close-mouthed.'**
36:18	Any **food**, the throat eats —but **there is 'eating' that will be more delightful than food.**
36:19	The palate examines flavors of a thing —and the heart understands 'flavors' of a lie.
36:20	A deceived heart will give pain —and a straightforward man will restore it for himself.
36:21	Any wind-fall, a wild beast will eat —but there is a 'blow' that will be more delightful than a blow.
36:22	**Form of a wife and face causing-light** —and upon all that **greatly-delights** the eye, (a heart) will grow strong.
37:20	And there is a wise-man rejected for his words —and from any **'food,' pleasure is withheld**.
37:24	A wise-man will **have his fill of pleasure** for his own self —and all who see him, they will call him happy.
40:19c	Bearing and planting cause a name to blossom —and more than both, **a wife who is desired.**
40:20	**Wine** and mead cause a heart to exult —and more than both, **she who loves love-making.**
40:21	Flute and harp cause a song to blend —and more than both, a voice that is clear.
40:22	Grace and beauty cause an eye to delight —and more than both, flowers of the field.
40:23	Friend and companion lead your steps —and more than both, an intelligent wife.

5.5.3 Wisdom, the Sage, and the "Intelligent Wife"

The Hebrew verb-roots קנא ("to be jealous"), קנה ("to gain/acquire"), and קנן ("to nest") form a nexus of wordplay in the Book of Ben Sira, and gender-focal instances of these verbs occur, almost exclusively, in the passages represented in chart 5-13, below.[56] The chart shows three paired Wisdom/wife verses (keyed with arrows after the verse numbers) that share one of the verbs: BBS 14:26 (Wisdom) and 36:26c (wife) share קנן; BBS 51:18 (Wisdom) and 9:1 (wife) share קנא; and BBS 51:21 (Wisdom) and 36:24 (wife) share קנה. The permutations of קנא\קנה\קנן are relevant for interpretations of their individual poetic units and, as a linked set of operative motifs, they also demonstrate a relationship among the passages. The verbs interconnect to the extent that one can masquerade as another—BBS 9:2 spells קנה like קנא, the verb in the preceding verse.[57] The distribution of these verbs between the figures of Wisdom and the "intelligent wife," plus their strong interconnections, support a contention that the "intelligent wife" replicates, on a human scale, some of the functions and activities of Wisdom. The 'boxed' section of chart 5-13 shows a close lexical match between excerpts from a poetic unit for Wisdom (BBS 14:20–15:8, from chart 3-4) and excerpts from the unit that also links the "intelligent wife" to Eve (BBS 36:18–26, from chart 5-6).

Chart 5-13: Similar verses for two females: Wisdom and the "intelligent wife"
KEY: Arrow (→) by verse-number means verb קנה, קנן, or קנא is present.

WISDOM (*SIRACH* FROM NETS)	"INTELLIGENT WIFE"
4:15 "One who hearkens to me will be judged true—and one who listens to me will encamp in the **most-interior chambers** of the house."	26:16 Sun rising in the heights of the heavens—beautiful a wife in the chosen **holy-of-holies**.
Sir 24:10 "In a **holy tent** I ministered before Him—and thus in Zion I was firmly set."	26:17 Lamp burning upon the **holy candlesticks**—splendor of face upon tallness of stature.
6:28b For in the end, you will find her repose—and she will be changed for you, into **pleasure**.	37:24 A wise-man will have his fill of **pleasure** for his own self—and rewards of his knowledge are upon his person.

---

56 Forms of קנא ("to be jealous") appear a total of twelve times, קנה ("to gain") eleven times, and קנן ("to nest") three times. Twelve of the twenty-six occurrences relate to *gender*, and eleven of those twelve are concentrated in four poetic units: BBS 9:1–16 (paired poetic units) has two gendered instances of "jealous" and one of "acquire"; BBS 14:20–15:8 (paired units) has one instance of "nest"; BBS 36:18–26 and 37:16–26 (another pair of poetic units) has two instances of "gain" and one of "nest"; and BBS 51:13–22 has three instances of "gain" and one of "jealous." For a chart of all instances of the three roots, see the chart AppLex-11, in the Appendix.

57 See chart 4-9, in chapter 4.

14:26 → And he has established **his nest** in her foliage —and in her branches he will lodge. 14:27 And takes refuge in her shade from **parching heat**—and in her abodes he will dwell. 15:3 And **she will feed him** with bread-of-intelligence—and water-of-understanding she will give him to drink. 15:4 And **he will lean upon her**, and will not stumble—and in her he will trust, and will not be ashamed.	36:26c → Thus a man who has no '**nest**'—settling where he'll be-at-nightfall. 36:25 Without a wall, an orchard will **be burned**—and without a wife, **weak and wandering**. 36:18 Any **food**, the throat eats— but there is 'eating' that will be more delightful than food. 36:24 *[also last sec.]* Gaining a wife is beginning of gain—**help**, and citadel, and **pillar of support**.
15:6 She will bring gladness and joy—and **an everlasting name she will cause him to possess**.	40:19 Child and city **establish a name** —more than both, **finding Wisdom**. Bearing and planting **cause name to blossom** —more than both, **a wife who is desired**.
51:14 She came to me in her **form**—and until the end-of-time I will study her.	36:22 **Form** of a wife and face causing-light —and upon all that greatly-delights the eye, (heart) will grow strong.
51:18 → I have resolved, and may I celebrate—I have been (**z/j)ealous** in **pleasing**, and I will not stray.	9:1 → Do not **make jealous** the wife of your bosom—lest she learn evil concerning you. 26:13 Grace of **a wife 'pleases' her husband** —and her intelligence will fatten [?].
51:21 → My belly is 'fired-up' like an oven in regarding her—in order that thus **I gained her, a good gain**. 51:22 YYY gave to me, **mead** (for) my lips—and with my tongue I will praise/thank Him.	36:24 → *above* **Gaining a wife** is the **beginning of gain**—help, and citadel, and pillar of support. 40:20 **Wine and mead** cause a heart to exult—more than both, she who loves love-making (דודים).

Passages for the "intelligent wife" and for Wisdom share these six elements: references to the Temple in terms of "inner chambers;" being a source of "pleasure" for the sage; being (or providing) a "nest" as a safe refuge for the sage; establishing his name; "pleasing" the sage and/or being "pleased" by him; and being a significant "gain" for the sage.

In the first section of paired verses, for Wisdom the "most-interior chambers of the house" corresponds to the "holy-of-holies" for the wife, allowing the spaces that the two figures inhabit to overlap. For both verses of the second section, the word תענוג ("pleasure") is used with erotic overtones, though it is not erotic elsewhere in BBS.

The third section is 'boxed' to emphasize that the two parts are excerpts from two complete poetic units. This section, like the first, concerns a habitation. In this case the sage will establish his "nest" in Wisdom's "foliage," while the man who "has no nest" has no lodging. If the two poetic units are related semantically as well as lexically, then it could be the human wife—the man's "nest"—whose presence allows the sage to "dwell" in Wisdom's abodes. Further, verses BBS 15:3 and 36:18 may link Wisdom and the "intelligent wife" to Eve because the "bread of intelligence" and "water of understanding" sound like kin of the "fruit of the knowledge of good and evil." The "food" and "'eating'" in 36:18 can refer to both the 'eating' of new knowledge and to sexual experience—two kinds of "knowing," as in Genesis (Gen 2:9 for "tree of the knowledge…"; 4:1 for sexual "knowing"). Wisdom and the wife both are sources of strength and stability for the sage (BBS 15:4 and 36:24).

The fourth section links Wisdom and the "intelligent wife" as agents for establishing the "name" of the sage, and the fifth section links the figures through shared motifs of the sage's visual pleasure and the mutual sexual-'pleasing.' The sixth and final section of chart 5-13 shows equivalent applications of "gaining" the female figure as an excellent "gain." Elsewhere in the Book of Ben Sira, the formulation of "gaining" a person is used for "gaining" a male friend, and in no instance does it indicate that the person is possessed like an object. The last pair of verses are read in conjunction with Song 1:2, "Oh, that he will kiss me, the kisses of his mouth—for better is your love-making (דֹּדֶיךָ), than wine!" Therefore, an alternate translation for שכר שפתותי in BBS 51:22 is "mead (for) my lips" (שֵׁכָר), in addition to "a reward of my lips" (שָׂכָר).

Though chart 5-13 demonstrates significant overlap in the lexical ranges for Wisdom and the "intelligent wife," and implies an equivalent semantic overlap, one distinction between real and figural women is apparent through the different functions of the "yoke" motif. In the case of Wisdom, Ben Sira (or another sage) puts on Wisdom's single-yoke to demonstrate that he has become her "servant"—as in BBS 4:14 "those who serve the HolyOne are serving her."[58] In the case of the human wife, whom the verse names as the "intelligent wife": "Happy is the husband of an intelligent wife—he is not plowing like ox-with-ass" (BBS 25:8). The "plowing" refers to the double-yoke of Deut 22:10, interpreted as a metaphor for spouses who are as badly-matched as an ass yoked together with an ox, with the counter-expectation that a well-matched pair would 'pull together.'[59]

---

58   For Wisdom, "yoke" verses include 6:30 (chart 3-2); 51:17, 30 (chart 3-5).

59   The Hebrew from BBS and from Deuteronomy is given in a footnote in section 2.2.2 of chapter 2.

5.6 The Book of Ben Sira and the Song of Songs

Ancient texts have survived, or disappeared, by combinations of chance and intent. One item in the "intent" module of the equation is ideology, about which Osiek comments that the "amount of ancient Israelite or early Christian life [that] is reflected in the texts that have survived … [is probably] very little, and what has survived, we can almost say with certainty, is biased. Indeed, that is probably exactly *why* it has survived."[60] Against this background of the pervasive bias of texts, her answer to how we might see past the "veneer of male dominance" is that we should take note of "possible hints of matrilocality and matrifocality preserved in … ancient texts" such as Gen 2:24 ("a man shall leave his father and his mother and shall cling to his wife") and Song 3:4 ("I brought him to my mother's house").[61] This hint is particularly relevant to the current study because Ben Sira uses images from the early chapters of Genesis and shares a significant set of eroticized vocabulary with the Song of Songs.

Bergant reports that "an analysis [of the Song of Songs] according to the gender-defined categories of honor and shame" yields unexpected results: the social relationships "are anomalous, if the honor/shame model is the norm." [62] One significant similarity between the Song of Songs and the Book of Ben Sira is that neither uses the Greek gender trope of plowing, by which the woman becomes (non-human) soil that functions as an incubator for seed deposited in her by the plowman.[63] Though the Song of Songs is unquestionably the only ancient Jewish text that is—in its entirety—a "rhapsodic affirmation of sexual love,"[64] I suggest that parts of the Book of Ben Sira can also be described in this way because BBS shares significant vocabulary with Song: a set of words with erotic connotations that contribute to an 'erotic sensibility' BBS shares with Song. Chart 5-14, below, presents a maximal set of these instances of shared vocabulary.

---

60 Osiek, "New Handmaid," 276 (emphasis original).

61 Osiek, "Women, Honor, and Context," 333.

62 Bergant, "My Beloved Is Mine," 37.

63 Walsh makes this point about Song, mentioning "agricultural imagery that does not render the woman an inert field" (*Exquisite Desire*, 85). I make the same point for BBS through its taxonomy (chapter 1) and the use of the "yoke" metaphor.

64 Collins, "Marriage, Divorce, and Family," 136. Collins considers that Song "stands alone." Camp ("Woman Wisdom and the Strange Woman," 99), however, declares that Prov 1–9 "is remarkable for bringing the vocabulary and the forms of the Song of Songs into its portrayal of both Woman Wisdom and the beloved wife."

Chart 5-14: The Book of Ben Sira and the Song of Songs (verse-sequences are boxed)

BBS → WISDOM	SONG OF SONGS
4:15b חדר "and one listening to me will encamp in the **innermost-chambers** of the house."	3:4b חדר [bring him] to the house of my mother, to the **innermost-chamber** of she-who-conceived-me.
6:28b תענוג and it/she will be changed for you, to **pleasure**.	7:7 תענוג "How beautiful and how + *wife* delightful, love, with **pleasures**"

14:23a החלונה He looks down through **her window** …	2:9 הַחַלֹּנוֹת Behold him, standing behind our wall—gazing through **windows**
14:25a אהל And spreads out **his aloe** near her	4:14 אֲהָלוֹת [her emanations are rare spices] … myrrh and **aloes**
14:26b לין and in her branches **he will lodge**.	1:13b לין between my breasts **he will lodge**.
14:27 צל, ישב And shelters in **her shade** from parching heat— and in her abodes **he will dwell**.	2:3b צל, ישב —in **his shade** I have greatly-delighted and **I will dwell**.

51:15c רגל **My foot** advanced on level ground	5:3cd רגל Shulamite: "I have bathed **my feet**—must I soil them?"
51:20c יד, פתח **My hand has opened** her gates	5:4a יד, חר My beloved reached out **his hand** towards the hole
51:20d חדר and **I will be surrounded by her**, and I will regard her.	5:5a פתח I, myself, arose **to open** to my beloved

BBS → "INTELLIGENT WIFE"	SONG OF SONGS
26:15b צרורה —and there is no weighing for one (f.) who is '**close**-mouthed.'	1:13a צרור A **bundle**-of myrrh my beloved is to me
37:24a תענוג A wise-man will have his fill of **pleasure** for his own self	7:7 תענוג "How beautiful and how + *Wisd.* delightful, love, with **pleasures**"
40:20 יין, דודים **Wine** and mead will cause a heart to exult —**more than** both, she who loves **love-making**.	1:2b יין, דודים —for **better** is your (m.) **love-making**, than **wine**.
	4:10 —let us extol your (f.) **love-making, more than wine**.

In the Book of Ben Sira, verses about Wisdom and about the human wife share the vocabulary (and its semantic range) of verses in the Song of Songs. In Wisdom's verses, the first shared word in chart 5-14 is חדר ("innermost-chamber," BBS 4:15b), the domestic locale for sexual intimacy. The second shared word, תענוג ("a pleasure," BBS 6:28b), is shared also with a verse about the "intelligent wife" (BBS 37:24a). The third section is a boxed span of verses about Wisdom (BBS 14:23a, 25a, 26b, and 27) that matches verses of Song at four points: the man looking through the female figure's window(s); the rare spice אהל / אֲהָלוֹת ("aloe/s")[65] that is used to perfume bedding and other fabrics; the verb לין ("to lodge (for the night)"); and a double parallel, "dwelling" (ישב) in someone's "shade" (צל). Note that BBS 14:20–15:8—the poetic unit that provides the sequence of verses for Wisdom—is the same unit shown in chart 5-13, where it is boxed together with verses from a poetic unit about the "intelligent wife" (BBS 36:18–26, the unit with strong allusions to Eve).

For Wisdom, the most significant parallel to Song of Songs is given in the fourth section, in the pair of clearly-erotic verses (BBS 51:15, 20) that are boxed together with verses from Song. The BBS sequence matches Song 5:3–5 at three points.[66] First, the word רגל ("foot") doubles as "genitals" for the male in BBS, possibly, and definitely for the female in Song; second, the word יד ("hand") signifies "penis" in BBS 51:20c and also in Song 5:4a, *if* the "hole" is the woman's vagina,[67] as דלת in Song 5:4a and שארים in BBS 51:20c both represent the vaginal opening;[68] and third, both texts speak of the woman "opening," or "surrounding" the man at the touch of (or in anticipation of) his "hand."

An equally-exact parallel exists for the "intelligent wife" (BBS 40:20) and, like that for Wisdom, the site is part of the poetic unit that is the clearest erotic statement for that figure. The shared set of words for the human wife centers on "love-making" (דודים), which is said to be "better than" (טוב) "wine" (יין). The word דודים occurs in the Hebrew Bible only in the Song of Songs (six times), Proverbs (twice), and Ezekiel (twice)—the Book of Ben Sira is the only post-biblical text.[69] A reader's sense of the strong presence of דודים in Song is bolstered by at least thirty instances of the singular form דוד

---

65   For a possible double-reading of אהל "tent" as "aloes" see chart A3-4 in the Appendix.

66   Muraoka ("Sir 51,13–30," 173) notes shared vocabulary, especially the use of יד as "a possible sexual overtone."

67   See Bloch and Bloch (*Song of Songs*, 181) who interpret שָׁלַח יָדוֹ מִן־הַחֹר as "literally 'stretched his hand through the hole,' most likely the keyhole." They state that keyholes in the wooden doors in Near Eastern villages were "large enough for a man to put his hand through it."

68   For דלת as "vaginal opening," see the closing comment by Hicks ("Door of Love," 158), who calls the דלת "the sublime 'door to love.'" The plural שארים ("gates") in BBS 51:20c could be an image of the vaginal labia as the two sides of a gate.

69   Statistics are from the entries in *DCH* 2:423. The verses in Song are given in the chart. Other biblical instances are Prov 5:19; 7:18; and Ezek 16:8; 23:17 (used in polemics).

"beloved." The only other instance of דוד from the Hebrew Bible is Isa 5:1.[70] Because דדים is a rare word and because both it and the singular form דוד occur preponderantly in Song of Songs, the use of either word in later Hebrew literature must be evaluated as a possible evocation of that text.

1:2	כִּי־טוֹבִים דֹּדֶיךָ מִיָּיִן	… for your (m.) love-making is better than wine
1:4	נַזְכִּירָה דֹדֶיךָ מִיַּיִן	… let us extol your (m.) love-making, more than wine.
4:10a	מַה־יָּפוּ דֹדַיִךְ	… how beautiful is your (f.) love-making!
4:10b	מַה־טֹּבוּ דֹדַיִךְ מִיַּיִן	… how good is your (f.) love-making, more than wine!
5:1	אִכְלוּ רֵעִים שְׁתוּ וְשִׁכְרוּ דוֹדִים	Eat, companions, drink! and be drunk with love-making!
7:13	שָׁם אֶתֵּן אֶת־דֹּדַי לָךְ	… there I will give my love-making to you (f.).

In chart 5-14, the two strongest parallels between figures in the Book of Ben Sira and those in Song of Songs—"foot/hand/opened" for Wisdom and "wine/better/ love-making" for the "intelligent wife"—are exact beyond the likelihood of coincidence. To rephrase that proposition, an author of Ben Sira's era would probably have avoided these sets of words if he (or she) did *not* wish to evoke erotic sensibilities like those of the Song of Songs. These two prime examples strengthen the case for the whole set of parallels as indications of substantial erotic content in the Book of Ben Sira, content that aligns with the view of erotic delights expressed in Song. The eroticism of the Song of Songs is a special combination of flavors: "so voluptuous [and] so full of innocent delight;"[71] and again, "ripe sensuality and delicacy of expression and feeling."[72] Whether Ben Sira read or heard a version of Song of Songs that resembles the MT, or else availed himself of a standardized "vocabulary of love" from which the images in both texts were crafted, in either case, a semantic equivalence between the Book of Ben Sira and the Song of Songs matches the similarity of language.

---

70   The word דוד is also King David's name, דָּוִד "Beloved One." An instance of דוד in 4Q522 1.2:7 is said to be "'beloved' … unless דָּוִד 'David'" (*DCH* 2:423a,b).

71   Bloch and Bloch, *Song of Songs*, 4 (from section by C. Bloch, "The Garden of Delights").

72   Alter, "Afterword," 119 (from Bloch and Bloch, *Song of Songs*).

Chapter 6
The Discourse of *Gender* in the Book of Ben Sira

The product of the current study is a semantic analysis of the discourse of *gende*r in the Book of Ben Sira, based on analyses of gender-focal passages. Most of these passages also exhibit "relational gender"—meaning that the categories *feminine* and *masculine* are produced in relation to each other, together, in contrast to the common situation in which *feminine* is produced as the boundary of what is not *masculine*. Before beginning the large-scale analysis of the discourse of *gender*, I will briefly summarize the hermeneutical steps that created a frame of reference for the analyses of the individual poetic units.

Because the Book of Ben Sira is doubly-enmeshed with Greek social models—from its Hellenistic origins and from frequent interpretation, now, according to the "Mediterranean honor/shame theory"—I have demonstrated particular points at which the Book of Ben Sira differs from prevalent social models derived from classical Greece and Hellenism. Major differences are that the social model for extant Hebrew texts of Ben Sira is non-agonistic, includes a perception of "un-limited good" that is contingent on God and/or Wisdom, has positive values of *shame* for males, and is not phallogocentric (though the model is phallocentric). Further, to clarify distinctions between a passage's form and its semantic content, I introduced a category of "impersonal speech" to evaluate types of statements that may or may not correspond directly to an author's personal opinions. "Impersonal speech" in the Book of Ben Sira includes monovocal genres (*praise* and *blame*), schematic devices, and proverbial statements. Instances of "impersonal speech" do not all have the same discursive purposes or address the same topic, but they are similar in hiding personal opinion behind an implied attribution to sources outside themselves and in deriving their semantic content from the current context. A final element that influences my translations and interpretations is Ben Sira's colonial situation, since his writings were produced within—and against—the influence of Hellenistic Greek claims to cultural superiority.

6.1 Relational-Gender Passages

Raw material for a full-scale analysis of the discourse of *gender* comes from the analyses of seventeen gender-focal passages. Of the seventeen units, eleven are examples of relational-gender—four paired-units and three separate ones. The paired-units, in which the same topic is presented once with reference to women and once with reference to men, are my prime examples of relational-gender.[1] The second example is from Sirach; therefore, although the pattern of relation between what is said for a man and for a woman is clear from the Greek, its inclusion is conjectural. There are six non-relational units, of which the four that feature Wisdom are non-relational by definition, since this construction of non-human *femininity* has no *masculine* counterpart in the Book of Ben Sira. Another non-relational unit is a fragment (BBS 26:13–17) and the last is a special case (BBS 42:9–14) that is discussed later in the chapter. Chart 6-1, below, has information about all seventeen passages; the paired units are linked at the left-hand margin.

Chart 6-1: Gender-focal passages in the Book of Ben Sira

KEY: Units **with** relational gender; units **without** relational gender.

BBS #'S	FIGURE	TOPIC(S)	RELATIONAL GENDER?	MSS + MISC.
4:11–19 → 3-1	Wisdom, *erotic*.	Erotic, but not relational.	MS A
6:18–31 → 3-2	Wisdom, *erotic*.	Erotic, but not relational.	MSS A (C...)
7:18–26 → 4-8	Friend/wife.	Exchange friend ‖ reject wife.	MSS A (C)
9:1–9 → 4-9	Wife.	Replace wife (make jealous)	MS A
9:10–16 → 4-10	Friend.	is ‖ replace old friend.	
14:20–15:8→ 3-4	Wisdom, *erotic*.	Erotic, but not relational.	MSS A (B)
Sir 23:16–21 → 4-13	Adulterer.	Standard of *adultery* for a	Sirach
Sir 23:22–27 → 4-13	Adulteress.	man ‖ to that for a woman.	

---

1   The juxtaposed units are BBS 9:1–9 and 9:10–6, on the topic of *disloyalty* in replacing a wife or friend (charts 4-9 to 4-11); Sir 23:16–21 and 23:22–27, on *adultery* (chart 4-13); and BBS 36:18–26 and 37:16–26, on the sage's wife and the sage (charts 5-6 to 5-8). In the third example, the paired verses are separated by a jumble of related verses (see the discussion before chart 5-6). The fourth pairing has a major gap between the male-figure passage (Sir 22:9–15) and that for the female-figures (BBS 25:13–26:3).

Sir 22:9–15 → 2-4	Fool (W. Wife).	Hyperbolic version of	MS C
25:13–26:3 → 2-11	Wrong Wife, Right Wife.	relational gender, as *(in)appropriate marriage.*	anomalous BBS 25:24
26:13–17 → 5-11	Wife, *erotic.*	Wife likened to Temple items, but not relational.	MS C
33:20–30 → 4-5	Wife/friend.	Neither "rules over" sage.	MS B
36:18–26 → 5-6	Wife of sage.	Allusions to Gen. 1–4, for wife.	MSS B
37:16–26 → 5-7	Sage.	*Speech* and *erotic,* both units.	(C, D)
40:18–27 → 5-9	Wife+sage, *erotic.*	Recip. *erotic,* "wife who's desired" + "she who loves love-making." Comparable advisors, "friend and companion" and "intelligent wife."	MSS B, M
42:9–14 → 4-16	Daughter, father, *gender, shame, speech.*	Not relational gender. Father worries because daughter is slandered, innocent or guilty.	MSS B, M. anomalous BBS 42:14
51:13–30 → 3-5	Wisdom, *erotic.*	Erotic, but not relational.	MSS B, 11QPs[a]

All passages concern how a (Jewish) man should choose close associates and treat them. Several topics that are shared by more than one relational-gender unit are *rejection or replacement* (begin BBS 7:18 and 9:1); *adultery* (begin BBS 9:1 and Sir 23:16); and *appropriate associates* (begin BBS 9:1; 25:13, and 40:18; Sir 22:9). Though "wife" and "friend" are constituted similarly, BBS 7:18–26 exposes an entailment to the equation—the fact that the man is said to "accept" a wife for his son (v. 23) shifts the trope of *appropriate marriage* for cases where the man's father chooses the wife, and also explains the statement in v. 26 "Your wife—do not abhor her—or, hating her, do not trust her." If the father chooses an inappropriate wife for the son, the son might, indeed, abhor her and not trust her.[2] No such advice is needed for friendship, which would always be the man's own choice.

One relational-gender unit, BBS 25:13–26:3, is an atypical unit that represents a different mode of relation. The passage displays relational-gender in schematic fashion, making its rhetorical tone much more strident. A comparison of the schematic units BBS Sir 22:9–15 and 25:13–26:3 (the Fool, Wrong Wife and Right Wife) with realistic units BBS 9:1–9 and 10–16 (a

---

2   The lack of trust mentioned in BBS 7:26b can explain the recommendation in BBS 42:6a that for a man married to the "Wrong Wife, [it is prudent to have] a seal."

man's wife and his male friend) shows their similarities and differences clearly.[3] Both sets of male/female passages apply the trope of *appropriateness* to the sage's closest chosen affiliates—his wife and his close friend—and give examples of bad choices. The schematic units are formed as solid blocks of hyperbolic *blame* or *praise*, while the paired units in chapter 9 compare a man's rejecting his wife by choosing a sexual relationship with another woman to his rejecting an old friend in favor of a new one. Among females in BBS 9:1–9, bad choices such as prostitutes, singers-of-satires, and adulteresses contrast with the appropriate choice, the wife; among males in BBS 9:10–16, the bad choices include wicked men, insolent men, and a man "who has power to kill," contrasted with the appropriate choices, wise-men and the "discerning" man. The mode for the schematic units is caricature, or hyperbole, and the characters have categorical designations like those in proverbs—Fool, Wrong Wife ("bad woman/wife") and Right Wife ("good woman/wife"). Though the male and female schematic passages are not sequentially linked, the negative figures of the Wrong Wife and the Fool receive the same style of vituperative portrayal, with some shared accusations.[4] The mode of relation in BBS 9:1–16, which is shared with the other units that typify relational gender, is both more complex and more subtle than that of the genre-driven litanies of *blame* and *praise* in Sir 22:9–15 and BBS 25:13–26:3.

In order for my description of a discourse of *gender* to have explanatory power, the labels for members of the group I refer to as "schematic figures" must designate fixed, rather than mutable, qualities. According to my interpretations, members of the affinity-schema—labeled as the Right Wife ("good wife"), the Fool, and the Wrong Wife ("bad wife")—can act only within discursive constraints equivalent to the physical limitations of clockwork ornaments.[5] The constraints occur at the level of genre: if BBS 25:13-24 approximates a ψόγος γυναικῶν ("blame of women") then, by definition, the Wrong Wife cannot change, nor can the Right Wife change in her genre of *praise*. The Right Wife, the Wrong Wife, and the Fool do not act in any way outside the definitions provided by their labels. In contrast, the non-schematic figures of the "intelligent wife," the male "friend," the male "companion," and

---

3   For Sir 22:9–15, see chart 2-4 and for BBS 25:13–26:3 see charts 2-11 and 2-12. For BBS 9:1–16, see charts 4-9 to 11. The distinction between "schematic" and "realistic" characters is made in chart 2-2. The designation of BBS 25:13–26:3 as relational gender is a borderline case, but the comparison with chapter 9 demonstrates at least a minimal semantic overlap.

4   See chart 2-4 for a comparison of verses about the two figures. Sir 22 is not extant in Hebrew.

5   The Sage figure participates in the schema as its focal-point, but is less constrained than the others. For the full discussion of the schematic figures, see section 2.2.2 of chapter 2.

the sage (in his lower-case incarnation) are capable of change. The sage is capable of change toward "the wife of [his] bosom" (BBS 9:1) and, though she is an example of the well-matched wife, she is likely to change toward him if the sage makes her jealous; in parallel, the sage is pictured changing toward an old friend (BBS 9:10). Ben Sira also speaks of the suffering experienced when a friend or companion becomes an enemy:

6:8	יש אוהב נהפך לשנא	There is a friend who is changed to a hater—
(MS A) : ואת ריב חרפתך יחשוף		and in time of strife he'll bare your reproach.
37:2	הלא דין מגיע על מות	Is it not a judgment unto death—a companion
(MS B) : ריע כנפש נהפך לצר		like a self changed to an enemy?

No such comment is made about the schematically-labeled Right Wife (the אשה טובה "good wife") turning "bad." Likewise, the Fool is not expected to change in the direction of wisdom. The word for the young men Ben Sira invites to his "house of instruction" as potential students (BBS 51:23) is סכלים, "confused-ones," which is not the label for the Fool (כסל).[6] There is, however, no conclusive evidence in either direction for the fixity or mutability of the Fool, or the Right Wife and Wrong Wife, and the potential for "a good wife" to become "a bad wife" is precisely the discursive instability Camp sees as fundamental to an analysis of *gender* in BBS/Sirach.[7] The investigative strategies she uses lead to her conclusions, and my strategies lead to my alternate views.

Relational-gender is demonstrated in the large-scale compositions of chart 6-1, but also in individual verses with equivalent statements for women and men. Chart 6-2, below, matches vocabulary used for a female in the units listed in chart 6-1 with that used for a male in verses that are *not* part of chart 6-1.[8] These all are instances in which approved behaviors for males and for females are formulated with equivalent vocabulary.

---

6   Note that סכל can be a pun on the homophone שכל ("intelligent," a word Ben Sira uses often) to imply that the "confused-ones" who follow his teachings may be transformed into "intelligent-ones." It is unlikely that the word סכלים could be a scribal error for כסלים. The poetic unit is an acrostic—the line above begins with נתן and the line below with עד. The word סכלים is third in the line, but *that* could be a scribal error! Another meaning of שכל is "be foolish" (from סכל), and in BBS 14:16g, שכלות is used instead of סכלות for "confusion/folly."

7   C. Camp, in conversation 18 October 2006.

8   These sets of equivalent statements are from chart 4-6.

Chart 6-2: *Identical vocabulary for females and males in the Book of Ben Sira*
KEY: *Italicized* verse numbers are from passages in chart 6-1.

MOTIF(S)	VOCABULARY	VERSE #'S
A wise man avoids people who have no self-control in speech—who **speak without thinking** or who reveal secrets.	אשת לשון or איש לשון	Female = wife *25:20.* Male = ? 8:3; 9:18.
A **God-fearing** man is "given" a wife (by God) and also will "reach" a friend.	ירא יי' or ירא אל	Female = wife *26:3.* Male = student 6:15.
Modest behavior (includes sexuality and speech) leads to approval ("**grace**") by the community. Such a person is beyond price ("there's **no weighing**" for them).	ביישת or בייש + חן / אין משקל ל-	Female = wife *26:15.* Male = student 42:1 and friend 6:14.
A man is said to **gain** a wife, and a friend.	קנה	Female = wife *36:24.* Male = student 6:6.
In potentially dangerous situations, a pious person will **be extra careful to behave righteously** ("be afraid-before-God").	פחד	Female = daughter *42:14.* Male = son 4:20; student 37:12.

The full group of these solidly-demonstrated examples of relational-gender, shown in charts 6-1 and 6-2, forms the background for an analysis of the virulent verses BBS 25:24 and BBS 42:13–14.

6.2 'Anomalous' Verses— BBS 25:24 and BBS 42:13 and 14

The poetic unit BBS 42:9–14, though heavily gender-focal, is not a site of relational gender. Several themes intersect in this passage, which sits as the final link in a chain of units on the topic of the double-nature of *shame* and is, also, the last comment on human females. The complex intertwining of *shame* and *speech* in BBS 42:9–14 produces a motif of *slander* that is my key for interpreting the passage. *Appropriate marriage* is a focus for the gender discourse in this poetic unit, but, though the daughter is pictured with either an appropriate husband or one who is incompatible, the categories *masculine* and *feminine* are not products of the discourse; the male/female pair is a father and daughter, adding a second taxonomic imbalance of power—parent/child—that de-emphasizes relational gender. The final verses of this passage require further comment, as does BBS 25:24, another verse that is notorious for gender-bias.

BBS 25:24 (MSS B, M)   מאשה תחלת עון ובגללה גוענו יחד
"From a woman is the start of iniquity
—and because of her, we waste away, all alike."

BBS 42:13–14 (MS M)   כי מבגד יצא עש ומאשה רעת אשה :
          טוב רע איש מטיב אשה(מטוב) ובת מפחדת מכול חרפה

13 For "from a garment goes forth a moth"
—and from a woman, the evil of a woman.
14 "Better the evil of a man than the goodness of a woman"
—but a daughter who is afraid-before-God (is better) than any taunt.

These verses are anomalous in the overall picture of gendered discourse as demonstrated in charts 6-1 and 6-2. Against that semantically-even background of recommendations for "modest" behaviors for men and for women, the three verses stand out in sharp contrast. They are anomalies—very loud anomalies, and very interesting. What is the function of these verses, if any? Do these passages share any features other than tone? Is there any viewpoint from which these passages make sense as part of the total discourse of *gender*?

All three of the verses are examples of "impersonal speech." Specifically, each is, in whole or in part, a proverbial statement. And, the statements have meaning only in context, since their semantic range depends on that of the surrounding poetic unit. Each verse functions as a focal-point for the theme of its passage. The verse BBS 25:24 is the essence of the genre "blame of women." The theme of double-natured *shame* organizes the gendered discourse in BBS 42:9–14, and vv. 13 and 14 are examples of "taunts" that can be directed as *slander* against the female protagonist. Since the two passages that include the verses participate in the total discourse of *gender* for the Book of Ben Sira, these verses are not anomalous when viewed in context. However, there is no direct relation between these verses and the opinions of the author—evaluating the verses depends on interpreting the passages from which the verses derive meaning.

6.3 *Gender* in the Book of Ben Sira

In the Book of Ben Sira, the sexual code for males is not constituted in contrast to expectations for females but in parallel with them. In other words, the taxonomy of the Book of Ben Sira prioritizes values that it expects from both women and men because the primary taxonomizer is Piety, rather than Sex. All conduct that is under the rubric of Piety, including sexual expression, is thus roughly equivalent for the two gender-categories in the taxonomy. The discourse of *gender* shifts expectations for men's conduct to be more like that expected for women, using marriage-motifs derived from the early chapters of Genesis. Emphasis on male self-restraint in sexual matters is explicit because the biblically-sanctioned default would be permission for liaisons with any unmarried female not under a father's authority. The examples in charts 4-6, 6-1, and 6-2 show equivalent expectations for males and females with regard to mannerisms of speech and affect that are labeled as "modest." Thus, at the level of taxonomy, gender-performance is not strongly differentiated.

Nevertheless, concurrent with the focus on pious behavior, all other scales of value are ignored. The Book of Ben Sira stresses the importance of "fearing God" and being faithful to the Torah/Law as requirements for every Jew but does not spell-out what would be meant by following Torah, except in terms of piety.[9] The layer of discourse at which the different real-life social roles for males and females are constituted through interpretations of Torah is invisible in the Book of Ben Sira although the book functions as an etiquette manual for young men studying to become scribes or sages. Why would a book that devotes entire passages to polite behavior at banquets say nothing specific about what the people wore, or ate? If Ben Sira and his followers were not distinguishable from other Jews by appearance or behavior, then the monumental absence of regulations for daily life could mark a boundary of Ben Sira's teachings. In this scenario, guidelines for "how to live a good (Jewish) life" are divided into two sets of lore, each with a distinct set of experts who interpret and teach. Priests interpret Torah for issues such as dietary laws, appropriate attire, and matters of ritual-purity, and sages interpret those aspects of Torah that answer questions about our place in the universe and our relations with other humans and with God. Sages would have authority for questions of *meaning* and priests would have authority for *practices*. Therefore, in the Book of Ben Sira, the important discursive activity that Connell identifies as "the maintenance of practices that institutionalize men's dominance over women" is not available for analysis,[10] at least not within the parameters of the current study.

Although Ben Sira uses the same vocabulary of piety for women as for men, in terms of recommendations for living as "one who fears-God," one difference is that the phrase כנפש\כנפשך (like a self / like yourself) is never used for a female. The phrase appears five times for males: twice for an "intelligent slave" (עבד מסכיל BBS 7:21; 10:25); twice for a "companion" (רע

---

9   Further, there was no single set of standards among all groups of Jews. Schwartz' formulation captures this amorphous situation: "the 'Torah' was a series of negotiations between an authoritative but opaque text and various sets of traditional but not fully authorized practice" (*Imperialism and Jewish Society*, 68 [entire quote italicized in book]).

10   Connell, *Gender and Power*, 185.

רֵעַ \ BBS 34:15; 37:2); and once for a "friend" (אוֹהֵב BBS 34:2). The taxonomizer in this case is clearly *gender*, indicating a boundary for the author's imagining his "self," though the framework of an intensely homosocial society could render such idioms reflexive.

In contrast, the verses that rank the "wife" with a man's closest male associates, or designate the "intelligent wife" as the best confidant/counselor of her sage-husband, move the discursive boundary closer to the sage's self.[11] The inclusion of a female in that particular category—'appropriate confidant'— is counter-taxonomic for the Greek model of *gender* and, for the Hebrew/BBS model, brings the spousal discourse out of the realm of predictable taxonomic generalities. In addition to receiving the highest status as a confidant/e, the "intelligent wife" is counter-taxonomic because there is no mention of her procreative potential. Thus, two factors in the Greek model of *gender* are reversed: a positive value usually assigned to a male figure (that is, a man's closest relationship of intellectual intimacy) is assigned to a female, and a positive value expected for a female (that is, the function of childbearing) is missing. In spite of the emphasis in the Hebrew Bible on child-bearing as a major concern of women, chapters 2 and 3 of Genesis do not mention that the value of the woman is related to her ability to bear children, nor does the Book of Ben Sira or the Song of Songs. "Ben Sira does not mention procreation as the purpose for marriage"[12]—but what, then, *is* the purpose of marriage? One unequivocal answer I see in the Book of Ben Sira is that the purpose of marriage is to ensure that a man will not be "weak and wandering" like Cain was before his marriage. This is companionship-as-a-preventative, but companionship nonetheless. The erotic poetry presents an image of companionship-as-an-achievement, an image in which another purpose of marriage is to replicate, on a human scale, the union of the female and male aspects of God. If the man wishes to follow Wisdom, then the "union of male and female aspects" comes into play as his wife's semantic territory overlaps with that of Wisdom.

One area of semantic territory that maintains distinctions between Wisdom and the "intelligent wife" is the vocabulary chosen to portray the erotic aspects of each figure. The double-valued hands and gates that appear in the verses about Wisdom are not part of the semantic range of the "intelligent wife" whose erotic qualities are made evident through direct reference to her as "she who loves love-making." And, her body-parts are likened to the temple but are not 'handled.' To me, this greater reticence in the verses about the "intelligent wife" indicates that she is figured as though she

---

11   See, especially, chart 5-9, in chapter 5. See also charts 4-5, 4-7, 4-8, in chapter 4.

12   Collins, "Marriage, Divorce, and Family," 127.

were an actual woman/wife. She is enough of a real person that the anatomical double-meanings are less appropriate for speaking about her. Applying the erotic terminology for Wisdom to the "intelligent wife" would not be ביישׁ— decorous and modest—the term used in the verse that mentions the "intelligent wife" as "'close-mouthed,'" and signals the limits of candor (BBS 26:15a).

"One who reads a verse of the Song of Songs and makes it like a secular song—and one who reads a verse in a banquet-house, unseasonably—brings evil to the world," according to the Babylonian Talmud (*b. Sanh.* 101a). "Unfortunately," as Collins notes, "we know practically nothing about the people who sang in banquet halls or their sexual morality."[13] This is, indeed, unfortunate. Bergant suggests that the Song of Songs "might serve as an interpretive key to unlocking the revelatory possibilities of other texts," if "the sexual relationship depicted here is more characteristic than previously believed."[14] I have followed her suggestion and compared erotic tropes in the Book of Ben Sira with those from the Song of Songs, finding a small but significant set of shared vocabulary. An even clearer overlap for the Book of Ben Sira is the use of specific vocabulary from the early chapters of Genesis, though Ben Sira's interpretations of Genesis 1–4 seem to be entirely positive. In light of later interpretations of these Genesis texts as a "fall" of humanity into a degraded condition, the Book of Ben Sira provides a radically-different viewpoint. Yet, we do not know whether Ben Sira's ideas were radical during his lifetime or were standard interpretations for some Jews. The current study of *gender* demonstrates a range of attitudes that the Book of Ben Sira shares with biblical literature, including Prov 5:15–23 for attitudes toward *adultery* and erotic marital relationships; Song 5:3–5 (with other verses) for erotic tropes, and Genesis 1–4 for the stories of Eve, Adam, and Cain. In his role as an interpreter of Torah, Ben Sira incorporates selective readings of those texts and others—readings that may ignore major elements of the stories.[15] Thus, in rather subtle ways, the Book of Ben Sira takes wisdom literature along different paths—though in a seemingly-familiar vehicle.

---

13 Collins, "Marriage, Divorce, and Family," 137.

14 Bergant, "My Beloved Is Mine," 37.

15 The statement presumes a large degree of continuity between Ben Sira's sources and these parts of our MT. Selective readings are a common basis for interpretation—still, it is startling to see נע ונד ("weak and wandering," Gen 4:12, 14) used with reference to Cain's need for a wife, with no mention of fratricide.

Appendix
Lexical Studies and Annotated Translations

Details of background information are grouped here, for reference, so that they do not clutter the chapters. The section on lexical lists includes discussions of several of the topics; the section on translations includes all Hebrew variants for the most complex poetic units translated in the chapters, as well as the most speculative translations.

A.1 Lexical Studies

Results of lexical studies and other analyses are mentioned in the chapters, but the studies themselves appear here. Note that the chart-numbers for this section are not keyed to chapters, but are labeled sequentially: "AppLex-1," "AppLex-2," etc. The most complex lexical study is that made for Hebrew words and phrases related to the commonly-binary pair טוב and רע, because meanings for words related to רעע shifted over time.

A.1.1 טוב and רע: Good and Bad/Evil in the Book of Ben Sira

The paired words are "good" and "evil" in Genesis 1–11, but the range of meaning is different in the Book of Ben Sira. Because allusions to Eve are part of the gender-discourse of the Book of Ben Sira,[1] it is important to note differences in the semantic ranges of vocabulary shared by Genesis and the Book of Ben Sira. In Genesis, the word רע does not appear in the story of the eating of the forbidden fruit (Gen 3:1–19) or even in conjunction with Cain's killing of Abel (Gen 4:8–16); it is introduced later, to categorize unspecified human actions that cause God to despair of human behavior and send the flood to cleanse the earth (Gen 6:5). There, the semantic range for רע *begins* at a level of guilt *above* unpremeditated murder. In the Book of Ben Sira, the

---

1   See chapter 5, "Human Female, Biblical Females."

semantic range for רע is below that crime, frequently paired with טוב as "adversity" and "prosperity."

Both טוב and רעע seem to have rather mundane connotations in the Book of Ben Sira and the extremes of goodness or of evil are categorized with other labels. For example, Ben Sira's highest praise is for "one who fears YYY," and the adjective רע does not seem to include physical violence. Labels for violent men include עז (fierce), שונא (a hater), and[ג]איש [שלי]ט להרון (a man who has the power to kill), and the categories explicitly associated with blood are the איש בליעל (a destroyer), the אַכְזָרִי (cruel man), the אוֹיֵב (enemy), and the בעל אף (master-of-anger). The word רָשָׁע that I translate "wicked-man" (opposite צַדִּיק, "righteous-man") is a major category, with a semantic range between the use of רע in BBS and its use in the early chapters of Genesis.[2]

The *Dictionary of Classical Hebrew* defines the adjective רַע as "bad, i.e., displeasing," and the nouns רָעָה and רֹע as "(ethical) evil," listing "BBS 12:10; 25:17; 42:14" as examples (*DCH* 7:505a–509b; 513b; 521a–525a; the root רעע 529b–531b). However, though BBS 12:10 has רוע (רֹע), BBS 25:17 has רע (רַע or רֹע) and BBS 42:14 has רע (רַע or רֹע) in MSS M and B^m, with only MS B having רוע (רֹע). Thus, in most cases the word could be translated either as "bad" (רַע) or as "evil" (רֹע).

"Good" is not analyzed further because the range of meaning is less extreme. The chart AppLex-1, below, gives summaries of the definitions for "evil" from Muraoka,[3] for Greek (italics denote my preferred definitions).

AppLex-1: Greek words in BBS/Sirach related to "evil"

κακόω **to treat harshly, cause difficulty, harm**

ענה 13 times (12 pi., 1 pu.); רעע 10 times (9 hi., 1 ni.); יגה 1 time (hi.).

κακός adj. *1. bad in effect (B.) misfortune, misery.* 2. morally bad, evil, wicked; (B.) improper, unacceptable (of action). רָעָה 17 times; רַע 16 times.

κακία n. 1. moral evilness, vice. 2. physically hard or distressful circumstance. רָעָה 21 times; רֹע 1 time; עָנָה 1 time.

πονηρεύομαι **to conduct oneself immorally**

רעע 2 times (1 qal, 1 hi.); זמם 1 time (qal); נכל 1 time (hith.).

נפש עזה (BBS-A 6:3; C 19:2); פי עז (BBS-M 40:30), שונא (BBS-A 5:15; 6:3,8,12; 12:8,9,10; C 20:23; B, E, F 33:2; E, F 33:6), איש בליעל (BBS-A 11:32); אַכְזָרִי (BBS-A 8:15, 13:12; B 35:22; B, D 37:11); בעל אף (BBS-A 8:16); אוֹיֵב (BBS-A 12:16). Related categories are: גאוה ("proud" BBS-A 10:6,7,8; 13:20; 16:8; A, C 7:17), זד ("insolent" BBS-A 10:22; 12:7; A, B 11:9; B, F 32:18), and לץ ("mockers" BBS-A 3:28; 8:11; 11:30; 13:1; A, B 15:8; B 31:26; 37:7; B, E, F 32:18).

3   Muraoka, *Greek-English Lexicon of the Septuagint: Chiefly of the Pentateuch.*

πονηρός adj. *1. morally or ethically wrong, evil. 2. harmful or injurious. 3. out of favor. 4. deficient, of poor quality.* רַע 68 times; רֹע 2 times; רָעָה 4 times; רְעַע 2 times.

πονηρία n. *evil design and intention. (B.) pl. wicked, evil deeds.* רָעָה 2 times.

Another aspect of the Good/Evil language in BBS/Sirach deserves special attention. Ben Sira uses a set of four human figures in his schema of affinities: חכם (the sage), אשה טובה (the good wife/woman), כסיל (the fool), and אשה רעה (the bad wife/woman).[4]

AppLex-2: "Bad" or "good" + " wife/woman" in BBS and Sirach

# (MS C)	BOOK OF BEN SIRA	SIRACH
25:13	[?] רעת [n.] **badness**-of-[wife]	πονηρίαν γυναικός [n.] **evilness**-of-wife
25:16	*[Verse not in extant Hebrew.]*	γυναικὸς πονηρᾶς [adj.] **evil** wife
25:17	רע אשה [n.] wife-**badness**	πονηρία γυναικὸς [n.] **evilness**-of-wife
25:19	רעת אשה [n.] **badness**-of-wife	κακίαν γυναικός [n.] **badness**-of-wife
25:23	*[Verse not in extant Hebrew.]*	γυνὴ πονηρά [adj.] **evil** wife
25:25	*[Verse not in extant Hebrew.]*	γυναικὶ πονηρᾷ [adj.] **evil** wife
26:1	אשה טובה [adj.] **good** wife	γυναικὸς ἀγαθῆς [adj.] **good** wife
26:3	אשה טובה [adj.] **good** wife	γυνὴ ἀγαθὴ [adj.] **good** wife
26:7	*[Verse not in extant Hebrew.]*	γυνὴ πονηρά [adj.] **evil** wife
42:6 (B)	אשה רעה [adj.] **bad** wife	γυναικὶ πονηρᾷ [adj.] **evil** wife
42:13 (BM)	רעת אשה [n.] **badness**-of-wife	πονηρία γυναικὸς [n.] **evilness**-of-wife

The semantic range of the words linked with "wife" in the Greek translations does not match the range in Hebrew because the Greek translations use two words, πονηρία and κακία, to translate רע(ה). The range of meaning for forms of πονηρία is closer to the use of רע(ה) in the early chapters of Genesis, as "evil" or "wicked(ness)," than to the use of רע(ה) in BBS as "bad(ness)" or "misfortune."[5] For forms of κακία, the semantic range is close enough to that of רע(ה) in BBS that the words can share a translation as "bad(ness)."

---

4   See section 2.2.2, in chapter 2, for detailed discussions of the special translations used for the female figures of the schema.

5   However, in the matched comments on the Flood sequence, the LXX of Genesis uses κακία for Gen 6:5 and πονηρός for Gen 8:21, but the Hebrew is רע(ה) both times.

Because only one of the nine instances in the Greek translation of (ה)רע has
κακία (BBS 25:19), it appears from chart AppLex-2 that the more extreme
interpretation of (ה)רע has prevailed. The binary opposition רע \ טוב in Gen
1–8 of the MT is translated by καλός / πονηρός in the LXX of Genesis, yet the
same Hebrew binary in the Book of Ben Sira is translated in Sirach by ἀγαθός
/ κακός. Moreover, an apparent distinction between רעה and רע in Gen 6:5 is
seemingly replicated in the LXX by κακία and πονηρός. Thus, since רע \ טוב
in BBS is consistently ἀγαθός / κακός in Sirach, the preference in Sirach for
translating combinations of רעה or רע with "wife" as πονηρ- instead of κακ-
strongly suggests an intensification of the meaning, from "bad" to "evil."
Such an intensification would fit the genre of "blame of women," where the
excessiveness of describing a wife who talks too much as "evil" takes it out
of ordinary semantic boundaries into the territory of irony.

The chart AppLex-3, below, compares summarized information from the
chart AppLex-2 with vocabulary from the MT and LXX of Genesis.

AppLex-3: Translations of טוב *and* (ה)רע *from BBS and Genesis*

BINARIES AND "WIFE" VERSES	BBS	SIRACH
~~BBS~~ / Sir 17:7	n/a	ἀγαθός → κακός
BBS A / Sir 11:14	טוב ← רע	ἀγαθός → κακός
BBS E / Sir 33:14	[?] ← טוב	κακός → ἀγαθός
BBS C (7 items) / Sir (11 items) "+ wife"	(ה)רע	πονηρ- (10); κακ- (1)
BBS C (2 items) / Sir (2 items) "+ wife"	טובה	ἀγαθ-
BINARIES AND MISC.	MT GENESIS	LXX GENESIS
Gen 2:9, 17; 3:5, 22	טוב ← רע	καλός → πονηρός
Gen 2:18	טוב	καλός
Gen 6:5	רעה ← רע	κακία → πονηρός
Gen 8:21	רע	πονηρός

A.1.2 Eve and the Vocabulary of BBS 25:24

Arguments on one topic are covered in this section: details for why the
Hebrew text BBS 25:24 cannot allude to the biblical character Eve as the
woman responsible for sin and death. In chapter 5, a number of verses in the
Book of Ben Sira are proposed as allusions to Eve on the basis of Ben Sira's
use of rare words and phrases that occur in Genesis 1–4. These are the exact
same criteria by which I reject BBS 25:24 as a allusion to Eve, since none of
the words from Eve's stories are present in v. 24, nor is the vocabulary
neutral and available for assignment, since the vocabulary of that verse has
strong links to other stories.

The graphic below shows the Hebrew and Greek verses divided into units according to the Hebrew text. The top-most row notes whether the Greek translation of the unit is a "minor" or "MAJOR" divergence from the Hebrew. For each word-pair, I compare the vocabulary of BBS/Sirach with that of words associated with Eve in Genesis 2 and 3, using the MT and LXX of Genesis.

=	MINOR	MAJOR	=	MAJOR	MINOR
מאשה	תחלת	עון	ובגללה	גוענו	יחד
From woman	start of	iniquity	and because of her	we waste away	all alike
ἀπὸ γυναικὸς	ἀρχὴ	ἁμαρτίας	καὶ δι'αὐτὴν	ἀποθνῇσκομεν	πάντες
From woman	begin'g of	sin	and because of her	we die	all

The only equivalent word pair is the first, in which the Greek and Hebrew words translated as "woman/wife" have similar semantic ranges and are both available for allusions to Eve. The pair בגלל and διά, "because of," are functionally equivalent.[6] However, בגלל does not occur in the early chapters of Genesis.

Two of the differences between Hebrew and Greek word-units are minor. The Hebrew/Greek word pair תחלה and ἀρχὴ translate as "beginning" and "start," but the Greek word ἀρχὴ can allude to Gen 1:1 because it is the word used in LXX Genesis to translate ראשית (beginning). According to Collins, ראשית "carries a sense of hierarchical as well as temporal primacy," but the Hebrew word in BBS 25:24, תחלה, "has a more strictly temporal sense."[7] The word ראשית would evoke the creation stories of Genesis, but תחלה cannot do so.[8] In the other set of minor differences, יחד and πάντες, πάντες corresponds to Hebrew כל or כלנו, "all" or "all of us." The word יחד is comparatively rare. The translation is "together" or "as one" when it indicates *unity*; "all at once" to show *temporal similarity*; and "all alike" to show *similarity of circumstances*. There is no instance of יחד in the early chapters of Genesis.

The two major divergences are the Greek words translated as "sin" and "die." The word translated as ἁμαρτία (sin) is the Hebrew word עון. However, this is not the Hebrew word one would expect from reading the Greek translation of 25:24. The expected word would be חטא. The word חטא is semantically close to the Greek ἁμαρτία because both relate to "missing (a

---

6   Thanks to B. G. Wright for that information.

7   Collins, "Before the Fall," 298.

8   The word תחלה cannot evoke the first chapters of Genesis because it does not occur there—thus, it is not available in the system through which Ben Sira alludes to a particular biblical text by using a rare word that belongs to that text.

mark)." In Sirach, a noun or verb-form of ἁμαρτάνω always translates חטא. In the Book of Ben Sira, עון occurs twelve times, and ten times out of twelve the translation in Sirach is ἁμαρτία, once ἄδικος and once λύπη. However, the word עון, though often used in parallel with חטא, seems to have its own distinct semantic range that centers on "iniquity" but includes "guilt (for iniquity)" and/or "punishment (for iniquity)."

And—whatever the similarities and differences between "iniquity" and "sin"— neither עון nor חטא is ever used in connection with Eve. Both words appear first in connection with Cain. In Genesis 4:7, God tells Cain that "'לפתח חטאת רבץ,'" which means something like "an opening for sin awaits," and in verse 13 Cain cries out "'גדול עוני מנשא,'" which can mean both "my punishment is too great to bear" and "my iniquity is too great to take away."[9] Thus, the introduction of both sorts of transgression occurs in conjunction with the character Cain and can relate to Eve only by association—and then only through the interpretation that her eating the fruit of the Tree is the first sin.

Of the six Hebrew/Greek word pairs for BBS/Sir 25:24, גוע and ἀποθνῄσκω have the least overlap of semantic range. The verb root גוע means "to expire," "to breathe one's last breath," or "to waste away." Sometimes גוע results in death, or is itself a result of death as "a body," but classical Hebrew almost always uses the verb root מות to express "death," and "mortality" in contrast to "immortality." Thus, מות is close to the Greek θάνατος and ἀποθνῄσκω. In Genesis, Eve's association with death is through words from the verb root מות. The link originates in the prohibition against eating the fruit of the Tree of the Knowledge of Good and Evil (Gen 2:17) and continues in her conversation with the Serpent (Gen 3:3-4). Eve has no association with the word גוע, which is part of the story of the Flood (Gen 6–8). In Genesis 7, all land-creatures slowly suffocate, as the waters rise in response to God's plan "to destroy all flesh that has in it the breath of life, from under the heavens—each that is upon the earth, it shall expire (יגוע)" (Gen 6:17; also 7:21). The connection between "breath" and גוע is clear; therefore, "expire" is an appropriate translation.[10]

---

9   There is no consistent pattern for matches between the words in BBS/Sir 25:24 and those in the MT or LXX of Genesis. BBS 25:24 (עון) matches Gen 4:13 (עון) but not 4:7 (חטא). Sir 25:24 (ἁμαρτία) matches 4:7 (ἁμαρτάνω) but not 4:13 (αἰτία; "responsibility, mostly in a bad sense, guilt, blame, or the imputation thereof ... i.e., an accusation" [Liddell, et al., Greek-English Lexicon, 44a-b]).

10   See DCH 2:335b, גוע 2. 'gasp,' ... גוענו "we are at the last gasp." Thus, the phrase ובגללה גוענו יחד could be translated as "and because of her, we are at the last gasp, all alike."

Nine verses in the Book of Ben Sira use גוע.[11] The semantic range includes three verses with unambiguous conditions of death (BBS 8:7, 38:16, and 48:5); the Septuagint translates these by the Greek words νεκρός and σῶμα. One verse, in which the choice between "expire" and "waste away" is unclear, is translated by τελευτάω (BBS 4:18). Each of the remaining five verses uses גוע for a condition that is not death, and in each case the context indicates that "waste away" is a better translation than "expire." BBS 25:24 is among these verses because its context is a sequence of debilitations that befall the husband. Therefore, I translate גוע in 25:24 as "waste away." In the verses I translate as "waste away," the LXX translates גוע twice as ἀποθνῇσκω, once as λύπη, once as τελευτάω, and once not at all—there is no related word in the Greek translation.

Comparing the Ben Sira texts with Genesis confirms the evidence that גוע is a misfit within Greek semantic categories. Translations of גוע in LXX Gen 6 and 7 are not consistent: the same event is translated in Gen 6:17 (when the flood is announced) as τελευτάω, yet the phrase ויגוע... מתו in Gen 7:21 (when the flood occurs) is translated twice as ἀποθνῇσκω though the verbs are different. However, the Hebrew death-words associated with Eve—those from מות—are uniformly translated in LXX Genesis 3 and 4 as words related to ἀποθνῇσκω. Muraoka distinguishes between ἀποθνῇσκω and τελευτάω on the basis that ἀποθνῇσκω could imply a natural death—simple mortality—while τελευτάω means the end of life, but "not as a result of natural death."[12] He notes that, in his sources, forms of ἀποθνῇσκω translate מות one hundred and seventy-one times and גוע only three times; τελευτάω translates מות forty times and גוע twice.[13] Interestingly, the verb ἐκλείπω—"to die out, perish" or "to lose strength, physically, as in old age"—which translates גוע six times in Muraoka's sources but never translates מות—is not used for any of the instances of גוע in the Book of Ben Sira nor for those in chapters 2 to 7 of Genesis.[14] The Hebrew verb גוע seems to occupy a semantic niche between the Greek verbs τελευτάω and ἐκλείπω. It often indicates the end of life, but in terms of the process of dying rather than the state of death, which is מות. The instances of גוע are gradual movements toward death, such as suffocation (in the Flood of Genesis) or extreme debilitation due to illness or old age (in

---

11 See chart AppLex-4, for the lexical list for גוע.

12 Muraoka, *Greek-English Lexicon of the Septuagint: Chiefly*, 53–54. Muraoka's complete edition of the lexicon (*A Greek-English Lexicon of the Septuagint*, 2009) lacks the earlier versions' "Section D," which gives the Hebrew equivalents; however, the 2009 edition gives the same definitions as those cited here.

13 Muraoka, *Greek-English Lexicon of the Septuagint: Chiefly*, 552.

14 Muraoka, *Greek-English Lexicon of the Septuagint: Chiefly*, 164.

the Book of Ben Sira). The only possible allusive connection between Eve and *death* for the MT of Genesis would be through the verb מות used in Gen 3:3-4 in her speech and the serpent's speech to her—גוע cannot allude to Eve.[15]

AppLex-4: All extant instances of גוע in BBS

# (MS)	GREEK	HEBREW	TRANSLATION OF THE HEBREW
8:7 (A)	νεκρός	אל תתהלל על גוע זכר כלנו נאספים :	Do not gloat on account of one who *expires* —remember: all of us are "being gathered."
38:16 (B)	σῶμα	כמשפטו אסוף שארו ואל תתעלם בגויעתם :	According to his sentence, his body is being gathered—and do not withdraw yourself from *their* (?) *corpse*.
48:5 (B)	νεκρός	המקים גוע ממות וממשאול כרצון יִיַ	The one who raises one who *expires* from death—and from Sheol by the will of YYY.
14:18 (Aᵐ)	τελευτάω	גוע ואחר גומל	*expire* / **waste away** and after become ripe.
14:17 (A)	θάνατος + ἀποθνῇσκω	כל הבשר כבגד יבלה וחוק עולם גוע יגועו :	All flesh like a garment will wear out— and the decree forever: "Surely they will **waste away**!"
25:24 (C)	ἀποθνῇσκω	מאשה תחלת עון ובגללה גוענו יחד	From a woman is the beginning of iniquity—and because of her, we **waste away**, all alike.
37:2 (B)	λύπη	הלא דין מגיע על מות רע כנפשך נהפך לצר :	Is it not a sentence of **wasting-away** towards [D = unto] death—a companion like your soul [D = a soul], changed to an enemy?
37:30 (B)	—	כי ברוב תענוג.יקנן חולי והמרבה יגיע אל זרא :	For with increase of pleasure, sickness is gained—and an excessive-one will **waste away** to nausea.
37:30 (D)		כי ברב אובל יקנון חולי והמזיע יגוע על זרא :	For with much eating, sickness is gained— and a trembling-one will **waste away** from nausea.
37:31 (B)	τελευτάω	בלא מוסר רבים יגועו והנשמר יוסיף חיים :	Without discipline, many will **waste away** [D= have **wasted away**]—and one who is heedful will prolong life.

For 8:7a, גוע is pointed as a participle. For 48:5b, reading גוע as a participle.

---

15 As mentioned previously, the Greek text of Sir 25:24 probably refers to Eve.

A.1.3 Miscellaneous Lexical Studies

AppLex-5: Instances of the word ראש in the Book of Ben Sira

KEY: **F** = first/best; **D** = dignity/submission; **B** = body part; **T** = top/chief.

#MS	ראש	GREEK	
D 4:7A	ולשלטון עוד הכאף ראש:	κεφαλή	—and to those having more power, bend the head. (|| "incline ear to the poor")
T 10:2A	וּבְרֹאשׁ עִיר כֵּן יוֹשְׁבָיו :	ἡγέομαι (pt.)	—and as is the head of a city, thus are his co-habitants.
T 10:20AC	בין אחים ראשם נכבד	ἡγέομαι (pt.)	Among brothers, the chief/head of them is honored (—and more than him, one fearing God.)
D 11:1AB	חכמת דל תשא ראשו	κεφαλή	Wisdom of a poor-man lifts-up his head
F 11:3ABB[m]	וראש תנובות פריה :	ἀρχή	(Feeble among flyers is the bee)—and best/head of produce is her fruit.
D 11:13A	נשא בראשו וירממהו	κεφαλή	God lifts-up [a poor man's] head and exalts him
B 12:18A	ראש יניע והניף ידו	κεφαλή	[an enemy] will shake [his] head, and he will wave his hands
B 13:7A	ובראשו יניע אלוך :	κεφαλή	—and [a rich man] will shake his head at you.
F 15:14B	הוא מֹראש ברא אדם	ἀρχή	He, from the beginning/head created a human/Adam
15:14B[m]	[ם מבראשית] ברא אדם [4]]	ἀρχή	[God?] from "the beginning"/ from b'reishit created a human/Adam
F 16:26A	כברא אל מעשיו מראש על חייהם	ἀρχή	For God created His works from the beginning, concerning their lives
D 30:12B	כיף ראשו בנערותו	—	Bend-down [your son's] head in his youth
F 31:28B	והוא לגיל נחלק מראש :	—	—and [wine] was apportioned from the beginning/head, to cause to rejoice.
B 31:29B	כאב ראש לענה וקלין	—	Pain of the head, bitterness, and dishonor
D 33:26E	ואם נשא ראשו יבג[4]	—	—and if he lifts-up his head, he will betray you[?]
T 36:10B	השבת ראש פאתי מֹואב [אויב]	κεφαλή	Cause-to-desist the head of the regions of Moab [B[M] enemy]
F 36:15B	תן עדות למראש מעשיך	ἀρχή	Give testimony on Your works from-the-beginning.
F 37:9B	זֹק[5] [ראשֶׁךְ :] להביט רישֶׁךְ :	—	—and [?] to behold your poverty. [B[M] your beginning/head.]

F 37:16B (2x)	ראש כל מעשה דבר וראש — כל פועל היא מחשבת	ἀρχή	Beginning/head of every work, is a word—and the beginning/head of every action? it is a plan.
37:16B^mD	[ראש כל מעשה מאמר]	ἀρχή	Beginning/head of every work, a saying
D 38:3B	דאת רופא תרים ראשו	κεφαλή	The knowledge of a physician raises-up his head
F 39:25B	לטוֹב חלק מראש [3]	ἀρχή	[?] for a good-one, a portion from the beginning/head [Beentjes: וב[5]]
F 39:32B	על כן מראש התיצּבתי	ἀρχή	Therefore, from the beginning I've positioned-myself
D 44:22B	וברכה נחה על ראש ישראל: (v. 23 "Jacob")	κεφαλή	—and He guided a blessing, upon the head of Israel.

TOTALS: **First** = 9 of 22; **D**ignity = 7 of 22; **B**ody = 3 of 22; **T**op = 3 of 22.
- For BBS 10:20, the entry for אח at *DCH* 1:174b gives "colleagues."

From *DCH* 7:365–66, the list of meanings for ראש I includes the categories of *body-part* (head of a person); *topmost* (head or summit of a mountain); *status* (head person, chief); *place* (front one, headwater of a river); and *time* (first one, beginning). The list for the second meaning, ראש II, consists of *poison*, with particular poisons from plants and the venom of snakes. The Greek of Sirach 25:15 seems to be translated from a Hebrew text that mentioned "poison" of "a serpent"; however, the translator gave ראש as "head" (of "a serpent").

The "head" metaphor in BBS seems more like "top/bottom ‖ important/ less important," rather than "head/body ‖ mental/physical" (the head/body of the Great Chain of Being). The Book of Ben Sira does not share the Great Chain of Being schema. Though the important/less important binary could combine with head/body binary, as in the Greek form, it does not combine here in BBS.

AppLex-6: Words related to fool *(כסיל) in the Book of Ben Sira*

	HEBR.		GREEK	TRANSLATION OF GR.
20:7, MS C	כסיל	opp. חכם	ἄφρων	foolish, ignorant
20:13, MS C	כסיל	opp. חכם	μωρός	foolish, stupid
31:20, MS B	כסיל	—	ἄπληστος	glutton; immoderate-man
31:30, MS B	כסיל	—	ἄφρων	foolish, ignorant
42:8, MSS B, M	כסיל	contrast? with פותה	μωρός	foolish, stupid
6:20, MS A	אויל	parallel לב	ἀπαίδευτος	ignorant, untaught
8:4, MS A	אויל	—	ἀπαίδευτος	ignorant, untaught
31:6, MS B	אויל	parallel פותה	ἄφρων	foolish, ignorant (v. 7)
41:5, MS B	אויל	—	—	—
8:15, MS A	אולת	parallel ?? אכזרי	ἀφροσύνη	foolish, lacking in sense
20:22, MS C	אולת	—	ἄφρων	foolish, ignorant
30:13, MS B	אולת	—	ἀσχημοσύνη	indecency
41:15, MSS B, M	אולת	~ with חכם	μωρία	folly
47:23, MS B	אולת	—	ἀφροσύνη	foolish, lacking in sense
11:16, MS A	שכלות	—	—	—
51:23, MS B	סכלים	—	ἀπαίδευτος	ignorant, untaught
8:17, MS A	פותה	—	μωρός	foolish, stupid
16:23, MS A	פותה	contrast חסדי־לב (misspelled חסרי־תב?)	ἄφρων	foolish, ignorant
31:6, MS B	פותה	parallel אויל	ἄφρων	foolish, ignorant
42:8, MSS B, M	פותה	contrast? with כסיל	ἀνόητος	foolish, silly
6:20, MS A	חסר־לב	parallel אויל	ἀκάρδιος	lacking-heart

AppLex-7: Spoken vs. written contexts, proverb-related words in BBS

KEY: **S** = spoken; **W** = written; **(?)** = unknown

CONTEXT		משל PROVERB	חידה RIDDLE	שיח DISCOURSE	אומר SAYING
3:29	heart perceives proverb ‖ *ear hearkens* to wisdom	S	—	—	—
4:24	wisdom known in saying ‖ understanding from *tongue*	—	—	—	S
6:35	*listen* to each discourse ‖ proverb not escape you	S-	- - - -	-S	—
8:8	*not leave* discourse of sages ‖ teach self their riddles	—	S-	-S	—
9:17	wise handiwork ‖ *teller*-of-proverbs makes people wise [16]	S	—	—	—
11:8	listen before speaking ‖ don't *speak* amid discourse	—	—	S	—
12:12	understand my saying in future ‖ sigh for my sighing	—	—	—	S
13:11	not confide in nobleman ‖ not trust his discourse	—	—	S	—
13:12	his abundant discourse is test ‖ he will spy on you	—	—	S	—
13:26	good heart + shining face ‖ magnify discourse + plan	—	—	(?)	—
15:10	sage *speaks* hymn ‖ will teach proverb with it	S	—	—	—
31:22	son, do not despise me ‖ understand my saying, at end	—	—	—	(?)
32:4	do not *pour out* discourse instead of wine	—	—	S	—
33:4	prepare saying, do it ‖ prepare restful house, make shine	—	—	—	(?)
35:17	God won't reject orphan ‖ nor reject widow's discourse	—	—	S	—
42:15	by a saying, God did works ‖ His will enacts instruction	—	—	—	S
44:4	sages of discourse + <u>book</u> ‖ proverb-*tellers* + proverbs	S-	- - - -	-W	—
44:5	psalmists + chord ‖ composers of proverbs + <u>writing</u>	W	—	—	—
47:17	Solomon praised for song, proverb, riddle & figure	(?)	(?)	—	—
50:27	timely *telling*-of-proverbs = Ben Sira's profession	S	—	—	—

---

16   The word מושל can also be translated as "ruler" wherever it occurs (this verse, 15:10, and 44:4).

AppLex-8: Ben Sira's writing activities: The roots כתב *and* ספר

כתב

39:32b (MS B)   והתבוננתי ובכתב —and I have considered and I have put
                        הנחתי : it **in writing**.

42:7b (B[M])   : ומתת ולקח הכל בכתב —and of giving and taking, everything
                        in writing.

44:5b (B [M])   : נושאי משל בכתב —composers of proverb, **in writing**.

45:11cd (B)   כל אבן יקרה לזכרון בכתב חרות Each stone ... with engraved

(Ben-Hayyim) (: שׁבֹ[טי יש[ראל) :]ראל[5] למספר **writing**—for the number of
                        the tribes of Israel.

48:10a (B)   הכתוב נכון לעת It is written: (you) who are ready for the time

ספר

31:11b (B)   : ותהלתו יס[פר קה[ל —and the assembly will recount his praise.

38:24a (B)   חכמת סופר תרבה חכמה The wisdom of **the scribe** increases
                        "wisdom"

42:7a (B)   על מקום תפקד יד תספור Concerning a place you entrust/appoint
                        a hand, you will count

42:15b (B)   : וזה חזיתי ואספרה —and what I have beheld, may I recount.

42:17b (B [M])   : לספר נפלאות יײ —to recount the wonders of YYY.

43:24a (B)   ויורדי הים יספרו קצהו And those who go down to/travel the
                        sea will recount its entirety

44:15b (Bᵐ, M)   : ותהלתם יספר קהל —and the assembly will recount their
                        praise.

51:1a (B)   אספרה שמך מעוז חיי May I recount your Name, fleeing in
                        haste (for) my life

AppLex-9: Concepts linked with honor *in the Book of Ben Sira*

(Grey rows show verses not extant in the Hebrew manuscripts.)

	Honor	Humility	Dishonor	Shame	Violence	Riches	Poverty	Fear-of-God	Wisdom
2:10 no **shame** if trusting God				no				@	
4:13 honor from God, if wise	@								@
4:21 there is a shame that is honor	@			@					
6:31 Wisdom gives honor	@								@
10:19 dishonor if not-Fear-of-God			not					@	
10:20 honor if Fear-of-God	@							@	
10:23a do not honor violent men,	not				@				
10:23b ...do not dishonor poor men			not				@		
10:24 honor for F-of-G > high rank	@							@	
10:28 honor if humility	@	@							
10:29 not honor one dishonor. his soul	not		@						
10:31a honor of poor man greater	@						@		
10:31b ...than honor of rich man	@					@			
15:04 no **shame** if trust Wisdom				no					@
24:22 no **shame** if obey Wisdom				no					@
32:24 no **shame** if trusting Lord				no				@	
37:26 inherit honor, if wise	@								@
44:1-7 honored for kindliness	@				not				
51:17 Wis., know. and prayer → honor	@								@
51:25 choose Wisdom, not money						not			@

AppLex-10: Words for slander in BBS and Sirach

HEBREW	GREEK
דבה slander	καταψευσμόν calumny
רוכל gossip; defamation	ψίθυρον slanderous whispering
רגל a spy/slanderer	δίγλωσσον double-tongued
נרגן a whisperer	διαβολή slander

5:14bA	ובלשונך אל תרגל רע: —and by your tongue don't **slander** a companion. *[no clear Greek equiv.]*
11:29A	רוכל [3]פ רבו ומה : (פִּצְעֵי) —and how wounds of a **defamer** multiply!
11:30A	אורב הרוכל כדוב לבית לצים The **defamer** lurks like a bear near a house of scoffers—and like a **spy** he'll see וכמרגל יראה ערוה: *[no clear Greek equiv.]* vulnerability/nakedness.
26:5 διαβολὴν πόλεως	**Slander in the city**, the gathering of a mob, and false accusation—all these are worse than death.
28:13 ψίθυρον δίγλωσσον	Curse the **gossips** and the **double-tongued**, for they destroy the peace of many.
28:14 γλῶσσα τρίτη	**A meddlesome tongue** has ... destroyed strong cities, and overturned the houses of the great.
28:15 γλῶσσα τρίτη	**A meddlesome tongue** can drive virtuous women from their homes and rob them of the fruit of their toil;
41:5B[m]	כי כן נאמס דבת ערים ... **slander** of cities *[no clear Greek equiv.]*
42:11B	דבת עִיר וק[2]ת עם **Slander** of a city and an assembly of the people λαλιὰν ἐν πόλει ... a **byword** in the city
46:7B	ולהשבית דבה רעה (Caleb) quieted evil **slander**
51:2B	דבת עם + דבת לשון ...**slander** of the people + **slander** of the tongue διαβολῆς γλώσσης ... **slander** of the tongue

AppLex-11: Gendered use of roots קנה, קנן, and קנא, poetic units of BBS

KEY: ♀ = gendered instance (Wisdom or woman/wife); ♂ = gendered instance (male); @ = non-gendered instance; poetic units chosen for analysis.

Verse	gain קנה	a gain קְנָיָן	nest קנן	a nest קֵן	jeal's קנא	envy קִנְאָה	Poetic units
6:6a (A, 2x)	@@						
9:1a (A)					♀		Ch. 9 = paired units: ‖ bet.
9:2a (A)	♀						replacing wife (vv. 1–9) and
9:11a (A)					♂		replacing old friend (10–18).
12:11cd (A)						@	
14:26a (A)				♀			14:20–15:8, pursuing Wisd.
20:23b (C)	@						
30:24a (B)						@	
33:31d (E)					@		
36:24a (B)	♀	♀					36:18–26, on women/wife ‖
36:26c (B)				♀			"wise-man," 37:16–26
37:10b (D)					@		
37:11d (B)	@						
37:30a (B)			@				
40:5a (B)						@	
45:18b (B)					@		
45:23c (B)					@		
48:2b (B)						@	
51:18a (11QPsᵃ)					♀		51:13–30, poem spoken by
51:20f (B)	♀						Ben Sira about Wisdom; vv.
51:21b (B)	♀	♀					13–21 are erotic.
51:25b (B)	♀						
51:28b (B)	@						
Total all, 26	10	2	1	2	7	4	Totals, each (♀+ ♂+ @)
Total all, 12	5	2	0	2	3	0	Gender totals (♀+ ♂)
	4/5	2/2	—	2/2	3/3	—	poetic gender/Gender ratio
	<all	all	none	all	all	none	

38:16b (B) has קינה from קין "to mourn or wail." (only instance).

AppLex-12: The name שמעון

BBS 50:27   מוסר שכל ומושל אופנים   לשמעון בן ישוע בן אלעזר בן סירא :

Intelligent instruction and the timely telling-of-proverbs
—[belonging] to Simeon, son of Yeshua, son of Eleazar, son of Sira.

BBS 5:30   עד הנה דברי שמעון בן ישוע שנקרא בן סירא :

Thus far, the words of Simeon son of Yeshua—who is called "son of Sira."

חכמת שמעון בן ישוע בן אלעזר בן סירא :

The wisdom of Simeon son of Yeshua son of Eleazar son of Sira.

יהי שם יי מבורך מעתה ועד עולם :

Let the name of YYY be blessed, from now and until forever!

The personal name of the author "who is called 'son of Sira'" is the subject of debate. His name is given as "Simeon" twice in the Hebrew text (MS B) but never in Greek versions. Those who dispute the possibility of the name "Simeon" for Ben Sira often claim that the word is a scribal duplication of the name of the high priest who is the subject of BBS 50:1–20. However, the name Simon/Simeon was in frequent use by the Common Era—thus it is quite possible that "Simeon" is the high priest's personal name and also Ben Sira's.

Fitzmyer states that, in lists of Jewish names found in "Egypt, Josephus, the Palestinian ossuaries, the New Testament and the new texts from Murabba'at," in each list the variants of the name "Simon" are the most frequently attested, among these much-used names for men: "Joseph, Judah, John, Eleazar, Jesus, Matthias, Jonathe, Zachary, Azariah, Jairus, Menahem.."[17]

---

17 Fitzmyer, "The Name Simon," 4, citing the work of Józef Tadeusz Milik and Bellarmino Bagatti (Gli scavi del 'Dominus Flevit' (Monte Oliveto - Gerusalemme): Part I, La necropoli del periodo romano [Pubblicazioni dello Studium Biblicum Franciscanum XIII; Jerusalem, 1958], p. 108). Fitzmyer includes a list of minor corrections, and a tally of all variants, citing Pierre Benoit, Józef Tadeusz Milik and Roland de Vaux (*Les Grottes de Murabba'at*; Discoveries in the Judaean Desert II; Oxford: Clarendon Press, 1961).

AppLex-13: Verses in Sir 51:13–22 that diverge from BBS 51:13–22

KEY→ MS 11QPsᴬ default for Hebrew through v. 20b, then MS B; Ben-Hayyim.

#	BBS 51:17, 19–21	#	Sɪʀ 51:17, 19–21 (NETS)
17	: וֹעלה היתה לי למלמדי אתן הודי And she was *an ascent* for me —to my teacher I will give my splendor.	17	προκοπὴ ἐγένετό μοι ἐν αὐτῇ τῷ διδόντι μοι σοφίαν δώσω δόξαν. I made progress in her; to him who gives me wisdom I will give glory.
18	זמותי ואשחקה קנֹאתי בטוב ולוֹא אשוב: I have planned so that I may be joyful—(for) I have been zealous in pleasing, and I will not turn back.	18	διενοήθην γὰρ τοῦ ποιῆσαι αὐτὴν καὶ ἐζήτησα τὸ ἀγαθὸν καὶ οὐ μὴ αἰσχυνθῶ. For I intended to practice her, and I sought the good, and I will never be ashamed.
19	: חריתי נפשי בה ופני לוא השיבֹותי I kindled my desire/soul for her —and my face I have not turned away.	19	διαμεμάχισται ἡ ψυχή μου ἐν αὐτῇ καὶ ἐν ποιήσει νόμου διηκριβασάμην. My soul has grappled with her, and in the performance of the law I was exacting.
20	: טרתי נפשי בה וברומיה לוֹא אשלה I have kept my desire/soul for her —and *at her exaltation* I will not be slack.	20	τὴν ψυχήν μου κατεύθυνα εἰς αὐτὴν καὶ ἐν καθαρισμῷ εὗρον αὐτήν. I directed my soul to her, and in purification I found her.
20c (B)	ידי פתחה שעריה ולה אחדֹר ואביט ב[ה]: My hand has opened her gates— and I will be surrounded by her, and I will regard her.	19c	τὰς χεῖράς μου ἐξεπέτασα πρὸς ὕψος καὶ τὰ ἀγνοήματα αὐτῆς ἐπενόησα. I spread out my hands on high, and I thought about ignorance of her.

The trope of Wisdom as "an ascent" (17a) for Ben Sira that culminates "at her exaltation" (20b) is missing from Sirach, as is the ability to identify Wisdom as the "teacher" to whom he will give his "splendor" (17b).[18] The major change occurs in Sir 19bcd, where the Greek text is semantically unrelated to any phrase of BBS 19b and 20cd in either Hebrew MS though it mixes some words here and there.

---

18   Note that BBS 4:11 opens with חכמות למדה בניה "Wisdom has taught her sons," linking the figure's explicit name (not the usual "wisdom/Wisdom") with the verb root למד, "to teach."

AppLex-14: Modifiers for אשה *in the Book of Ben Sira*

KEY: Left-hand set is taken from the complete group on the right, in which the less relevant entries are shaded.

FREQUENCY OF MODIFIER	SEQUENTIALLY, BY VERSE ([MS] #:#)
3x אשה משכלת intelligent wife	[A]7:19 אשה משכלת intelligent wife
2x אשה טובה good wife	[A]7:23 וְשָׁם לָהֶם נשים wives for sons
>1x אשה רעה bad wife (missing?)	[A]7:26 אשה לך your wife
1x אשה לך your wife	[A]9:1 אשת חיקך wife of your bosom
1x אשת חיקך wife of your bosom	[A]9:3 אשה זרה strange(r) woman
1x אשה זרה strange(r) woman	[A]9:8 אשת הן graceful woman
1x אשת הן graceful woman	[A]12:14 אשת זדון insolent wom'n/wife
1x אשת זדון insolent woman/wife	[AB]15:2 אשת נעורים wife of y'r youth
1x אשת נעורים wife of your youth	[C]25:8 אשה משכלת intelligent wife
1x אשת לשון talkative wife	[C]25:17 רע אשה wife-trouble
1x אשת חיל valorous wife	[C]25:18 רעת אשה badness of wife
1x אשה ביישת modest wife/wom'n	[C]25:20 אשת לשון talkative wife
1x אשה נחשקת desired wife	[C]25:22 אשה מכלכלת wife who supports
	[C]25:23 אשה לא תאשר wife not pleasing h.
	[C]26:1 אשה טובה good wife
13 modifying words = 16 instances of אשה with a modifier	[C]26:2 אשת חיל valorous wife
	[C]26:3 אשה טובה good wife
	[C]26:13 אשה מֹטיב בעלה w. does-good to h.
	[C]26:15 אשה ביישת modest wife/wom'n
	[B]40:19 אשה נחשקת desired wife
	[B]40:23 אשה משכלת intelligent wife
	[B]42:6 אשה רעה bad wife
	[BM]42:13 רעת אשה evil of wife

These are the unmodified instances of אשה in the Book of Ben Sira: BBS 9:2, 8 (MS A); 10:18 (MS A) ("Pride is not fitting for a mortal-person—nor strong anger to one-born-of-woman"); 19:2 (MS C) ("Wine and women will make a heart reckless—and a warlike spirit will ruin its master"); 25:24 (MS C); 26:16 (MS C); 33:28 (MS E); 36:22,24, 25 (MSS B,C); 37:11 (MSS B,D); 42:12 (MS B); 42:14 (MSS B, M); 47:19 (MS B).

A.2 Fully-Annotated Translations of Passages
from the Book of Ben Sira

Chart numbers for the translation section are the same as the version in the text, but prefixed with "A".

NOTE: For square brackets in all Hebrew examples and their translations, numbers approximate the number of missing letters, and letters or words indicate conjectures about the letters missing from the Hebrew MSS.

A.2.1 Fully-Annotated Chart for Chapter 1

Chart A1-2: BBS 33:14–15 (MS E) and 42:24–25 (MSS B, M)

KEY→ BBS 33:14–15 (MS E) and 42:24–25 (MS B, {B^m}; <u>MS M</u>): Ben-Hayyim

33:14	טֹוב [6]	[Opposite bad-things are] good
	: וְנוכח חיים מות	—and opposite life is death.
	רשע [3] איש [3]	Opposite a good man is a wicked-man (נֹזבֹח איש טֹוב)
	ונוכח האור [4]	—and opposite light, darkness. (חֹ[שד]:)
33:15	אל כולם אל כל מ[3]	Regard all the works of God (מעֹשֹה) (הֹבֹט) all
	שנים שנים זה לעומת [2]	of them in pairs, this-one close by [that-one זה?].
42:24	כלם שונים זה מזה ולא	All of them in pairs, this-one by that-one
	עשזה מהם שו[1]כלם [10]	—and He has not made any of them
	לעמת זה	[deceptive שוא?].
42:25	{זה על זה חלף טוב טובם}	{This-one according to that-one renews their
	[ו]מי ישבע להביט הודם	goodness}—and who can have enough of beholding their splendor?

NOTES for chart A1-2:
- Note that the missing word Ben-Hayyim fills in as טֹוב could as easily be צדיק, the usual opposite for רשע. The other three-letter space is filled in with a four-letter word, נֹזבֹח.
- For the verb חלף in 42:25a, the subject could be the first זה, "this-one"; or could be God ("He renews their goodness"), who is the subject of the verb עשה in 24b; or could be טוב, so that "this-one according to that-one, their goodness passes by," which accords with 25b's reference to "beholding their splendor." Multiple translations are possible for חלף and the rest of the colon. *DCH* 3:238b gives "חלף pass by, pass away, be renewed ... SUBJ זה this one Si 42:25 ... OBJ טוב goodness ... PREP על on behalf of, + זה this one Si 42:25." *CDCH* 120a gives "exchange goodness Si 42:25 (+ על, with)."

A.2.2 Fully-Annotated Charts for Chapter 2

FORMATTING KEY FOR TRANSLATIONS:

MS X = default MS, plain text

{X^m} = marginal notes of default MS, plain text in curly brackets.

<u>MS Y</u>, {<u>Y$^{\underline{m}}$</u>} = 2nd MS & marg., underlined plain text for Hebrew and translation.

[#] = gaps in Hebrew MS with # of spaces; [?text?] is best-guess translation.

([#]א) = Ben-Hayyim's Hebrew; text is translation based on Ben-Hayyim.

text = translation from Greek of Sirach, bolded white text on dark grey ground.

Chart A2-1: "The oppressed-man's cry for help" BBS 35:21–26 (MS B)

KEY→ MS B is default, {B^m}; Ben-Hayyim; Greek.

35:21 עבים חלפה} שועת דל ענן חל The oppressed/poor-man's cry for help
{כי} : עם ועד תגיע לא תנוח   {pierces the clouds}—and until it will
arrive, it shall not rest silent.

לא תמוש עד יפקוד אל ושופט It shall not give-way until God will inspect
{עושה} : צדק יעשה משפט   —and the Righteous Judge will make judgment.

35:22 אדון} גם אל לא יתמהמה God, also, shall not delay—and like
{מה} : וכגבור לא יתאפק   a powerful-one, He'll not be patient.

מפני} עד ימחץ מתני Until He shall strike through, {on account of} the
: אכזרי ולגוים ישיב נקם cruel-one—and He'll repay vengeance on the nations.

35:23 שבטי} אד יוריש שבט זדון Till He'll dispossess the scepter of insolence
{רשעים} : ומטה רשע גדוע יגדע   —and staff of wickedness, surely, hew-down.

35:24 עד ישיב לאנוש פעלו Till He'll repay to the person his actions—and
: וגמול אדם כמזמתו recompense of a human, according to his scheme(s).

35:25 [5] ריב עמו ושמחם [Till He judges? ἕως κρίνῃ] quarrel of His people
{וישמחם} : בישועתו —and {cause them to rejoice} in His deliverance.

35:26 [12] [9] ז[ו]ב[ז]מן [His mercy is apt? ὡραῖον ἔλεος … αὐτου] (in time of)
מצוקה כעת חזיים בעת distress—as a season of thunderclouds, in a season of
: בצורת drought.

Charts 2-2 through 2-6 do not require annotation.

Chart A2-7: "My son, in a time of tumult" BBS 4:20–28 (MSS A, C)

KEY→ MS A is default, {A^m}; <u>MS C.</u>

4:20	בני עת המון שמר ופחד	My son, in a time of tumult, watch and be wary
	מרע ואל נפשך אל תבוש :	of evil—and don't be ashamed for yourself.
4:21	כי יש בֹשֶׁאֹת משאת עון	For there is shame that is a burden of guilt
	ויש בשת כבוד וחן :	—and there is shame that is honor and grace.
4:22	אל תשא פניך על נפשך ואל	Do not favor yourself—and do not be
	תכשל למכשוליך: <u>ואל תבוש</u>	tripped by your stumbling-blocks.
4:23	אל תמנע דבר בעולם	Do not withhold a word forever
	<u>ואל תקפוץ</u> : אל תצפין את חכמתך	—do not conceal your wisdom.
4:24	כי באומר נודעת חכמה	For in speaking, wisdom is known—and
	ותבונה במענה לשון :	understanding in the answer of the tongue.
4:25	אל תסרב עם האל	Do not be obstinate with TheGod
	ואל אלהים היכנע :	—and to God, humble-yourself.
4:26	אל תבוש לשוב מעון ⁽∙∙⁾	Do not be ashamed to turn from guilt
	ואל תעמוד לפני שבלת :	—and do not stand against a torrent/"Shibbolet."
4:27	אל תצע לנבל נפשך	Do not 'fetter' yourself to an impious-fool
	⁽∙∙⁾ ואל תמאן לפני מושלים:	—and do not act defiantly before rulers.
	אל תשב עם שופט עול	Do not remain with an unjust judge
	כי כאשר כרצונו תשפט עמו	—for you'll be judged by his disposition, with him.
4:28	עד המות היעצה על הצדק	Until death, strive for righteousness
	וייי נלחם לך – אל תקרא בעל	—and YYY will fight for you.

NOTE for chart A2-7:
- There are three small dots at the right margin of v. 26 and similar dots at the left margin of v. 27. Beentjes notes that the "function of the three-dotted symbol ... is not clear here" (*Book of Ben Sira in Hebrew*, 25, n.2).

Chart A2-8: "Listen, children ..." BBS 41:15c–42:1d (MSS B, C, M→ no 20)

KEY→ MS M is default; <u>MS B</u>, {B<u>ᵐ</u>}; MS C (v. 16, only); Ben-Hayyim.

41:15c	מוסר בשת שמע בנים	Listen, children, to an instruction on shame
	[3]לּ[1]וּ ([והכ]לָמֹו) על משפטי :	—and be abased according to my judgment.
41:16	לשמר \ לא כל בשת נאה לבוׁש	Not every shame is fit to retain
	ולא כל הכלם נבחר :	—and not every abasement, to be chosen.
41:17	בוש מאב ואם אל פחז	Be ashamed before father and mother, for
	מנשיא ושר אל [בחש]	recklessness—before prince and chief, for deceit.
41:18	מאדון וגבר[ת] על שקר	Before lord and lady, concerning a lie—before
	מעדה ועם [ע]לֹ [פ]שע :	assembly and people, concerning a transgression.
	משותף ורע על מעל	Before partner and companion, concerning treachery
	וממקום תגור [2]יד (עֹ[ל] יד)	—and in the place you sojourn, concerning theft.
41:19	מהפֹר אלה וברית	For breaking stipulation and covenant
v. 20	וממטֹה אציל על לחם	—and reclining to dine, concerning fighting.
	ממ[3]תת (ממנֹ[ע] מתת) שאלה ומהשיב את	For refraining from granting a request
	פני שׁארך\מחשֹׁב אפי רעד : {מיהשע פי}	—and turning away the face of your kin.
41:21	מ(ח)שות מחל(ק)ת מנה	For keeping quiet at the allotment of a share
	זֹמשאל שלום החריׁש	—and for 'not hearing' one who greets [you].
	{אשה} מהביט [13]	For regarding {a woman/wife}
	זֹמהתבונן אל זרה	—and for looking at a stranger-woman.
41:22	מהתעשק [5]הֹ לך	For occupying yourself with your female servant
	ומהתקומם על יציעיה	—and for 'rising up' upon her bed. *[absent MS B]*
	מאהב על דברי חסד	Before a friend, concerning disgraceful words
	ומאחר מתת חרף	—and after a gift, reproaching.
	{דבר חסד} מאוהב על [2]רֹי חרפה ומאחרי מ[תת] א[ל תֹנֹ]אֹץ : {שאלה}	
42:1	משנות ד[ב]רֹ תשמע ומחשף כל דבר	For repeating a word you'll hear—and
	עצה \ ומחסוף כל סוד עצה {על סוש}	for making bare each word of counsel.
	תֹ \ [4]והיית בייש באמת	And you will become truly modest
	ומצא חן בעיני כל חי	—and find grace in the eyes of all the living.

NOTES for chart A2-8:

- Where MSS B and M differ semantically I note both versions; otherwise, MS M is the default because MS B has same texts but includes incoherent variants.
- For 41:19b: Kister ("Some Notes," 160 n. 3) translates as "be ashamed to fight someone with whom you dine," reading ממטֹה as a participle and לחם as לֶחֶם (battle, war), The usual translation "for stretching out your elbow at a meal" breaks the context (for example, Skehan and Di Lella, *Wisdom*, 476.)
- For מחשות in 41:21a, Beentjes (*Book of Ben Sira in Hebrew*, 116 n. 79) states: "Under the *waw* of מחשות, an - *aleph* was originally written."

Chart A2-9: "However, for these (matters) ..." BBS 42:1e–8 (MSS B, M)

KEY→ MS M is default; <u>MS B</u>, {B<u>ᵐ</u>}; Ben-Hayyim.

42:1e	על אלה אל [2] <u>אַד עַל</u> {אַל}	However, for these do not be put to shame
	תבוש ואל תשא פנים וחטא	—and do not show partiality, and sin.

42:2	על תורת עליון וחק	Concerning Torah of the MostHigh, and statute
	ועל משפט להצדיק רשע	—and concerning judgment to acquit wicked-man.

42:3	על חשבון שותף ודרך	Concerning reckoning of a partner and a path—
	ועל מחלקת נחלה ויש	and concerning allotment of inheritance and property.

42:4	על שחקי מזנים ופלס	Concerning accuracies of scales and a balance
	ו[ע]ל תמחי איפה ואבן	—and concerning cleansing of measure and weight.

[3]ל [ב]ר בין מקנה על\	Concerning acquiring, between much to little
תגר ממכר מחיר[3מ] <u>למעט</u>	—and concerning the price of something sold by a
: <u>תגר</u>[3ר ממחיר ועל</u>	vendor.

42:5	רע ועבד ה[13] [?]	*{Greek is about discipline of children}*
	וצלע מהלכת	—and a bad servant and who limps because of beatings.

42:6	ומקום חותם: ת[10]	Concerning the Wrong Wife, a seal
	ידים רבות מפתח	—and a place of many hands, a key.
: תפתח רפות ידים ומקום חכם: חותם רעֹה אשה על} {טפשה}	

42:7	מספר פקיד[7]	Concerning a place where you deposit, an accountant
	בכתב: הכל ת[6]ש	—and for giving and taking, everything in writing.
{ותתה ושואה: בכתב הכל ולקח ומתת תסגור יד תפקד מקום על {תחשוב יד מספר}	

42:8	וכסיל נאיוה ותה פ[4 מ]מוסר על	Concerning instruction of naïve-man and Fool
	בזנות ענה כושל ב[ש]	—and grey-haired stumbler, busy with whoring.
ואיש באמת זהיר והיית	And you will become truly enlightened
: ח[י] כל לפֿנֿי [8] 'צנוע	—and a man who is humble before all the living.

NOTES for chart A2-9:

- For אל תבוש in 42:1e, translating as "do not be ashamed" makes sense only if a positive value is assumed for each "concern," such as "[fulfilling] the Torah" in v. 2a, "a [just] reckoning" in v. 3a, and "[maintaining] accuracies" in v. 4a. *DCH* 2:130b translates the Qal stem of בוש as "be ashamed, be put to shame" and, in the present instance, the latter option covers the ambiguous phrasing of the "concerns."

- For 42:5b, note slight possibility of an allusion to Eve, as a "rib" who "goes about." This is from *DCH* 2:556a "Pi. go, walk about <SUBJ>…appar. עָבַד servant Si 42:5(M) (or perh. subj. = צֵלָע rib, i.e. wife)."

Chart A2-10: BBS 44:1–6 (MSS B, M), from "Praise of the Fathers"

KEY→ MS B is default, {B^m}; MS M; Ben-Hayyim.

[Not in MS M] שבח אבות עולם   An encomium, of the fathers of ancient-time:

44:1	אהללה נא אנשי חסד Let me praise men of piety/kindliness/
	{את} : את אבותינו בדורותם disgrace—our fathers in their generations.
44:2	{להם} רב כבוד חלק עליון Abundant honor has the Most High apportioned
	וגדלה : וגדלו מימות עולם [for them]—and they became great, from days of ancient-time.
44:3	{רודי} דורי ארץ במלכותם Governors of the earth, in their reign —and
	{בגבורם} : ואנשי שם בגבורתם men of renown, in their might. *[not MS M]*
	{יו'} ^50 היועצים בתבונתמסויעצים Counselors, in their understanding
	וחזי : וחוזי כל בנבואתם —and those 'seeing' all, in their prophecy.
44:4	שרי גוים במזמתמסשרי גוי Chiefs of nations, in their discretion
	במחקקן[תם]ורוזנים במחקרותם —and princes, in their <u>decrees</u>.
	{במס'} חכמי שיח בספֿרתם Wise-men of discourse, in their narration
	ומושלים במשמֿחֿותם : —and proverb-tellers, in their 'nails.'
44:5	חקֿרי {חֿקֿן} חוקרי מזמור על חוק על Searchers of psalm, by <u>chord</u>
	קו ונשאי : נושאי משל בכתב —composers of proverb, in writing.
44:6	וסומכי כֿחֿאנשי חיל וסומכי כח Men of valor and supporters of strength—
	ושוקטים על מכונתם : and tranquil-men, on their dwelling place.

NOTES for chart A2-10:

- For דורי in BBS 44:3a, see דֻּוָּר *DCH* 2:428a "'governor' Si 44:3."
- For במשמֿחֿותם in BBS 44:4d, there is some disagreement over the identity of the fifth letter in במשׁמֿרֿותם, which Yadin (*Ben Sira Scroll from Masada*, 36) reads as ח. Corley ("Sirach 44:1-15" p. 166), Skehan ("Staves, Nails, Scribal Slips," 69), and Beentjes (*Book of Ben Sira in Hebrew*) are among those who read the letter as ר, though Beentjes has both versions: במשׁמֿרֿותם on page 77 for MS B, but במשׁמֿחֿותם on page 174 for MSS B and M, while Ben-Hayyim gives both as alternate versions (*Book of Ben Sira*, 53). See מַסְמֵר in *DCH* 5:367a (six instances: Isa 41:7; Jer 10:4; Qoh 12:11; 1 Chron 22:3; 2 Chron 3:9; CD 12:17) and אֲסֻפָּה in *DCH* 1:350a. There may be an echo of colon 4d in Qoh 12:11, where "nails" are linked with "goads." Also, Qohelet's association of "goad" with "shepherd" is similar to the reading of BBS 38:25a where the מלמד as both "an ox-goad" and "a teacher."
- For מושלים in BBS 44:4d, Skehan ("Staves, Nails, Scribal Slips," 69) translates as "proverb-makers" and notes the link between Ben Sira and this verse in Qohelet but interprets along different lines.
- For BBS 44:3c Beentjes (p. 77, n. 50) notes that "some illegible characters follow."

Chart A2-11: "Any wound, not like a heart's wound" BBS 25:13–26:3 (MS C)

KEY→ MS C; Ben-Hayyim.

25:13	כל מכה ולא כ[4] לב	Any wound, and not like [wound of?] the heart
	כל רעה ולא כר[5] ([עת] [3])	—anything bad, and not like badness of [a wife?].
25:17	רע אשה ישחיר מראה	Wife-badness darkens the appearance of husband
	איש ויקדיר פ[2]ז לדוב (פנֵיו)	—and englooms his countenance like a bear.
25:18	בין רעים ישב בעלה	Her husband dwells among bad-things
	ובלא טעמו יתאנח	—and without his "taste," he bemoans himself.
25:19	מעט רעה כרעת אשה	There is little badness like a wife's badness
	גורל חוטא יפול עליה	—may a sinner's lot befall her!
25:20	כמעלה חזק לאיש ישיש	Like a hard ascent for an old man
	אשת לשון לאיש מך	—a talkative wife for a diminished husband.
25:21	אל תפול אל יופי אשה	Do not fall for a woman's beauty
	ועל יש לה [1]ל תמהר	—and [do not] hasten to what is hers.
25:22	כי בעדה [5] בושת	For in the assembly [?] shame
	אשה מכלכלת [2] בעלה	—a wife sustaining [?] her husband.
25:23	רפיון ידים [2]שלון ברכים	Slackness of hands and [weakness] of knees
	([וכ]) אשה לא תאשר את בעלה	—a wife who won't make her husband happy.
25:24	מאשה תחלת עון	From a woman is the start of iniquity
	ובגללה גועגו יחד	—and because of her, we waste away, all alike.
26:1	אשה טובה אשרי בעלה ומספר	A good wife—happy is her husband
	ימיו כפלים	—and the number of his days is doubled.
26:2	אשת חיל תדשן לבעלה	A "valorous wife" fattens her lord-husband
	ושנו[6]שמנ[1] (ושנוֹת[4]ת[שמנ]ח[:])	—and [his] years [?] she will make joyful.
26:3	אשה [1]ובה ([ט]ובה) מנה [3]	A good wife is a good gift—and may she
	ובחלק ירא ייי תנת[1] (תנתן)	be given in portion of one-fearing-YYY.

NOTES for chart A2-11:
- For רע אשה in BBS 25:17a, I translate רע elsewhere as "trouble" because, in the situation of changing the husband's appearance, "badness" could imply that the wife used sorcery ("evil eye") against the husband, a charge that does not fit the rest of the passage.
- For טעם in BBS 25:18b: *DCH* 3:372b "'taste; discernment; decree' … Si 25:18 'he sighs without his discernment.'" I translate as "'taste'" because the English word can include "discernment" and also allows sexual connotations, as in Prov. 30:20 and rabbinic discussions of texts such as *m. Ket.* 5:9.
- For BBS 25:22, the meaning of the Hebrew is uncertain. Words are missing, but the idea is that a man who marries for money (v. 21) is shamed.
- For תדשן in BBS 26:2, see *DCH* 2:477a "דשן Qal 1. 'make fat' i.e., 'anoint' (Ps 23:5), 'refresh, enrich' (Pr 15:30; Si 26:13; 43:22), 'bring joy' (Si 26:2)."

A.2.3 Fully-Annotated Charts for Chapter 3

FORMATTING KEY FOR TRANSLATIONS:

MS X = default MS, plain text

{X^m} = marginal notes of default MS, plain text in curly brackets.

<u>MS Y</u>, {<u>Y^m</u>} = 2nd MS & marg., underlined plain text for Hebrew and translation.

[#] = gaps in Hebrew MS with # of spaces; [?text?] is best-guess translation.

([#]א) = Ben-Hayyim's Hebrew; text is translation based on Ben-Hayyim.

text = translation from Greek of Sirach, bolded white text on dark grey ground.

Chart A3-1: "Wisdom has taught her sons" BBS 4:11–19 (MS A)

	Hebrew	Translation
4:11	חכמות למדה בניה	Wisdom has taught her sons
	ותעיד לכל מבינים בה :	—and she has exhorted all who perceive her.
4:12	אהביה אהבו חיים	Those who love her love life—and those who
	ומבקשיה יפיקו רצון מייי :	seek her will obtain favor from YYY.
4:13	ותמכיה ימצאו כבוד מייי	And those holding her will find honor from YYY
	ויחנו בברכת ייי :	—and they'll be graced with the blessing of YYY.
4:14	משרתי קדש משרתיה	Those who serve the Holy One are serving her
	ואלהו במא ויהא	—and (those serving) God are among those who desire her.
4:15	שומע לי ישפט אמת	"One who hearkens to me will be judged true
	ומאזין לי ייחן בחדרי	—and one who listens to me will encamp in the
	מבית :	most-interior chambers of the house. *[no v. 16]*
4:17	כי בהתנכר אלך עמו	For when he has made himself known, I'll walk
	ולפנים יבחרנו בנסיונות :	with him—and face-to-face he'll choose us by tests.
4:18	ועד עת ימלא לבו בי	And till the time his heart is filled with me,
	אשוב אאשרנו	I will return, I will lead us
	וגליתי לו מסתרי :	—and I will reveal to him my secret-place.
4:19	אם יסור ונטותיהו	If he deviates then I will reach out to him
	ויסרתיהו באסורים :	—and I will warn him, on forbidden-things.
4:19c	אם יסור מאחרי אשליכנו	If he deviates from following me, I'll reject him
	ואסגירנו לשדדים :	—and I will deliver him to marauders."

NOTES for chart A3-1:

- For קדש in 4:14a, *DCH* 7:203 gives קדש "18c. 'Holy One, God,' <CSTR> משרתי קדש 'servants of the Holy One' Si 4:14."

- For BBS 4:14b, *DCH* 1:149a amends to אל אוהב מאויה, "God loves those who desire her." A less-complex reading is ואלוה במאויה; with אלהו as אלוה, "God," translated as "and (those serving) God (are) among those who desire her." Ben-Hayyim has "?" for each unit of Hebrew (pp. 332, 323, 336).

- For ייחן in BBS 4:15b: *DCH* 3:268a gives "חנה I, 'encamp'… חֶדֶר … 'innermost chamber' Si 4:15 (A)."

Chart A3-2: "...you will reach Wisdom" BBS 6:18–31 (MSS A, C, 2Q18)

KEY→ MS A is default; <u>MS C</u>; 2Q18 has only last letters, matching MS A.

6:18a [not in Hebrew]	**Child, from your youth welcome education, and**	
[6:18b, top of III recto]	**until gray hairs you'll find wisdom** (Sirach, NETS).	
6:18b	... תשיג חכמה	... you will reach w/Wisdom.
6:19	כחורש וכקוצר קרב	Like one who plows and like one who reaps, approach
	אליה וקוה לרב תבואתה :	her—and hope for her produce to become abundant.
6:19c	כי בעבדתה מעט תעבוד	For in her service you will scarcely work
	ולמחר תאכל פריה :	—and quickly, you will eat her fruit.
6:20	עקובה היא לאויל	To a foolish-man, she is 'rough going'
	ולא יכלכלנה חסר לב :	—and one lacking heart will not hold her.
6:21	כאבן משא תהיה עליו	Like a carried stone she will be to him
	ולא יאחר להשליכה :	—and he will not delay to cast her off.
6:22	כי המוסר כשמה כן הוא	For "the discipline/teaching" is like her name,
	ולא לרבים היא נְכוֹחָה :	thus it is—and she's not straightforward to many.
6:23-25	*[not in Hebrew]*	*[ch 27:5,6 inserted here—does not fit context]*
6:26	הט שכמך ושאה	Bow down your neck and accept her
	ואל תקץ בתחבולתיה :	—and do not cut off her guidance.
6:27	דרש וחקר בקש ומצא	Investigate and search out, seek and find—
	והחזקתה ואל תרפה :	and be attached to her, and don't let (her) fall.
6:28	כי לאחור תמצא מנוחתה	For in the end, you will find her repose—and
	ונהפך\ <u>ותהפד</u> לך לתענוג :	it/<u>she</u> will be changed for you, into pleasure.
6:29	והיתה לך רשתה מכון עז	And her net'll become for you a site of strength
	וחבלתה בגדי כתם :	—and her ropes, garments of fine-gold.
6:30	עלי זהב עולה	A yoke of gold is her yoke
	ומוסרתיה פתיל תכלת :	—and her fetters, a cord of blue-purple.
6:31	בגדי כבוד תלבשנה	As garments of honor you'll wear her—and as a
	ועטרת תפארת תעטרנה :	crown of glory you'll encircle her (round you).

NOTES for chart A3-2:
- For 6:19a: both Hebrew MSS have קצר, "to reap," yet Skehan and Di Lella (*Wisdom of Ben Sira*, 190–91) translate as "plowing and sowing," apparently reconstructing with זרע, "to sow," from the Greek σπείρω. Their translation is used by Webster ("Sophia," 70) who adds a sexual interpretation of the "plowing and sowing," and she is cited by Balla (*Ben Sira on Family*, 22). Substituting "sow" for "reap" changes the gender discourse to the Greek "incubator" model of reproduction in which the man = plowman and the woman = soil (see chap. 3), and adding "reap" and "eat her fruit" to that model produces grotesque scenes of 'harvesting' and 'eating.' I read BBS 6:19 in relation to 6:26–30, where the sage is "yoked" in service to Wisdom.

- For 6:20, "foolish-man" and "lacking-heart" are the categories of men who try to reach Wisdom but give up—a "fool" (כְּסִיל) probably does not try.
- For נְבוֹחָה in BBS 6:22b, reading as "straightforward, i.e., easy" from נָכֹחַ (*DCH* 5:692a, "adj. fem. sing. (Si נְבוֹחָה)"; though 4:209a "יכח Ni. 'be adjudged, be understood (Si 6:22)'").
- For 6:22, see BBS 4:18b, Wisdom discloses herself "from my concealment."
- For 6:28b in MS A, the subject of נהפך is מוסר, "teaching/discipline" (6:22a).
- For 6:31, the f. s. suffix with תלהשנה and תעטרנה refers to Wisdom. See *DCH* 6:351b "עטר Pi. 2. 'wear as a crown' OBJ: 'wisdom' Si 6:31." I translate as "encircle her" instead of repeating "wear her," but the translation would be better using "circlet" for עטרת.   [NOTES for chart A3-2 end.]

Chart 3-3 does not require annotation.

Chart A3-4: "Happy the person who will meditate on Wisdom" BBS 14:20–15:8 (MSS A,B)

KEY→ MS A is default; <u>MS B</u> extant 15:1–10 matches MS A except as noted, {<u>B</u>^m}.

14:20	אשרי אנוש בחכמה יהגה	Happy the person who will meditate on Wisdom
	ובתבונה ישעה :	—and he will pay attention to understanding.
14:21	השם על דרכיה לבו	Who sets his heart upon her paths
	ובתבונתיה יתבונן :	—and he'll consider her [understandings][plans].
14:22	לצאת אחריה בחקר	To go forth after her with searching
	וכל מבואיה ירצד :	—and all her entrances he'll observe-jealously.
14:23	המשקיף בעד חלונה	Who looks down through her window—and because of
	ועל פתחיה יצותת :	her openings he can [listen carefully] [be set afire].
14:24	החונה סביבות ביתה	Who encamps roundabout her house
	והביא יתריו בקירה :	—and brings his tent-cords to her wall.
14:25	ונטה אהלו על ידה	And spreads out [his tent] [his aloe] near her
	ושכן שכן טוב :	—and he will dwell, a good dwelling.
14:26	וישים קנו בעופיה	And he has established his nest in her foliage
	ובענפיה יתלונן :	—and in her branches he will lodge.
14:27	וחוסה בצלה מחרב	And takes refuge in her shade from parching
	ובמעונותיה ישכן :	heat—and in her abodes he will dwell.
15:1	כי ירא ייי יעשה זאת	For one who fears YYY will do this
	ותופש תורה ידריכנה :	—and one holding to Torah will attain to her.

15:2	וקדמתהו כאם וכאשת	And she'll meet him like a mother
	נעורים תקבלנו :	—and like the wife of his youth she'll accept him.
15:3	והאכילתהו לחם שכל	And she'll feed him with bread-of-intelligence—and
{תבונה} : ומי תבואה תשקנו	water-of-understanding she'll give him to drink.
{ומתבואתה} : ומי תבונה תשקנו	—and from her produce she'll give him to drink.
15:4	ונשען עליה ולא ימוט	And he'll lean upon her, and won't stumble
	ובה יבטח ולא יבוש :	—and in her he'll trust, and won't be ashamed.
15:5	ורוממתהו מרעהו	And she will exalt him more than his companion(s)
	ובתוך קהל תפתח פיו :	—and she'll open his mouth within the congregation.
15:6	ששון ושמחה ימצא	He'll find gladness and joy
	{ימצא} תמצא	*[MS B = she'll bring]*
	ושם עולם תורישנו :	—and she'll cause him to possess an everlasting name.
15:7	לא ידריכוה מתי שוא	Men-of-untruth will not attain to her
	ואנשי זדון לא יראוה :	—and men-of-insolence will not see her.
15:8	רחוקה היא מלצים	She is far from scoffers
	ואנשי כזב לא יזכרוה :	—and men-of-deceit will not remember her.

NOTES for chart A3-4:

- For a parallel to המשקיף בעד החלונה in 14:23a, see Song 2:9, which matches at חלון and has a synonym for "wall" (v.24b): הִנֵּה־זֶה עוֹמֵד אַחַר כָּתְלֵנוּ מַשְׁגִּיחַ מִן־הַחַלֹּנוֹת מֵצִיץ מִן־הַחֲרַכִּים (כֹּתֶל)—"Behold him, standing behind our wall (כֹּתֶל), gazing from/through the windows (חַלֹּון), peeking through the screens (חָרָךְ)."

- For יצת in 14:23b, see Ben-Hayyim, p. 351, "צות → עתיד פולל. צות = יצותת." DCH 7:111a gives "צות I 'listen'—Pol. Impf. Si יצותת 'listen carefully' <PREP> על 'at' + פתח 'door' Si 14:23" and "צות II 'set on fire,' byform of 'kindle'" can provide conjectural translation with Pol. Impf. "he will be kindled/set on fire."

- For אהל in 14:25 as "aloe" (אֲהָל, used in plural form), the scented wood that perfumes a bed in Prov 7:17 (DCH 1:146a–b). The woman dressed like a harlot says to the young man, "I have perfumed my bed with myrrh, aloes and cinnamon" נַפְתִּי מִשְׁכָּבִי מֹר אֲהָלִים וְקִנָּמֹון .

- For מְעוֹנָה in 14:27, DCH 5:390a has "dwelling-place, abode" of Y. (Ps 76:3; 4Q392 1:5), of king (Jer 21:13), of Wisdom (Sir 14:27)." Other instances of the word are used with regard to wild animals (Amos 3:4; Nathan 2:13; Ps 104:22; Job 37:8, 38:40), light (1QH 12:5), and darkness (1QH 12:7). In this group of those who inhabit a מעונה, the unifying factor is their non-humanness—the king is part of the list because the use is derisive.

Chart A3-5: "I was a young man, before I had wandered" BBS 51:13–30
(MSS B, 11QPs[a])

KEY→ For 51:13–20b, MS 11QPs[a] is default (MS B given only for v. 17).
For 51:20c–30, MS B is default (MS 11QPs[a] ends with v. 20cde, + fragment
of v. 30); Ben-Hayyim.

51:13	אני נער בטרם תעיתי (תעי\ותי) ובקשתיה	I was a young man, before I had wandered about—and I sought her.
51:14	באה לי בתרה ועד / סופה אדורשנה	She came to me in her form—and until [the end- of-time] [her end] I will study her.
51:15	גם גרע נץ בבשול ענבים ישמחו לב /	Likewise, when blossom diminishes with the ripening of grapes—they will rejoice a heart.
51:15c	דרכה רגלי במישור כי מנעורי ידעתיה	My foot advanced [in equity] [on level-ground] —for from my time-of-youth I have known her.
51:16	הטיתי כמעט / אוזני והרבה מצאתי לקח	I inclined my ear just a little —and abundantly I found knowledge.
51:17	ועלה היתה לי למלמדי אתן הודי / (הודו\י)	And she was [an ascent] [the Most High] for me —to my teacher I will give my splendor.
	עלה היתה לי לכבוד ולמלמדי אתן הודאה :	[She was an ascent] [Her yoke was] for me to honor —and to my teacher I will give my splendor.
51:18	זמותי ואשחקה קנאתי בטוב ולוא אשוב	I've planned and may I [celebrate] [be joyful]—(for) I've been zealous in pleasing, and I'll not turn back.
51:19	חריתי / נפשי בה ופני לוא השיבותי : (הש[יב]ותי)	I kindled my desire for her —and my face I have not turned away.
51:20	טרתי נפשי בה וברומיה לוא / אשלה	I have kept my desire with her —and at her exaltation I will not be slack.
MS B ↓	MS 11QPs[a] v. 20cd עֲרמיה אתבונן [2][7] ידי פת	
51:20cd	ידי פתחה שעריה ולה אח[2] ואביט ב[4] (ולה אחדֹּר ואביט ב[ה] :)	My hand has opened her gates—and I'll be surrounded by her, and I'll regard her.
	MS 11QPs[a] colon 20e (may not be complete) / כפי הברותי אל	
51:20ef	ובטהרה מצאתי ולב קניתי לה מתחלתה	And in purity I found—and a heart I gained by her, from her beginning.
51:21	מעי יהמו כתנור להביט בה בעבור כן קניתיה קנין טוב :	My inmost-parts are 'fired-up' like oven, regarding her—in order that thus I gained her, a good gain.
51:22	נתן ייי לי שכר שפתותי ובלשוני אהודנו :	YYY gave to me my lips' [reward] [mead]—and with my tongue I will praise/thank Him.
51:23	פנו אלי סכלים ולינו בבית מדרשי	"Confused-ones! Turn to me —and lodge in my house-of-study.
51:24	עד מתי תחסרון מן אילו	How long will you lack some of these things, and

	: ואילו ונפשכם צמאה מאד תהיה	these?—and your soul(s) will be very thirsty."
51:25	פי פתחתי ודברתי	I've opened [my] mouth and I have spoken concerning
	: בה קנו לכם חכמה בלא כסף	her—"Gain for yourselves Wis., without money.
51:26	וצואריכם בעלה הביאו	Bring your necks within her yoke
	: ומשאה תשא נפשכם	—and her burden will lift up your soul.
	קרובה היא למבקשיה	She is close to those who seek her
	: ונותן נפשו מוצא אתה	—and one who gives himself finds her.
51:27	ראו בעיניכם כי קטן הייתי	See with your eyes: for I was a young-one
	: ועמדתי בה ומצאתיה	—and I persisted with her and I found her.
51:28	רבים שמעו למודי בנערותי	Hear many-things taught me in my youth
	: וכסף וזהב תקנו בי	—and silver and gold you'll gain with me.
51:29	תשמח נפשי בישיבתי	My soul rejoices in my [academy] [habitation]
	: ולא תבושו בשירתי	—and you'll not be ashamed, by means of my song.
51:30	מעשיכם עשו בצדקה והוא	Your works are made with righteousness—
	: נותן לכם שכרכם בעתו	and He gives to you your reward, in His time."
	ברוך ייי לעולם	Blessed be YYY forever—and exalt
	: ומשובח שמו לדר ודר	His name to generation and generation!
	עד הנה דברי שמעון בן	Thus far, the words of Simeon son of Yeshua,
	: ישוע שנקרא בן סירא	who is called "son of Sira."
	חכמת שמעון בן ישוע בן	The wisdom of Simeon son of Yeshua
	: אלעזר בן סירא	son of Eleazar son of Sira.
	יהי שם ייי מבורך מעתה	Let the name of YYY be blessed,
	: ועד עולם	from now and until forever!

NOTES for chart A3-5:

- For תר in 14a, translating תור and תאר consistently as "form" rather than "beauty," which is the translation for יפה in the current study.

-For עד סופה in 51:14b: see *DCH* 6:133b "סוף n. m. 'end' 2. of time (Ec 3:11, Si 51:14)"; reading סופה as "time's end" with the feminine noun עֵת ("time") implied. Alternate: "until her [Wisdom's] end," to match 20f "from her beginning"—though it is unlikely that Wisdom would "end," so the first three verses would apply better to the human wife.

- For אדורשנה in 51:14b, see *DCH* 2:474a "דרש Qal 7. 'seek with interest, be intent on, study, interpret.'"

- For במישור in 51:15c, see *DCH* 5:263b "מִישׁוֹר 2. 'plain,' as place of safety and confidence (... Si 51:15). 3. 'equity' (*[no mention of BBS]*)."

- For עלה in 51:17a, *DCH* 6:296b–7a gives "עוֹל I Qal 2. noun, 'one that gives suck, wet nurse,' in ref. to … wisdom Sir 51:17 (11QPsª) … (in B עלה = 'her yoke')." Other possibilities are: (1) in *DCH* 6:408b "עלה I 14. inf. cstr. as noun, 'ascent'" or ibid. 418a–b עלה II "n. f. 'ascent'"; and (2) as a feminine form of *DCH* 6:398b "עָלִי III 'High One, Most High, Sublime One' = "And she was (the) Most High, for me." The choice between these possibilities depends on the translator's assumptions: "wet nurse" could be chosen as a counterpoint to "my teacher" if one presumes the teacher is YYY. The translation I prefer is "ascent," to build on v. 15c, "my foot advanced on *level ground*."

- For הוד in 51:17b, I read "splendor" with a second meaning as "erect penis."
- For אשחקה in 51:18a, see *DCH* 8:121ab "שחק Pi. 1. 'play, celebrate' ... 3b. 'rejoice, be happy,' of Ben Sira Si 51:18."
- For בטוב in 51:18a, see *DCH* 3:349b "טוב Qal—'be good, be pleasing, be appropriate, be happy ...,'" reading as a masc. sing. active participle.
- For חריתי נפשי in 51:20a, see *DCH* 3:313b "חרה Qal—2. trans. 'kindle' SUBJ Ben Sira Si 51:19 (11QPs[a]). OBJ נפש 'soul,' i.e., desire." See also BBS 6:1 for נפש as "desire."
- For אשלה in 51:20b, see *DCH* 8:364:a "שלה Ni. 'be slack.'"
- For רומיה in 51:20b, see *DCH* 7:449a "רום sf. Si רומיה 1. 'height, loftiness, exaltation,'" interpreting as "'her ...orgasm'" (Muraoka, "Sir 51,13–30," 172).
- For יד in 51:20c: see *DCH* 4:85a "יד 2. perh. 'penis.'" In 15c, רגל (foot) might also be read as "penis." However, the juxtaposition of "flesh," "hand," and "foot" in BBS 51:2b is a warning against too quick a choice of "penis": "You have spared my flesh from the pit-of-destruction, and from the hand of Sheol You have delivered my foot."
- For אחדר in 51:20d, reading as Ni. אֶחָדֵר "be surrounded/enclosed by." See *DCH* 3:163 "חדר I Qal 'surround, encircle,' perh. 'enter, penetrate deeply' SUBJ: Ben Sira Si 51:20 (B) (unless חדר II 'keep oneself') PREP: ל introducing object ... חכמה 'wisdom' Si 51:20 (B)" and *DCH* 4:484a "ל 13. in passive constructions, of agent 'by (the agency of).'"
- For 51:20cd–21 (MS 11QPs[a]): עָרמיה[2] J. A. Sanders reads מַעֲרֻמֶּיהָ "her nakedness," making another erotic element of the poetic unit. I chose the verse from MS B as the place to change MSS in part for the purely subjective reason that the translation of 20d in MS B is experimental and, if acceptable, moves the discourse of *gender* in interesting directions.
- Cola 51:20e and 20f are transposed, to continue the acrostic. There is no "כ" line in MS B, though 11QPs[a] has the partial line [?] [?] כפי הברותי אל as 20e.
- For 52:20f ולב קניתי לה מתחלתה, see BBS 4:18 ועד עת ימלא לבו בי אשוב אאשרנו וגליתי לו מסתרי : "And till the time his heart is filled with me, I will return, I will lead us—and I will reveal to him my secret-place."
- For מעי in 51:21a, See *DCH* 5:382a–b "מֵעֶה 1. often as source of procreation in body of a man, perh. 'genitals' ...6. 'inner person, self,' ...perh. of sexual arousal or yearning ...of man, Si 51:21." In this case, I think the term could mean both "genitals" and "body-core," but I translate as "my belly is 'fired-up' like an oven" to convey the sense of the current phrase "have a fire in one's belly" as having a passionate commitment to achieve some abstract or physical goal. In this sense, the author could speak of both "wisdom" and "Wisdom."

- For יהמו in 51:21a, translations for the root המה from *DCH* 2:565b are "1a. 'be in a tumult, commotion, turmoil, uproar'" and "4. 'murmur, moan, stir' of heart, soul, etc." and those for הום (*DCH* 2:504b) and נהם (*DCH* 5:631a) have a similar range of uproar and/or noises. Though bellies can be in an uproar and make noises, none of these images match the stolid qualities of a clay or brick oven, a hollow object with several openings, which is heated and retains heat at a steady rate while food is cooked inside it. This description fits food digesting in a belly, but is not analogous to a man's genitals.

- For בית מדרשי in 51:23b, see *DCH* 5:150a "[מִדְרָשׁ] ... בית מדרשי 'house of my study,' i.e. my academy Si 51:23." See the note for ישיבתי in 51:29a.

- For ודברתי בה in 51:25a, see *DCH* 2:392b "בְּ 'concerning,' + perh. 'wisdom' Si 51:25."

- For 51:26b, ומשאה תשא נפשכם, the sequence of words could be (1) "object, verb, subject" or (2) "subject, verb, object." Option (1) yields "your soul will lift up her/its burden" and option (2) is "her [Wisdom's] burden will lift up your soul." Because colon a has put the necks of the addressees into Wisdom's yoke, option (2) makes sense as a playful reversal of meaning: Wisdom's yoke is a burden that lessens the mental load.

Reading משאה as "from ruin" (*DCH* 8:206a "שׂאָה, see שׁוֹאָה 'disaster; ruin'") yields "she [Wisdom] will lift up your soul from ruin" or "your soul will be lifted up from ruin." However, the "soul" is "thirsty," which is not necessarily a state of "ruin" or "disaster."

- For ישיבתי in 51:29a, see *DCH* 4:332b "[יְשִׁיבָה] n. f. 'sitting'—sf. Si ישיבתי —'sitting of teacher,' i.e. 'teaching,' perh. 'academy.'" The existence of v. 23's "houses of study" in Ben Sira's time is an unresolved question, but the presence of ישיבה—a second pedagogical word whose later use indicates a formal set of practices—bolsters the likelihood that the *concepts* of such teaching methods existed in Ben Sira's time regardless of how many actual instances of the *practices* occurred then. The terms "my house of study" and "my sitting" can indicate a set of relations between teacher and students without identifying exact locales. On the basis of these terms, I presume that a group of students gathered at prearranged times to experience the "teaching" of a particular person, probably at a location favored by the teacher such as his (or her) home or a public space. Thus, these terms could indicate that the standard pedagogical model for a sage was not that in which a tutor was hired to instruct one student at that student's family's home. Another possible translation for ישיבתי is "my habitation," referring to the author's "dwelling" with Wisdom (BBS 14:25–27).

- For בשירתי in 51:29b, see *DCH* 2:131a "בוש I ... <PREP> בְּ of agent/instrument, 'by (means of),' or of cause, 'because of, through,' + שִׁירָה 'song' Si 51:29." I interpret the preposition's function as *agency*, in the sense that the song will protect them from shame. [NOTES for chart A3-5 end.]

The remaining charts in chapter 3 (3-6 through 3-9) require no annotation.

A.2.4 Fully-Annotated Charts for Chapter 4

FORMATTING KEY FOR TRANSLATIONS:

MS X = default MS, plain text

{X^m} = marginal notes of default MS, plain text in curly brackets.

MS Y, {Y^m} = 2nd MS & marg., underlined plain text for Hebrew and translation.

[#] = gaps in Hebrew MS with # of spaces; [?text?] is best-guess translation.

([#]א) = Ben-Hayyim's Hebrew; text is translation based on Ben-Hayyim.

text = translation from Greek of Sirach, bolded white text on dark grey ground.

Chart A4-1: "... honors his mother" Sirach 3:1–6 (NETS), BBS 3:6b–16 (MSS A, C)

KEY→ MS A is default, {A^m}; MS C.

3:1 Ἐλεγμὸν πατρὸς ἀχούσατε, τέχνα, καὶ οὕτως ποιήσατε, ἵνα σωθῆτε.	Listen to a father's reproof, children, and act accordingly so you may be safe.
3:2 ὁ γὰρ κύριος ἐδόξασεν πατέρα ἐπὶ τέχνοις καὶ κρίσιν μητρὸς ἐστερέωσεν ἐφ᾽ υἱοῖς.	For the Lord has glorified father over children, and [H]e has confirmed a mother's judgment over sons.
3:3/4 ὁ τιμῶν πατέρα ἐξιλάσεται ἁμαρτίας, καὶ ὡς ὁ ἀποθησαυρίζων ὁ δοξάζων μητέρα αὐτοῦ.	He who honors father will atone for sins, and like one who lays up treasure is he who glorifies his mother.
3:5 ὁ τιμῶν πατέρα εὐφρανθήσεται ὑπὸ τέχνων, καὶ ἐν ἡμέρα προσευχῆς αὐτοῦ εἰσακουσθήσεται.	He who honors his father will be gladdened by children, and in the day of his prayer, he'll be heard.
3:6 ὁ δοξάζων πατέρα μακροημερεύσει, καὶ ὁ εἰσακούων κυρίου ἀναπαύσει μητέρα αὐτοῦ.	He who glorifies father will prolong his days, and he who listens to the Lord will give rest to his mother.
3:6b מכבד אמו :	...honors his mother.
3:8 בני במאמר ובמעשה כבד אביך עבור ישיגוך כל ברכות :	My son, honor your father in speech and deeds —so that he'll bring you near all blessings.
3:9 ברכת אב תיסד שרש וקללת אם תנתש נטע :	A father's blessing will found a root —but a mother's curse will uproot a plant.
3:10 אל תתכבד בקלון אביך כי לא כבוד הוא לך :	Do not honor yourself with the dishonor of your father—for it is not an honor to you.
3:11 כבוד איש כבוד אביו ומרבה חטא מקלל אמו :	His father's honor is a man's honor—and he who curses his mother multiplies sin.

3:12   בני התחזק בכבוד   My son, strengthen yourself with your father's honor
אביך ואל תעזבהו כל ימי חייך :   —and don't forsake him all the days of your life.

3:13   וגם אם יחסר מדעו עזוב   Even if his intellect should fail, forsaking him
לו ואל תכלים אותו כל ימי חייו :   —yet don't humiliate him all the days of his life.

3:14 {תנטע} צדקת אב לא תמחה   The righteousness of a father won't be blotted
ותמור חטאת היא תנתע :   out—and it will change sin; {it will be planted}.

<u>צדקת אב אל תשכח ותחת   Don't forget the righteousness of a father—and</u>
<u>[ ] ענותו תתנצל   instead of his affliction you'll [protect נצר] yourself.</u>

3:15   ביום צרה תזכר לך כחם   In day of anguish it'll be remembered for you
על כפור להשבית עוניך :   —like heat upon frost, to abolish your guilts.

<u>ביום יזכר לך וכחורב על קרח   In the day it will be remembered for you—like</u>
<u>נמס חטאתיך :   drought upon ice, your sins will be melted.</u>

3:16   כי מזיד בוזה אביו   For one who acts proudly despises his father—
ומכעיס בוראו מקלל אמו   and provokes his Creator, who curses his mother.

<u>כמגדף העוזב אביו   Like one who reviles is the one forsaking his father—and</u>
<u>וזועם אל יסחוב אמו   irritating God, he who drags away/abuses his mother.</u>

NOTES for chart A4-1:
- 3:14a *DCH* 5:215a "מחה Nif. 'be wiped out' OBJ: צדקה 'righteousness' Si 3:14 (A)."
- 3:14b *DCH* 5:677b "נטע Nif. 'be planted' SUBJ: צדקה 'righteousness' Si 3:14 (A) (corrected from תנתע appar. 'it will be broken')."

Chart 4-2 is not annotated—see chart 4-8 for the full passage.

Chart A4-3: "Do not give him rulership in his youth" BBS 30:11–13 (MS B)

KEY→ MS B, {Bᵐ}; additions in GII of Sirach (from an HTII source).

30:11   אל תמשילהו בנעוריו   Do not give him rulership in his youth
ואל תשא לשחיתותיו : {מש־}   —and do not show favor, ruining him.

30:12   כפתן על חי תפגע   You'll meet with hostility like a viper against a living-
רציץ מתניו שעודנו נער: thing—crush his/its strength while he's still a youth.

30:12c   כיף ראשו   Bend down his head in his youth—[and tear apart his loins/
בנערותו   strength, like he was a little-one.] [and tear (him) apart(from)
ובקע מתניו כשהוא קטן :   those-who-indulge/permit-him like he was a little-one.]

30:12e   {יקשיח, ישקיח} למה ישקה   Why will he {show stubbornness}
ומרה בך ונולד {ולד} ממנו מפח   and be rebellious against you?
נפש : {ולוד, ממך}   {—and disappointment is born to you.}

30:13   יסר בנך והכבד עולו פן   [Discipline your son and make his yoke heavy]
באולתו יתלעבך : {יתעל}   [Instruct your son and bring his yoke to honor]
—lest, in his folly, {he will exalt himself}.

NOTES for chart A4-3:

- For מתניו in 30:12b, see *DCH* 5:573 "מֹתֶן, du. only 'loins,' or perh. rather 'musculature' linking upper part of body with lower" and *DCH* 5:571 מֹתֶן "'strength'" (though "מֹתֶן 'hip' Si 30:12" in *DCH* 2:249a). In this verse מתניו is translated from מָתְנַיִם because it makes sense to "crush" the "strength" or "musculature" of a "viper."

- For בקע in 30:12d, *DCH* 2:249a gives "בקע I Pi. 'split, cut up, tear apart,' also (Si 30:12) 'strike' loins, i.e., beat child." Yet, the violence perpetrated in other instances of this verb is fatal: literally "splitting apart" people (e.g., pregnant women) and other creatures. Thus, I think the verse is cited in *DCH* with an anomalous definition that matches the Greek verse. If "strike" were intended, there are Hebrew verbs that have that exact meaning, so why use this one?

- For 30:12d, מתניו has a second translation, unlike that in v. 12b, because to "split/cut up/tear apart" is not coherent with "loins/strength" and "like a little-one." I suggest a possible translation of מתניו as an unattested Hifil participle of נתן or as the preposition מ, "from," with some form that permits a stem of תנ'. The word would be comparable to the Qal of נתן in *DCH* 5:810b "7. 'allow, permit, enable' to do something, to be, to have."

- For 30:12f, see מַפָּח in *DCH* 5:430b-431a 'expiring' (1) 'breathing out' of life (2) 'breathing out' of the life, i.e., 'heartache, disappointment' Si 30:12. SUBJ pass. 'be born' Si 30:12 (B^m), ni. 'be born,' i.e., caused."

- For BBS 30:13a, see *DCH* 4:351b "Hi. impv. Si הכבד; 'make heavy…bring to honour, glorify'… Si 30:13." The use of "yoke" as a metaphor for marriage could provide a secondary meaning based on the biblical prohibition against plowing "with an ox and an ass together" (Deut 22:10). Because males are said to be restrained by marriage (becoming less like Cain), and in parallel with BBS 7:23 in chart A4-8 (בנים לך יסיר אותם ושׂא לָהֶם נשׁים בנעוריהם :), "Your sons—discipline/instruct them—and accept/find wives for them, in their youth," a double reading is possible.

Chart A4-4: "Do not yearn for…worthless youths" BBS 16:1–4 (MSS A,B)

KEY→ MS A is default; MS B not used (damaged, extant is close match); Ben-Hayyim.

16:1	אל תתאוה תואר נערי שוא ואל תשמח בבני עולה :	Do not yearn for the appearance of worthless youths—and do not rejoice in unjust sons.
16:2	וגם אם פרו אל תבעבם אם אין אתם יראת ייי :	Moreover, if they multiply, do not seek for them —if they have not the fear-of-YYY.
16:3	אל תאמין בחייהם ואל תבטח בעקבותם :	Do not have confidence in their living —and do not trust in their deceits/cheatings.
16:3c	כי לא תהיה להם אחרית טובה כי טוב אחד עושה רצון מאלף	For there won't be a good end for them—for better 1 who does the divine-will, than 1000.
16:3e	ומות ערירי ממי שהיו לו בנים רבים ומאחרית זדון [עֹז]לה :	And to die childless, than someone with many unjust sons—and posterity that is insolent.
16:4	מאהד ערירי ירא ייי תשב עיר וממשפחת בגדים תחרב:	From one childless-person who fears-YYY, a city will be established—and from a clan of traitors, it will be devastated.

NOTES for chart A4-4:

- For תבע בם in 16:2: see *DCH* 8:591a "תבע [perh. byform of בעה II 'seek'] 'claim.'"

- Di Lella (*Wisdom*, 58) considers 16:3 a retroversion from Syriac. He notes that Rüger (*Text und Textform in hebräischen Sirach*, esp. 1–11) disagrees with a Syriac origin and argues it is "similar to what Kearns calls HTI and HTII."

Chart A4-5: "Son and wife, friend and companion" BBS 33:20–30 (MS E)

KEY→ MS E; Ben-Hayyim.

33:20	בן ואשה אהב ורע	Son and wife, friend and companion
	אל תמשיל בחייך	—do not cause to rule over your life.
33:21	עד עודך חי ונשמה בך	While you are still alive and breath is in you
	אל תשלט בך כל [3]	—do not empower over you any [?].
33:21c	אל תתן שלך לאחר :	Do not give that which belongs to you to another
	לשוב לחלות א[5]	—to return to entreat [?].
33:22	כי טוב לחלות בניך פניך	For it is better for your sons to entreat your face
	מהביטך על ידי [4]	—than you accepting, at the hand of [your sons?].
33:23	בכל מעשיך היה עליון :	In all your deeds, be excellent
	ואל תתן מום בכ[4]	—and do not put/give a stain on [your honor?].
33:24	בעת מספר מצער ימיך :	At the time your days are a small number
	ביום המות הנח[5] (הנח[ל] [3])	—at the day of death [cause to inherit] [?].
33:25	מספוא ושוט ומשא לחמור	Fodder and whip and burden for an ass—and
	ומרדות מלאכה לע[2]	chastisement רדה [in] labor for a servant/slave.
33:26	העב[1] עבדך שלא יבקש	Cause your servant to work, so he
	חת (נחת) ואם נשא ראשו[1]	doesn't seek [repose?] —and if his head's
	יבג[1] (יבג[ד])	lifted, [he'll betray?].
33:27	העב[1] עבדך שלא ימרוד	Cause your servant/slave to work, so he does
	כי הרבה רעה עז[6]	not rebel מרד —for badness/evil increases [?].
33:28	[7] חוטר תומכו	[?] a rod holding him
	על עבד רע הר[7]	—concerning a bad servant/slave, [?].
33:29	*[no space on MS]*	
33:30	אל תותר על כל אדם :	Do not act-excessively against any human
	ובלא משפט [10]	—and without judgment, [?].

NOTES for chart A4-5:
- For עד עודך חי in 33:21a see *DCH* 6:294b "עַד עוֹד a. 'while still' … 'while you are still alive' Si 33:21; followed by verb, שלט hi. 'allow to rule.'"
- For 33:21d, see *DCH* 3:229a.
- For 33:28a, see *DCH* 3:202a "חטר 'cut' Qal Ptc. … 'that which supports,' i.e. neck Si 33:28 [Ben-Hayyim 30:35] (unless חֹטֶר 'shoot, rod')." ALTERNATE: "חֹטֶר (חוטר)'shoot, rod' תמך 'support' Si 33:28."

Charts 4-6 and 4-7 do not require annotation.

Chart A4-8: "Do not exchange a friend for a price" BBS 7:18–26 (MSS A, C)

KEY→ MS A is default; <u>MS C.</u>

7:18	אל תמיר אוהב במחיר	Do not exchange a friend for a price
	ואח תלוי בזהב אופיר :	—or lend a brother for the gold of Ophir.
7:19	אל תמאס אשה משכלת	Do not reject an intelligent woman/wife
	וטובת חן מפנינים :	—and a good-one is grace more than pearls.
7:20	<u>אל תר[־] עבד עובד אמת</u>	<u>Do not treat badly a slave serving honestly</u>
	<u>וכן שכיר נותן נפשו</u>	<u>—and thus a hireling giving his soul/self.</u>
7:21	עבד משכיל חבב כנפש	An intelligent slave—cherish like a self
	[־]ל תמנע ממנו חפש :	—do not withhold from him freedom.
7:22	בהמה לך ראה עיניך	Your animal—inspect (with) your eyes
	ואם אמנה היא העמידה :	—and if it is faithful, maintain it.
7:23	בנים לך יסיר אותם	Your sons—discipline/instruct them
	וְשָׂא לָהֶם נשים בנעוריהם :	—and accept/take for them wives in their youth.
7:24	בנות לך נצור שארם	Your daughters—protect their body/flesh
	<u>בנים לך נצור שאר[־]</u>	<u>Your sons— protect their body/flesh</u>
	ואל תאיר אלהם פנים :	—and don't [show favor] [be overindulgent] to them.
7:25	הוצא בת ויצא עסק ואל נבון	Marry a daughter and a duty fulfills
	גבר חברה : ג[2] <u>נבון זבדה</u>	—but unite her to a <u>discerning fellow.</u>
7:26	אשה לך אל תתעבה	Your wife—do not abhor her
	ושנואה אל תאמן בה :	—or, hating her, do not trust her.

NOTES for chart A4-8:

-For תלוי in 7:18b, reading it as (variant form of) a 2ms verb *DCH* 4:523a "לוה I Hi. 'lend.'" *DCH* 8:636:a gives "תלה Qal 1. 'hang' someone ... 3c. pass. ptc. as adj. 'dependent,' used attributively of אח brother, i.e., relative Si 7:18."

- For גבר in 7:25: *DCH* 2:313a "usu. man as distinct from woman" [no BBS examples, but 8 times in BBS]. The only instance of גבר in association with a female figure is BBS 7:25 (MSS A, C), "Marry a daughter and a duty fulfills—and unite her to a discerning fellow." The modifier נבון, "discerning," indicates a man similar to the גבר מבין, the "perceptive fellow" who will not reject the medicines God "brought forth from the earth" (BBS 38:4 (MS B), and who sounds like a student of Wisdom.

- For תאמן in 7:26, Ben-Hayyim gives "Hifil future." See *DCH* 1:316a, אמן I "Hi. 1a. 'believe, trust' someone …Si 7:26." Perhaps אל תאמן בה could also be translated as "do not be established with her," as a euphemism for "divorce her"?

Chart A4-9: "Do not make jealous…" BBS 9:1–9 (MS A)

KEY→ MS A; Ben-Hayyim.

9:1	אל תקנא את אשת חיקך	Do not make jealous the wife of your bosom
	פן תלמד עליך רעה :	—lest she learn evil concerning you.
9:2	אל תקנא לאשה נפשך	Do not allow yourself to acquire a woman
	להדריכה על במותיך :	—to 'attain to' her upon your 'high places.'
9:3	אל תקרב אל אשה זרה	Do not approach a stranger-woman
	פֶּן תִּפּוֹל בִּמְצוֹדְתֶיהָ :	—lest you fall in her nets.
9:3c	[עָ]ם זוֹנָה אַל־תִּסְתַּיָּיד	With a prostitute do not 'take counsel'
	פֶּן תִּלָּכֵד בִּלְקוֹחָתֶיהָ :	—lest you be captured in her traps.
9:4	עִם מְנַגִּינֹת אַל תִּדְמֹוךְ	With singers-of-satires do not sleep
	פֶּן יִשְׂרְפֶךָ בְּפִיפִיֹתָם :	—lest they burn you with their 'mouths.'
9:5	בבתולה אל תתבונן	An unmarried girl, do not observe
	פן תוקש בעונשיה	—lest you be ensnared by her fines.
9:6	אל תתן לזונה נפשך	Do not give your soul/self to a prostitute
	פן תסוב את נחלתך :	—lest you besiege your inheritance.
9:7	להתנבל במראה עיניך	To befool your eyes with her appearance
	ולשומם אחר ביתה :	—and to 'play the fool' behind her house.
9:8	העלים עין מאשת חן	Cover the eye from a graceful-woman
	ואל תביט אל יפי לא לך :	—and do not regard beauty that is not yours.
9:8c	בעד אשה [ה]שחתו רבים	Through a woman/wife, many will be destroyed
	וכן אהביה באש תלהט	—and thus her lovers with fire she will set ablaze.
9:9	עם בעלה אל תטעם [3]ו : ב	With a mistress-of-the-house don't 'taste'—and
	עמו שכור : (וא[ל ת[סֹב)	don't recline-at-table with him/her, intoxicated.
9:9c	פֶּן תטה [2]יה לב (א[ליה))	Lest you turn aside to her (your) heart
	ובדמים תטה אל שחת :	—and in blood turn aside to destruction.

NOTES for chart A4-9:
- For תקנא in 9:1a, see *HALOT-SE* 1109b "MHeb. pi. to make jealous, show jealousy"; Jastrow 1390b "Pi. 2. to arouse jealousy; to provoke." BBS 9:1 would be an early instance of this usage. However, *DCH* lists קנא in 9:1 as the husband's jealousy of the wife (*DCH* 7: 263b–64a "קנא Pi 2. 'be jealous of,' in rivalry, a. in love or affection, of a sexual partner (…Si 9:1) <SUBJ> 'son' Si 9:1 <OBJ> 'woman' Si 9:1."). Camp ("Understanding," 20–22) states that, instead of "do not be jealous of the wife of your bosom," she translates as "'zealous, or passionate, for' "—interpreting the colon as a semantic continuation of BBS 9:3–9, which deals with the man's sexual self-control—and thus, "the evil a wife learns from her husband's ardor is sexual desire itself. ... she may find that other men also inspire her ardor."
- For 9:1b, תלמד, see *DCH* 5:549a "(Qal) <PREP> על concerning, against Si 9:1."

- For תקנא in 9:2a: reading as קנה Hi., with Ben-Hayyim (p. 269b) and *DCH* 7: 268b "קנה I Hi. 2. 'allow to acquire,' i.e., 'give' <SUBJ> 'son' Si 9:2. <OBJ> 'soul,' i.e., self Si 9:2. <PREP> לְ of direction, 'to,' + אִשָּׁה 'woman' Si 9:2." Kister ("Genizah MSS," 45) also reads תקנא as a Hifil of קנה, and לאשה as an indirect object. These translations interpret לאשה as "(give yourself) to a woman," and I interpret the preposition as a לְ of possession, "(allow yourself to acquire) a woman/wife."

- For להדריכה in 9:2b, see DCH 2:464a "דרך Hi. 3. 'reach, attain to, obtain' Si 15:1, 7." BBS 15:1 and 7 both refer to Wisdom: ותופש תורה ידריכנה "and one who holds-fast to Torah will attain to her" (v. 1) and לא ידריכוה מתי שוא 'men-of-untruth will not attain to her" (v. 7)." The phrase appears also in BBS 46:9: "And He gave to Caleb strength—and until old age, it remained with him. To [attain to] [trample] them upon the 'high places' of the earth—and likewise his seed took possession of an inheritance" (MS B: להדריכם על במותי ארץ Ben-Hayyim). If BBS 9:2 and 46:9 are translated in parallel, then the one who tramples in 9:2 cannot be the woman. See also DCH 2:463b–64b "Hi. 2. 'allow to trample' (Si 9:2) <SUBJ> not specified. <OBJ> אשה 'woman' Si 9:2. <PREP> על 'upon' + במה 'high place' Si 9:2").

- For 9:5 a: See 41:21 (MS M), 3:22 -- התבונן ב.

- For לשומם in 9:7b, see *DCH* 8:445a "שמם I Po. 4. 'cause appalment,' by going to house of prostitute ... Si 9:7"; or *DCH* 8:446a "שמם II Po. 'play the fool' ... Si 9:7."

- For עמו in 9:9b, see *DCH* 6:107a "9. 'gather around' a table to dine, 'recline,' PREP עם with, + בעלה lady Si 9:9 (אל ת[סֹב עמו שכור) do not recline drunken with her)."   [NOTES for chart A4-9 end.]

Chart A4-10: "Do not reject an old friend" BBS 9:10–16 (MS A)

KEY→ MS A; Ben-Hayyim.

9:10	אל תטש אוהב ישן	Don't reject an old friend—for a new one won't [cause
	כי חָ[ד]ש לא יד[2]קֹ[1] :	you to adhere?].([ד])(ס)(יֹ[י]עָ[ו]ד[י]) [? be known to you?]
9:10c	חדש אוהב חדש [וֹ]יי	New wine, new friend—and you will drink it
	וישן אחר תֹ[1]תִינו :	after it is grown old. (תִינוּ[ש]ת)
9:11	תקנא באיש רשע [2]	[? Do not ?] be envious/jealous with a wicked man
	כי לא [ת]דע מה יומו	—for you do not know what is "his day."
9:12	בזדון מצליח זכר [4] אל	Do not [??] with insolence leading to success—
	כי עת מֹות לא ינקה :	remember (at) time of death he won't be guiltless.
9:13 [ג]להרו[3]ט	רחק מאיש	Be far from a man [? who has the power ?] to kill
	ואל תפחד פחדי מות	—and do not fear the terrors of death.
9:13c	ואם קרבת לא תאשם	And if you have approached you must not
	פן יקח [א]ת נשמתך :	trespass —lest he will take your breath!
9:13e	דע כי בין פחים תצעד	Know that among snares you will step
	ועל רשֹת תתהלך :	—and you will walk about upon fowling-nets.
9:14	ככחך ענה רעך	As is your strength, answer your companion
	ועם חכמים הסתייד :	—and take counsel with wise-men.
9:15	עם נבון יהי חשֹבונך	With a discerning-man be your conversation
	וכל סודך בינותם :	—and all your counsel, their insights.
9:16	אנשי צדק בעלי לחמך	Men of righteousness (are) your table-companions
	וביראת אלהים תפארתך :	—and in the fear-of-God, your glory.

NOTES for chart A4-10:
- For 9:10b, Beentjes sees יד[2]קֹ[1], probably reading as ידביקך (DCH 2:386a דבק
Hi. 1. 'cause to cling, adhere'"), and Ben-Hayyim sees a Qal passive participle of
ידע (p. 155a).
- For באיש רשע תקנא in 9:11a, the Piel of קנא with the preposition בְּ introducing
the object gives the meaning "be jealous of, be envious of." See DCH 7:263b "קנא
Pi. 1a. <SUBJ> 'son' Si 9:11."

Charts 4-11, 4-12a, 4-12b, and 4-13 do not require annotation.

Chart A4-14: Double translation, poetic fragment BBS 38:24–27, MS B, {B^m}

KEY → MS B, {B^m}; Ben-Hayyim.

BOTH VERSIONS

חכמת סופר תרבה חכמה
24 The wisdom of the scribe increases 'wisdom'
וחסר עסק הוא יתחכם :
—but/and one lacking business, he will make himself wise.

VERSION 1: "TEACHER" ◤		◥ VERSION 2: "CATTLE-HERD"
25 How can he make himself wise, who maintains teaching	מה יתחכם תומך מלמד	**25** How can he make himself wise, who holds a [cattle] goad
—and boast, who tests [בחן] a trembling-one [Hi. pt. רעד]?	ומתפאר בחנית מרעיד :	—and boast, a trembling-one with a spear [חנית]?
With a close-companion he will go forward, {and he will return with a song}	{וישובב בשיר} באלוף ינהג ישׁוּבב [לשדד] בּשׁור	With a cow he will drive forward, he will turn about [to harrow] with a bull
—and his delights [שעע] with [?]	ושעיותיו עם בנֹ[4] :	—and his looking-abouts [שעה] with [?]
26 And his wakefulness for brides, a 'stall'	ושקידתו לכלות מרבק	**26** And his watchfulness to finish [fatten calves, in] a stall
— (his) vigor [לְשָׁד] will set a heart [?].	(לֵב) לב יָשִׁית לשד[ד 7] :	—he will set [his] heart to harrow [שדד][?].
27 Although he makes [?] —that/who {will go forward} in the evening.	[6]שב (ח)[ה]רש וחו[שב] אשר ליל[5] : {ינהג} (ליל[ה] 4)	**27** אף עשה [6]שׁה *[?]* *[?]*

NOTES for chart A4-14:

- In BBS 38:25a, מלמד as both "teacher" and "ox-goad" may echo Qoh 12:11, as does BBS 44:4d where "nails" are linked with "goads." Qohelet's association of "goad" with "shepherd" is similar to this reading of BBS 38:25a where the מלמד as both "an ox-goad" and "a teacher."

- For באלוף in BBS 38:25c, *DCH* 1:289a translates אלוף "III. 1. 'companion, friend' ... 'companion of her youth' Pr 2:17." Other instances are Prov 16:28, about a man who "alienates a friend" (מַפְרִיד אַלּוּף), and 17:1, "[a man] who seeks love forgives a transgression, and one who harps upon a matter alienates a friend" (מְכַסֶּה־פֶּשַׁע מְבַקֵּשׁ אַהֲבָה וְשֹׁנֶה בְדָבָר מַפְרִיד אַלּוּף) . ("Harps upon" is from *DCH* 8:492b, שנה II.)

- For שעע in BBS 38:25d, the meaning "to flatter someone" is associated with the Hifil form (*HALOT-SE* 1613a cites BBS 13:6) and "to delight, to caress" with the Pilpal form, so I am stretching the translation.

Chart A4-15a: "Do not bring every man to a house" BBS 11:29–31 (MS A)

KEY→ MS A; Ben-Hayyim.

11:29	לא כל איש להביא אל בית	Do not bring every man to a house—and (this
	רוכל [3]פ רבו ומה : (פֹּצֵעַ)	is) how the wounds of a defamer multiply!

11:29c–11:30f → incomplete and/or less pertinent to the motif of slander.

11:30g	אורב הרוכל כדוב	The defamer lurks like a bear near house of scoffers
	לבית לצים וכמרגל יראה ערוה :	—and like a spy he'll see vulnerability/nakedness.
11:31	גן[2] יהפך טוב לרע (נרגן)	Good to bad, a whisperer will pervert—and
	ובמחמדיך יתן קשר :	against your delights he will send treachery.

NOTES for chart A4-15a:

- For פצעי in 11:29b, the slanderer inflicts "wounds" rather than receiving them.
- For "defamer" (רוכל) in 11:29b and 30g is not the word "slander" in BBS 42:5 (דבה). See *DCH* 7:493a "*רכל II.Qal Ptc. רוכל 'slander,' ptc. as noun Si 11:29,30." The semantic range for דבה is "evil report, gossip, defamation" (DCH 2:383b–384a), but both דבה and רוכל seem more serious than "gossip," which is not always malicious.
- For לצים in 11:30g, see *DCH* 2:156b "'house of scoffers' Si 11:30."
- For ערוה in 11:30h, see *DCH* 6:555a "2. 'nakedness, vulnerability' of person Si 11:30."
- For נרגן in 11:31a, see *DCH* 7:416a "Ni. 2. ptc. as noun, 'whisperer, ... gossip.'"
- For 11:31b, see *DCH* 5:802a "נתן 4h. 'afflict with, send against'" and *DCH* 5:221b מחמד "PREP בְּ of place, 'against' + נתן 'give' Si 11:31."

Chart A4-15b: "Let me declare Your name" BBS 51:1–2 (MS B)

51:1	אספרה שמך מעוז חיי	Let me declare Your name, Refuge-of-Life
	כי פדית ממות נפשי	—for You have ransomed my soul from death.
51:2	חשכת בשרי משחת	You've spared my flesh from the pit-of-destruction
	ומיד שאול הצלת רגלי :	—and from the hand of Sheol, delivered my foot.
51:2c	פציתני מדבת עם	You've rescued me from the slander of the people,
	משוט דבת לשון	from the spreading of slander-of-the-tongue—and
	ומשפט שטי כזב :	from the judgment of the spreaders of false-report.

NOTE for chart A4-15b:

- Di Lella (*Wisdom*, 58) notes that Kearns ("Ecclesiasticus," 548) considers 51:1 a later addition to the original Hebrew text, comparable to the GII additions.
- For "slander" in 51:2, this is the word in BBS 42:5 (דבה).

Chart A4-16: "A daughter is a deceptive treasure" BBS 42:9–14 (MSS B, M)

KEY: **No default**. MS B and {B̲ᵐ}; MS M; (Ben-Hayyim); *"slander" version.*

#	MS B, B̲ᴹ	MS M
9ab	{מְטַמוֹן} בת לאב מֹטמנת שקר דאֹגה תפ[7] : {וְדאֲגֲתה} Daughter is a deceptive treasure to father Daughter is a <u>treasure-falsehood</u> to father —{and} anxiety {(about) her} will [?]	בשׁ[1] לאב מטמון שׁ[3] [ב̲[2]] [8]יד נומה [Shame] [daughter?] is a deceptive hidden-treasure to a father— [?] slumber

FINAL   A daughter is a deceptive treasure to a father (B)
            —and anxiety about her will [disperse] slumber. (B, M)

NOTES for BBS 42:9ab
- For 9a, see *DCH* 5:239b "מַטְמֹנֶת 'treasure.'" *DCH* 5:239a "מַטְמֹוֹן 'treasure.'"
DCH 8:557a "שֶׁקֶר 'falsehood, deceit, deception.'" Translating as "treasure-
falsehood" fits my interpretation of שקר presaging the slander, דבה. Thus, both
nouns can stand as they are, without מטמון being read as מֹטמנת, the construct
form. However, I use the less literal "deceptive treasure" in the text.
- For 9b, combine [8]יד נומה (M) → וְדאֲגֲתה[7]תפ (Bᵐ, B) + תפ[ר]יד נומהוְדאֲגֲתה .

#	MS B, B̲ᴹ	MS M
9cd [4]	בנעוריה פן תגור ובבתוליה פן [4] In her girlhood, lest she sojourn /stray—and as a maiden, lest [?]	בֹנֹ[1] וריה פן [ת]מאס (בנֹעֹוריה) ובֹ[2]יה פן [4] In her girlhood lest she will reject/be rejected— [?]

FINAL   As a girl, (B, M) lest she will reject (M)
            —and as a maiden, lest (B) she be profaned (10a, MS M)

#	MS B, B̲ᴹ	MS M
10ab	{תתפתה} בבתוליה פן תפֹותה ובֹין[8] (ובֹית [2]לֹ[2]לֹ[2] ( ) {בבתוליה פ־ תֹתֹפֹתֹה בית בע־ ל תֹנֹשֹה} In her maidenhood, lest she be seduced —and in [the house of] [?](10a in B, 10c in Bᵐ) <u>In her maidenhood, lest she be seduced</u> (Bᵐ) <u>—the house of lord-husband, she will be</u> <u>forgotten.</u> (Bᵐ)	בבתוליה פן תחל ועל אישֹה [2] תשׁט[1] (תשטה) In her maidenhood, lest she be profaned—and concerning her man- husband, [lest?] she be faithless.

FINAL   As a maiden, lest she be seduced (B)
            —and in (B) <u>house of a lord-husband, [lest] she'll be forgotten.</u> (Bᵐ)

NOTES for BBS 42:10ab
- For פתה in 10a, see *DCH* 6:798b Pu. (B) and 799a Htp. (Bᵐ) "be seduced
(sexually) …Si 42:10.'"
- For תֹנֹשֹה in 10b, see Ben-Hayyim 225a "נשה Nifal future, BBS 42:10." *DCH*
5:777a "Ni. 'be forgotten.'"

42: **10cd**	{א־ פחזה ֿבבית אביה פן [5ᵒ] ובבית א[8]} {בבית אביה פ[3] ובב־ איש פ־ תעׇצֵּר}	בית אבֹיׇה פן תזריע ובעל[7]

| In the house of her father, lest she was reckless {B =10c, Bᵐ =10a} —and in the house of a man-husband [?] In the house of her father, lest [?] (Bᵐ) —and in the house of a man-husband lest she be restrained/barren. (Bᵐ) | In the house of her father, lest she "propagate" —and a/her lord-husband [?] |

FINAL In the house of her father, lest she "propagate" (M)
   —and in house of a man-husband lest she be restrained/barren. (Bᵐ)

11ab	[4]ל[3]ל[6]ל[4]) [4]ל[3]ל[2]ל מֹשמֹר (8] שם סרֹה: {סרח} {דבת ע־ ב־ החזק משמר פ־ תע־ מֹ־ לא־}	[5] בת חז[1] משמֹר ([3] עֹל בֹת} {חז[ק] ([13] [פ]ן ת[-----] (:)

| ? (B) [(B) = [?] one who guards] —[?] a name of rebellion/apostasy. Slander of [?], strengthen one who guards (Bᵐ) — [?] a rotting name. (Bᵐ) | [Slander?] concerning a daughter, make firm one who guards —lest [?] |

FINAL Slander concerning a daughter, make firm one who guards (Bᵐ, M)
   —lest [?] (M) a rotting name. (Bᵐ)

NOTES for BBS 42:11ab
- In 11a, reading דְּבָּה עַל instead of construct form דבת (Bᵐ), to fit with עַֹל [3]
בת in MS M, since the construct form would conflict with the preposition עַל.

11cd	דבת עֹ֖ר וק[2]ת עם (וק[ה]לת) והושבתך [2]דת שער : {והובישתך} ([2]עֹדת) {דבת ע־ וק־ ע־ והבשת בעדת שער}	דבת עיר וקהלת עם [13]ֹר

| Slander of a city and an assembly of the people —and it (slander) // she (daughter) may/will cause you shame, in the congregation of the gate. —and the shame, in the congregation of the gate. (Bᵐ) | Slander of a city and an assembly of the people — [?] |

FINAL Slander of a city and an assembly of the people (B, M) —and she
   (daughter) will cause you shame, in the congregation of the gate. (B)
   *Slander of a city, and an assembly of the people (B, M) —and it
   (slander) may cause you shame, in the congregation of the gate. (B)*

NOTES for BBS 42:11cd
- In MS B, colon-d has והושבתך (from ישב) in the text and והובישתך (from בוש)
in the margin. *DCH* 4:328a has "ישב Hi. 'cause to sit, allow to sit, place' …בַּת.
daughter Si 42:11 (B) (והובישתך; Bmg 'and she will shame you,' i.e. בוש hi.)."
- Because "daughter" is not mentioned in this bicola, the entity that causes
"shame" in 11d would be דבה. The presence of "daughter" in 11a allows
"daughter" to be another antecedent of the feminine pronouns that follow.

42: 11ef	[[מ[ו]קֺום תגור אל יהי אשנב ([[ת[שֹב]]) ובית מביט מבוא סביב :	מקום תגור אל יהי [15]ב

Let there not be a lattice (in) a place she will sojourn —and "a house looking out brings in the neighborhood." *Let there not be a lattice—a place it (slander) will attack—and "a house looking out brings in the neighborhood."*		A place she will sojourn, do not be— [?] *Let there not be a place it (slander) will sojourn—[?]*

FINAL   Let there not be a lattice (in) a place she will sojourn (B)
—and "a house looking out brings in the neighborhood."(B)
Let there not be a lattice—a place it (slander) will attack (B)
—and "a house looking out brings in the neighborhood." (B)

NOTES for BBS 42:11ef
- For גור in 11e as "attack" see *DCH* 2:336b, "גור II 'attack' [no mention of BBS]."
- For אשנב in 11f, two words in *DCH* are translated as "window," אשנב and חלון. HALOT-SE translates אשנב as "vent in a wall, (barred) window" (96b) and חלון as "hole in the wall for air and light, window" (318a). In BBS 14:23, the sage who seeks Wisdom "looks down through her window (חלון)…"

12ab	{תזכר} לכל זֺכֺר אל תתן תאר ובית נשים אל תסֺתֺויד : {תסתיד}	לכל זכר אל תבן תאר [16] —

For any male, don't permit a form—and among women // in house of women, let her not consult. *For any (slander), remember! Don't allow (that) it will break through//spy around—and among forgetting-ones, // in a house of forgetting-ones, do not consult.*		For any male, do not let discern a form— [?] *For everything, remember—to/like chaff [it (כל)] goes round.*

FINAL   For any male, do not permit (her) form (B)
—and (in) a house of women, do not let her take counsel. (B)
For all (slander), remember—do not allow (that) it will break through
(B, B^m) —and (in) house of men-who-forget, do not take counsel. (B)

NOTES for BBS 42:12ab
- For תאר 12a as "break through," see Jastrow 31b אור I "to perforate, break through, shine." Reading as תָאֵר [3rd per. f. s. Qal imperf.] "do not allow [that] it will break through."
- For תאר in 12a as "spy-around," see HALOT-SE 1676a "תאר I, root comparable with תור" and *DCH* 8:610b–611a "תור 1. 'spy out, explore.' 2a. 'search out, investigate.'"
- Reading נשים in 12b as נֹשִים "forgetting-ones" (Qal m. pl. participle), see *DCH* 5:776b–777a, נשה "Qal 'forget.'" The verb appears in BBS 42:10b, in the Nifal.

- For בית as "among" in 12b, see *DCH* 2:164a בֵּית "prep. 'between, among,'"
with verb... סוד htp. 'take counsel' Si 42:12."
- For תסתיד in 12b, see *DCH* 6:125b "סוד Htp. Impf. 'take counsel, consult.'
בֵּית 'among' + אשה 'woman' Si 42:12 'among women let her not take
counsel' unless בית נשים '[at] the house of women.'"

כי מבגד יצא עש סס [4]ה רעת [1]שֹה ([א]שֹׁה) כי מבגד יצא עש עש ומאשה רעת אשה: **13ab**	

For "from a garment goes forth a moth"—and from a wife-woman, the evil/bad-things of a wife-woman. *For "from a garment goes forth a moth"* *—and from a wife, the female-companion of a wife.*	For from a garment goes forth a moth —[?] evil/badness of a wife/woman.

FINAL   For "from a garment goes forth a moth" (B, M)
    —and from a woman, the evil of a woman. (B, M)
    For "from a garment goes forth a moth" (B, M)
    —and from a wife, the female-companion of a wife. (B, M)

מטוב רוע איש מטיב אשה ובית מחרפת תביע **14ab** אשה : {טוב רע איש מחפרת מטוב אשה} {ובית מחרפת תביע חרפה :}	טוב רע איש מטיב אשה(מטֹב) ובת מפחדת מכול חרפה

"Better(?) is the evil of a man/husband than the goodness of (?) a woman/wife" —and a house, than the reproaches a woman/wife will utter. Better is evil/badness of a man than goodness of a woman being ashamed (B^m) —and a house than reproaches of a reproach. (B^m)	"Better is the evil/badness of a man/husband than the goodness of a woman/wife" —and a daughter who is afraid-before-God, than any taunt / reproach.

FINAL   "Better the evil of a man than the goodness of a woman" (M)
    —but daughter who's afraid-before-God (is better) than any taunt. (M)

NOTES for BBS 42:14ab
- For מפחדת in 14b, see *DCH* 6:674a "פחד Pi. 1. 'be (continually) afraid,'
before Y. <SUBJ> 'man' Si 37:12 (D)." If איש מפחד is "a God-fearing man"
("a man who feels-afraid-before God") then בת מפחדת is "a God-fearing
daughter." See also HALOT-SE 922a, "פחד Pi. pt. 'be in terror, feel timid'
before God ... Si 37:12." A more nuanced translation makes a parallel with
BBS 37:12a, אך אם איש מפחד תמיד אשר תדע שומר מצוה, "but (be) with a man
who always-feels-afraid-before-God—that you will understand keeping a
commandment."
- For חרפה in 14b, see *DCH* 3:321a "חרפה 1. 'reproach, taunt' of enemy" and
3:321b "PREP:מן ... of cause, 'at,' + פחד 'be in dread' Si 42:14 (M)."(Though
DCH 6:674a is slightly different: "חרף 'taunt,'" plus מן, "on account of".)
            [NOTES for chart A4-16 end.]

A.2.5 Conjectural Translation of BBS 42:14

In addition to the proposed translation of BBS 42:9–14 given in chart 4-16, I offer a conjectural translation of v. 14 that would function as separate closing for the "slander" version. This translation—which is entirely conjectural—forms my boundary for interpretation. The word רע in colon 14a is "purpose/thought," and the מן of מכול in 14b has a privative function.[19] The word מטיב, translated as "one who pleases," is a masculine singular Hifil participle of the root טוב that occurs also in BBS 26:13a: אשה[3] מֹטיב בעלה, "[Grace] of a wife pleases her lord-husband."

> BBS 42:14 (MS M) טוב רע איש מטיב אשה (מטוב) ובת מפחדת מכול חרפֹה
>
> Good is the purpose of a man/husband who pleases מטיב (his) woman/wife —and of a daughter who is afraid-before-God, without any reproach.

For this conjectural translation, the happiness of the daughter is of equal concern with the reputation of the father. In BBS 42:9–14, the problem of slander arises, in part, from the situation of a bad marriage (colon 10b); the problem is resolved in v. 14 by the combination of a correct husband and a correct daughter/wife, whose harmonious relationship will disempower slander, if not prevent it.

Charts 4-17a and 4-17b do not require annotation.

A.2.6 Fully-Annotated Charts for Chapter 5

FORMATTING KEY FOR TRANSLATIONS:

MS X = default MS, plain text

{X^m} = marginal notes of default MS, plain text in curly brackets.

MS Y, {Y^m} = 2nd MS & marg., underlined plain text for Hebrew and translation.

[#] = gaps in Hebrew MS with # of spaces; [?text?] is best-guess translation.

([#]א) = Ben-Hayyim's Hebrew; text is translation based on Ben-Hayyim.

text = translation from Greek of Sirach, bolded white text on dark grey ground.

---

19   See *DCH* 7:513a "רַע" and for מִכּוֹל, *DCH* 5:341b מן 6. 'without, away from.'"

Chart A5-1: "Do not say 'my transgression ...'" BBS 15:11–20 (MSS A, <u>B</u>)

KEY→ MS A is default; <u>MS B</u>, {B^m}; Ben-Hayyim.

15:11	אל תאמר מאל פשעי Do not say "My transgression is from God"
	כי את אשר שנא לא עשה : —for that which He hates, you shall do.
	<u>אל תאמר מה פעלתי</u> Do not say "What have I committed?
	<u>[כי את אשר שנא לא אעש]1</u> —for that which He hates, I would not do."
15:12	פן תֹּאמר הוא התקילני Lest you'll say "He, Himself, caused me to stumble"
	כי אין צורך באנשי חמס : —for there is no need for men-of-violence.
	<u>כי אין לי חפץ באנשי חמס :{צ]3[}</u> —for He has no delight in men-of-violence.
15:13	רעה ותועבה שנא יײ YYY hates evil and abomination—and He will not
	ולא יאננה ליראיו : allow it to happen to those who fear Him.
15:14	<u>הוא מראש ...</u> He, from the start/beginning, created Adam/a human
	ברא אדם God from "the beginning" created Adam/a human
	אֱלֹהים מבראשית א ברא —and He appointed for him the power of his snatcher
	אדם וישתיהו ביד חותפו *[colon b is prob. also pres. MS B]*
	ויתנהו ביד יצרו : —and He gave to him the power of his inclination.
15:15	אם תחפץ תשמר מצוה If you choose, you shall keep commandment(s)
	ותבונה לעשות רצונו : —and understanding (is) to do His will.
	<u>ואֱמֹונה לעשות רצֹון אל : {ותבונה לע רצונו}</u> —and faithfulness (is) to do God's will.
15:15c	אם תאמין בו If you are faithful with Him
	גם אתה תחיה —indeed, you shall live.
15:16	מים ואשמוצק לפניך אש ומים ... Before you are displayed fire and water
	באשר תחפץ שלח ידך : <u>water and fire</u>—whichever you'll choose, reach out your hand.
15:17	לפני אדם חיים מוות Before a human, life and death—that
	אשר יחפץ ינתן לו : which he shall choose will be given to him.
15:17c (MS B only)	כי ל]3[חכמת יײ (לר]ו[ב) For <u>abundant</u> is the wisdom of YYY
	אל בגבורה ומביט לכל : —God-in-power, and beholding <u>all</u>.
15:18	ספקה חכמת יײ אמיץ Overflowing is wisdom of YYY—firm
	גברות וחוזה כלם : ...<u>וחזה כל :</u> of powers and perceiving everything <u>all</u>.
15:19	עיני אל יראו מעשיו The eyes of God see His works—and He, Himself,
	והו יכיר על כל מפעל איש : will find out concerning every action of a man.
	<u>יכיר כל מפעל אנוש : ...</u> —... will find out every action of humankind.
15:20	לא צוה אנוש לחטא He did not command humankind to sin
	ולא החלים אנשי כזב : —and He did not strengthen men-of-falsity.
	<u>ולא למד שקרים ל... </u> —and He did not teach lies to men-of-falsity.
15:20c	ולא מרחם על עושה And He does not have mercy upon those making
	שוא ועל מגלה סוד : falsehood—and upon those who reveal a secret.

Charts 5-2, 5-3, 5-4a, 5-4b, and 5-5 do not require annotation.

Chart A5-6: "Any food the throat eats" BBS 36:18–26 (MSS B, C, D)

KEY→ MS B is default, {B^m}; <u>MS D</u>, vv. 24–26; MS C vv. 19, 22–26 not different.

36:18 כל מאכל אוכל גרגרת אך יש [פֿ]	Any **food**, the throat eats	
(נע]ים) ל[2][1][2]) :ל[3][4]ל[4]ל אוכֹל	—but there is 'eating'	
{אך יש מֹאֹכל ממאכל תנעם}	{that will be more delightful than food.}	
36:18c ל[1]ק[4]ל[1] [?]		
{: אך יש אשה יפה} : [14] [?]	{—but there is a beautiful wife/woman.}	
36:19 חיך בוחן מטעמי דבר	The palate examines flavors of a word/thing	
: ולב מבין מטעמי כזב	—and the heart understands 'flavors' of a lie.	
36:20 לב עקוב יתן עצבת	A deceived heart will give **pain**—but	
[ואיש ותיק ישיֹבֹנה בו : [ישיבנו	a faithful man will restore it for himself.	
36:21 (נכס\ֹד) כל נבֹד תאכל חיה	Any wind-fall, a **wild beast** will eat—but there	
: אך יש מכה ממכה תנעם	is a 'blow' will be more delightful than a blow.	
36:22 [תואר אשה והֹליל פנים [יהלל	Form of **wife** and face causing-light	
: ועל כל מחמד עין יגבר	—and on all that **greatly-delights** the eye,	
	(the heart) will grow strong.	
36:23 ועד אם יֹש מרפא לשון [בֹה]	And further, if she has speech that heals	
: אין אֹשָה מבני אדם	—**her man** is not among the sons-of-**Adam**.	
36:24 קנֹה אשה ראשית קנין עזר [קונה]	**Gaining** a wife is **beginning of gain**	
[וֹמבצר ועמוד משען : [עיר מבצר	—**help**, and citadel, and pillar of support.	
36:25 באין גדיר יבוער כרם	Without a wall, an orchard will be burned	
: ובאין אשה נע ונד	—and without a wife, **weak and wandering**.	
36:26 מי יאמין גדוד צבא	Who will trust an army's marauder	
: המדלג מעיר אל עיר	—leaping about from city to city?	
36:26c [[שֹר אין לו] כן איש אשרֹ	Thus is a man who <u>has no 'nest'</u>	
: לא קן המרגיע באשר יערב	—settling where he will be-at-nightfall.	
<u>כן איש אשר אין לו קן</u>		

NOTES for chart A5-6:
- For 36:18a ‖ Gen 3:6, eating the fruit.
- For 36:18b, see *DCH* 5:705 "Qal 3fs Si תנעם, 'be pleasant, delightful, lovely,' perh. specifically 'be sweet' SUBJ 'food' appar. Si 33:23(B^m).'"
- For 36:20a ‖ Gen 3:16,17, עִצָּבוֹן as "pain, toil."
- For ותיק in 36:20b, see Jastrow 376ab "וָתִיק 'enduring; trusty; strong;

distinguished... faithful.'" Or, *DCH* 2:599 "וְתִיק adj. 'experienced'—Si 36:20."
- In 36:21a, translating by analogy to חיה "wildlife" as an allusion to the
serpent, חַיַּת הַשָּׂדֶה (Gen 3:1). For נבד see *DCH* 1:99b "אבד 4. 'be lost,
stray'... כל האובד 'any missing thing' CD 9:10, האובד בשדה 'what has gone
astray in the field' (of fallen fruit, etc.) 10:22." Ben-Hayyim's נכס "wealth"
and נכד "progeny" do not accord with an allusion to Genesis.
- For 36:22b ‖ Gen 2:9, perhaps 3:6: Genesis has the verb root חמד in the form
נחמד, and here Ben Sira uses a phrase with a related noun מחמד עין. Each use
in Genesis relates to the tree(s) in Eden—the close match is 2:9, where the
trees are **"delightful to the eye."** Gen 3:6 is less similar because "eye" is
replaced by "insight"—Eve notices that נֶחְמָד הָעֵץ לְהַשְׂכִּל the forbidden Tree is
"desirable for intelligence," and eats from it. BBS 25:8 has אשרי בעל אשה
משכלת, "happy is the husband/master of an intelligent wife."
- For 36:23 ‖ Gen 3:6: Ben Sira usually uses בעל for "husband." Here he
uses איש, the word used in Genesis 2, 3, and 4 to mean both "man" and
"husband" as אשה means both "wife" and "woman." MS B has אשה, adding
the dagesh that indicates "her husband" rather than "wife." The vowelled
word, surrounded by unvowelled text, emphasizes this reading. אשה occurs in
Genesis 3:6, where Eve ate the fruit and "gave it to **her man** with her, and he
ate." Thus Ben Sira alludes to the exact verse in which Eve eats the fruit, but
he makes no reference to "sin" or "death."
- For 36:24a ‖ Gen 4:1: The word "gain" is from the root קנה used by Eve in
Genesis 4:1, in explaining the name she chose for her son Cain. Ben Sira's
words קנה אשה are very similar to Eve's קניתי איש "I have gained a
man/husband." In BBS, קנה occurs two other places as "gaining" with regard
to a female figure: BBS 51:20 לב קניתי לה "I gained a heart from/by her" and
51:21b קניתיה קנין טוב "I have gained her, a good gain," both times for his
"gain" of Wisdom. For "gaining" a male friend, קנה occurs twice in BBS 6:6.
- In 36:24a, the word ראשית parallels Gen 1:1.
- For 36:24b ‖ Gen 2:18, 20: עזר "a help," in conjunction with "wife" may
allude to Gen 2:18 and 20, where Adam's future companion is described as
עזר כנגדו "a help as his opposite." This instance is the only occurrence of עֵזֶר
in BBS. MSS Bᵐ, C, and D have עיר מבצר, "city of fortification (fortified
city)," as in 1 Sam 6:18, rather than עזר ומבצר.
- For 36: 25 ‖ Gen 4:12,14: The expression נע ונד "weak [trembling] and
wandering" occurs only twice in the Hebrew Bible—in Genesis 4:12 and 14,
God's cursing of Cain and Cain's reiteration of the curse.
- For 36:26c: MS B has לא קן "do not nest [?]" MS C has אין לו קין "he has no
gain," and MS D has אין לו קן "he has no nest." I use MS D's version of this
phrase, though both meanings are probably present.

[NOTES for chart A5-6 end.]

Chart A5-7: "The source of every deed ..." BBS 37:16–26 (MSS B, C, D)

KEY→ MS D is default, {D[m]}; <u>MS B</u>, vv. 16–25; MS C, vv. 19, 22, 24, 26 (incomplete).

37:16	ראש כל מעשה מאמר לפני כל	The source of every deed is <u>a word</u>
	<u>ר־ כל מ־ דבר</u> : פועל היא מחשבת	—before every act, it is a plan.
37:17	עקר תחבולות לב	The root of guidance is the heart
	: ארבעה שרביטין[1] יפריח	—four branches spring up:
37:18	טוב ורע מות וחיים	Good and evil, death and life—and the
	: ומשלח בם כליל לשון	sender of them, completely, the tongue.
37:19	יש חכם לרבים נחכם	There is a wise-man making many wise
	: ולנפשו הוא נואל	—and for his own self, he is foolish.
37:20 <u>נמאס</u>	ויש חכם בדברו ימאס ב־ <u>נמאס</u>	And there's a wise-man rejected for his
	: ומכל מאכל תענוג נבצר	words—and from all pleasant food, he is cut off.
37:22 (no 21)	ויש חכם לנפשו נֶחֳם ל־ <u>יחכם</u>	And there is a wise-man who is wise for
	: זֹפֶֿרֽי דעתו על גוין[2]	his own self—and the rewards of
	<u>פרי ד־ על גויתו</u> :	his knowledge are upon <u>his person</u>.
37:23 {ויש חכם לעמו יכחם}	{ויש חכם לעמו יכחם}	{And there's a wise-man who'll make his people wise
	{פרי דעתו בגויתם} :	—the reward of his knowledge is in their persons.}
37:24	חכם לנפשו ישבע	A wise-man will have his fill of pleasure for own self
	: תענוג ויאשריהו כל רואיהו	—and all who see him, they will call him happy.
	{גויתהן מספר יש [2]מֽים וגוית שם ימי אין מספר}	
37:25	חיי אנוש ימים מספר	The life of humankind is a number of days
	וחיי ישורון ימי אין מספר	—and the life of Yeshurun, days without number.
37:26	חכם עם ינחל כבוד	A wise-man of the people will inherit honor
	: ושמו עומד בחיי עולם	—and his name endures in everlasting life.

NOTES for chart A5-7:

- For v. 20, *DCH* 8:660b gives "מאכל תענוג *food of delight*, i.e., delightful food Si 37:20." *DCH* 2: 247 gives "בצר Ni. *be cut off, withheld* <SUBJ> מאכל *food* Si 37:20 <PREP> מן *from ... wise (one)* Si 37:20;" however, "wise-man" fits better as the subject.

- Vv. 24 and 25 are transposed in both MS B and MS D, though the numbering is as above.

Chart 5-8 does not require annotation.

Chart A5-9: "A life of abundance ..." BBS 40:18–27 (MSS B, M)

KEY→ Ben-Hayyim; MS B is default, {MS Bᵐ}; <u>MS M</u>; Sirach

40:18	חיי יתר [1]כר ימתקו Life of abundance and reward שכר will be sweet
	{יותר שכל} חיי יןˆ ושכר ימתקו Life of {abundance and intelligence} will be sweet
	{סימה} : ומשניהם מוצא אוצר —more than both, finding treasure.
40:19	ילד ועיר יעמידו שם Child and city will establish a name
	ומשניהם מוצא חכמה —more than both, finding Wisdom.
40:19c	שגר ונטע יפריחו שם Bearing and planting will cause name to blossom
	ומשניהם אשה נחשקת —more than both, a wife who is desired.
40:20	[2]ן ושכר יעליצו לב [Wine] and mead will cause a heart to exult
	ומשניהם אהבת דודים : —more than both, she who loves love-making.
40:21	{חליל} [3]ל ונבל יעריבו {Flute} and harp will cause a song to blend
	שיר ומשניהם לשון ברה : —more than both, a clear tongue/speech.
40:22	[7 יע]מידו [9]מידו עין Grace and beauty will cause an eye [חמד to
	{שדי} : ומשניהם צמחי שדה delight]—more than both, flowers of the field.
40:23	[9]ת ינהגו Friend and companion will lead your steps
	ומשניהם אשה משכלת : —more than both, an intelligent wife.
40:24	אח [11] צרה ומשנˆיהם Brother and help will reduce distress
	{צדקה} : צדק מצלת —more than both, {alms} that rescue.
40:25	זהב וכס[9]ל Gold [and silver] will make a foot steady
	ומש[11] —more than both, excellent council.
40:26	חיל וכח יג[3] לב Valor and strength will uphold a heart
	ומשניהם [6]הים : —more than both, the fear-of-God.
40:26c	אין [1]יראת יי מחסור There is no want in the fear-of-YYY
	ואין לבקש עמה [3]ן : משען —and nothing to seek with it (as) a support.
40:27	יראת אלהים כעדן ברכה וכן The fear-of-God is like an Eden of blessing
	ועל כל כˉ חˉ : כל כבוד חפתה —and its bridal-canopy is over all the glory.

NOTES for chart A5-9:

- For נחשקת in 40:19d, see *DCH* 3:333 "חשק Ni. 'be desired, be loved;' SUBJ אשה 'woman' Si 40:19."

- For אהבת in 40:20b, see *DCH* 1:138a "אהב Qal ptc. אֹהֶבֶת" and p. 139a "אֹהֶבֶת רֵעַ 'a woman who loves a neighbor.'" An alternate translation for אהבת is אַהֲבָה "love" in construct form: "more than both, the love of love-making."

- For דודים in 40:20b, see HALOT-SE 215a-b "3. דודים 'love (lust)' ... Sir 40:20." I translate the plural as "love-making." However, see *DCH* 1:141b "אַהֲבָה <CSTR> דודים 'of friends' Si 40:20;" and *DCH* 2:423b "אהבת דודים 'love of friends' Si 40:20."

- For ברה in 40:21b, see Jastrow 189 "בַּר III (b. h. ברר) 'clear, bright, ... pure.'"

- For משען in 40:26d (MS M), see *DCH* 5:552b "**support** ... 'in reverence for

Y. there is no lack and no need to seek [additional] support beside it'" (lists
verse number as 42:26).   [NOTES for chart A5-9 end.]

Chart 5-10 does not require annotation.

Chart A5-11: "Grace of a wife pleases her husband" BBS 26:13–17 (MS C)

KEY→Ben-Hayyim; conjecture from Greek text.

26:13	(מֵטִיב) יב[2] אשה[3]	[Grace of] a wife "pleases" her lord-husband
	בעלה [4] ידשן שכלה	—and her intelligence will fatten [?].
26:14	*[no extant Hebrew]*	
26:15אשת ביישת	חן ע[3] (ע]ל ב[2])	Grace [upon grace], a modest wife—and there
	ואין משקל לצרורת פה :	is no weighing for one who's 'close-mouthed.'
26:16 במרומי	שמש [5] (זור[חת])	Sun rising in the heights of the heavens—
בדביר בחור	מעל יפה א[2] (א[שה])	beautiful a wife in the chosen holy-of-holies.
26:17	נר שרף על מנורת קדש	Lamp burning upon the holy candlesticks
	הוד פנים על קומת תוכן :	—splendor of face upon tallness of stature.

NOTE for chart A5-11:
- For מטיב in 26:13a, see *DCH* 3:350b–351a "טוב Hi. ptc. מֵטִיב …also
transitive, 'please' (Si 26:13)."
- For צרורה in 26:15b, see *DCH* 7:166a "צרר Qal 3a. 'be small, be narrow.'"
Reading as Qal f. s. pass. part. of צרר, "narrowed"—"one who is 'narrowed' of
mouth." Disagree with *DCH* 7:386a "צרר 5.ptc. pass.as noun,'one who is
closed up' of mouth,i.e., who keeps her mouth shut Si 26:15."

Charts 5-12, 5-13, and 5-14 do not require annotation.

The charts for chapter 6 do not require annotation.

Select Bibliography

Reference Works Consulted

Clines, David J. A., ed. *The Dictionary of Classical Hebrew*. 8 vols, *Aleph* to *Sin–Taw*. Sheffield: Sheffield Academic Press, 1993–2011. [Cited as: *DCH* vol.#: page# column.]

Dotan, Aron, ed. *Biblia Hebraica Leningradensia: Prepared According to the Vocalization, Accents, and Masora of Aaron Ben Moses Ben Asher in the Leningrad Codex*. Peabody, MA: Hendrickson, 2001.

Jastrow, Marcus, comp. *A Dictionary of the Targumim, the Talmud Babli and Yerushalmi, and the Midrashic Literature*. Peabody, MA: Hendrickson, 2005, 1943.

Koehler, Ludwig, Walter Baumgartner, and Johann Jakob Stamm. *The Hebrew and Aramaic Lexicon of the Old Testament: Study Edition*. Edited by M. E. J. Richardson. 2 vols. Leiden: Brill, 2001. [Cited as: *HALOT-SE* page# column]

Kohlenberger, John R., III. *The Parallel Apocrypha: Greek Text, King James Version, Douay Old Testament, the Holy Bible by Ronald Knox, Today's English Version, New Revised Standard Version, New American Bible, New Jerusalem Bible*. New York: Oxford University Press, 1997.

Liddell, Henry George, comp., Robert Scott, comp., Henry Stuart Jones, and Roderick McKenzie. *A Greek-English Lexicon*. Rev. ed. Oxford: Clarendon Press; New York: Oxford University Press, 1996.

Muraoka, Takamitsu. *A Greek-English Lexicon of the Septuagint: Chiefly of the Pentateuch and the Twelve Prophets*. Louvain: Peeters, 2002.

Pietersma, Albert, and Benjamin G. Wright, eds. *A New English Translation of the Septuagint and the Other Greek Translations Traditionally Included under that Title*. New York and Oxford: Oxford University Press, 2007. [Cited as NETS.]

Sources Cited

NOTE: Abbreviations for sources are from *The SBL Handbook of Style* (Peabody, MA: Hendrickson, 1999).

Academy of the Hebrew Language and the Shrine of the Book, The. *See* Ben-Hayyim, Zeev.

Adam, A. K. M., ed. *Postmodern Interpretations of the Bible: A Reader*. St. Louis, MO: Chalice Press, 2001.

Adler, Elkan N. "Some Missing Chapters of Ben Sira [7, 29–12,1]." *JQR* 12 (1899–1900): 466–80.

Aitken, James K. "Divine Will and Providence." In *Ben Sira's God*, edited by Renate Egger-Wenzel, 282–301. Berlin: Walter de Gruyter, 2002.

Aletti, Jean-Noël. "Séduction et parole en Proverbes 1–9." *VT* 27, no. 2 (1977): 129–44.

Alter, Robert. "Afterword." In *Song of Songs*, by Ariel A. Bloch and Chana Bloch, 119–131. New York: Random House, 1995.

Angel, Andrew. "From Wild Men to Wise and Wicked Women: An Investigation into Male Heterosexuality in Second Temple Interpretations of the Ladies Wisdom and Folly." In *A Question of Sex?*, edited by Deborah W. Rooke, 145–61. Sheffield: Sheffield Phoenix Press, 2007.

Archer, Léonie J. "The 'Evil Women' in Apocryphal and Pseudepigraphical Writings." In *Proceedings of the 9th World Congress of Jewish Studies, Jerusalem, Aug 1985: Division A: Period of the Bible*, edited by Raphael Giveon, H. Jacob Katzenstein and Moshé Anbar, 239–46. Jerusalem: World Union of Jewish Studies, 1986.

Argall, Randal A., Beverly A. Bow, and Rodney A. Werline, eds. *For a Later Generation: The Transformation of Tradition in Israel, Early Judaism, and Early Christianity*. Harrisburg, PA: Trinity Press, 2000.

Aristotle. *Aristotle: The "Art" of Rhetoric*. Translated by John Henry Freese. London: Heinemann; New York: G. P. Putnam's Sons, 1926.

Arthur, Marylin B. "The Dream of a World without Women: Poetics and the Circles of Order in the *Theogony* Proemium." *Arethusa* 16, no. 1/2 (1983): 97–116.

Augustine, Saint. *Against Julian (Contra Julianum)*. Translated by Matthew A. Schumacher. Writings of Saint Augustine 16; FC 35. Washington, DC: Catholic University of America Press, 1974.

Austin, John L. *How to Do Things with Words*. 2nd ed, The William James Lectures Delivered at Harvard University in 1955. Cambridge, MA: Harvard University Press, 1975.

Baillet, Maurice, Jósef T. Milik, and Roland de Vaux, eds. *Les "petites grottes" de Qumrân: Exploration de la falaise, les grottes 2Q, 3Q, 5Q, 7Q À 10Q, le rouleau de cuivre*. DJD 3. Oxford: Clarendon Press, 1962.

Baker, Cynthia M. *Rebuilding the House of Israel: Architectures of Gender in Jewish Antiquity*. Divinations. Stanford, CA: Stanford University Press, 2002.

Balla, Ibolya. *Ben Sira on Family, Gender, and Sexuality*. DCLS 8. Berlin: De Gruyter, 2011.

Bauman, Richard. *Verbal Art as Performance*. Series in Sociolinguistics. Rowley, MA: Newbury House, 1977.

Beal, Timothy K., and David M. Gunn, eds. *Reading Bibles, Writing Bodies: Identity and the Book*. Biblical Limits. London and New York: Routledge, 1997.

Beentjes, Pancratius C. *The Book of Ben Sira in Hebrew: A Text Edition of All Extant Hebrew Manuscripts and a Synopsis of All Parallel Hebrew Ben Sira Texts*. VTSup 68. Leiden: Brill, 1997. [Cited as: Beentjes (*Book of Ben Sira in Hebrew*).]

————, ed. *The Book of Ben Sira in Modern Research: Proceedings of the First International Ben Sira Conference, 28–31 July 1996, Soesterberg, Netherlands.* BZAW 255. Berlin: Walter de Gruyter, 1997.

————. "Canon and Scripture in the Book of Ben Sira (Jesus Sirach/Ecclesiasticus)." In *Hebrew Bible/Old Testament* (Vol. 1, Pt. 2), edited by Christian H. W. Brekelmans, Menaham Haran and Magne Saebø, 591–605. Göttingen: Vandenhoeck & Ruprecht, 2000.

————. "Errata Et Corrigenda." In *Ben Sira's God*, edited by Renate Egger-Wenzel, 375–77. Berlin: Walter de Gruyter, 2002. [Applies to *The Book of Ben Sira in Hebrew*.]

————. *"Happy the One Who Meditates on Wisdom" (Sir. 14,20): Collected Essays on the Book of Ben Sira.* CBET 43. Leuven and Paris: Peeters, 2006.

————. "Hermeneutics in the Book of Ben Sira: Some Observations on the Hebrew Ms. C." *EstBib* 46 (1988): 45–60.

————. "Reconstructions and Retroversions: Changes and Challenges to the Hebrew Ben Sira Text." In *Texts and Versions of the Book of Ben Sira*, edited by Jean-Sébastien Rey and Jan Joosten, 23–35. Leiden: Brill, 2011.

————. "Some Major Topics in Ben Sira Research." In *"Happy the One Who Meditates on Wisdom" (Sir. 14,20)*, 3–16. Leuven and Paris: Peeters, 2006.

Ben-Amos, Dan, and Kenneth S. Goldstein, eds. *Folklore: Performance and Communication.* Approaches to Semiotics 40. The Hague: Mouton, 1975.

Ben-Hayyim, Zeev. *The Book of Ben Sira: Text, Concordance and an Analysis of the Vocabulary*, with a foreword in English by Zeev Ben-Hayyim. The Historical Dictionary of the Hebrew Language. Jerusalem: The Academy of the Hebrew Language and the Shrine of the Book, 1973. [Cited as: Ben-Hayyim (*Book of Ben Sira*).]

Bergant, Dianne. "'My Beloved Is Mine and I Am His' (Song 2:16): The Song of Songs and Honor and Shame." In *Honor and Shame in the World of the Bible*, edited by Victor H. Matthews, et al., 23–40. Atlanta, GA: Scholars Press, 1996.

Bhabha, Homi K. *The Location of Culture.* London: Routledge, 1994.

Bickerman, Elias J. *The Jews in the Greek Age.* Cambridge, MA: Harvard University Press, 1988.

Bloch, Ariel A., and Chana Bloch. *The Song of Songs: A New Translation with an Introduction and Commentary.* Afterword by Robert Alter. New York: Random House, 1995.

Botha, P. J. "Through the Figure of a Woman Many Have Perished: Ben Sira's View of Women." *OTE* 9 (1996): 20–34.

Boyarin, Daniel. *Carnal Israel: Reading Sex in Talmudic Culture.* The New Historicism: Studies in Cultural Poetics 25. Berkeley and Los Angeles: University of California Press, 1993.

————. "Torah Study and the Making of Jewish Gender." In *A Feminist Companion to Reading the Bible*, edited by Athalya Brenner and Carole R. Fontaine, 515–46. Sheffield: Sheffield Academic Press, 1997.

Brekelmans, Christian H. W., Menaham Haran, and Magne Saebø, eds. *Hebrew Bible/Old Testament: The History of Its Interpretation.* Vol. 1, *From the*

Beginnings to the Middle Ages (until 1300), Pt. 2, *The Middle Ages*. Göttingen: Vandenhoeck & Ruprecht, 2000.

Bremmer, Jan N. "Pandora or the Creation of a Greek Eve." In *Creation of Man and Woman*, edited by Gerard P. Luttikhuizen, 19–33. Leiden: Brill, 2000.

Brenner, Athalya, and Carole R. Fontaine, eds. *A Feminist Companion to Reading the Bible: Approaches, Methods and Strategies*. FCB 11. Sheffield: Sheffield Academic Press, 1997.

Brod, Harry. "Studying Masculinities as Superordinate Studies." In *Masculinity Studies & Feminist Theory*, edited by Judith Kegan Gardiner, 161–75. New York: Columbia University Press, 2002.

Brooke, George J., ed. *Women in the Biblical Tradition*. Lewiston, NY: Edwin Mellen Press, 1992.

Brown, Teresa R. "Sinners, Idol-Worshippers and Fools among the Men of Hesed: Ben Sira's Pedagogy In Praise of the Fathers (Sir 44–50)." PhD dissertation, Graduate Theological Union; Berkeley, CA, 1998.

Burkes, Shannon. *God, Self, and Death: The Shape of Religious Transformation in the Second Temple Period*. JSJSup 79. Leiden: Brill, 2003.

Butler, Judith. *Gender Trouble: Feminism and the Subversion of Identity*. New York: Routledge, 1999. Reissue of 1990 book with extra preface.

———. "The Question of Social Transformation." In *Undoing Gender*, 204–31, 60. New York: Routledge, 2004.

Calduch-Benages, Núria. "Animal Imagery in the Hebrew Text of Ben Sirach." In *Texts and Versions of the Book of Ben Sira*, edited by Jean-Sébastien Rey and Jan Joosten, 55–71. Leiden: Brill, 2011.

———. "'Cut Her Away from Your Flesh': Divorce in Ben Sira." In *Studies in the Book of Ben Sira*, edited by Géza G. Xeravits and József Zsengellér 81–95. Leiden: Brill, 2008.

———. "Fear for the Powerful or Respect for Authority." Translated by Jan Liesen. In *Der Einzelne und seine Gemeinschaft bei Ben Sira*, edited by Renate Egger-Wenzel and Ingrid Krammer, 87–102. Berlin: Walter de Gruyter, 1998.

———. "Trial Motive in the Book of Ben Sira with Special Reference to Sir 2,1–6." In *The Book of Ben Sira in Modern Research*, edited by Pancratius C. Beentjes, 135–52. Berlin: Walter de Gruyter, 1997.

Calduch-Benages, Núria, and Jacques Vermeylen, eds. *Treasures of Wisdom: Studies in Ben Sira and the Book of Wisdom; Festschrift M. Gilbert*. BETL 143. Louvain: Leuven University Press; Peeters, 1999.

Cameron, Averil M., and Amélie Kuhrt, eds. *Images of Women in Antiquity*. 2nd ed. Detroit, MI: Wayne State University Press, 1993.

Camp, Claudia V. *Ben Sira and the Men Who Handle Books: Gender and the Rise of Canon-Consciousness*. Hebrew Bible Monographs 50. Sheffield: Sheffield Phoenix Press, 2013.

———. "The Female Sage in Ancient Israel and in the Biblical Wisdom Literature." In *The Sage in Israel and the Ancient Near East*, edited by John G. Gammie and Leo G. Perdue, 185–203. Winona Lake, IN: Eisenbrauns, 1990.

———. "Female Voice, Written Word: Women and Authority in Hebrew Scripture." In *Embodied Love*, edited by Paula M. Cooey, Sharon A. Farmer and Mary Ellen Ross, 97–113. San Francisco, CA: Harper and Row, 1987.

———. "Honor and Shame in Ben Sira: Anthropological and Theological Reflections." In *The Book of Ben Sira in Modern Research*, edited by Pancratius C. Beentjes, 171–88. Berlin: Walter de Gruyter, 1997.

———. "Storied Space, or Ben Sira "Tells" A Temple." In *'Imagining' Biblical Worlds*, edited by David M. Gunn and Paula M. McNutt, 64–80. London and New York: Sheffield Academic Press, 2002.

———. "Understanding a Patriarchy: Women in Second Century Jerusalem through the Eyes of Ben Sira." In *"Women Like This"*, edited by Amy-Jill Levine, 1–39. Atlanta, GA: Scholars Press, 1991.

———. *Wise, Strange, and Holy: The Strange Woman and the Making of the Bible*. JSOTSup 320; Gender, Culture, Theory 9. Sheffield: Sheffield Academic Press, 2000.

———. "Woman Wisdom and the Strange Woman: Where Is Power to Be Found?" In *Reading Bibles, Writing Bodies*, edited by Timothy K. Beal and David M. Gunn, 85–112. London and New York: Routledge, 1997.

Charles, Ronald. "Hybridity and the *Letter of Aristeas*." *JSJ* 40, no. 2 (2009): 242–59.

Charlesworth, James H. "Lady Wisdom and Johannine Christology." In *Light in a Spotless Mirror*, edited by James H. Charlesworth and Michael A. Daise, 92–133. Harrisburg, PA: Trinity Press, 2003.

Charlesworth, James H., and Michael A. Daise, eds. *Light in a Spotless Mirror: Reflections on Wisdom Traditions in Judaism and Early Christianity*. Faith and Scholarship Colloquies. Harrisburg, PA: Trinity Press, 2003.

Charlesworth, James H., Lee Martin McDonald, and Blake A. Jurgens, eds. *Sacra Scriptura: How "Non-Canonical" Texts Functioned in Early Judaism and Early Christianity*. London: T & T Clark, forthcoming November 2013.

Collins, John J. "Before the Fall: The Earliest Interpretations of Adam and Eve." In *The Idea of Biblical Interpretation*, edited by Hindy Najman and Judith H. Newman, 293–308. Leiden: Brill, 2004.

———. *Jewish Wisdom in the Hellenistic Age*. OTL. Louisville, KY: Westminster John Knox Press, 1997.

———. "Marriage, Divorce, and Family in Second Temple Judaism." In *Families in Ancient Israel*, edited by Leo G. Perdue, et al., 104–62. Louisville, KY: Westminster John Knox Press, 1997.

———. "Towards the Morphology of a Genre." *Semeia* 14; Apocalypse: The morphology of a genre (1979): 1–20.

Connell, R. W. *Gender and Power: Society, the Person, and Sexual Politics*. Stanford, CA: Stanford University Press, 1987.

Cooey, Paula M., Sharon A. Farmer, and Mary Ellen Ross, eds. *Embodied Love: Sensuality and Relationship as Feminist Values*. San Francisco, CA: Harper and Row, 1987.

Corley, Jeremy. *Ben Sira's Teaching on Friendship*. BJS 316. Providence, RI: BJS, 2002.

———. "Friendship According to Ben Sira." In *Der Einzelne und seine Gemeinschaft bei Ben Sira*, edited by Renate Egger-Wenzel and I. Krammer, 65–72. Berlin: Walter de Gruyter, 1998.

———. "An Intertextual Study of Proverbs and Ben Sira." In *Intertextual Studies in Ben Sira and Tobit*, edited by Jeremy Corley and Vincent Skemp, 155–82. Washington, DC: Catholic Biblical Association of America, 2005.

———. "Sirach 44:1–15 as Introduction to the Praise of the Ancestors." In *Studies in the Book of Ben Sira*, edited by Géza G. Xeravits and József Zsengellér, 151–81. Leiden: Brill, 2008.

Corley, Jeremy, and Harm W. M. van Grol, eds. *Rewriting Biblical History: Essays on Chronicles and Ben Sira in Honor of Pancratius C. Beentjes*. DCLS 7. Berlin: De Gruyter, 2011.

Corley, Jeremy, and Vincent Skemp, eds. *Intertextual Studies in Ben Sira and Tobit: Essays in Honor of Alexander a Di Lella, O.F.M.* CBQMS 38. Washington, DC: CBA, 2005.

Cornwall, Andrea, and Nancy Lindisfarne, eds. *Dislocating Masculinity: Comparative Ethnographies*. Male Orders. London: Routledge, 1994.

Cornwall, Andrea, and Nancy Lindisfarne. "Dislocating Masculinity: Gender, Power and Anthropology." In *Dislocating Masculinity*, edited by Andrea Cornwall and Nancy Lindisfarne, 11–47. London: Routledge, 1994.

Cowley, Arthur E., and Adolf Neubauer, eds. *The Original Hebrew of a Portion of Ecclesiasticus*. Oxford: Clarendon, 1897.

Crenshaw, James L. "A Proverb in the Mouth of a Fool." In *Seeking Out the Wisdom of the Ancients*, edited by Ronald L. Troxel, Kelvin G. Friebel and Dennis Robert Magary, 103–15. Winona Lake, IN: Eisenbrauns, 2005.

Davidson, Andrew B. "Sirach's Judgment of Women." *ExpTim* 6 (1894–1895): 402–04.

Davies, Philip R., and John M. Halligan, eds. *Second Temple Studies 3: Studies in Politics, Class and Material Culture*. JSOTSup 340. London: Continuum, 2002.

Day, John, Robert P. Gordon, and Hugh G. M. Williamson, eds. *Wisdom in Ancient Israel: Essays in Honour of J. A. Emerton*. Cambridge: Cambridge University Press, 1995.

Day, Peggy L., ed. *Gender and Difference in Ancient Israel*. Minneapolis, MN: Fortress Press, 1989.

Dean-Jones, Lesley Ann. *Women's Bodies in Classical Greek Science*. Oxford: Clarendon Press; New York: Oxford University Press, 1996 (paperback edition).

Dely, Carole. "Jacques Derrida: The Perchance of a Coming of the Otherwoman (the Deconstruction of 'Phallogocentrism' from Duel to Duo)." In *Sens[public] International Web Journal*, 1–15. Translated by Wilson Baldridge (quoted section is from Derrida's "Autrui est secret parce qu'il est autre"). www.sen-public.org, accessed 2 April 2008.

Derrida, Jacques. "Autrui est secret parce qu'il est autre." Interview by Antoine Spire. *Le Monde de l'éducation* 284 (2000): 14–21.

———. "Chorégraphies." Correspondence with Christie V. McDonald. In *Points de suspension. Entretiens*, 95–115. Paris: Galilée, 1992.

Derrida, Jacques, and Christie V. McDonald. "Interview: Choreographies: Jacques Derrida and Christie V. Mcdonald." *Diacritics* 12, no. 2 (1982): 66–76. Translated by Christie V. McDonald.

Deutsch, Celia. "The Sirach 51 Acrostic: Confession and Exhortation." *ZAW* 94, no. 3 (1982): 400–09.

———. "Wisdom in Matthew: Transformation of a Symbol." *NovT* 32, no. 1 (1990): 13–47.

Dever, William G., and Seymour Gitin, eds. *Symbiosis, Symbolism, and the Power of the Past: Canaan, Ancient Israel, and Their Neighbors from the Late Bronze Age through Roman Palestina.* Winona Lake, IN: Eisenbrauns, 2003.

Diamond, James A. "Nahmanides and Rashi on the One Flesh of Conjugal Union: Lovemaking vs. Duty." *HTR* 102, no. 2 (2009): 193–224.

Dieleman, Jacco. "Fear of Women? Representations of Women in Demotic Wisdom Texts." *Studien zur altägyptischen Kultur* 25 (1998): 7–46.

Diesel, Anja A., Reinhard G. Lehmann, Eckart Otto, and Andreas Wagner, eds. *"Jedes Ding hat seine Zeit": Studien zur israelitischen und altorientalischen Weisheit.* BZAW 241. Berlin: Walter de Gruyter, 1996.

Dihi, Haim. "Non-Biblical Verbal Usages in the Book of Ben Sira." In *Diggers at the Well*, edited by Takamitsu Muraoka and John F. Elwolde, 56–64. Leiden: Brill, 2000.

Di Lella, Alexander A. "The Newly Discovered Sixth Manuscript of Ben Sira from the Cairo Geniza." *Bib* 69 (1988): 226–38.

———. "Review: *Ben Sira's View of Women: A Literary Analysis.*" *CBQ* 46, no. 2 (1984): 332–34.

———. "Use and Abuse of the Tongue: Ben Sira 5,9 – 6,1." In *"Jedes Ding hat seine Zeit,"* edited by Anja A. Diesel, et al., 33–48. Berlin: Walter de Gruyter, 1996.

———. "The Wisdom of Ben Sira: Resources and Recent Research." *CurBS* 4 (1996): 161–81.

Dubisch, Jill, ed. *Gender and Power in Rural Greece.* Princeton, NJ: Princeton University Press, 1986.

duBois, Page. *Sowing the Body: Psychoanalysis and Ancient Representations of Women.* Women in Culture and Society. Chicago: University of Chicago Press, 1991; hardcover edition 1988.

Ebeling, Jennie R., and Yorke M. Rowan. "The Archaeology of the Daily Grind: Ground Stone Tools and Food Production in the Southern Levant." *Near Eastern Archaeology* 67, no. 2 (2004): 108–17.

Edwards, Douglas R., and C. Thomas McCollough, eds. *The Archaeology of Difference: Gender, Ethnicity, Class and the "Other" In Antiquity: Studies in Honor of Eric M. Meyers.* AASOR 60/61. Boston, MA: ASOR, 2007.

Edwards, Denis. *Jesus the Wisdom of God: An Ecological Theology.* Ecology and Justice Series. Maryknoll, NY: Orbis, 1995.

Egger-Wenzel, Renate. "The Absence of Named Women from Ben Sira's Praise of the Ancestors." In *Rewriting Biblical History*, edited by Jeremy Corley and Harm W. M. van Grol, 301–17. Berlin: De Gruyter, 2011.

————, ed. *Ben Sira's God: Proceedings of the International Ben Sira Conference, Durham, Ushaw College 2001*. BZAW 321. Berlin: Walter de Gruyter, 2002.

————. "The Change of the Sacrifice Terminology from Hebrew into Greek in the Book of Ben Sira: Did the Grandson Understand His Grandfather's Text Correctly?" *BN* 140 (2009): 69–93.

————. "Ein neues Sira-Fragment des MS C." *BN* 138 (2008): 107–14.

Egger-Wenzel, Renate, and Jeremy Corley, eds. *Prayer from Tobit to Qumran: Inaugural Conference of the ISDCL at Salzburg, Austria, 5–9 July 2003*. DCLY 2004. New York: De Gruyter, 2004.

Egger-Wenzel, Renate, and Ingrid Krammer, eds. *Der Einzelne und seine Gemeinschaft bei Ben Sira*. BZAW 270. Berlin: Walter de Gruyter, 1998.

Eisenbaum, Pamela M. "Sirach." In *Women's Bible Commentary: Expanded Edition*, edited by Carol A. Newsom and Sharon H. Ringe, 298–304. Louisville, KY: Westminster/John Knox Press, 1998.

Elizur, Shulamit. "Two New Leaves of the Hebrew Version of Ben Sira." *DSD* 17, no. 1 (2010): 13–29.

Ellis, Teresa Ann. "Is Eve the 'Woman' in Sir 25:24?" *CBQ* 73, no. 4 (2011): 723–42.

————. "Negotiating the Boundaries of Tradition: The Rehabilitation of the Book of Ben Sira in *b. Sanhedrin* 100b." In *Sacra Scriptura*, edited by James H. Charlesworth, Lee Martin McDonald, and Blake A. Jurgens, n.p. London: T & T Clark, forthcoming November 2013.

Eron, John Lewis. "'That Women Have Mastery over Both King and Beggar' (Tjud. 15.5)—the Relationship of the Fear of Sexuality to the Status of Women in Apocrypha and Pseudepigrapha: I Esdras (3 Ezra) 3–4, Ben Sira and the Testament of Judah." *JSP* 9 (1991): 43–66.

Fitzmyer, Joseph A. "The Name Simon." *HTR* 56, no. 1 (1963): 1–5.

Fonrobert, Charlotte Elisheva. *Menstrual Purity: Rabbinic and Christian Reconstructions of Biblical Gender*. Contraversions. Stanford, CA: Stanford University Press, 2000.

Fontaine, Carole R. "The Proof of the Pudding: Proverbs and Gender in the Performance Arena." *JSOT* 29, no. 2 (2004): 179–204.

————. "Proverb Performance in the Hebrew Bible." *JSOT* 32 (1985): 87–103.

————. *Traditional Sayings in the Old Testament: A Contextual Study*. Bible and Literature Series 5. Sheffield: Almond Press, 1982.

Foucault, Michel. *The Archaeology of Knowledge; and, the Discourse on Language*. Translated by A. M. Sheridan Smith. New York: Pantheon Books, 1972. Originally published in French, *L'archéologie du savoir* and *L'ordre du discours*, n.p.: Gallimard, 1969.

Foucault, Michel. *Dits et écrits: 1954–1988 / Michel Foucault*. Edited by Daniel Defert, François Ewald and Jacques Lagrange. 4 vols, Bibliothèque des sciences humaines. Paris: Gallimard, 1994.

————. "Prisons et asiles dans le mécanisme du pouvoir" (1974). In *Dits et Écrits*, vol. 2, edited by Daniel Defert, François Ewald and Jacques Lagrange, 523–4. Paris: Gallimard, 1994.

Foxhall, Lin. "Household, Gender and Property in Classical Athens." *CQ* 39, no. 1 (1989): 22–44.

Frankel, Rafael. "The Olynthus Mill, Its Origin, and Diffusion: Typology and Distribution." *AJA* 107, no. 1 (2003): 1–21.

Freeland, Cynthia A., ed. *Feminist Interpretations of Aristotle*. Re-Reading the Canon. University Park, PA: Pennsylvania State University Press, 1998.

Fuller, Reginald Cuthbert, Leonard Johnston, and Conleth Kearns, eds. *A New Catholic Commentary on Holy Scripture*. London: Nelson, 1969.

Gammie, John G. "Paraenetic Literature: Toward the Morphology of a Secondary Genre." *Semeia* 50 (1990): 41–77.

Gammie, John G., and Leo G. Perdue, eds. *The Sage in Israel and the Ancient Near East*. Winona Lake, IN: Eisenbrauns, 1990.

Gardiner, Judith Kegan, ed. *Masculinity Studies & Feminist Theory: New Directions*. New York: Columbia University Press, 2002.

Gaster, Moses. "A New Fragment of Ben Sira [Parts of Chaps. 18, 19 and 20]." *JQR* 12 (1899–1900): 688–702.

Gilbert, Maurice. "Ben Sira et la femme." *RTL* 7 (1976): 426–42.

———. "Ben Sira, Reader of Genesis 1–11." In *Intertextual Studies in Ben Sira and Tobit*, edited by Jeremy Corley and Vincent Skemp, 89–99. Washington, DC: Catholic Biblical Association of America, 2005.

———. "The Book of Ben Sira: Implications for Jewish and Christian Traditions." In *Jewish Civilisation in the Hellenistic-Roman Period*, edited by Shemaryahu Talmon, 81–91. Sheffield: JSOT Press, 1991.

———. "God, Sin and Mercy: Sirach 15:11–18:14." In *Ben Sira's God*, edited by Renate Egger-Wenzel, 118–35. Berlin: Walter de Gruyter, 2002.

———. "The Review of History in Ben Sira 44–50 and Wisdom 10–19." In *Rewriting Biblical History*, edited by Jeremy Corley and Harm W. M. van Grol, 319–34. Berlin: De Gruyter, 2011.

Giveon, Raphael, H. Jacob Katzenstein, and Moshé Anbar, eds. *Proceedings of the 9th World Congress of Jewish Studies, Jerusalem, Aug 1985: Division A: Period of the Bible*. Jerusalem: World Union of Jewish Studies, 1986.

Goering, Gregory W. Schmidt. *Wisdom's Root Revealed: Ben Sira and the Election of Israel*. JSJSup 139. Leiden: Brill, 2009.

Greenberg, Moshe. *Ezekiel 1–20: A New Translation with Introduction and Commentary*. AB 22. Garden City, NY: Doubleday, 1983.

Gregory, Bradley C. *Like an Everlasting Signet Ring: Generosity in the Book of Ben Sira*. DCLS 2. Berlin: De Gruyter, 2010.

Gruen, Erich S. *Heritage and Hellenism: The Reinvention of Jewish Tradition*. Hellenistic Culture and Society 30. Berkeley and Los Angeles: University of California Press, 2002; hardcover edition 1998.

Gunn, David M., and Paula M. McNutt, eds. *'Imagining' Biblical Worlds: Studies in Spatial, Social and Historical Constructs in Honor of James W. Flanagan*. JSOTSup 359. London and New York: Sheffield Academic Press, 2002.

Hardin, James W. "Understanding Domestic Space: An Example from Iron Age Tel Halif." *Near Eastern Archaeology* 67, no. 2 (2004): 71–83.

Hasan-Rokem, Galit. *Tales of the Neighborhood: Jewish Narrative Dialogues in Late Antiquity*. The Taubman Lectures in Jewish Studies 4. Berkeley and Los Angeles: University of California Press, 2003.

Headlam, Walter. "Prometheus, and the Garden of Eden." *CQ* 28, no. 2 (1934): 63–71.

Hempel, Charlotte, and Judith Lieu, eds. *Biblical Traditions in Transmission: Essays in Honour of Michael A. Knibb*. JSJSup 111. Leiden: Brill, 2006.

Henze, Matthias, ed. *A Companion to Biblical Interpretation in Early Judaism*. Grand Rapids, MI: Eerdmans, 2012.

Hesiod. *Hesiod, the Homeric Hymns, and Homerica*. Trans. Hugh G. Evelyn-White. London: Heinemann; New York: Macmillan, 1914.

Hicks, R. Lansing. "The Door of Love." In *Love and Death in the Ancient Near East*, edited by John H. Marks and Robert M. Good, 153–58. Guilford, CT: Four Quarters, 1987.

Himmelfarb, Martha. "The Wisdom of the Scribe, the Wisdom of the Priest, and the Wisdom of the King According to Ben Sira. " In *For a Later Generation*, edited by Randal A. Argall, Beverly A. Bow and Rodney A. Werline, 89–99. Harrisburg, PA: Trinity Press International, 2000.

Horsley, Richard A. *Scribes, Visionaries, and the Politics of Second Temple Judea*. Louisville, KY: Westminster John Knox Press, 2007.

Horsley, Richard A., and Patrick Tiller. "Ben Sira and the Sociology of the Second Temple." In *Second Temple Studies 3*, edited by Philip R. Davies and John M. Halligan, 74–107. London: Continuum, 2002.

Hymes, Dell H. "Breakthrough into Performance." In *Folklore: Performance and Communication*, edited by Dan Ben-Amos and Kenneth S. Goldstein, 11–74. The Hague: Mouton, 1975.

Ilan, Tal. *Integrating Women into Second Temple History*. Texts and Studies in Ancient Judaism 76. Tübingen: Mohr Siebeck, 1999.
———. "'Wickedness Comes from Women' (*Ben Sira* 42:13): Ben Sira's Misogyny and Its Reception by the Babylonian Talmud." In *Integrating Women into Second Temple History*, chapter 5. Tübingen: Mohr Siebeck, 1999.

Judaic Classics Library. Version 2.2, March 2001. (The Soncino Talmud, The Soncino Midrash Rabbah, and The Soncino Zohar), copyright 1991–2001 Institute for Computers in Jewish Life, Davka Corporation, and/or Judaica Press, Inc.

Kearns, Conleth. "Ecclesiasticus, or the Wisdom of Jesus the Son of Sirach." In *A New Catholic Commentary on Holy Scripture*, edited by Reginald Cuthbert Fuller, Leonard Johnston and Conleth Kearns, 547–50. London: Nelson, 1969.

Kennedy, Robinette. "Women's Friendships on Crete: A Psychological Perspective." In *Gender and Power in Rural Greece*, edited by Jill Dubisch, 121–38. Princeton, NJ: Princeton University Press, 1986.

Kister, Menahem. "Genizah Manuscripts of Ben Sira." In *Cambridge Genizah Collections*, edited by Stefan C. Reif, 36–46. Cambridge: Cambridge University Press, 2002.

———. "Some Notes on Biblical Expressions and Allusions and the Lexicography of Ben Sira." In *Sirach, Scrolls, and Sages*, edited by Takamitsu Muraoka and John F. Elwolde, 160–87. Leiden: Brill, 1999.

Krammer, Ingrid. "Scham im Zusammenhang mit Freundschaft," in *Freundschaft bei Ben Sira*, edited by Friedrich V. Reiterer, 171–199. Berlin: Walter de Gruyter, 1996.

Kübel, Paul. "Eva, Pandora und Enkidus 'Dirne.'" *BN* 82 (1996): 13–20.

Kugel, James L. *Traditions of the Bible: A Guide to the Bible as It Was at the Start of the Common Era*. Cambridge, MA: Harvard University Press, 1998.

Kvam, Kristen E., Linda S. Schearing, and Valarie H. Ziegler, eds. *Eve and Adam: Jewish, Christian, and Muslim Readings on Genesis and Gender*. Bloomington: Indiana University Press, 1999.

Labendz, Jenny R. "The Book of Ben Sira in Rabbinic Literature." *AJS Review* 30, no. 2 (2006): 347–92.

Lachs, Samuel Tobias. "The Pandora-Eve Motif in Rabbinic Literature." *HTR* 67, no. 3 (1974): 341–45.

Laqueur, Thomas. *Making Sex: Body and Gender from the Greeks to Freud*. Cambridge, MA: Harvard University Press, 1992 (paperback edition).

Lee, Thomas R. *Studies in the Form of Sirach 44–50*. SBLDS 75. Atlanta, GA: Scholars Press, 1986.

Leiman, Shnayer (Sid) Z. *The Canonization of Hebrew Scripture: The Talmudic and Midrashic Evidence*. 2nd ed, Transactions of the Connecticut Academy of Arts and Sciences 47. New Haven, CT: Connecticut Academy of Arts and Sciences, 1991.

Lévi, Israel. "Fragments de deux nouveaux manuscrits hébreux de l'Ecclésiastique." *REJ* 40 (1900): 1–30.

Lévinas, Emmanuel. *Du sacré au saint: Cinq nouvelles lectures talmudiques*. Collection Critique. Paris: Éditions de Minuit, 1977.

———. "Et Dieu créa la femme." In *Du sacré au saint*. Paris: Éditions de Minuit, 1997.

———. "Le judaïsme et le féminin." In *Difficile liberté*. Paris: A. Michel, 2006.

Levine, Amy-Jill, ed. *"Women Like This": New Perspectives on Jewish Women in the Greco-Roman World*. Early Judaism and Its Literature 01. Atlanta, GA: Scholars Press, 1991.

Levison, John R. "Is Eve to Blame: A Contextual Analysis of Sirach 25:24." *CBQ* 47, no. 4 (1985): 617–23.

———. *Portraits of Adam in Early Judaism. From Sirach to 2 Baruch*. JSPSup 1. Sheffield: JSOT Press, 1988.

Liesen, Jan. "'With All Your Heart': Praise in the Book of Ben Sira." In *Ben Sira's God*, edited by Renate Egger-Wenzel, 199–213. Berlin: Walter de Gruyter, 2002.

Lincoln, Bruce. "Competing Discourses: Rethinking the Prehistory of *Mythos* and *Logos*." *Arethusa* 30, no. 3 (1997): 341–67.

———. *Discourse and the Construction of Society: Comparative Studies of Myth, Ritual, and Classification.* New York and Oxford: Oxford University Press, 1989.

———. "Gendered Discourses: The Early History of Mythos and Logos." *HR* 36, no. 1 (1996): 1–12.

———. "The Tyranny of Taxonomies." In *Occasional Papers of the University of Minnesota Center for Humanistic Studies 1*, edited by Susan McClary and Nancy Kobrin, 1–18. Minneapolis: University of Minnesota, 1985.

Loader, William R. G. *Sexuality and the Jesus Tradition.* Grand Rapids, MI: Eerdmans, 2005.

Long, A. A. "The Concept of the Cosmopolitan in Greek & Roman Thought." *Daedalus* 137, no. 3 (2008): 50–58.

Loraux, Nicole. *The Children of Athena: Athenian Ideas About Citizenship and the Division between the Sexes.* Translated by Caroline Levine. Princeton, NJ: Princeton University Press, 1993.

Loraux, Nicole. "On the Race of Women and Some of Its Tribes: Hesiod and Semonides." In *The Children of Athena*, 72–110. Translated by Caroline Levine. Princeton, NJ: Princeton University Press, 1993.

Luttikhuizen, Gerard P., ed. *The Creation of Man and Woman: Interpretations of the Biblical Narratives in Jewish and Christian Traditions.* Themes in Biblical Narrative 3. Leiden: Brill, 2000.

MacCormack, Carol P., and Marilyn Strathern, eds. *Nature, Culture, and Gender.* Cambridge: Cambridge University Press, 1980.

Mack, Burton L. *Wisdom and the Hebrew Epic: Ben Sira's Hymn in Praise of the Fathers.* CSJH. Chicago: University of Chicago, 1985.

Malina, Bruce J. *The New Testament World: Insights from Cultural Anthropology.* 3rd rev. ed. Louisville, KY: Westminster/John Knox Press, 2001.

Marböck, Johannes. "Structure and Redaction History in the Book of Ben Sira: Review and Prospects." In *The Book of Ben Sira in Modern Research*, edited by Pancratius C. Beentjes, 61–80. Berlin: Walter de Gruyter, 1997.

———. *Weisheit im Wandel: Untersuchungen zur Weisheitstheologie bei Ben Sira.* BZAW 272. Berlin: Walter de Gruyter, 1999.

Marcus, Joseph. "A Fifth MS of Ben Sira." *JQR* 21 (1931): 223–40.

Marks, John H., and Robert M. Good, eds. *Love and Death in the Ancient Near East: Essays in Honor of Marvin H. Pope.* Guilford, CT: Four Quarters, 1987.

Margoliouth, George. "The Original Hebrew of Ecclesiasticus 31:12–31, and 36:22–37:26." *JQR* 12 (1899–1900): 1–33.

Martone, Corrado. "Ben Sira Manuscripts from Qumran and Masada." In *The Book of Ben Sira in Modern Research*, edited by Pancratius C. Beentjes, 81–94. Berlin: Walter de Gruyter, 1997.

Marttila, Marko. *Foreign Nations in the Wisdom of Ben Sira: A Jewish Sage between Opposition and Assimilation.* DCLS 13. Berlin: De Gruyter, 2012.

Matthews, Victor H., Don C. Benjamin, Claudia V. Camp, and Dianne Bergant, eds. *Honor and Shame in the World of the Bible.* Atlanta, GA: Scholars Press, 1996.

Matthews, Victor H., Bernard M. Levinson, and Tikva Simone Frymer-Kensky, eds. *Gender and Law in the Hebrew Bible and the Ancient Near East,*. JSOTSup 262. London and New York: T & T Clark, 2004.

McClure, Laura. *Spoken Like a Woman: Speech and Gender in Athenian Drama.* Princeton, NJ: Princeton University Press, 1999.

———. "'The Worst Husband:' Discourses of Praise and Blame in Euripides' Medea." *CP* 94, no. 4 (1999): 373–94.

McCreesh, Thomas P. "Wisdom as Wife: Proverbs 31:10–31." *RB* 92, no. 1 (1985): 25–46.

McInerney, Jeremy. "Plutarch's Manly Women." In *Andreia*, edited by Ralph M. Rosen and Ineke Sluiter, 319–44. Leiden: Brill, 2003.

McKeating, Henry. "Jesus Ben Sira's Attitude to Women." *ExpTim* 85, no. 3 (1973): 85–87.

McKinlay, Judith E. *Gendering Wisdom the Host: Biblical Invitations to Eat and Drink.* JSOTSup 216. Gender, Culture, Theory 4. Sheffield: Sheffield Academic Press, 1996.

Meyers, Carol. "Contesting the Notion of Patriarchy: Anthropology and the Theorizing of Gender in Ancient Israel." In *A Question of Sex?*, edited by Deborah W. Rooke, 84–105. Sheffield: Sheffield Phoenix Press, 2007.

———. "Engendering Syro-Palestinian Archaeology: Reasons and Resources." *Near Eastern Archaeology* 66, no. 4 (2003): 185–97.

———. "From Field Crops to Food: Attributing Gender and Meaning to Bread Production in Iron Age Israel." In *The Archaeology of Difference*, edited by Douglas R. Edwards and C. Thomas McCollough, 67–84. Boston, MA: ASOR, 2007.

———. "Material Remains and Social Relations: Women's Culture in Agrarian Households of the Iron Age." In *Symbiosis, Symbolism, and the Power of the Past*, edited by William G. Dever and Seymour Gitin, 425–44. Winona Lake, IN: Eisenbrauns, 2003.

Mieder, Wolfgang. *Proverbs: A Handbook.* Greenwood Folklore Handbooks. Westport CT: Greenwood Press, 2004.

Mieder, Wolfgang, and Alan Dundes, eds. *The Wisdom of Many: Essays on the Proverb.* Madison: University of Wisconsin Press, 1994 (1981 by Garland Press).

Moore, Stephen D., ed. *In Search of the Present: The Bible through Cultural Studies.* Semeia 82. Atlanta, GA: SBL, 1998.

Moxnes, Halvor. "Honor and Shame." In *The Social Sciences and New Testament Interpretation*, edited by Richard L. Rohrbaugh, 19–40. Peabody, MA: Hendrickson, 1996.

———. "Honor and Shame." *BTB* 23, no. 4 (1993): 167–76.

Muraoka, Takamitsu. "Sir 51, 13–30: An Erotic Hymn to Wisdom." *JSJ* 10, no. 2 (1979): 166–78.

Muraoka, Takamitsu, and John F. Elwolde, eds. *Diggers at the Well: Proceedings of a Third International Symposium on the Hebrew of the Dead Sea Scrolls and Ben Sira.* Studies on the Texts of the Desert of Judah 36. Leiden: Brill, 2000.

Muraoka, Takamitsu, and John F. Elwolde, eds. *Sirach, Scrolls, and Sages: Proceedings of a Second International Symposium on the Hebrew of the Dead Sea*

Scrolls, Ben Sira, and the Mishnah, Held at Leiden University, 15–17 December 1997. Studies on the Texts of the Desert of Judah 33. Leiden: Brill, 1999.

Murphy, Roland E. "The Personification of Wisdom." In *Wisdom in Ancient Israel,* edited by John Day, Robert P. Gordon and Hugh G. M. Williamson, 222–33. Cambridge: Cambridge University Press, 1995.

———. *Proverbs.* Word Biblical Commentary 22. Nashville, TN: Thomas Nelson, 1998.

Nacht, Jacob. סמלי אשה — Simle ishah bi-mekorotenu ha-ʿatikim, be-sifrutenu ha-hadashah uve-sifrut ha-ʿamim : Mehkere torah ve-emunot, minhagim ve-folklor. Tel-Aviv: Hotsaat vaʿad talmidav va-hanikhav shel ha-mehaber, 1959.

Najman, Hindy, and Judith H. Newman, eds. *The Idea of Biblical Interpretation: Essays in Honor of James L. Kugel.* JSJSup 83. Leiden: Brill, 2004.

Newsom, Carol A. "Wisdom and the Discourse of Patriarchal Wisdom: A Study of Proverbs 1–9." In *Gender and Difference in Ancient Israel,* edited by Peggy L. Day, 142–60. Minneapolis, MN: Fortress Press, 1989.

Newsom, Carol A., and Sharon H. Ringe, eds. *The Women's Bible Commentary: Expanded Edition.* Louisville, KY: Westminster/John Knox Press, 1998.

Obeng, Samuel Gyasi. "The Proverb as a Mitigating and Politeness Strategy in Akan Discourse." *AnL* 38, no. 3 (1996): 521–49.

Ortner, Sherry B. "So, *Is* Female to Male as Nature Is to Culture?" In *Making Gender,* 173–80, 234–35. Boston: Beacon Press, 1996.

Osiek, Carolyn. "The New Handmaid: The Bible and the Social Sciences." *TS* 50 (1989): 260–78.

———. "Women, Honor, and Context in Mediterranean Antiquity." *HvTSt* 64, no. 1 (2008): 323–37.

Osiek, Carolyn, and Margaret Y. MacDonald, with Janet H. Tulloch. *A Woman's Place: House Churches in Earliest Christianity.* Minneapolis, MN: Fortress Press, 2006.

Owens, J. Edward. "'Come, Let Us Be Wise': Qoheleth and Ben Sira on True Wisdom, with an Ear to Pharaoh's Folly." In *Intertextual Studies in Ben Sira and Tobit,* edited by Jeremy Corley and Vincent Skemp, 227–40. Washington, DC: CBA, 2005.

Pakkala, Juha, and Martti Nissinen, eds. *Houses Full of All Good Things: Essays in Memory of Timo Veijola.* Publications of the Finnish Exegetical Society 95. Göttingen: Vandenhoeck & Ruprecht, 2008.

Passaro, Angelo, and Guiseppe Bellia, eds. *The Wisdom of Ben Sira: Studies on Tradition, Redaction, and Theology.* Deuterocanonical and Cognate Literature Studies 1. Berlin: De Gruyter, 2008.

Penchansky, David. "Is Hokmah an Israelite Goddess, and What Should We Do About It?" In *Postmodern Interpretations of the Bible,* edited by A. K. M. Adam, 81–92. St. Louis, MO: Chalice Press, 2001.

Perdue, Leo G. "Ben Sira and the Prophets." In *Intertextual Studies in Ben Sira and Tobit*, edited by Jeremy Corley and Vincent Skemp, 132–54. Washington, DC: Catholic Biblical Association of America, 2005.

———. "The Book of Ben Sira and Hellenism." Manuscript, pp. 1–16; 24 January 2009.

———. *Proverbs*, Interpretation Bible Commentary. Louisville, KY: John Knox, 2000.

———. *The Sword and the Stylus: An Introduction to Wisdom in the Age of Empires*. Grand Rapids, MI: Eerdmans, 2008.

———. *Wisdom and Creation: The Theology of Wisdom Literature*. Nashville, TN: Abingdon Press, 1994.

———. *Wisdom Literature: A Theological History*. Louisville, KY: Westminster John Knox Press, 2007.

Perdue, Leo G., Joseph Blenkinsopp, John J. Collins, and Carol Meyers, eds. *Families in Ancient Israel*. The Family, Religion, and Culture. Louisville, KY: Westminster John Knox Press, 1997.

Peristiany, John G., and Julian Pitt-Rivers, eds. *Honor and Grace in Anthropology*. Cambridge Studies in Social and Cultural Anthropology. Cambridge: Cambridge University Press, 2005.

Peskowitz, Miriam. "Engendering Jewish Religious History." *Shofar* 14, no. 1 (1995): 8–34.

———. *Spinning Fantasies: Rabbis, Gender, and History*. Contraversions 9. Berkeley and Los Angeles: University of California Press, 1997.

Philo. *Philo*. Translated by F. H. Colson and G. H. Whitaker. Vol. 1, "On the Creation." London: Heinemann; New York: Putnam, 1929–1962.

Phipps, William E. "Eve and Pandora Contrasted." *ThTo* 45, no. 1 (1988): 34–48.

Pilch, John J. "'Beat His Ribs While He Is Young' (Sir 30:12): A Window on the Mediterranean World." *BTB* 23, no. 3 (1993): 101–13.

———, ed. *Social Scientific Models for Interpreting the Bible: Essays by the Context Group in Honor of Bruce J. Malina*. Biblical Interpretation Series 53. Leiden: Brill, 2001.

Pistone, Rosario. "Blessing of the Sage, Prophecy of the Scribe: From Ben Sira to Matthew." In *The Wisdom of Ben Sira*, edited by Angelo Passaro and Guiseppe Bellia, 309–53 Berlin: De Gruyter, 2008.

Rabinowitz, Isaac. "The Qumran Hebrew Original of Ben Sira's Concluding Acrostic on Wisdom." *HUCA* 42 (1971): 173–84.

Rajak, Tessa, Sarah Pearce, James K. Aitken, and Jennifer M. Dines, eds. *Jewish Perspectives on Hellenistic Rulers*, Hellenistic Culture and Society 50. Berkeley and Los Angeles: University of California Press, 2007.

Reif, Stefan C., ed. *The Cambridge Genizah Collections: Their Contents and Significance*. Cambridge University Library Genizah Series 1. Cambridge: Cambridge University Press, 2002.

Reif, Stefan C. "The Discovery of the Cambridge Genizah Fragments of Ben Sira: Scholars and Texts." In *The Book of Ben Sira in Modern Research*, edited by Pancratius C. Beentjes, 1–22. Berlin: Walter de Gruyter, 1997.

Reiterer, Friedrich V. "Aaron's Polyvalent Role According to Ben Sira." In *Rewriting Biblical History*, edited by Jeremy Corley and Harm W. M. van Grol, 27–56. Berlin: De Gruyter, 2011.

——, ed. *Freundschaft bei Ben Sira: Beiträge des Symposions zu Ben Sira Salzburg 1995*. BZAW. Berlin: Walter de Gruyter, 1996.

——. "Review of Recent Research on the Book of Ben Sira (1980–1996)." In *The Book of Ben Sira in Modern Research*, edited by Pancratius C. Beentjes, 23–60. Berlin: Walter de Gruyter, 1997.

Rey, Jean-Sébastien, and Jan Joosten. *The Texts and Versions of the Book of Ben Sira: Transmission and Interpretation*. JSJSup 150. Leiden: Brill, 2011.

Rogers, Susan Carol. "Gender in Southwestern France: The Myth of Male Dominance Revisited." *Anthropology* 9, no. 1/2 (1985): 65–86.

Rohrbaugh, Richard L. ed. *The Social Sciences and New Testament Interpretation*. Peabody, MA: Hendrickson, 1996.

Rollston, Chris A. "Ben Sira 38:24–39:11 and the Egyptian *Satire of the Trades*: A Reconsideration." *JBL* 120, no. 1 (2001): 131–39.

Rooke, Deborah W., ed. *A Question of Sex? Gender and Difference in the Hebrew Bible and Beyond*. Hebrew Bible Monographs 14. Sheffield: Sheffield Phoenix Press, 2007.

Rosen, Ralph M., and Ineke Sluiter, eds. *Andreia: Studies in Manliness and Courage in Classical Antiquity*. Mnemosyne: Bibliotheca Classica Batava, Supplementum 238. Leiden: Brill, 2003.

Rüger, Hans Peter. *Text und Textform in hebräischen Sirach: Untersuchungen zur Textgeschichte und Textkritik der hebräischen Sirachfragmente aus der Kairoer Geniza*. BZAW 112. Berlin: Walter de Gruyter, 1970.

Russell, D. A. "Rhetoric and Criticism." *GR* 14, no. 2 (1967): 130–44.

Sanders, James A. *The Psalms Scroll of Qumrân Cave 11 (11QPsᵃ)*. Discoveries in the Judean Desert of Jordan 4. Oxford: Clarendon Press, 1965.

Sanders, Jack T. *Ben Sira and Demotic Wisdom*. SBLMS 28. Chico, CA: Scholars Press, 1983.

Satlow, Michael L. *Tasting the Dish: Rabbinic Rhetorics of Sexuality*. BJS 303. Atlanta, GA: Scholars Press, 1995.

Schechter, Solomon. "A Fragment of the Original Text of Ecclesiasticus." *Expositor* 5th Ser. 4 (1896): 1–15.

——. "A Further Fragment of Ben Sira [Ms C; Parts of Chaps. 4, 5, 25, and 26]." *JQR* 12 (1899–1900): 456–65.

Schechter, Solomon, and Charles Taylor. *The Wisdom of Ben Sira: Portions of the Book of Ecclesiasticus from Hebrew Manuscripts in the Cairo Genizah Collection Presented to the University of Cambridge by the Editors*. Cambridge: Cambridge University Press, 1899.

Scheiber, Alexander. "A Leaf of the Fourth Manuscript of the Ben Sira from the Geniza." *Magyar Könyvszemle* 98 (1982): 179–85.

Schirmann, Yafim. "Dap hadas mittok Seper ben-Sira ha-ibri." *Tarbiz* 27 (1957–1958): 440–43.

——. "Dappim nospim mittok Seper ben-Sira." *Tarbiz* 29 (1959–1960): 125–34.

Schmitt, Jean-Claude, and Jean-Pierre Vernant. *Eve et Pandora: La création de la première femme*. Le temps des images. Paris: Gallimard, 2002.

Schroer, Silvia. *Wisdom Has Built Her House: Studies on the Figure of Sophia in the Bible*. Translated by Linda M. Maloney and William C. McDonough. Collegeville, MN: Liturgical Press, 2000.

Schwartz, Seth. *Imperialism and Jewish Society, 200 B.C.E. to 640 C.E.* Edited by R. Stephen Humphreys, William Chester Jordan and Peter Schaefer. Christians, Jews, and Muslims from the Ancient to the Modern World. Princeton, NJ: Princeton University Press, 2001.

Scott, James C. *Domination and the Arts of Resistance: Hidden Transcripts*. New Haven and London: Yale University Press, 1990.

Séchan, Louis. "Pandora, l'Ève grecque." *BAGB*, no. April (1929): 3–36.

Seitel, Peter. "Proverbs: A Social Use of Metaphor." In *The Wisdom of Many*, edited by Wolfgang Mieder and Alan Dundes, 122–39. Madison: University of Wisconsin Press, 1994.

Sherwood, Yvonne. "Prophetic Scatology: Prophecy and the Art of Sensation." In *In Search of the Present*, edited by Stephen D. Moore, 183–224. Atlanta, GA: SBL, 1998.

———. *The Prostitute and the Prophet: Hosea's Marriage in Literary-Theological Perspective*. JSOTSup 212; Gender, Culture, Theory 2. Sheffield: Sheffield Academic Press, 1996.

Skehan, Patrick W. "Staves, and Nails, and Scribal Slips (Ben Sira 44:2–5)." *BASOR* 200 (1970): 66–71.

Skehan, Patrick W., and Alexander A. Di Lella. *The Wisdom of Ben Sira: A New Translation with Notes by Patrick W. Skehan: Introduction and Commentary by Alexander A. Di Lella, O.F.M.*. AB 39. New York: Doubleday, 1987. [cited as: Skehan and Di Lella (*Wisdom*) - OR - Di Lella (*Wisdom*)]

Smend, Rudolf. *Die Weisheit des Jesus Sirach erklärt*. Berlin: Georg Reimer, 1906.

Snaith, John G. "Biblical Quotations in the Hebrew of Ecclesiasticus." *JTS* 18, no. 1 (1967): 1–12.

Soncino Talmud. *See* Judaic Library.

Spatafora, Andrea. "Intelligent or Sensible Woman (Sir 25:8)?" *Theoforum* 31, no. 3 (2000): 267–81.

Stokes, Adam. "Life and After Life in the Book of Ben Sira." *Koinonia* 18 (2006): 73–91.

Talmon, Shemaryahu, ed. *Jewish Civilisation in the Hellenistic-Roman Period*. JSPSup 10. Sheffield: JSOT Press, 1991.

Tcherikover, Victor. *Hellenistic Civilization and the Jews*. Peabody, MA: Hendrickson, 1959, 1999.

———. "Jerusalem on the Eve of the Hellenistic Reform." In *Hellenistic Civilization and the Jews*, edited by Victor Tcherikover, 117–51. Philadelphia: Jewish Publication Society of America, 1959, 1961.

Tomes, Roger. "A Father's Anxieties (Sirach 42:9–11)." In *Women in the Biblical Tradition*, edited by George J. Brooke, 71–91. Lewiston, NY: Edwin Mellen Press, 1992.

Trenchard, Warren C. *Ben Sira's View of Women: A Literary Analysis*. BJS 38. Chico, CA: Scholars Press, 1982.

Troxel, Ronald L., Kelvin G. Friebel, and Dennis Robert Magary, eds. *Seeking Out the Wisdom of the Ancients: Essays Offered to Honor Michael V. Fox on the Occasion of His Sixty-Fifth Birthday*. Winona Lake, IN: Eisenbrauns, 2005.

Türck, Hermann. *Pandora und Eva: Menschwerdung und Schöpfertum im griechischen und jüdischen Mythus*. Weimar: Verus-Verlag, 1931.

Vernant, Jean-Pierre. "Hestia-Hermès: Sur l'expression religieuse de l'espace et du mouvement chez les grecs." *L'Homme* 3, no. 3 (1963): 12–50.

Voitila, Anssi. "For Those Who Love Learning: How the Reader Is Persuaded to Study the Book of Ben Sira as a Translation." In *Houses Full of All Good Things*, edited by Juha Pakkala and Martti Nissinen, 451–60. Göttingen: Vandenhoeck & Ruprecht, 2008.

Walker, Susan. "Women and Housing in Classical Greece: The Archaeological Evidence." In *Images of Women in Antiquity*, edited by Averil M. Cameron and Amélie Kuhrt, 81–91. Detroit, MI: Wayne State University Press, 1993.

Walsh, Carey Ellen. *Exquisite Desire: Religion, the Erotic, and the Song of Songs*. Philadelphia, PA: Fortress Press, 2000.

Webster, Jane S. "Sophia: Engendering Wisdom in Proverbs, Ben Sira and the Wisdom of Solomon." *JSOT* 78, no. 2 (1998): 63–79.

Westbrook, Raymond. "The Female Slave." In *Gender and Law in the Hebrew Bible and the Ancient Near East*, edited by Victor H. Matthews, Bernard M. Levinson and Tikva Simone Frymer-Kensky, 214–38. Sheffield: Sheffield Academic Press, 1998.

Whitley, James. *The Archaeology of Ancient Greece*. Cambridge World Archaeology. Cambridge: Cambridge University Press, 2001.

Wieringen, Willien van. "Why Some Women Were Included in the Geneologies of 1 Chronicles 1–9." In *Rewriting Biblical History*, edited by Jeremy Corley and Harm W. M. van Grol, 291–300. Berlin: De Gruyter, 2011.

Wikan, Unni. "Shame and Honour: A Contestable Pair." *Man* 19, no. 4 (1984): 635–52.

Winston, David. "The Sage as Mystic in the Wisdom of Solomon." In *The Sage in Israel and the Ancient Near East*, edited by John G. Gammie and Leo G. Perdue, 383–97. Winona Lake, IN: Eisenbrauns, 1990.

Winter, Michael M. "The Origins of Ben Sira in Syriac (Part 1)." *VT* 27, no. 2 (1977): 237–53.

———. "The Origins of Ben Sira in Syriac (Part 2)." *VT* 27, no. 4 (1977): 494–507.

Witt, Charlotte. "Form, Normativity and Gender in Aristotle: A Feminist Perspective." In *Feminist Interpretations of Aristotle*, edited by Cynthia A. Freeland, 118–37. University Park, PA: Pennsylvania State University Press, 1998.

Wright, Benjamin G., III. "B. Sanhedrin 100b and Rabbinic Knowledge of Ben Sira." In *Treasures of Wisdom*, edited by Núria Calduch-Benages and Jacques Vermeylen, 41–50. Louvain: Leuven University Press; Peeters, 1999.

———. "Ben Sira on Kings and Kingship." In *Jewish Perspectives on Hellenistic Rulers*, edited by Tessa Rajak, et al., 76–91. Berkeley and Los Angeles: University of California Press, 2007.

———. "Ben Sira on the Sage as Exemplar." In *Praise Israel for Wisdom and Instruction*, 165–82. Leiden: Brill, 2008.

———. "Biblical Interpretation in the Book of Ben Sira." In *A Companion to Biblical Interpretation in Early Judaism*, edited by Matthias Henze, 363–88. Grand Rapids, MI: Eerdmans, 2012.

———. "From Generation to Generation: The Sage as Father in Early Jewish Literature." In *Biblical Traditions in Transmission*, edited by Charlotte Hempel and Judith Lieu, 309–32. Leiden: Brill, 2006.

———. "Joining the Club: A Suggestion About Genre in Early Jewish Texts." *DSD* 17, no. 3 (2010): 289–314.

———. *No Small Difference: Sirach's Relationship to Its Hebrew Parent Text.* Septuagint and Cognate Studies Series 26. Atlanta, GA: Scholars Press, 1989.

———. *Praise Israel for Wisdom and Instruction: Essays on Ben Sira and Wisdom, the Letter of Aristeas and the Septuagint.* JSJSup 131. Leiden: Brill, 2008.

———. ""Put the Nations in Fear of You": Ben Sira and the Problem of Foreign Rule." In *Praise Israel for Wisdom and Instruction*, 127–46. Leiden: Brill, 2008.

———. "The Use and Interpretation of Biblical Tradition in Ben Sira's Praise of the Ancestors." In *Studies in the Book of Ben Sira*, edited by Géza G. Xeravits and József Zsengellér, 183–207. Leiden: Brill, 2008.

———. "Wisdom and Women at Qumran." *DSD* 11, no. 2 (2004): 240–61.

———. "Wisdom of Iesous son of Sirach." In *A New English Translation of the Septuagint*, edited by Albert Pietersma and Benjamin G. Wright, 715–62. New York and Oxford: Oxford University Press, 2007.

Xeravits, Géza G., and József Zsengellér, eds. *Studies in the Book of Ben Sira: Papers of the Third International Conference on the Deuterocanonical Books, Shimeon Centre, Pápa, Hungary, 18–20 May, 2006.* JSJSup 127. Leiden: Brill, 2008.

Yadin, Yigael. *The Ben Sira Scroll from Masada.* Jerusalem: Israel Exploration Society, 1965. Originally *Megillat ben-Sira mimmasada, Eretz Israel* 8 (1965) [The E. L. Sukenik Memorial Volume], 1–45.

Yankah, Kwesi. "Do Proverbs Contradict?" *Folklore Forum* 17, no. 1 (1984): 2–17.

———. "Risks in Verbal Art Performance." *Journal of Folklore Research* 22, no. 2/3 (1985): 133–53.

Zakovitch, Yair. "Through the Looking Glass: Reflections/Inversions of Genesis Stories in the Bible." *BibInt* 1, no. 2 (1993): 139–52.

Zeitlin, Froma I. "Playing the Other: Theater, Theatricality, and the Feminine in Greek Drama." *Representations* 11 (1985): 63–94.

Ziegler, Joseph, ed. *Sapientia Iesu Filii Sirach.* 2nd ed. Septuaginta: Vetus Testamentum Graecum 12:2. Göttingen: Vandenhoeck & Ruprecht, 1980.

Index of Modern Authors

Index of Ancient Sources

NOTES:
- entries don't distinguish between the Book of Ben Sira and Sirach;
- numbering for BBS/Sirach is according to Beentjes and the Hebrew texts;
- no verses from the lexical studies AppLex-5 to AppLex-14 are listed;
- each passage in section A.2 (Annotated Translations) is listed as a range of pages, without listings for individual verses.

Translated verses from the Book of Ben Sira

Index of Subjects

NOTE: Subjects mentioned in footnotes are listed by page only, without a footnote number.